ON THE WATER | PALISADE BAY

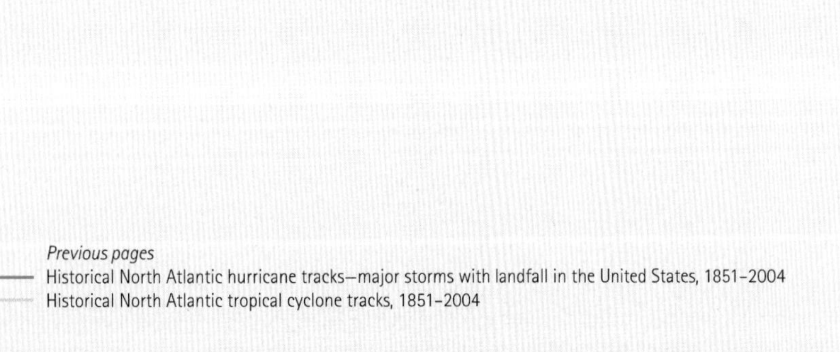
Previous pages
Historical North Atlantic hurricane tracks—major storms with landfall in the United States, 1851–2004
Historical North Atlantic tropical cyclone tracks, 1851–2004

ON THE WATER | PALISADE BAY

Guy Nordenson
Catherine Seavitt
Adam Yarinsky

with

Stephen Cassell
Lizzie Hodges
Marianne Koch
James Smith
Michael Tantala
Rebecca Veit

Foreword by Michael Oppenheimer
Afterword by Barry Bergdoll

PRINCETON UNIVERSITY
SCHOOL OF ARCHITECTURE

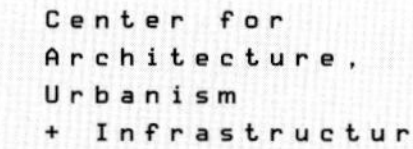

CONTENTS

ACKNOWLEDGMENTS

On the Water: Palisade Bay is published on the occasion of The Museum of Modern Art's exhibition *Rising Currents: Projects for New York's Waterfront* and as a record of the research and design work completed by the 2007 AIA College of Fellows Latrobe Prize team led by Guy Nordenson and Catherine Seavitt of Princeton University's School of Architecture, and Adam Yarinsky of Architecture Research Office.

Guy Nordenson was the overall project director and worked with James Smith, of Princeton University's Department of Civil and Environmental Engineering, and Michael Tantala to direct the engineering analyses and infrastructural design. Catherine Seavitt and Adam Yarinsky oversaw the urban planning, architecture, and landscape design, and Catherine Seavitt provided the ecological analyses.

James Smith and Mary Lynn Baeck worked with Jordan Hill and Ning Lin of the Department of Civil and Environmental Engineering on the computational fluid dynamic analyses used to test the performance of the design hypotheses. Michael Tantala directed a team of Princeton graduate and undergraduate architecture and engineering students to create a series of analytic maps derived from GIS software and data. These students, Keith Cochrane, Aaron Forrest, Marianne Koch, Ajay Manthripragada, Cynthia Michalak, and Jakob Rosenzweig, also performed much of the historical research on the bay region. Michael Tantala produced the HAZUS analysis which served as a basis for the initial hypotheses regarding flood damage assessment.

Megumi Tamanaha, Mikkel Bogh, Jejon Yeung, Rosalyne Shieh, Minna Koo, and Ariane Phipps-Morgan from Architecture Research Office worked under the direction of Adam Yarinsky and Stephen Cassell on much of the urban and architectural design development and representation throughout the book. Jejon Yeung is responsible for producing the detailed design section on Lower Manhattan.

Lizzie Hodges, Marianne Koch, and Catherine Seavitt compiled the research, design work, and text into this book with the input of Guy Nordenson and Adam Yarinsky. Marianne Koch and Ilana Altman worked on compiling the data used for the Edge Atlas. Marianne Koch completed the Edge Atlas and Ilana Altman developed a plan for a future transportation network in the bay. Rebecca Veit assisted by editing the text and coordinating the images with assistance from Laura Diamond, Jaffer Kolb, Rebecca Marriott, and Amie Shao of Princeton University.

On the Water: Palisade Bay has been generously funded by the AIA College of Fellows through the award of the 2007 Benjamin Henry Latrobe Prize. We would especially like to thank the 2007 Chancellor Frank E. Lucas, the 2008 Chancellor Carole J. Olshavsky, and Director Pauline Porter for their encouragement and enthusiasm, as well as Jury Chair Daniel Friedman and the members of the Latrobe Prize selection committee for their confidence in our project. We are also grateful to the High Meadows Sustainability Fund for Research, Education, and Civic Engagement Initiatives at Princeton University which provided additional funding for the project.

A generous contribution from Princeton University's Center for Architecture, Urbanism and Infrastructure (CAUI) helped to make this publication possible. Directed by Mario Gandelsonas, CAUI is a research center established by the School of Architecture to study the spatial effects of the distributed networks of communications, resources, finances, and migration that characterize the contemporary city. The Center fosters collective, interdisciplinary research across the University by hosting conferences, working sessions and publications. We would also like to acknowledge Rob Stewart '84 for his support of the Center's programs. Finally we thank our friends and colleagues at the School of Architecture, especially our dean, Stan Allen, for the community, resources, and support that have enabled this project from the beginning.

FOREWORD

The overleaf of *On the Water: Palisade Bay* tells the story: squiggly lines randomly draped across an impressionist's outline of the Atlantic coast, much like spaghetti fallen from the kettle. Actually, these are the historical, chaotic pathways taken by hurricanes. Most years New Yorkers were lucky and the spaghetti fell elsewhere. Once in a while, a strand fell close by, causing high winds and flooding as the storms pushed the water inland, with loss of life and costly damage to property.

Now the world is warming due to the buildup of the greenhouse gases. Sea level is rising, inexorably, as glaciers and polar ice sheets melt and ocean water expands. There may not be more hurricanes in the future, but those we do get are likely to be stronger and will be pushing an already higher sea surface further and further inland with greater and greater force.

Like residents of many other great cities, New Yorkers live by the sea but hardly know it's there until, during a hurricane or a nor'easter, its presence can't be ignored. A friend once called the city "one of the most astonishing meetings of land and water on earth." But this is now only evident from above. We have reconfigured and hardened the coast, building sea walls and filling wetlands, drawing a hard line between the water and ourselves. I have seen hundreds of aerial photos of my home town, but the ones in Palisade Bay, along with maps and photographs, make this point explicit: despite our best efforts, the city and the water remain one organism. As the sea rises and storms intensify, the water will break down the boundary again and again. The question is whether we should build faster and harder to keep it out, or find a way to gently merge ourselves with the water once again, transforming the hard boundary into a continuum, a smooth transition, a co-mingling rather than a battle zone. This is the challenge to which Palisade Bay rises.

I spend a lot of time at scientific meetings mulling over the newest temperature, storm, and sea level data, and at the endless negotiation sessions, most recently at Copenhagen, as governments struggle to design a response to global warming. Inevitably, we will grapple with the problem, emissions of the greenhouse gases will be reduced, and eventually, many, many decades in the future, the climate will stabilize. But most people don't follow the scientific details and don't care about the agonizingly slow process of governments. Rather, they worry about what's happening at home, and here at home in New York City, we are going to have to cope with a warming climate and a rising sea for a long time to come.

Like all the other great coastal cities, New Yorkers have been artful about their rough coexistence with the sea in the past, and have the option of being creative once again. The inclination will be to wait until the last minute with the water up to our knees, then defend ourselves with concrete and steel. But Palisade Bay provides an alternative vision that opts for the transition zone, with islands, wetlands, and graded embankments, allowing the city to cooperate with the sea, rather than trying, fruitlessly, to banish it.

Michael Oppenheimer, Albert G. Milbank Professor of Geosciences and Interntional Affairs
Princeton University

Soft infrastructure aims to synthesize solutions for storm defense and environmental enrichment along the coast.

Opposite
New York-New Jersey Upper Bay, 2009

INTRODUCTION

On the Water: Palisade Bay *is the research and design initiative of a team of engineers, architects, planners, professors, and students to imagine the transformation of the New York-New Jersey Upper Bay in the face of certain climate change. The work began during the summer of 2007 upon award of the 2007 Latrobe Prize, a biannual research grant awarded by the American Institute of Architects College of Fellows. This book is a product of our two-year collaboration.*

The New York-New Jersey Upper Bay is a large estuarine harbor fed by the Hudson River and connected to the Atlantic Ocean through the Verrazano Narrows and the Long Island Sound. Its surface area is approximately twenty square miles and it measures nearly four miles across at its widest point. This vast body of water is surrounded by the dense urban development of New York City—adjacent to the New York-New Jersey Upper Bay are the three boroughs of Manhattan, Brooklyn, and Staten Island, as well as Jersey City and Bayonne in Hudson County, New Jersey. With an estimated population of 20 million people, the greater metropolitan region is the largest in the United States. The island of Manhattan alone has almost 2 million residents, making it one of the most densely populated places in the country.

Within the next fifty years the New York-New Jersey Upper Bay is likely to see its waters rise by as much as one foot as a consequence of global climate change. In the next one hundred years, that rise could be as much as two feet. Furthermore, given the possibility of rapid and widespread melting of polar ice caps due to dynamic feedback mechanisms in the global climate system, it is quite possible that waters in the New York-New Jersey area could rise by more than four feet by the end of the century.[1]

Sea level rise in itself will lead to an increase in the occurrence of what is presently recognized as extreme flooding. Because of a higher baseline of water, the frequency and extent of flooding due to severe storms—hurricanes, tropical storms, and nor'easters—will increase dramatically. Within this century, what is currently considered the one-hundred-year flood could recur as often as every fifteen years, and the 500-year flood may recur closer to every 120 years.[2] Moreover, a rise in ocean surface temperatures could bring about an increase in the frequency and intensity of severe storms, escalating the threat of damaging storm surge far beyond that which we know today.

These climatic changes threaten our local infrastructures, ecosystems, and communities. A substantial portion of the area bounding the Upper Bay—and some of the most valuable real estate in New York City—lies just above sea level, and there is a prevalent risk that the city will be severely paralyzed due to predicted inundation and wave action associated with storm surge. Buildings and infrastructure at low elevations may face irreparable damages and public

MANHATTAN
NEW JERSEY
NEW YORK–NEW JERSEY
UPPER BAY
BROOKLYN
STATEN ISLAND

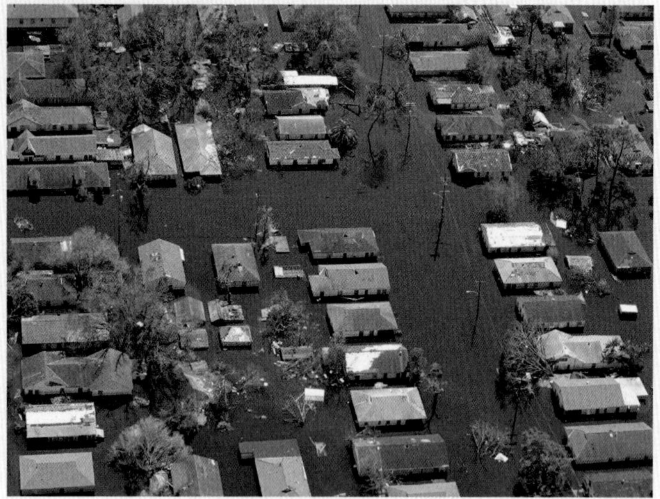

Flooding in New Orleans after Hurricane Katrina, 2005

Opposite
Combined observed and projected temperature, precipitation, and sea level rise, in *Climate Risk Information*, New York City Panel on Climate Change, Release Version, February 17, 2009

transportation, highways, and local streets will experience extreme delays or even shutdowns in the event of a major storm. Increased inflow to water control systems will result in overloaded wastewater treatment plants, increased discharge from combined sewer overflows, and flooding of brownfields will lead to heightened pollution. Saltwater intrusion into freshwater sources and wetlands will reduce the quality and availability of drinking water, increase erosion, and weaken precious ecosystems.

The need to address these risks provides an opportunity to rethink the relationship between infrastructure, ecology, and society in the urban environment. The conventional response to flooding has been hard engineering: cities fortify their coasts to protect real estate at the expense of nature. If this approach persists as the default solution, seawalls and bulkheads will be raised to define a clear boundary between dry land and deep water, while native tidal wetlands along the coast will erode and eventually wash away. The loss of these wetlands not only diminishes the variety of plants, invertebrates, fishes, and birds that inhabit them but also erases the naturally occurring buffer zone between land and water which mitigates the impact of fluctuating sea levels and lowers the risk of flood damage. Moreover, the hard engineering habit has proven costly, unreliable, and often ineffective. The disastrous failure of the levees in the aftermath of Hurricane Katrina speaks to our excessive reliance on this risky solution to flood control. Adequately protecting cities from the hazards posed by climate change and sea level rise requires a more holistic approach to coastal planning.

This study invents a "soft infrastructure" which aims to synthesize solutions for storm defense and environmental enrichment along the coast. It is an adaptable solution that adjusts to varying climatic conditions and urban demands by balancing environmental, technical, and economic priorities. Our goal is to layer these priorities throughout the harbor zones to not only create a comprehensive storm defense system but to also provide new places for recreation, agriculture, ecologies, and urban development. By arraying these activities on the water, the bay becomes a regional center, and the city refocuses on the body of water it embraces.

CHARACTERIZING DYNAMIC SYSTEMS

While the behavior of the earth's atmosphere is complex it can, like other complex systems, be modeled in ways that represent and bracket the possible consequences of various factors. Combinations of statistical and historical data analysis, derived mathematical models of atmospheric physics, and sensitivity analyses can provide a full and accurate understanding of the range and trend of future outcomes. In this fashion it is possible for models of complex natural systems to predict the probability that a parameter characterizing a natu-

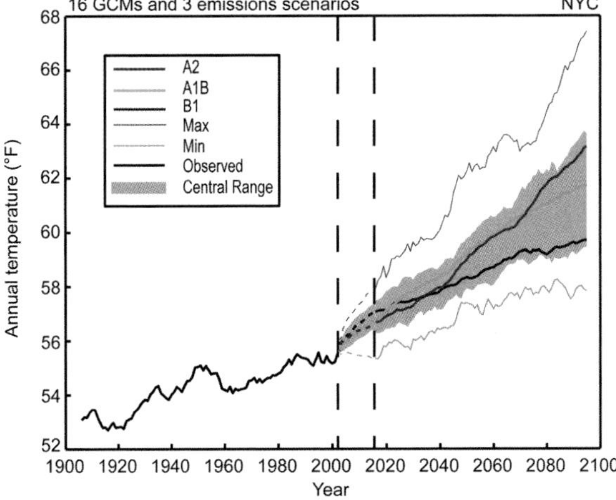

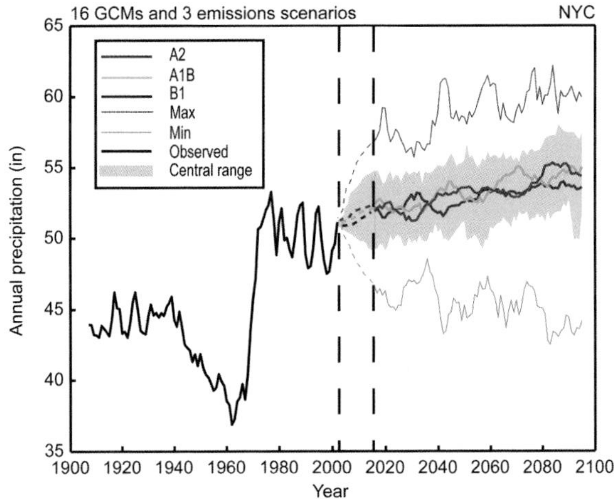

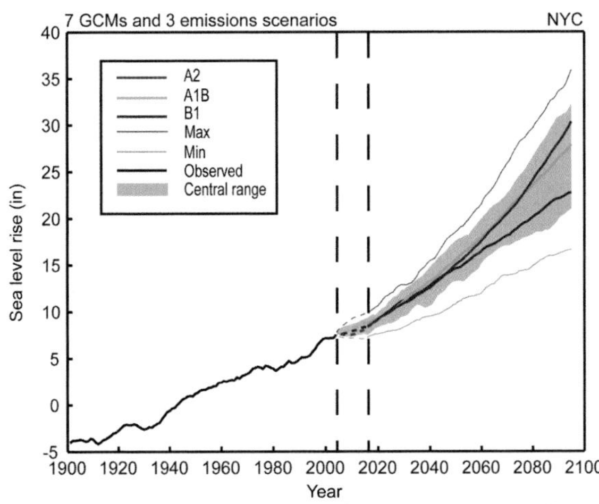

ral hazard—earthquake peak ground acceleration, peak hurricane wind velocity, or average flood height above mean sea level—will be exceeded in any period of time by some probability, say five percent in fifty years (475-year average return period). It is further possible to characterize the uncertainty of such predictions quantitatively by distributing the predicted outcomes around an average value, and then assigning a marginal rate by which the increase of a particular parameter, with an increased time exposure period, decelerates or remains steady. In short, it is possible to fully and realistically characterize the "complexion" of a complex environmental system.

The ability to thoroughly characterize complexity is important for two reasons. First, complex natural systems are dynamic, both as phenomena and in their patterns of recurrence. Second, the probability that any human settlement will survive a severe natural hazard is dependent on a broadly configured resilience to endure a disaster and fully recover its livelihood. A large aspect of developing this resilience is in calculating accurate predictions and designing appropriate tools and methods to withstand disaster. Doing this effectively may well be the clearest way that the enormous complexity of cities is both developed and put to the test. For example, depending solely on the construction of levees as a solution to flood control is not adequate. Appropriate maintenance and monitoring procedures must be enacted, and regularly reviewed contingency plans must be designed, for the built infrastructure to perform in response to a dynamic environmental system. In other words, a broad capacity in the built and natural environment, as well as in social policy, must be developed in order for survival and recovery to be successful.

SOFT INFRASTRUCTURE

If a device such as a bridge, buoy, or radio is excited by an alternating force, or other effect that is in synch with one of its own natural periods of vibration, it will resonate. This effect can be either beneficial or destructive. In the case of natural hazards, the "coupling" between systems—for example the buffeting of wind or the vibrations of the ground—needs to be identified and mitigated. Otherwise, such resonance may lead to a build-up of energy that will lead to systemic or local catastrophes.

System modeling often approaches static and dynamic effects separately. Flows of fluid or wind may be characterized as having both a steady velocity and resulting pressure and a separate turbulent or dynamic component. Often the steady state or "static" component can be understood with great simplicity and certainty, while the "dynamic" component is characterized in terms of probability distribution, spectra, or other nuanced descriptions. Thus, the resistance required to withstand either static or dynamic components is effectively different. Static demands require strength and stiffness

to assure that the response to loads is elastic (without lasting effect) and stable (without buckling or other instabilities). The resistance to dynamic demands also requires strength, stability, and stiffness, but it also needs devices to dissipate energy such as shock absorbers, fuses, or dampers to withstand unexpected peak demands or effects from resonance.

Natural ecologies are resilient, within the range of phenomena for which they have evolved; forests grow back after fires, animals recover from illness, and wetlands return to equilibrium after severe storms. This ability to recover from accidents and catastrophes over time is a direct consequence and distinct characteristic of complex ecologies. As a result, successful design for mitigating natural hazards is based on the sophisticated understanding and mimicry of such natural systems.

For example, the key insight in earthquake engineering during the mid-twentieth century was the realization that building structures could be designed and detailed to withstand the shock of earthquakes with considerable structural damage, but without collapse. Just as a car can be designed to protect the passengers inside when it is nearly destroyed in a severe crash, a building can be designed to "crumple" without collapse in the event of an earthquake to allow occupants to safely exit. This is accomplished by introducing ductility, or energy absorbing capability, into structural elements and connections. In the most sophisticated designs this capability is located in discrete elements that isolate the damage and allow the majority of the structure to survive with little or no damage. Through similar means, resilience can be implemented in urban settings which are vulnerable to floods and storm surges. A balanced combination of infrastructure, landscapes, and social policy can comprise a coastal defense system that is resilient to the volatility of sea level rise and severe storms.

Natural ecologies are resilient; forests grow back after fires, animals recover from illness, and wetlands return to equilibrium after severe storms.

CLIMATE CHANGE

There is ample evidence and general international agreement that the global climate is changing at an accelerating rate and that human-driven emissions of greenhouse gases into the atmosphere and shifts in land use are the main processes driving this trend. In the past century, the temperature in the New York–New Jersey metropolitan region has increased by 2.5°F.[3] Global climate models (GCMS) project that temperatures in and around New York City are likely to increase by 1.5 to 3°F by the 2020s, 3 to 5°F by the 2050s, and by 4 to 7.5°F by the 2080s.[4]

A recent Intergovernmental Panel on Climate Change (IPCC) assessment report gives estimates of between 1.8°C and 4°C for the change in global average temperature projected between 2000 and 2100.[5]

Wildflowers grow after a forest fire in the Kenai National Wildlife Refuge, 2001

Opposite
Observed annual temperature and precipitation in Central Park, 1901-2006, and sea level rise at the Battery tide gauge station, 1901-2006, in *Climate Risk Information*, New York City Panel on Climate Change, Release Version, February 17, 2009

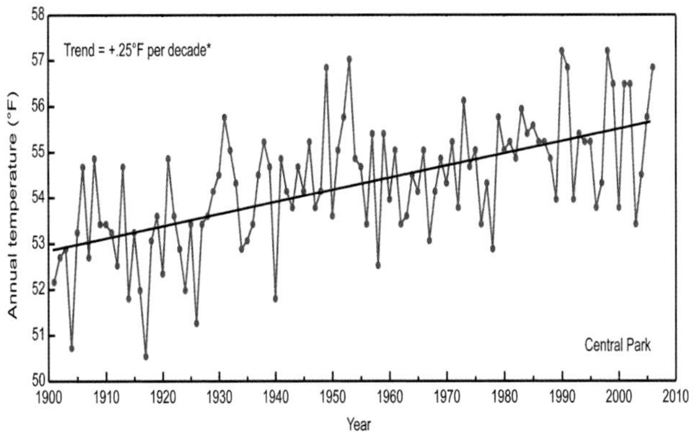

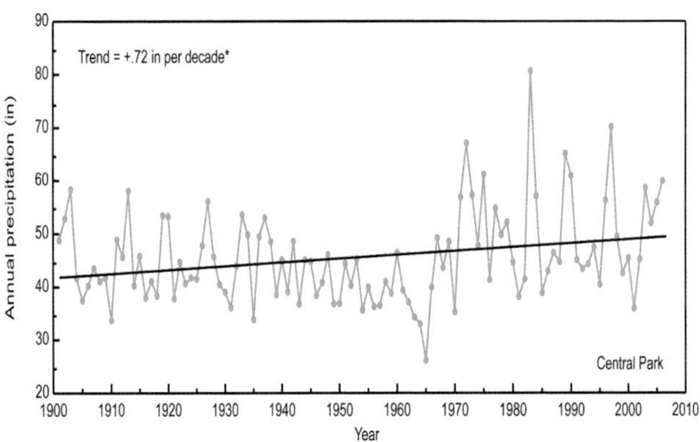

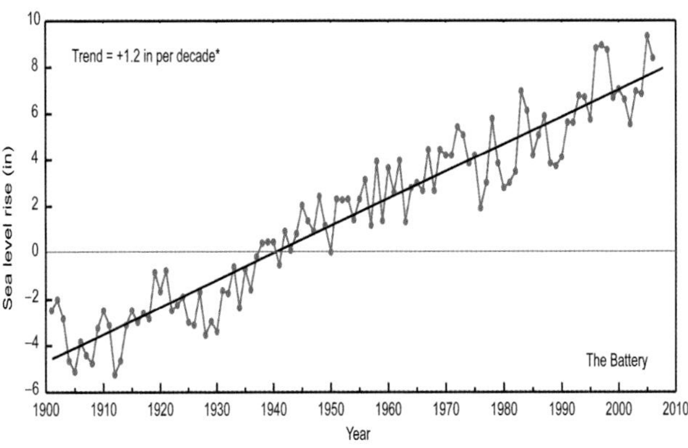

Global climate models project that the rate and amount of warming, as well as the frequency and severity of extreme events, such as heat waves and droughts, will increase over the twenty-first century as a result of this warming.

SEA LEVEL RISE

Although sea level has been rising along the Eastern Seaboard since the end of the last glaciation, the rise in the twentieth century can be attributed to both natural and anthropogenic factors. In New York City, the rate of relative sea level rise is currently 0.11 inches per year (2.73 millimeters/year).[6] This rate of sea level rise for the metropolitan area is greater than the rate for global sea level, most likely due to continuing regional subsidence of the land.

Future sea level rise will lead to greater damage from coastal floods, increased salinity of aquifers, and loss of coastal land. Taking projected climate change into account, it is extremely likely that sea level in the region will rise between 2 and 5 inches by the 2020s, between 7 and 12 inches by the 2050s, and between 12 and 23 inches by the 2080s. These higher predicted sea levels would lead to more damaging storm floods in coastal areas and a marked reduction in the return period for a given flood level.[7] In New York City, the one-hundred-year flood would have an average probability of occurring once in sixty-five to eighty years by the 2020s, once in thirty-five to fifty-five years by the 2050s, and once in thirty-five years to as often as once every fifteen years by the 2080s.[8]

FLOODING

Flooding is generally a result of tropical storms (hurricanes) and extra-tropical storms (nor'easters). Hurricanes are major tropical cyclones or low-pressure systems that intensify over the open ocean. The destructive power of hurricanes derives from their very high wind speeds of at least 74 miles/hour (119 kilometers/hour), flooding due to the high storm surge and wave action, as well as heavy rainfall.[9] The most prevalent climate extremes in the New York–New Jersey region are flooding events either occurring from heavy precipitation or, in coastal areas, from storm surges.

Nor'easters are the dominant type of storm producing major coastal flooding and beach erosion north of Chesapeake Bay, generally occurring between January and March. This type of storm gains wind speeds from the convergence of cold arctic air and the warmer gulf streams. While wind speeds are lower than in hurricanes, nor'easters cause considerable damage due to their greater areal extent and longer duration, often over several tidal cycles at a given location.[10]

The apparent increase in flooding is a consequence of the regional sea level rise, beach erosion, and coastal development over the last fifty years.

A stretch of 9th Street in Brooklyn after heavy rains, 2004

Opposite
New York City Hurricane Evacuation Zone Map, Office of Emergency Management, 2008

Precipitation has also increased over the past hundred years with a tendency towards greater extremes and may increase more rapidly in the future. Heavy rains falling during a very short period of time can overwhelm drains, causing flooding in streets, basements, and on subway tracks. The situation is worsened by the fact that antiquated New York City drainage infrastructure combines sewage and stormwater outlets, so uncontrolled combined sewage overflow (CSO) runoff flows into the Upper Bay in excess of federal and state CSO discharge allowances.

STORM SURGE

A storm surge is a dome of water produced by the pairing of low barometric pressure and strong wind shear on the right side of an advancing low-pressure system. High wind speeds push on the ocean surface and cause the water to rise up higher than the ordinary sea level. As a storm surge advances past the shore, the extent and impact of its damage is amplified if it coincides with the lunar high tide. Geographically, the New York City region is highly susceptible to storm surge. The right-angle bend between the New Jersey and Long Island coasts funnels surge waters towards its apex, the New York–New Jersey Upper Bay. Additionally, surge waters pile up at the western end of the Long Island Sound.

The National Hurricane Center forecasts storm surge using the SLOSH (Sea, Lake, and Overland Surges from Hurricanes) model. SLOSH-estimated surge levels have been computed using the effects of a hurricane surge for a worst-case scenario Category 3 hurricane (with wind speeds of 111–130 miles/hour on the Saffir-Simpson scale). Based on these calculations, maximum surge levels could reach 25 feet (7.6 meters) above the National Geodetic Vertical Datum at JFK Airport, 21 feet (6.4 meters) at the Lincoln Tunnel entrance, and 24 feet (7.3 meters) at the Battery.[11]

FREQUENCY

Within the last fifty years, storm frequencies along the Eastern Seaboard peaked in the late 1960s, decreased in the 1970s, and then rose again in the early 1990s. Twentieth-century tide-gauge records from Atlantic City, New Jersey and Charleston, South Carolina show no statistically significant trends in either the number or duration of storm surge events after accounting for tidal factors and long-term sea level rise.[12] The apparent increase in flooding is a consequence of the regional sea level rise, beach erosion, and coastal development during this period.

While hurricanes may occur less often than nor'easters in the Northeast, they are generally more destructive. Influenced by the

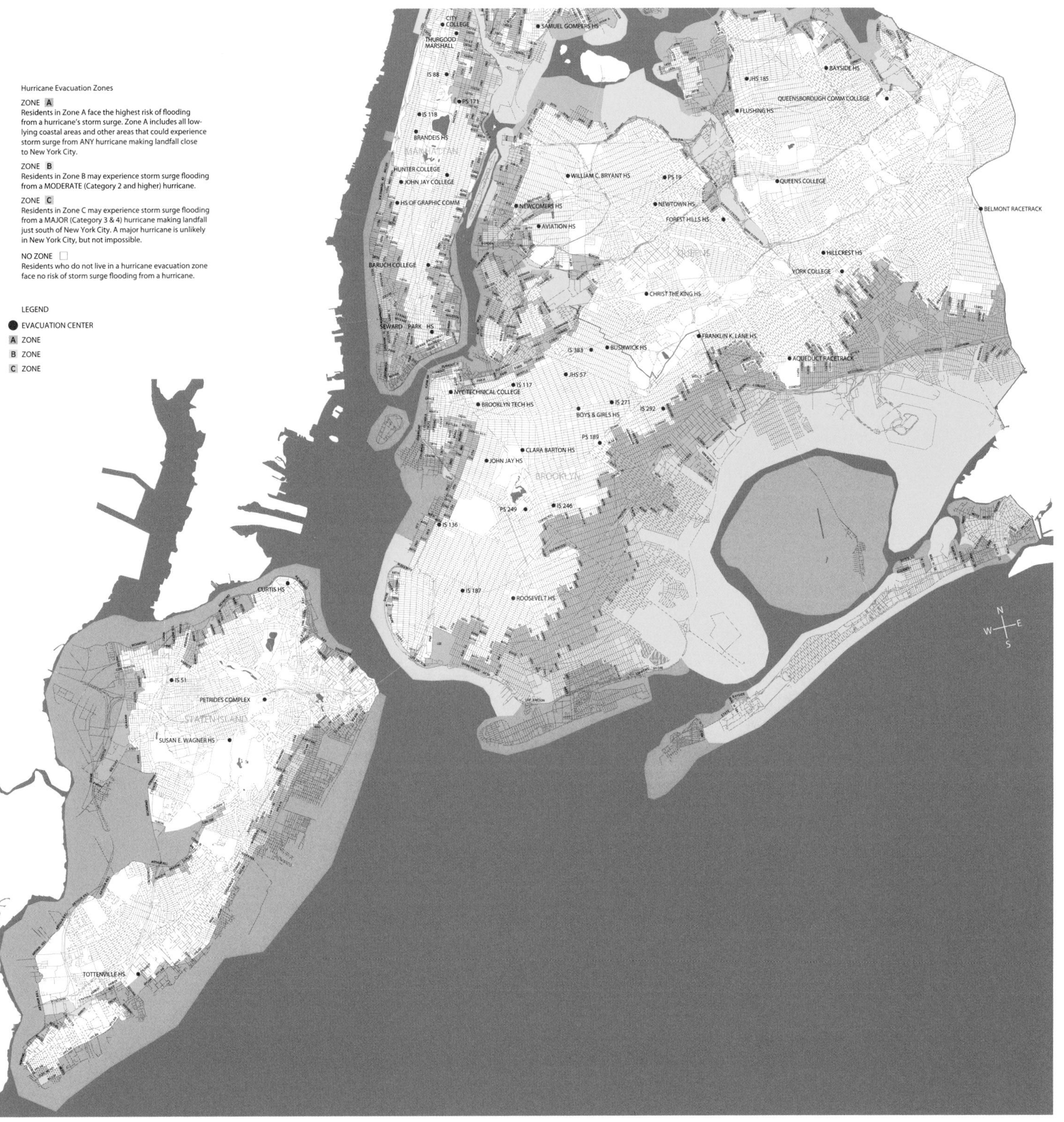

Hurricane Evacuation Zones
ZONE A
Residents in Zone A face the highest risk of flooding from a hurricane's storm surge. Zone A includes all low-lying coastal areas and other areas that could experience storm surge from ANY hurricane making landfall close to New York City.
ZONE B
Residents in Zone B may experience storm surge flooding from a MODERATE (Category 2 and higher) hurricane.
ZONE C
Residents in Zone C may experience storm surge flooding from a MAJOR (Category 3 & 4) hurricane making landfall just south of New York City. A major hurricane is unlikely in New York City, but not impossible.
NO ZONE
Residents who do not live in a hurricane evacuation zone face no risk of storm surge flooding from a hurricane.
LEGEND
EVACUATION CENTER
A ZONE
B ZONE
C ZONE
CITY COLLEGE
SAMUEL GOMPERS HS
THURGOOD MARSHALL
IS 88
PS 171
IS 118
BRANDEIS HS
HUNTER COLLEGE
JOHN JAY COLLEGE
HS OF GRAPHIC COMM
BARUCH COLLEGE
SEWARD PARK HS
JHS 185
BAYSIDE HS
QUEENSBOROUGH COMM COLLEGE
FLUSHING HS
WILLIAM C. BRYANT HS
PS 19
QUEENS COLLEGE
NEWCOMERS HS
NEWTOWN HS
FOREST HILLS HS
AVIATION HS
BELMONT RACETRACK
HILLCREST HS
YORK COLLEGE
CHRIST THE KING HS
FRANKLIN K. LANE HS
IS 383
BUSHWICK HS
AQUEDUCT RACETRACK
JHS 57
IS 117
NYC TECHNICAL COLLEGE
BROOKLYN TECH HS
IS 271
BOYS & GIRLS HS
IS 292
PS 189
CLARA BARTON HS
JOHN JAY HS
BROOKLYN
IS 246
PS 249
IS 136
IS 187
ROOSEVELT HS
CURTIS HS
IS 51
PETRIDES COMPLEX
STATEN ISLAND
SUSAN E. WAGNER HS
TOTTENVILLE HS
N
W
E
S

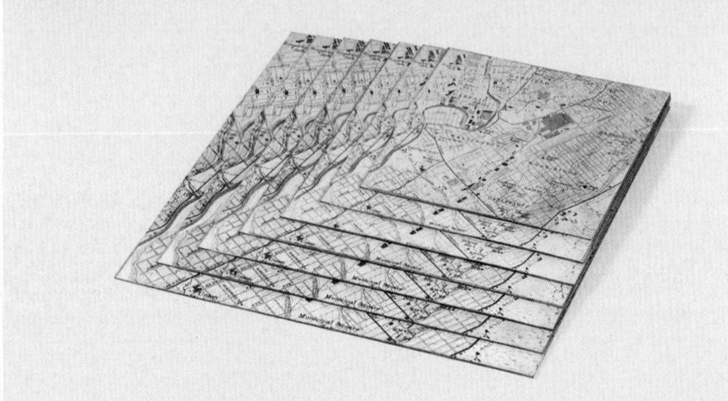

Debris along the Hackensack River, 2006

Robert Smithson, *Untitled (Map on Mirror—Passaic, New Jersey)*, 1967

Bruno Munari, from the book *The Sea as a Craftsman*, Corraini Edizioni, 1994

Opposite
Aerial view of Shooters Island, 2008

atmospheric shifts of the El Niño Southern Oscillation (ENSO), Atlantic hurricanes are thirty-six percent more likely to occur and six percent more intense during a La Niña phase than during an El Niño phase. In the last two centuries, nine or more hurricanes have struck the metropolitan New York City region, including major ones in 1893 and 1821 and the infamous Long Island Express of 1938.[13]

FLUX

An aerial view of Shooters Island, a 43-acre island at the end of the Kill Van Kull, displays the enigmatic ecological *informe* that speaks to the rich cycles of growth and decay within the harbor. In the image, remnants of wooden ships and piers, relics of the several shipbuilding companies that operated here from approximately 1860 through 1918, are gradually disintegrating into the water. The island has since been acquired by the NYC Department of Parks and Recreation and has been preserved as a bird sanctuary. From its state of industrial decay, the island now supports habitat for nesting pairs of wading birds such as herons, ibis, egrets, and double-crested cormorants.

The collection of found objects photographed in Bruno Munari's book, *The Sea as a Craftsman,* beautifully illustrates the observation that some of the most evocative objects are those which have been created by the ocean and its tides. The notion that the sea can be a craftsman suggests that un-authored processes can act on objects and develop unique phenomenona which cannot be predicted or copied.

Robert Smithson's work that evolved from his expeditions to the fringes of New Jersey is also a generative example. In his essay "A Provisional Theory of Non-Sites," written in 1968, Smithson notes that his three-dimensional works negotiate the space between actual sites and the systems of abstractions and logic which attempt to represent them. Within this "space of metaphoric significance," Smithson defines sites "in terms of esthetic boundaries rather than political or economic boundaries."[14] In his 1966 essay, "Entropy and the New Monuments," Smithson discusses contemporary art through the lens of entropy, the thermodynamic law that states energy is more easily lost than obtained. He notes that the monumental has caused us to forget the future rather than remember the past—it has eliminated the notion of time as decay. He argues for a new kind of sight which looks beyond conventional progressive scales of time and space, and into the possibility of alternative relationships between development and decay.

This work is inspirational to us as we begin to reinvent the Upper Bay for the future. Though the intervention is extensive, we do not aim for monumental development, nor do we look backward to emulate

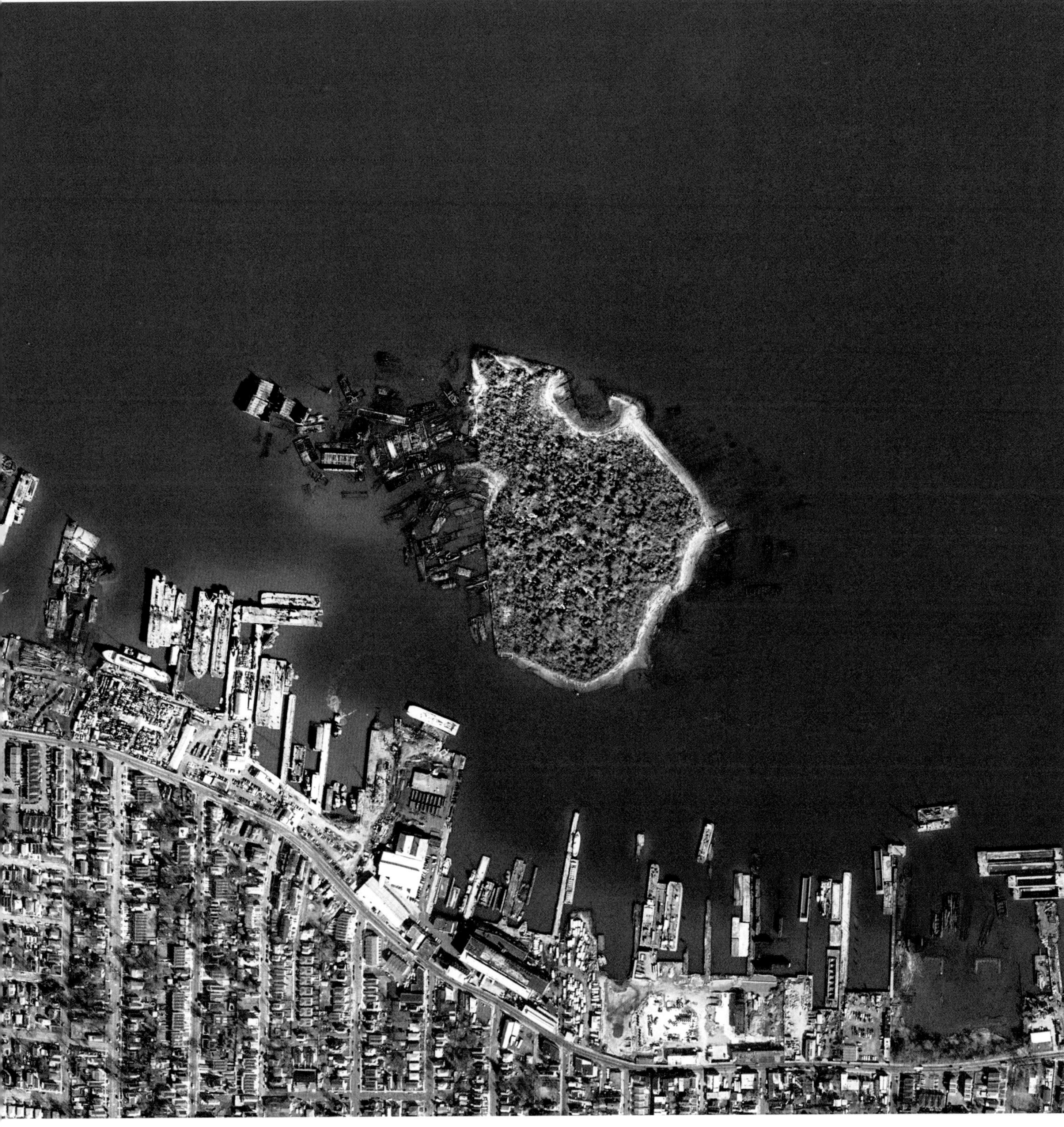

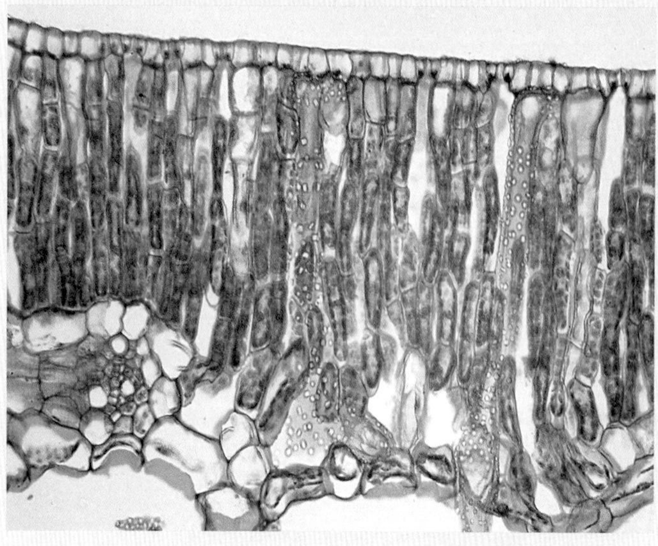

The Giant's Causeway, Northern Ireland, 2006

Palisade cells seen under a microscope

Opposite
Thomas Davies, *The Landing of the British Forces in the Jerseys 1776*, watercolor

a former condition. Rather, we insert our project within the current space of the harbor as a series of conditions which will be enveloped into the larger and uncertain processes of ecological transformation. The figure of the Upper Bay we envision is not fixed but is instead a fluid body with a porous boundary developed with soft infrastructure. The figure-ground relationship of the water and the land constantly changes as it is subject to forces ranging from diurnal tides, flood and dry seasons, and modes and intensity of use.

PALISADE

The word "palisade" derives from the Latin word *palus*, meaning stake. Within the framework of our proposal for the Upper Bay, the various definitions of the word speak to the ranging goals and interests our proposal assumes. The possibility of marking a porous boundary across both politically staked borders and along the edge where water meets land deeply influences this research and our design proposal.

Most commonly, palisade refers to a type of fortification dating back to ancient civilization. In this case, a palisade is a wooden fence made of tightly arrayed tree trunks sharpened to points and driven into the ground. Protecting the encampments of Greek and Roman militaries and many native settlements in the Southeastern United States, these defensive structures vary in robustness depending on the size and density of the stakes. Fences found today are not much different from the original forts, and range from structures defining suburban lawns to porous boundary markers defining zones on beaches and other park lands.

Palisade is also the geological description of the vertical cliffs rising steeply near our site above the western bank of the Hudson River. The New Jersey Palisade is a Triassic period rift which was uplifted during the breakup of Pangaea when molten magma intruded upward into sandstone. The sandstone was later eroded and the igneous columnar formation remains. The Lenape people, the original denizens of the region, called the cliff "we-awk-en," meaning "rocks that look like rows of trees." Similar volcanic formations exist throughout the world including at the Giants Causeway in Northern Ireland where columnar, volcanic formations are eroded by the ocean to form a stepped terrace which is exposed and revealed as the tide cycles from low to high.

In plant biology, a vertical array of cylindrical palisade cells makes up a layer of mesophyll below the upper epidermis of the leaves in dicot plants. The cells contain the chloroplasts necessary for photosynthesis and produce carbohydrates for the plant by absorbing light and harnessing solar energy. In this sense, palisade refers to a geometrical resemblance of the photosynthetic cells to the geological formations and aligns this formation with cellular level energy production.

Interconnected infrastructures and landscapes rethink the current thresholds of water, land, and city.

ON THE WATER | PALISADE BAY

This project is the initiative of a group of engineers, architects, planners, professors, and students to imagine a "soft infrastructure" for the New York–New Jersey Upper Bay by developing interconnected infrastructures and landscapes which rethink the thresholds of water, land, and city. Three objectives summarize the strategies we have developed:

Construct an archipelago of islands and reefs along the shallow shoals of the New York–New Jersey Upper Bay to dampen powerful storm currents as well as encourage the development of new estuarine habitats.

Revitalize the waterfront by designing a broad, porous, "fingered" coastline which combines tidal marshes, parks, and piers for recreation and community development.

Enact zoning formulae that adapt efficiently in response to the impact of storms in order to increase community resilience to future natural disasters.

These three principles—on the water, along the coast, and in the communities—comprise a proposal for a coastal planning strategy which seeks not only to protect the New York–New Jersey region from sea level rise and storm surge flooding, but also to re-conceptualize the relationship between infrastructure and ecology in the twenty-first century waterfront city. With looming climate change as the catalyst for this work, we seek to incorporate conclusions drawn from complex numerical analysis of dynamic systems, as well as formal sensibilities, into a comprehensive plan which enriches ecology and the health of the urban estuary to create a vibrant culture on the water.

Kenzo Tange, *A Plan for Tokyo*, 1960

Opposite
The proposed "soft infrastructure" transforms the Upper Bay into Palisade Bay.

1 FT INUNDATION

2 FT INUNDATION

Incremental inundation

Maps illustrating the incremental inundation of the New York-New Jersey Upper Bay and surrounding area. This GIS-generated map sequence was created by applying one-foot increases in water level to a merged elevational and bathymetric model. The eight-foot and ten-foot increases in water level roughly correspond to the inundation expected in the one-hundred-year and 500-year floods as described in the New York City Panel on Climate Change's Climate Risk Information report. The twelve-foot, twenty-foot, twenty-six-foot, and twenty-eight-foot increases correspond to inundation levels at the Battery caused by four SLOSH scenarios[15].

T INUNDATION

4 FT INUNDATION

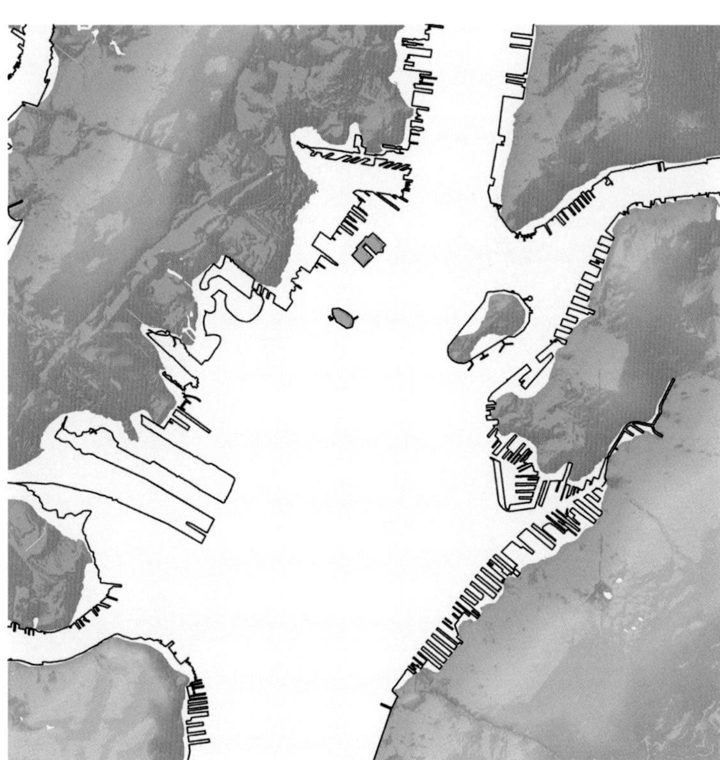

6 FT INUNDATION

8 FT INUNDATION—ONE-HUNDRED-YEAR FLOOD

FT INUNDATION—500-YEAR FLOOD / CATEGORY 1 HURRICANE

12 FT INUNDATION

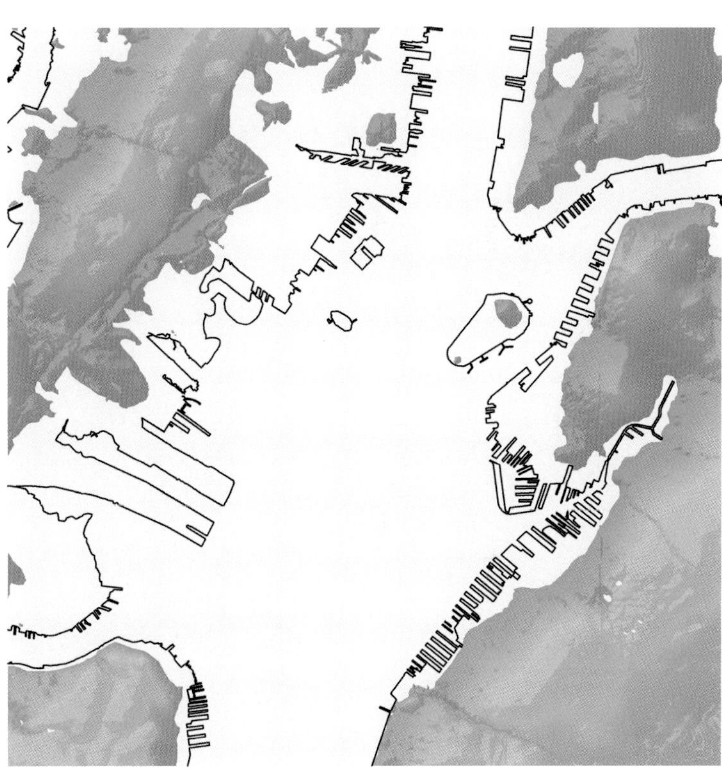

14 FT INUNDATION

16 FT INUNDATION—CATEGORY 2 HURRICANE

FT INUNDATION

20 FT INUNDATION

22 FT INUNDATION

24 FT INUNDATION—CATEGORY 3 HURRICANE

FT INUNDATION

28 FT INUNDATION—CATEGORY 4 HURRICANE

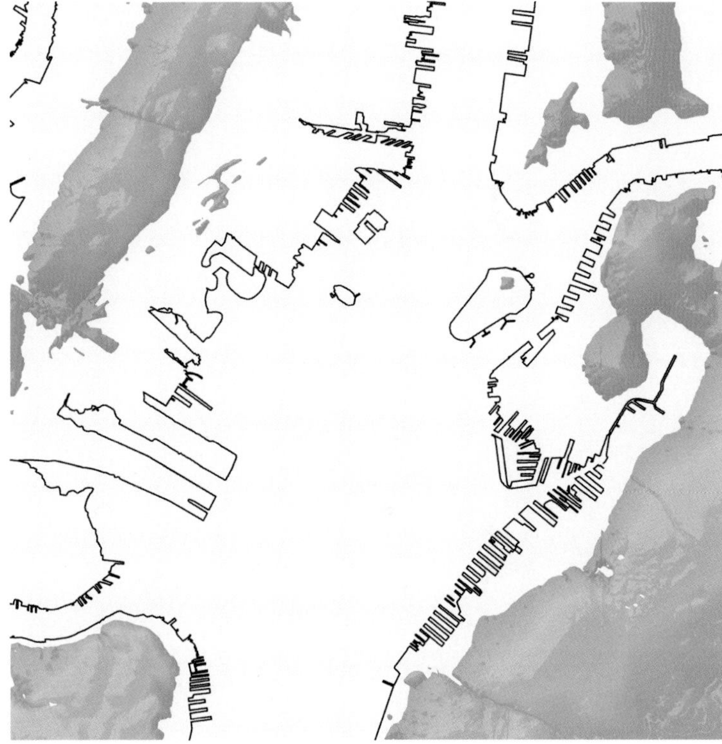

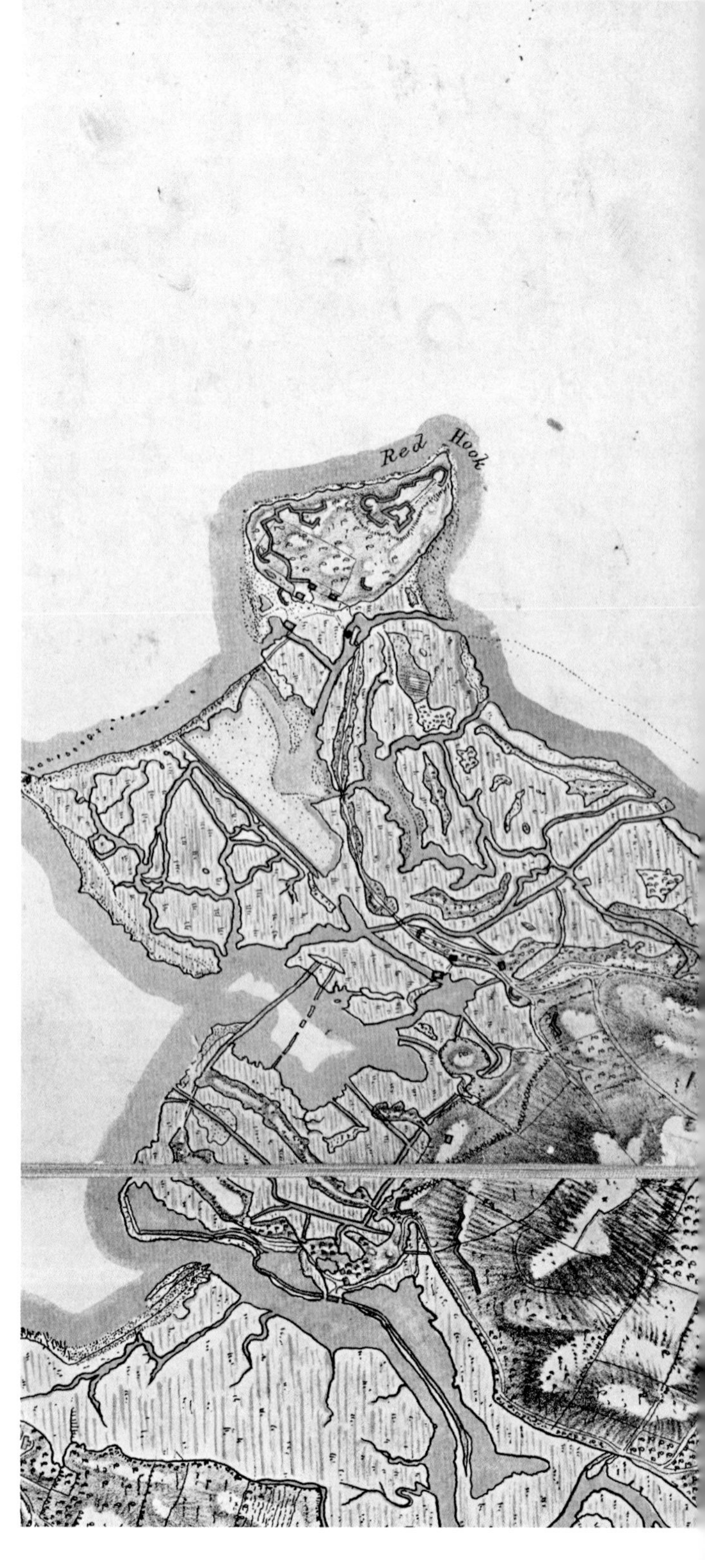
Red Hook

HISTORY AND CONTEXT

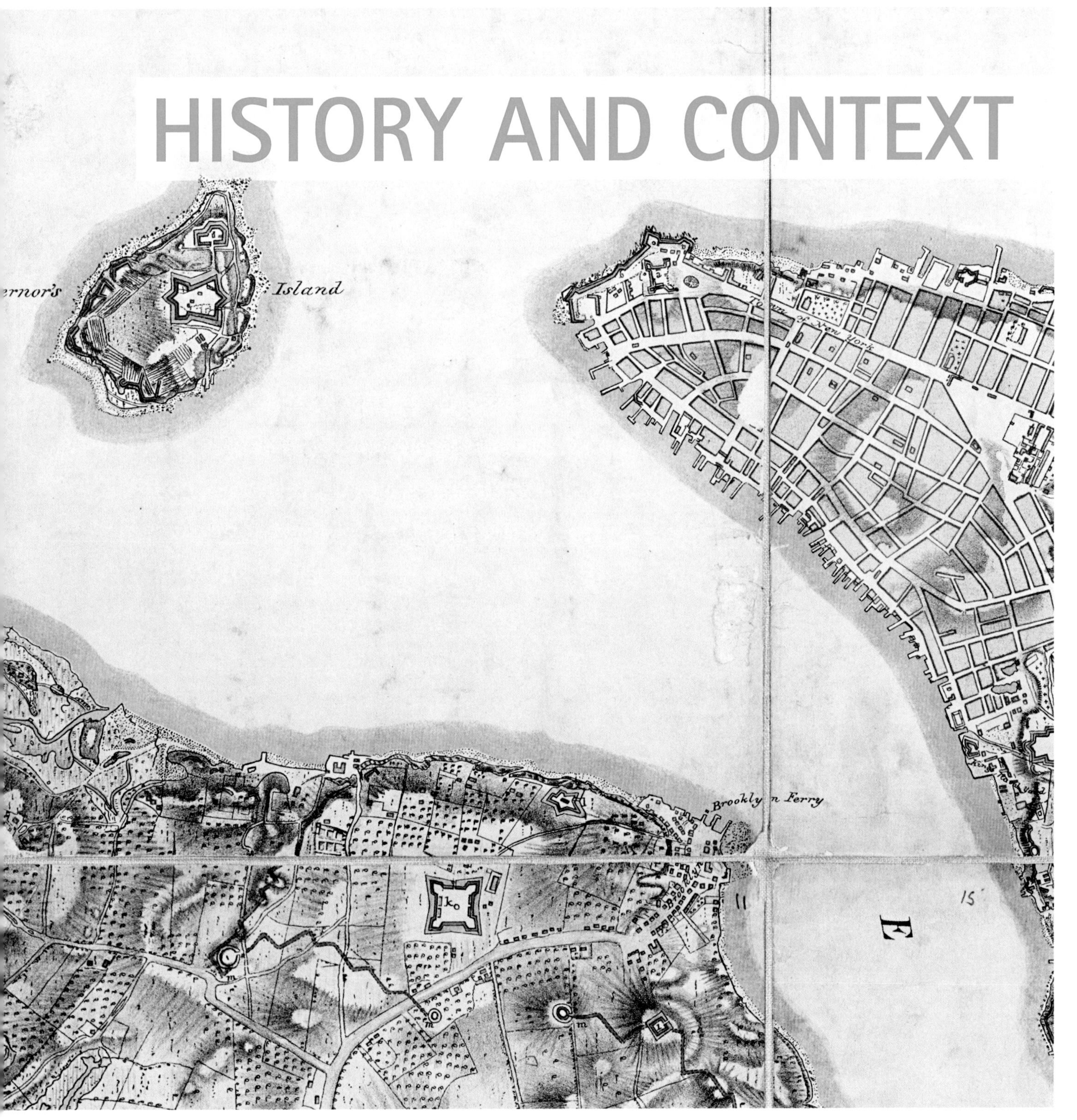

ORIGINS OF THE UPPER BAY

The focus of our project is the Upper Bay of the New York–New Jersey Bay. This estuarine bay is inextricably connected with and defined by the geological foundations of the region, the tidal rhythms of the Hudson River, the complexity of the ocean current, historic industrial and maritime uses, and recent remediation efforts.

GEOLOGICAL FOUNDATIONS

About 200 million years ago, the vast landmass called Pangaea began to break up into the continents as we know them today. The North American and African plates split along Cameron's Line, a band of fractured rock over one hundred feet wide and located more than 500 feet below the earth's surface. This ancient fault line has been mapped as running diagonally from the northeast to the southwest of North America. It runs through Manhattan, along the bed of the Bronx River, under Roosevelt Island, and finally bisects the New York–New Jersey Upper Bay before continuing south along the spine of Staten Island.

TERMINUS OF THE WISCONSIN ICE SHEET

The last great ice sheet in North America, the Wisconsin Glaciation, crept into the New York City region about 22,000 years ago. It moved from the northwest to the southeast, blanketing Manhattan, northern New Jersey, and the northern halves of Brooklyn, Queens, Staten Island, and Long Island. As the glacier advanced, it carved the deep bed of the Hudson River, and as it receded and melted, its great volume of water caused the sea to rise and flood the lowest areas of the region. The Wisconsin Glaciation terminated at the Verrazano Narrows, completely covering the Upper Bay and forcing the Hudson River into a deep gorge far below the surface of the ice. The channel it created, named the Hudson Canyon, remains an underwater trench 3,000 feet deep and extending into the Atlantic Ocean.

THE PRE-COLONIAL HUDSON RIVER MUHHEAKUNNUK

The source of the Hudson River is high in the Adirondack Mountains, 315 miles north of the Upper Bay. From the location of today's George Washington Bridge, south to the ocean, the water is an estuarine mix of both fresh and salt waters. Because the rise of sea level was induced by the melting of the last glacier, the river is essentially flooded by the ocean's tides two times every day with the ocean water flowing up the river and then out again. Thus, the region's first

Map showing the direction of ice movement in northern New Jersey, Geological Survey of New Jersey, 1902 (detail)

Opposite
Mark Tiddeman, *A Draught of New York from the Hook to New York Town*, 1737, engraving

Previous pages
Facsimile of the unpublished *British headquarters coloured manuscript map of New York & environs 1782*, 1900 (detail)

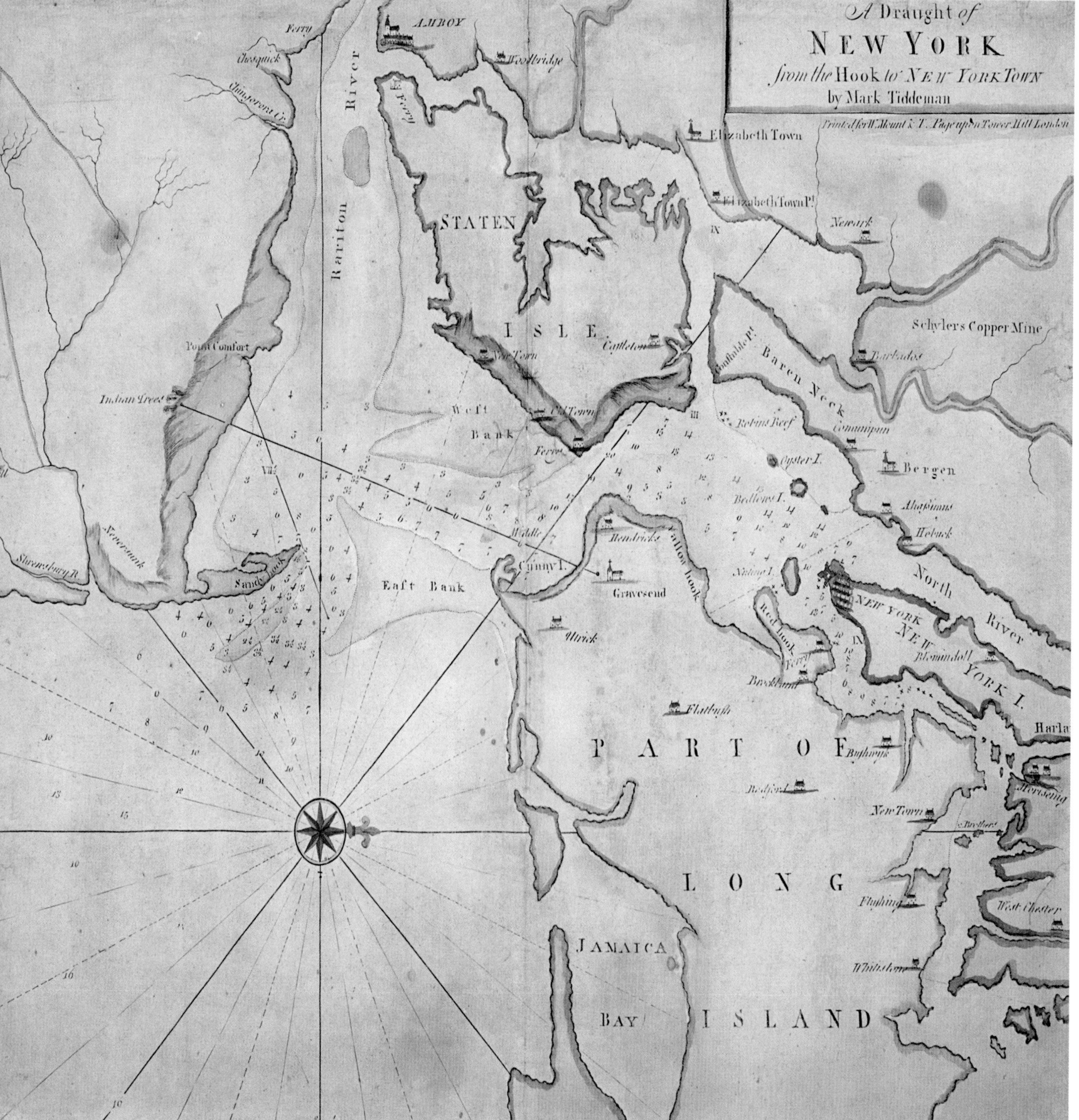

A Draught of
NEW YORK
from the Hook to NEW YORK TOWN
by Mark Tiddeman
Printed for W. Mount & T. Page upon Tower Hill London
AMBOY
Woodbridge
Ferry
Elizabeth Town
Elizabeth Town Pt.
Newark
Schylers Copper Mine
Barbados
Raritton River
STATEN
ISLE
Castleton
New Town
Old Town
West Bank
Ferry
Point Comfort
Indian Trees
Baren Neck
Robins Reef
Comunipau
Oyster I.
Bergen
Bedlows I.
Hebuck
North River
NEW YORK
NEW YORK I.
Blomindoll
Harla
Hendricks
Gravesend
Sandy Hook
East Bank
Conny I.
Utrick
Red hook
Ferry
Brookland
Flatbush
PART OF
LONG
ISLAND
Bedford
New Town
Flushing
West Chester
JAMAICA
BAY
Shrewsbury R.
Neversunk

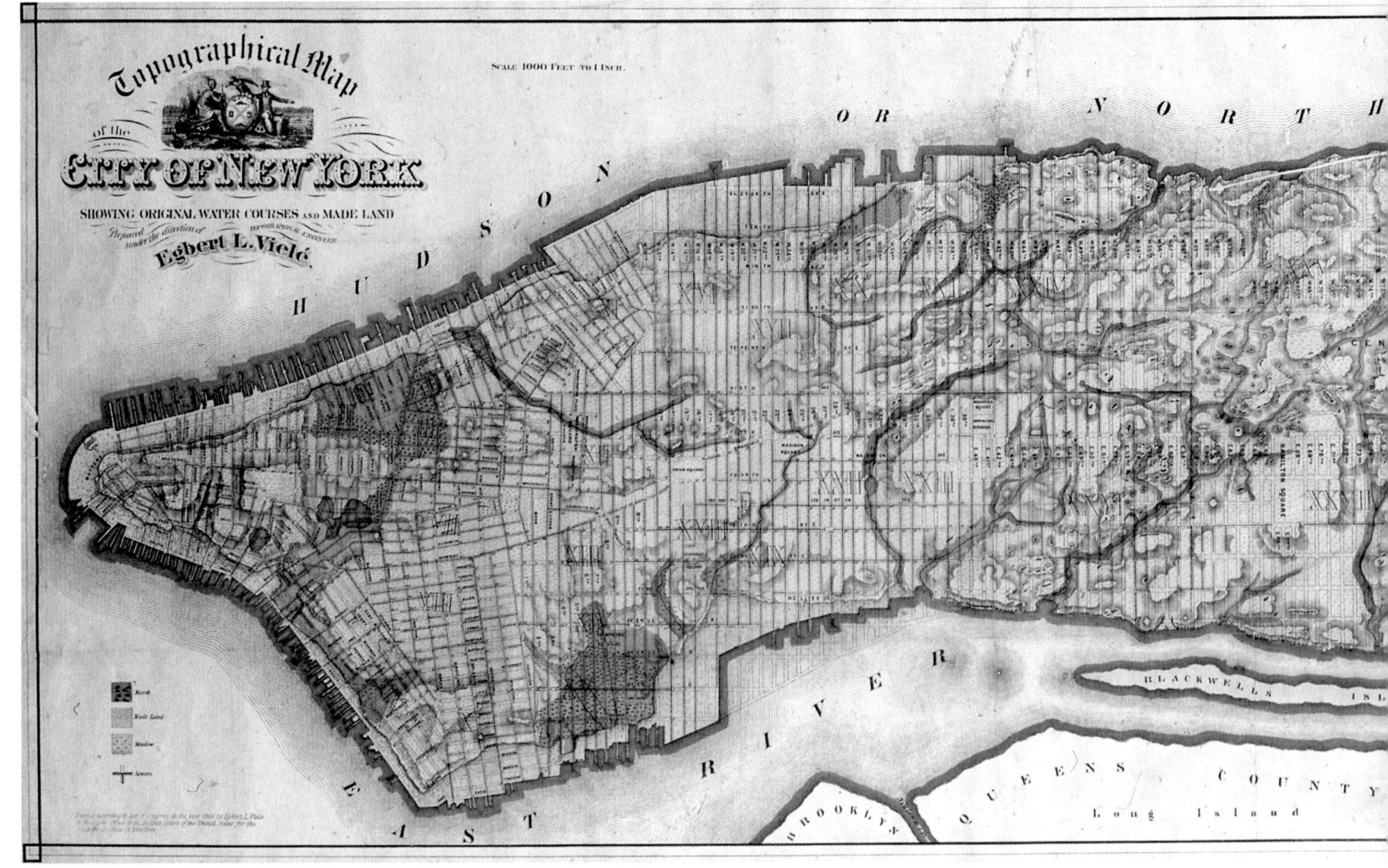

Egbert L. Viele, *Topographical map of New York showing watercourses and made land*, 1865

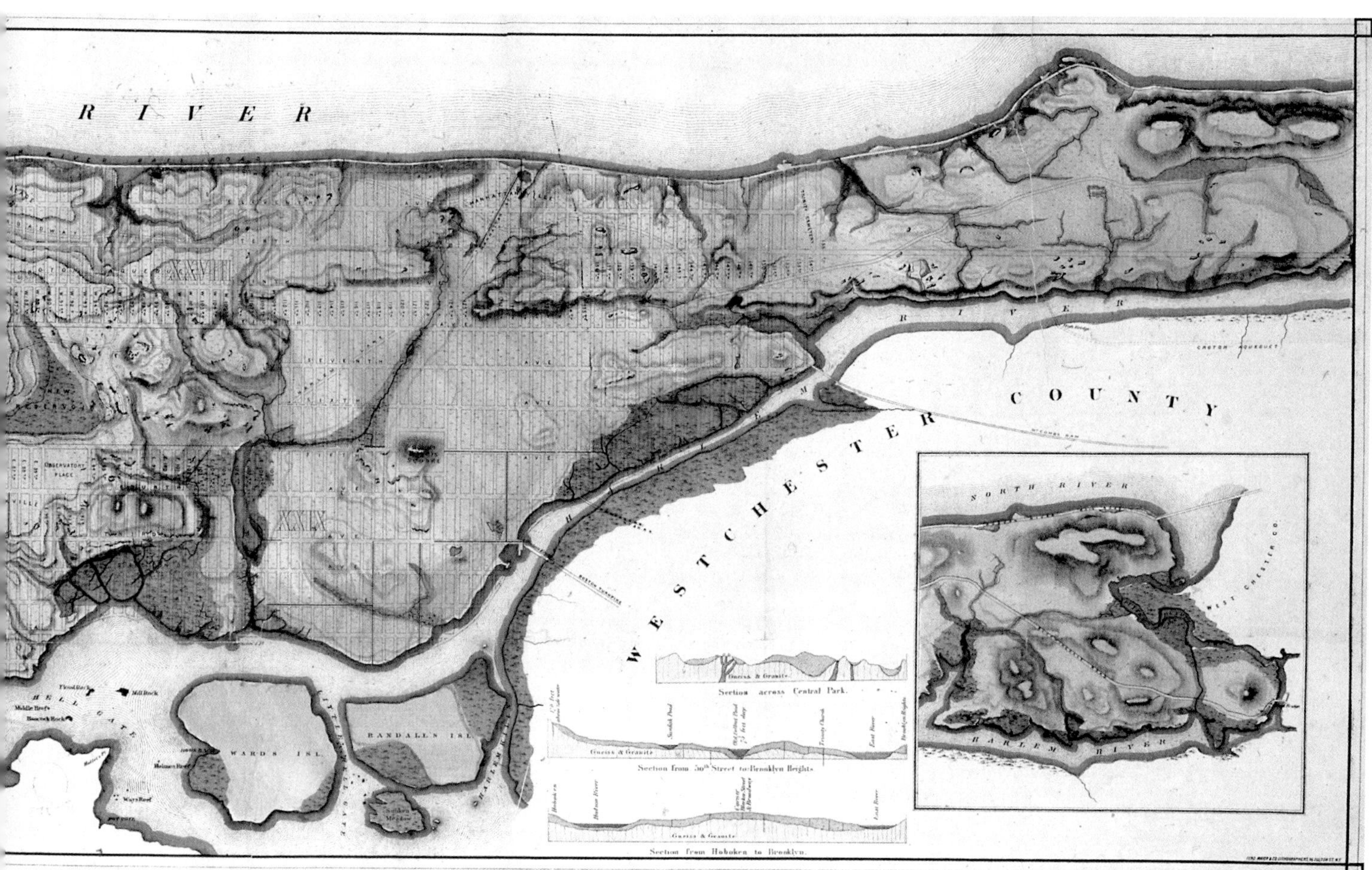
RIVER
XXVIII
XXIX
OBSERVATORY PLACE
SEVENTH AVE
RIVER
CROTON AQUEDUCT
COUNTY
WESTCHESTER
Gneiss & Granite
Section across Central Park.
Gneiss & Granite
Section from 50th Street to Brooklyn Heights
Gneiss & Granite
Section from Hoboken to Brooklyn.
HELL GATE
Mill Rock
WARDS ISL.
RANDALLS ISL.
HARLEM RIVER
NORTH RIVER
WEST CHESTER CO.
HARLEM RIVER

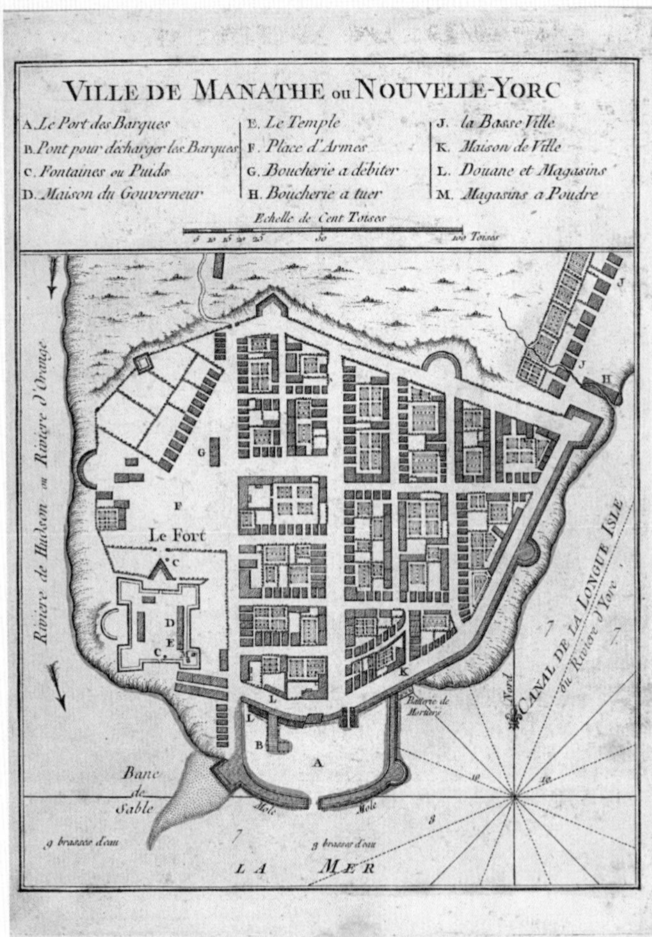

Jacques Nicolas Bellin, *Ville de Manathe ou Nouvelle-Yorc*, 1764

Opposite
Daniel Beard, "Opening of the Oyster Season," in *Harper's Weekly*, September 16, 1882

settlers, a Delaware tribe speaking a dialect called Munsee, named the river Muhheakunnuk, meaning "the river that runs both ways." 260 billion cubic feet of ocean water flow up through the Verrazano Narrows diurnally, while fresh water from the river and its tributaries flows out to sea with the low tide.[16] The river's current runs upstream all the way to the city of Albany and then flows back out to the Atlantic, creating a mixture of fresh and saline waters ideal for an estuarine ecosystem.

EUROPEAN EXPLORATION AND COLONIZATION

> At the end of a hundred leagues we found a very agreeable location situated within two prominent hills, in the midst of which flowed to the sea a very great river, which was deep at the mouth.
> —Giovanni da Verrazano

In 1524, Verrazano enjoyed a brief stay at the gate of the harbor before a strong wind forced his ship to turn around. The Florentine explorer, sailing under the French flag, noted the presence of a large "lake" and amiable native people.

HENRY HUDSON AND THE NORTHWEST PASSAGE

In 1609, the English explorer Henry Hudson and his crew arrived to the region aboard the Half Moon, in search of the legendary "Northwest Passage" to China and India. Upon entering the Upper Bay, he ventured further up the waterway which was subsequently named for him. Hudson reported back to his sponsor, the Dutch East India Company, that he had discovered a fine harbor, a wide river, and a pleasant region promising a prosperous fur trade.

THE COLONIAL PERIOD

Following Hudson's expedition, a small group of Dutch settlers colonized the island of Manhattan. In 1626, Peter Minuit purchased the land from the Native Americans, who had already inhabited the island, and established New Amsterdam. Within forty years, the Dutch lost the island to the British and it was renamed New York. The new colony took root in the complex topography between land, river, and ocean known as an estuary. The environment of the estuary is one rich in fauna, despite the need for estuarine creatures to adjust to a continually changing balance of fresh and saline waters. Currently over 330 species of birds and 170 different kinds of fish live in the estuary. Yet these wetlands have been greatly damaged since human colonization began. A map of the historic tidelands produced by the Regional Plan Association shows the pre-colonization extents of the

584 HARPER'S WEEKLY. VOLUME XXVI, NO. 1343.

1. Dredging through the Ice. 2. Oyster-Shell covered with Young. 3. Dredging from a Boat. 4. Drum-Fish. 5. Opening Oysters for Export. 6. Oyster Knives. 7. Star-Fish. 8. Dredge. 9. Young Oysters. 10. Oyster Sloops at foot of West Tenth Street.

OPENING OF THE OYSTER SEASON.—Drawn by Dan. Beard.—[See Page 582.]

wetlands. Reduced by more than 80 percent today, these ecologically rich zones between land and sea have been all but erased. The RPA's companion map of today's estuary indicates with gray coloring the significant amount of filled lands in the Upper Bay.

Perhaps the most accurate historic mapping of the original condition of Manhattan and the New York–New Jersey coastlines was prepared by the British during the Revolutionary War. Called the *British Headquarters Map* of 1782, the map's detailed depictions of wetlands, streams, and topographic features were rendered to aid the British in their defense of the island against George Washington's Continental Army. This map detail of Red Hook, Governor's Island, and the tip of Lower Manhattan indicates the marshy wetlands of Red Hook and Gowanus Creek, the original extent of Governor's Island, and the early development of the familiar feathered edge of piers and slips along Manhattan's East River coastline.

INDUSTRIALIZATION AND SANITATION

Shipping and maritime industries rapidly developed along the coastlines of the Upper Bay, because of the calm waters and the broad width and depth of the Hudson River. The estuary was soon transformed by human interventions, specifically by the process of channel dredging and filling. The edge of the shore was soon lined with a fringe of perpendicular piers and slips, and large extents of wetlands and small tributary waterways were drained and filled with earth, or covered over with streets and infrastructure.

In 1811, the Commissioners' Plan was proposed by the New York State Legislature for the development and sale of the land of Manhattan. A uniform street grid was implemented between 14th Street and Washington Heights, without regard for the existing topography of the island. This disconnect between actual topography and the abstraction of the grid led the civil engineer Egbert L. Viele to survey and produce a map entitled *Sanitary and Topographical Map of the City and Island of New York* in 1859. Concerned with the rise of water-borne disease, Viele sought to use this map, revised and republished in 1865 and again in 1874, to indicate areas of substandard sewage drainage in areas of former watercourses and marshes. Since the former streams and wetlands had been filled, the placement of sewage systems was often unknowingly set above the former streams, causing the streams to become stagnant and polluted with leached sewage. Today the Viele map is an invaluable document because it indicates the extent of historic tributaries and wetlands along the edge of Manhattan and the harbor, and superimposes this information with the street grid, extent of landfill, piers, and slips.

As shipping flourished and the population of the region increased, the waters became badly polluted by industrial processes, especially

Oyster beds once lined over 350 square miles of the harbor estuary.

New York Bay Pollution Commission, *Outline map of New York harbor & vicinity: showing main tidal flow, sewer outlets, shellfish beds & analysis points*, 1905 (detail)

Opposite
New York Bay Pollution Commission, *Outline map of New York harbor & vicinity: showing main tidal flow, sewer outlets, shellfish beds & analysis points*, 1905

by the dumping of raw sewage into the waters. The sewage problem became extreme, and as a result affected the habitat and health of the estuary's shellfish beds. Local oysters and clams had once been a significant economic product of the mercantile trade economy throughout the eighteenth and nineteenth centuries, with oyster beds lining over 350 square miles of the harbor estuary. These oysters and other mollusks served the estuary as one of nature's most efficient filtration systems. In 1905, a study was undertaken by the New York Bay Pollution Commission, which mapped the harbor's sewer outlets, shellfish beds, and compromised water quality. This map is significant because it represents both the extent of the shellfisheries' marketable clams and oysters, as well as the hundreds of adjacent sewer outlets. Clearly the two were incompatible; although also overharvested, the effects of raw sewage on the water quality led to the loss of the oyster population by the early twentieth century.

POLLUTION AND LANDFILL

With the development of containerized shipping in the late1950s, the shipping industry gradually shifted away from the Manhattan and Brooklyn waterfronts to the New Jersey ports, located on the opposite side of the Upper Bay. The only remaining active container and break-bulk shipping port in New York City today is Brooklyn's Red Hook Container Terminal, owned by the Port Authority of New York and New Jersey and operated by American Stevedoring Incorporated. A result of the overall increase in industrial manufacturing is the dumping of industrial wastes, especially toxic polychlorinated biphenyls (PCB's) and raw sewage in the form of combined sewage overflow (CSO) outfalls, which have continued to degrade the health of the estuary's environment throughout most of the twentieth century. The Gowanus Canal and Newtown Creek, both tributaries of the East River, and thus of the bay, are two of the United States' most polluted streams. The wetlands have also continued to be filled and developed throughout the estuary region, and the largest remaining protected wetland, Jamaica Bay, is shrinking at unprecedented rates.

THE CLEAN WATER ACT

In 1972, the first federal law governing water pollution was passed. The Clean Water Act authorized the Environmental Protection Agency to begin a National Estuary Program to protect, preserve, and restore American estuaries. This radically transformed the New York-New Jersey Harbor, as municipalities had previously dumped raw sewage directly into the estuary. The Clean Water Act stipulated that sewage must be treated and the water quality

CITY	DISCHARGING INTO	SEWER OUTLET NUMBERS	ESTIMATED POPULATION 1904	[illegible]
YONKERS	HUDSON RIVER	330-341	56000	6
CITY OF N.Y. MANHATTAN	"	1-53	823000	82
" "	HARLEM & EAST RIVERS	54-128	1234000	124
" THE BRONX	"	197-212	297000	30
" THE QUEENS	EAST RIVER	213-238	147000	15
" "	JAMAICA BAY		53000	5
" BROOKLYN	EAST RIVER	159-183	920000	92
" "	UPPER BAY	184-189	271000	27
" "	LOWER BAY	190-193	41000	4
" "	JAMAICA BAY	194-196	122000	12
" RICHMOND	KILL VAN KULL	242-260	35000	4
" "	UPPER BAY	261-278	20000	2
" "	LOWER BAY		8000	1
" "	ARTHUR KILL	239-241	12000	1
WEST N.Y., WEEHAWKEN, UNION, W. HOBOKEN, HOBOKEN, JERSEY C.	HUDSON RIVER " "	279-305	334000	33
JERSEY CITY	UPPER BAY	306-308	23000	2
BAYONNE	" "	309-311	15000	1
"	KILL VAN KULL	312-315	27000	3
ELIZABETH	ARTHUR KILL	342-347	91000	9
PERTH AMBOY	" "	316-329	22000	2
	TOTALS		4550000	455

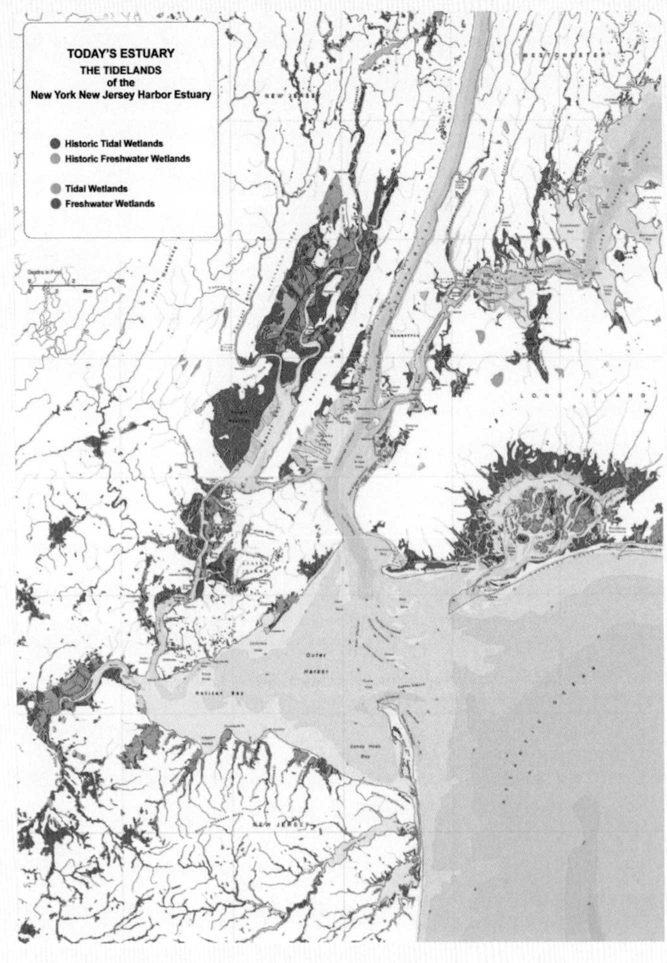

Regional Plan Association, *Today's estuary, the tidelands of the New York-New Jersey harbor estuary*, 2003

Opposite
Regional Plan Association, *Nature's estuary, the historic tidelands of the New York-New Jersey harbor estuary*, 2003

of the bay has since greatly improved. The Act has also worked to stop and reverse the loss of wetland zones. Additionally, the New York District of the United States Army Corps of Engineers (USACE) has begun the process of researching the development of new 'artificial' wetlands. In a further restoration effort, research is underway to develop new dredging strategies that minimize the disturbance of contaminants within the dredge spoils.

But New York City still does not comply with the federal Clean Water Act standards, primarily due to the discharge of raw sewage directly into its waterways when the combined sewer infrastructure is overwhelmed by storm water on rainy days. These CSO (combined sewage overflow) outfalls are the legacy of nineteenth century municipal engineering which collected both wastewater and storm water in the same pipes. New York City's current drainage plan still relies upon this system. As little as one-tenth of an inch of rain per hour can overwhelm this outdated infrastructure and cause major overflows. 450 CSO outlets exist around the city, and through them over 27 billion gallons of combined sewage overflows enter the city's waterways each year.

THE FUTURE

For at least twenty years, most states and the federal government have settled environmental disputes through "credit projects" that benefit the environment rather than funnel penalty dollars into a general fund. In the New York-New Jersey region, General Electric has repeatedly been a source of pollutants and the legal settlements which have resulted have required corporate sponsorship of local environmental remediation. One might argue that this arrangement has led to the birth of the local environmental movement as numerous non-governmental watchdog groups have established themselves throughout the region.

Another environmental transformation is evolving within the United States Army Corps of Engineers (USACE), the federal body which governs the distribution of permits for construction on wetlands. Rather than uphold the previous no-net-loss attitude of the past, the USACE has begun a program of reestablishing wetlands in order to achieve a net gain in wetland area. Currently the USACE is studying the feasibility of such a project for the Gowanus Canal in Brooklyn. The city is also supporting the protection and management of its remaining wetlands by preventing the development of city-owned properties containing wetlands.

To address the continuing problem of combined sewage overflow outfalls, the City's PlaNYC 2030 has addressed the issue through a "best management practice" strategy. This would harness natural strategies such as the implementation of permeable surfaces, bio-

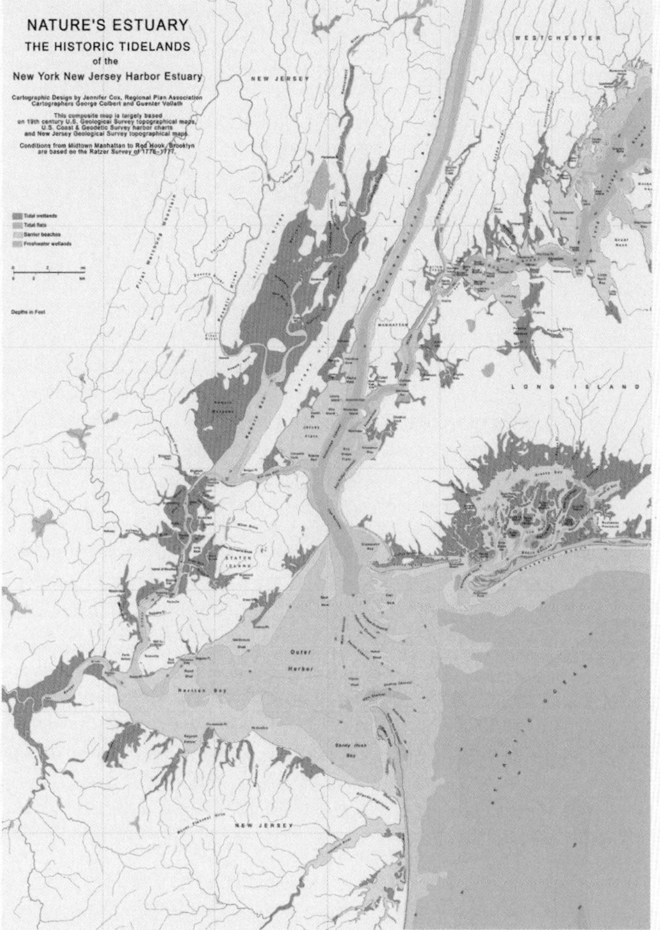
NATURE'S ESTUARY
THE HISTORIC TIDELANDS
of the
New York New Jersey Harbor Estuary
Cartographic Design by Jennifer Cox, Regional Plan Association
Cartographers George Colbert and Guenter Vollath
This composite map is largely based on 19th century U.S. Geological Survey topographical maps, U.S. Coast & Geodetic Survey harbor charts and New Jersey Geological Survey topographical maps.
Conditions from Midtown Manhattan to Red Hook, Brooklyn are based on the Ratzer Survey of 1776–1777.
Tidal wetlands
Tidal flats
WESTCHESTER
NEW JERSEY
LONG ISLAND
Outer Harbor
Raritan Bay
NEW JERSEY

The pre-colonization extents of the ecologically rich wetland zones has been reduced by more than eighty percent.

swales, and green roofs that, by retaining, detaining, or cleansing water, would help prevent storm water from entering the sewage system. Research is also being done to examine strategies of capturing CSOs before they enter the waterways. In addition, the city is beginning a pilot project to test the capability of mollusks to improve water quality by using twenty cubic meters of ribbed mussel beds in a tributary of Jamaica Bay.

Thus, efforts are being made with the goal of improving the water quality of the estuary and its role as ecological habitat. Yet the analysis of the effects of global warming, sea level rise, and storm surge on the Upper Bay, reveals the necessity for even more radical interventions at a large scale. These effects are transformative and real for both humans and marine and terrestrial ecosystems. Our project will propose new ideas about how we might mitigate, prevent, or accept these transformations in the Upper Bay.

Renderings of the waterfront and boating bay at Brooklyn Bridge Park, Michael Van Valkenburgh Associates

Opposite
Renderings of Governors Island Park, West 8, Rogers Marvel Architects, Diller Scofidio+Renfro, Quennell Rothschild, SMWM

CURRENT PROJECTS AND PROPOSALS

A range of projects, plans, and proposals from citizen groups, local government, architects, urban planners, and engineers are currently underway to enrich the waterfront with new park landscapes and wildlife habitats. The following projects are a selection of the schemes that include apt strategies for protecting against the effects of severe storms and providing new waterfront programs.

BROOKLYN BRIDGE PARK
Michael Van Valkenburgh Associates

As proposed, this park will extend over a mile along the East River between Atlantic Avenue and Jay Street, covering eighty-five acres on Brooklyn's pier-lined waterfront. The planned program incorporates playgrounds; acres of paddling waters; courts for basketball, handball, volleyball, and fields for sports such as soccer; water recreation areas for kayaking; a marina; bicycle paths; and a greenway and spaces for recreation.

The design integrates a number of features such as boardwalks, floating bridges, canals, hills, and levee-like land formations which act as sound barriers to the noisy Brooklyn-Queens Expressway. Water access is a primary asset of the park, and the inclusion of wetlands, freshwater swale, and marshlands as a design feature is innovative in its consideration of sustainable, functioning habitats. Another notable feature is the pair of "safe-water zones." These two connected basins, which cover approximately twelve acres, provide a secure water area for non-motorized boats. In these bays, marine structures, namely floating breakwaters, would serve to attenuate waves from passing boats.

The combination of piers, water, marshlands, and levees offers an important model for coastal development and storm protection. Piers act as breakwaters and energy dissipaters—i.e. fenders—and marshlands and levees as sustaining, and sustainable, ecologies and storm protection. The hard/soft fender pier and wetland combination will reappear as one of the two or three key strategies for this project.

EAST RIVER WATERFRONT
SHoP Architects, Ken Smith Landscape Architect, and ARUP

In contrast to the Brooklyn Bridge Park, the East River Waterfront Project is constrained by the decision to work with the elevated FDR Drive, and the resulting narrow strip of sunlit land along the waterfront. The proposal includes three elements: the piers, the esplanade, and the slipways. The existing Pier 15 is being rebuilt, possibly with two decks over some portions. The esplanade includes some planted areas along the east edge with a system for storm water collection

and filtering for reuse as irrigation. The slips are presented as "get downs" proposed at the locations of old docking slips (Peck Slip, Catherine Slip) to allow better visual access to the water from the far side of the FDR, as well as manifestations of tidal and sea level changes. A notable feature of the esplanade is an "archipelago walkway" that will connect outboard from the old Staten Island Ferry Terminal to the walkway north, around a place where the FDR ramps block the esplanade continuity.

PLANYC 2030
City of New York

Announced in December 2006, Mayor Bloomberg's PlaNYC 2030 pinpoints ten major goals for New York City. Three of these goals address climate change, transportation, and water quality, and will be particularly relevant to the future of the New York–New Jersey Upper Bay. Addressing climate change, the plan pledges to reduce global warming emissions by more than thirty percent, and to build up disaster preparedness, even entertaining the idea of a storm surge barrier. To improve transportation, it undertakes the task of expanding commuter ferry service.

GOVERNORS ISLAND PARK
West 8, Rogers Marvel Architects, Diller Scofidio+Renfro, Quennell Rothschild, SMWM

The Governors Island Park and Public Space design competition proposal by the West 8 team transforms the 172 acre island in Upper New York Bay. Formerly a military base and site for U.S. Coast Guard operations, Governors Island had long been an obscured landmark in the harbor. This proposal suggests demolishing non-historic buildings on the island's southern end and using the resulting demolition debris to raise the topography of the island and build new hills. In doing so, the new topography addresses challenges posed by climate change, rising sea levels and intensified storms. The resulting landscapes also frame views of new brackish habitats, play areas, and waterfront open spaces.

The West 8 team's ideas for gardens, terraces, open spaces and recreational uses build upon the potential of Governors Island to provide a unique vantage point on the harbor. The Great Promenade encircling the island connects visitors to the waterfront by providing unparalleled views of the harbor, Lower Manhattan, Brooklyn, and New Jersey.

GOWANUS WETLANDS
dlandstudio

The goal of this feasibility study is to review the potential for creating wetlands in the Gowanus Canal, a highly developed area in Brooklyn. The canal extends from the Bay Ridge Channel to the beginning of the Gowanus Creek Channel. Due to heavy industrial use, the canal is now predominantly characterized by poor water quality and pollution. The USACE proposal is the implementation of designed wetlands along the canal which will remove suspended pollutants, restore ecosystems, and provide new habitats for fish, wildlife and benthic vertebrates. These measures will substantially increase biodiversity and productivity in the canal. Different wetland types are being considered, including storm water wetlands, terraced wetlands, transitional wetlands, and turning basin wetlands.

NEW STAPLETON WATERFRONT
Marpillero Pollak Architects and Wallace Roberts Todd

Stapleton, a neighborhood in Staten Island just north of the Narrows, is slated to have its harbor front rehabilitated for public use. Although currently almost entirely inaccessible, a scheme has been proposed by Marpillero Pollak Architects in collaboration with WRT that features a pedestrian promenade. The 1,410 foot pier, diagonal to the shoreline and originally built for navy use, is also being restored. Along the walk will be a series of canopied outdoor seating areas and landscaped areas, which may seem to be randomly arranged, but are in fact carefully planned to create a loose boundary. The inclusion of a cove that will be used as a kayak launch reflects the goal to retain a waterfront that works ecologically.

BUSH TERMINAL PIERS PARK
New York City Economic Development Corporation (NYCEDC)

Encompassed by the Brooklyn Waterfront Greenway and located in the Sunset Park neighborhood of Brooklyn, the unique feature of this yet unfinished waterfront park is a set of "sinking piers"—piers which have been left to deteriorate in the harbor. With funding from the local, state, and federal governments, the New York City Economic Development Corporation will undertake the remediation, fill, planning, and construction of a twenty-three acre public park.

Susannah C. Drake, dlandstudio, Rendering of Gowanus Canal Open Space

Marpillero Pollak Architects and Wallace Roberts Todd, Rendering of New Stapleton Waterfront

Opposite
Bush Terminal Pier Park

James Corner Field Operations, Aerial view rendering of Fresh Kills Master Plan

ENVISIONING GATEWAY COMPETITION
Ashley Kelly, Rikako Wakabayashi

In 2007, the partnership of Van Alen Institute, National Parks Conservation Association and Columbia University Graduate School of Architecture Planning and Preservation held a competition for designers to reinvision the landscape of the Gateway National Recreation Area located along the southwestern shores of Long Island in Southern Brooklyn. The site covers 26,607 acres and was one of the first U.S. National Parks established to sustain both natural and urban ecologies.

The winning competition design was entered by Ashley Kelly and Rikako Wakabayashi. The design concept centers around the idea that wetlands are a landscape in constant flux. It employs a strategy of jetties, piers and marshlands, to create overlapping zones of ecological tension. The designers call these zones Ecotones and in concert, they comprise a layered landscape which reconceptualizes the Gateway site into a vital place where biological ecologies and urban decay can coexist.

FRESH KILLS PARK MASTER PLAN
James Corner Field Operations

The masterplan to transform what was formerly the world's largest landfill into a productive and beautiful cultural destination features a wide range of recreational activities and educational programs which address public concern for human impact on earth.

Situated on the site of a former landfill located on Staten Island, the 2,200 acre Freshkills Park will be almost three times the size of Central Park. Its development in itself is evidence of shifting public attitudes which seek to reconcile dense urban development and vast park landscapes.

While the park will continue to be constructed for another thirty years, development over the next several years will focus on providing public access to the interior of the site and showcasing its unusual combination of natural and engineered landscapes. The topography covers lands once used for landfill operations as well as coastal wetlands, open waterways, and unfilled lowland areas. The tops of the landfill mounds offer broad vistas of the expansive site, as well as views of downtown Manhattan.

CONTEMPORARY URBAN ESTUARIES

NEW YORK CITY
Hudson/East Rivers

Population:	8,214,000
Area:	469 square miles
Settlement:	1626

New York City contains the highest population of any city in the United States, with over twice the population of Los Angeles, the second-largest. Spread across the five boroughs of Manhattan, the Bronx, Queens, Brooklyn, and Staten Island, the city ranks as the second densest city in the country. The most dense is Union City, New Jersey, just across the Hudson River. Today, over 20 million people live within a 50 mile radius of New York Harbor. The New York-New Jersey Bay is the home to the largest port complex on the East Coast of North America—The Port of New York and New Jersey. In 2006, it handled over 149 billion dollars worth of cargo.

The New York Harbor estuary is geographically and ecologically complex. The harbor is also an estuarine complex where several estuaries meet. This includes the Hudson River, the Hackensack River, the Passaic River, and the Meadowlands, a drowned glacial valley; Jamaica Bay, a classic barrier beach wetland complex; the Arthur Kill and the Harlem Rivers, tidal straits; Raritan Bay, the northernmost Piedmont Province River Bay; Pelham Bay, the southernmost point of the New England Rocky Coast; and the East River, which connects to the Long Island Sound.

Both the lower Hudson River and the East River flow in and out of the tidal estuary of the Upper Bay. At this local level, the estuary is fed by two additional rivers in New Jersey via the Kill Van Kull and Newark Bay—the Hackensack and the Passaic. Our study area, bounded by the Bayonne Bridge at the western edge of the Kill Van Kull, the Holland Tunnel and the Manhattan Bridge at the north, and the Verrazzano-Narrows Bridge at the south, covers a water area of about 20 square miles. At its widest, it measures almost four miles across. Winding its way around piers and into inlets, the coastline of the Upper Bay measures just over 45 miles long. Unwound, the length of this waterfront is about the same as the travel distance between Princeton, New Jersey and Manhattan.

Landsat satellite aerial of the New York Harbor at 40 kilometer elevation

Aerial view of New York–New Jersey Upper Bay, 2008

LONDON
Thames River

Population:	8,500,000
Area:	609 square miles
Settlement:	A.D. 43

The thirty-seventh largest urban area in the world, London is facing the reality that a changing climate, resulting sea level rise, and consequentially more frequent and intense storms could flood the city and surrounding areas—putting approximately five million residents, as well as 400 schools, twenty-six underground stations, sixteen hospitals, and an airport at risk (with 1.25 million people, 400,000 homes, and 45 square miles in the city alone). The Thames River, which could not only flood the city but also produce tidal surges, is the greatest threat to London. In an effort to control this, the Thames Barrier was completed in 1983. The world's second largest movable flood barrier, it divides the Thames into fourteen navigable and non-navigable sections and operates by hollow steel and concrete members that rotate and fill with water when a flood threat of large enough proportion occurs. Though currently effective, the Barrier was designed to last through 2030 under the assumption that it would have to be closed once every two or three years.

Unfortunately, the number of times the barrier has been needed has exceeded projections (it was used about two times per year pre-1990 and four times/year post-1990, was closed for fourteen consecutive tides in 2003, and has been closed for a total of 114 times as of February 2009).[17] The city is thus planning for necessary changes. The Thames Estuary 2100 Project (TE2100) is developing a tidal flood risk management plan for the city and Thames Estuary, which includes a new system of floodgates to assist the Barrier. London is also planning to spend approximately 300 million pounds over the next fifteen years on flood defense.

Landsat satellite aerial of the Thames River at 40 kilometer elevation

Thames River Barrier, 2008

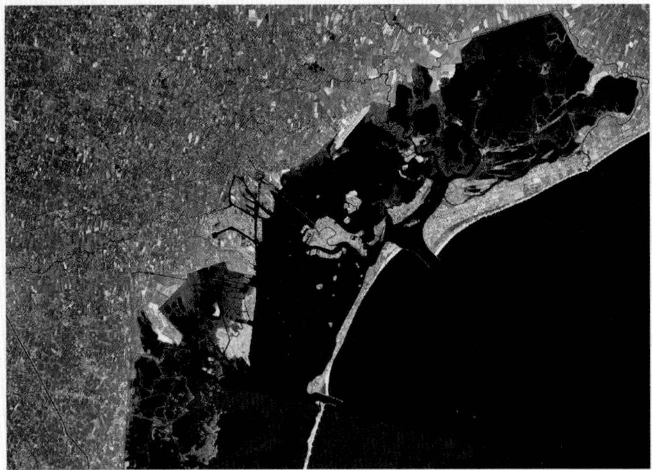

VENICE
Po/Piave Rivers

Population:	271,000
Area:	159 square miles
Settlement:	Ninth century

Venice has been battling the acqua alta, or high tide, since its inception. A collection of islands in a marshy lagoon, the city is separated from the Adriatic Sea by a strip of long narrow barrier islands with three openings or inlets into which the water flows. These high tides usually occur between October and February, although flooding at other times of the year is not unheard of. Though raised catwalks have been a somewhat effective solution to the problem in recent decades, the government has realized the need for a long-term solution that prepares for extreme conditions, such as the floods of 1966 and 2008, when the tide rose approximately five feet above its normal level.

The current proposal is to insert a series of inflatable floodgates at the three inlets. These would normally lie dormant at the seabed and be used only during an extreme high tide. When high tide is immanent, the seventy-nine modules, each 30 meters high and 20 meters wide, would fill with air and pivot around a stationary hinge so as to rise perpendicular to the incoming tide.

Landsat satellite aerial of the Venice Lagoon at 40 kilometer elevation

Venice's Piazza San Marco with the Doges' Palace under the acqua alta of December 1, 2008. This was the city's most significant flood event in the last twenty-two years, with the waters rising five feet before beginning to recede.

NEW ORLEANS
Mississippi River

Population:	485,000
Area:	350 square miles
Settlement:	1718

Draining over forty percent of the contiguous United States, the Mississippi River and its tributaries make up the third largest drainage basin in the world. At the mouth of the Gulf of Mexico is the expansive Mississippi River Delta, a 3 million acre spread of wetlands perched just around sea level. In the midst of this extreme environment is one of the nation's major ports, the port of New Orleans.

7,000 years ago, when the last ice age was ending and sea level was stabilizing, Mississippi River sediment began to accrete on the continental shelf lining the Gulf of Mexico, creating what we know today as southeastern Louisiana. About once every thousand years since then, the river has naturally changed its course to the next easiest route, depositing its sediment to form a total of seven delta "lobes." European explorers arriving in this territory in the 1500s encountered the Balize Delta, still the active lobe today. About 200 years later, French colonists established the city of New Orleans where a sliver of dry land on the east bank, a natural levee, sat just above the water and wetlands, one hundred miles upstream from the river mouth. Within a decade, three hurricanes and a handful of riverine floods swept through the small colony and forced the French to start anew. To protect the new town, a three foot tall artificial levee was erected atop the natural one. Privately constructed levees to control spring floods sufficed until the devastating flood of 1927 prompted the federal government to take action. It commissioned the US Army Corps of Engineers (USACE) to design and build a complex system of flood protection infrastructure to channel the meandering Mississippi River. Since the region depends heavily on the river, the USACE has maintained an artificial drainage split for over fifty years, with thirty percent of the waters directed toward the Atchafalaya—what would be its new natural route—and seventy percent directed toward the Mississippi River.

On August 30, 2005, Category 3 hurricane Katrina caused major devastation, significant damage, topographic loss, and human misery. The city's protection system, under construction since 1965, failed miserably to stop the overland storm surge and eighty percent of the city was flooded. As a result, the population of the city in 2007 was less than before Hurricane Katrina.

Landsat satellite aerial of New Orleans at 40 kilometer elevation

Flooding in New Orleans after Hurricane Katrina, 2005

ST. PETERSBURG
Neva/Moika Rivers/Gulf of Finland

Population:	4,661,000
Area:	234 square miles
Settlement:	1703

St. Petersburg, located at the eastern end of the Gulf of Finland, is often threatened by floods as most of its central territory is located just several feet above sea level. The city has experienced over 270 major floods since its founding in 1703. The city's flooding patterns are closely connected with the movement of low-pressure air masses over the Atlantic. The air moves in from the west, creating "long waves" that bring extra water into the gulf and the mouth of the Neva River. Strong westerly winds and ice then block the flow of water from the Neva, causing the river level to rise and spill its excess water over its banks and into the city.

In 1980, construction began on two massive storm surge barriers from an island in the center of the gulf to its northern and southern shores, isolating the region around St. Petersburg. Although halted for many decades, the project has recommenced and is nearing completion.

Landsat satellite aerial of St. Petersburg and the Gulf of Finland at 40 kilometer elevation

View along the Moika River, St. Petersburg, Russia, 2008

SAN FRANCISCO
Sacramento/San Joaquin Rivers

Population:	744,000
Area:	47 square miles
Settlement:	1776

The San Francisco Bay, formed from the Sacramento-San Joaquin River Delta—one of the few inverted deltas in the world—is a prime source of California's water supply. An inverted delta is narrower at its outlet and has a branching inflow structure. Through its history, the harbors and channels that comprise the estuary have experienced extensive dredging and pumping, which has drastically altered the conditions of the land and water flow, and formed bowl-like islands below sea level, with levees keeping the water from flooding fertile farmland. Over time, land has washed away, tides have become harder to ward off, and levees have been made even higher. The levees have led to the delta's water being diverted and heavily pumped to provide water for area farms and communities; this pumping can be so forceful as to cause channels to flow backward, the power being too much for weaker sea life which is consequentially endangered.

Over 1,000 miles of the delta is edged in earthen levees, which could breach, alter the freshwater of the delta, cause pumps to shut down, and leave an enormous number of Californians without water during a major flood or earthquake. Californians recognize these threats and voted to allot one billion dollars for delta levee maintenance in 2006. CALFED, a collaboration of many governmental and citizen groups, is another way in which California has made attempts to understand and fix the delta's issues. In conducting a scientific report, however, CALFED's findings only determined that the water is being spread thin. The allocation of water between competing users has had major impacts on the condition of the bay. Other problems faced by the delta are current and future urban development and pollution created by both residents and farmers.

Landsat satellite aerial of the San Francisco Bay at 40 kilometer elevation

View of the San Francisco waterfront, 2009

SHANGHAI
Yangtze River

Population: 13,447,000
Area: 2,046 square miles
Settlement: 1553

Shanghai is located at the mouth of the Yangtze River in southeastern China. It has one of the most rapidly growing urban economies in the world, stimulated in part by commerce through the Shanghai Harbor. The population of Shanghai municipality in 2005 was approximately 18 million with substantial growth projected for the period through 2030. Air and water quality problems present major obstacles to sustained growth in Shanghai. Overpumping of groundwater in Shanghai and nearby agricultural regions has worsened flood hazard problems through land subsidence, in a similar fashion to problems created in New Orleans by "drainage projects." Flood hazards in Shanghai are tied to both riverine flooding and storm surge from tropical cyclones. Completion of the upstream Three Gorges Dam promises to diminish hazards from river flooding. The continued expansion of population growth in low-lying regions adjacent to the Yangtze, combined with land subsidence and sea level rise, however, create acute hazards for the region.

A prominent waterfront development activity in Shanghai is the Dongtan "eco-city," which is planned for the island of Chongming, located near the outlet of the Yangtze River. Key objectives of Dongtan are to: adapt to and mitigate climate change, preserve wetland habitat, create an integrated and evolving city, work toward carbon neutrality, and manage resource use in an integrated manner. Dongtan is projected to have a population of 50,000 by 2010 and 500,000 by 2040 (a small fraction of the projected growth in the Shanghai region). Flood hazards due to rising sea level have become an important issue in design of the low lying city. The approach to flood hazards combines traditional floodwall development, modularization of development into elevated flood cells, construction of canals for efficient transport of water during flood periods (and provision of fill material for elevated land), and location of critical facilities (hospitals, police, etc.) on elevated landscapes.

Landsat satellite aerial of Shanghai at 40 kilometer elevation

View of the waterfront, Shanghai, China, 2008

Landsat satellite aerial of Rotterdam at 40 kilometer elevation

Aerial view of the Maeslantkering Barrier, Hoek van Holland, The Netherlands, 2008

ROTTERDAM
Rhine/Meuse Rivers

Population:	589,000
Area:	123 square miles
Settlement:	1340

Rotterdam's Europoort, an artificially constructed harbor on the Nieuwe Mass River in the Rhine-Meuse River Delta of the North Sea, serves as the waterborne-commercial gateway to Belgium, France, Switzerland, and the industrial Ruhr Area in Germany. It is the largest port in Europe, and the third largest in the world.

As early as the 1300s, Rotterdam was an established trans-shipment center for activity between Holland, England, and Germany. The Randstad region, which ties Rotterdam to other Dutch cities, is today the sixth largest metropolitan region in Europe. For thousands of years, the Rhine has been draining run-off and depositing sediment into the North Sea from as far into continental Europe as the Swiss Alps. Beginning in the 1200s, dams, canals, cutoffs, and groins were constructed along the river and its tributaries to maintain navigability, controlling the channels' historic lateral migration patterns and preventing its depths from silting-up. Since 1709, with the construction of the Pannerdens Kanaal, the discharge of the Rhine River has been artificially controlled. Today, a consistently divided distribution of the Rhine is maintained with artificial weirs: one-ninth gets to the North Sea via the IJessel River, two-ninths via the Nederrijn-Lek River, and the remaining six-ninths via the Waal River.

Settlement on the Rotte River, a tributary of the Nieuwe Maas River, which is itself a distributary of the Rhine, dates back to the 900s. Beginning in the 1100s, dams and dikes were constructed to protect the near sea level (often below sea level) flood prone areas of the Rhine-Meuse River Delta. The artificial augmentation of the delta compounded further in 1872, when the Nieuwe Waterweg was dredged to relieve the naturally silting Meuse and Rhine channels. Today, under the direction of Delta Works, Holland's national flood-protection and waterborne-navigation engineering squad, the region is a perplexing assemblage of natural and mechanical systems. Dams, sluices, locks, dikes, and storm surge barriers, such as the 500 million dollar Maeslantkering barrier installed at the mouth of the Nieuwe Waterweg in 1997, are among the types of infrastructure that both protect and engineer this complex landscape.

Another startling engineering feat in the Rotterdam Harbor is Maasvlakte, a 1970s land reclamation project that extended the port out into the North Sea on artificial fill. Currently, plans are being drawn up to extend the port out into the sea even further.

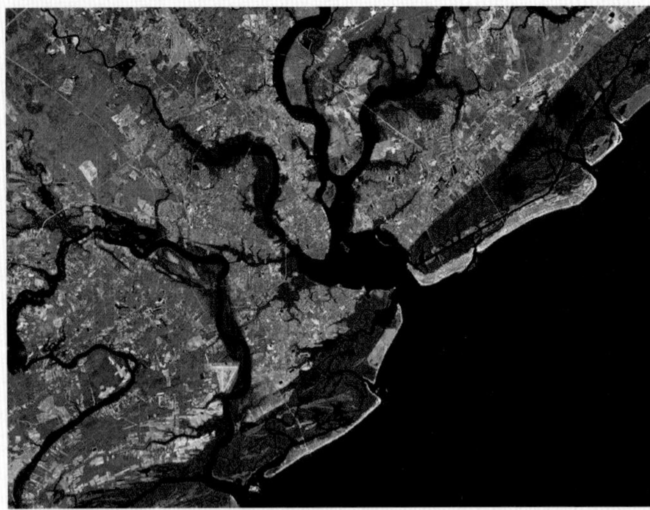

CHARLESTON
Ashley/Cooper Rivers

Population:	108,000
Area:	178 square miles
Settlement:	1670

Charleston, South Carolina is situated on a peninsula between the Ashley and Cooper Rivers, several miles inland from the Atlantic Ocean. The harbor is flanked by barrier islands along the coast, including Seabrook, Kiawah, and Folly Beach to the south and Sullivan's Island and Isle of Palms to the north. Charleston's deep rivers and the presence of a submerged offshore river delta indicate that the land sank or the ocean rose over time. The low elevation of the city, the shape of the harbor, and the position of the peninsula make Charleston prone to flooding from heavy rains, storm surges, and unusually high tides. Charleston was also the site of an 1886 earthquake—the largest recorded in southeastern North America, which caused significant loss of life and property damage. As in Manhattan, the oldest parts of the city, founded in 1672, are located near the tip of the peninsula. Daniel Island, a recently annexed area east and north of the city, is a new 4,500-acre suburban development designed by Cooper Robertson Partners.

The port of Charleston, consisting of five terminals, is one of the most active ports in North America. The maintenance of the waterways and harbor infrastructure of the city are under the jurisdiction of the US Army Corps of Engineers, Charleston District. The Folly Beach Shore Protection Project (2005) is an example of the USACE work. The USACE pumped offshore sand to create a nine foot tall, fifteen feet wide berm along 5.34 miles of existing beach, to address beach erosion caused by the 2004 hurricane season. In contrast to this natural erosion, the Isle of Palms to the north of the harbor is being augmented with new sand through natural processes. Other civil works include the Arthur Ravenel Jr. Bridge across the Cooper River, which is the largest cable stayed bridge in the US. Perhaps the most famous element in the harbor is Fort Sumter, which contained the Union Garrison where the first shots of the Civil War were fired.

Landsat satellite aerial of Charleston at 40 kilometer elevation

Aerial view of tidewater streams near Charleston, 1970

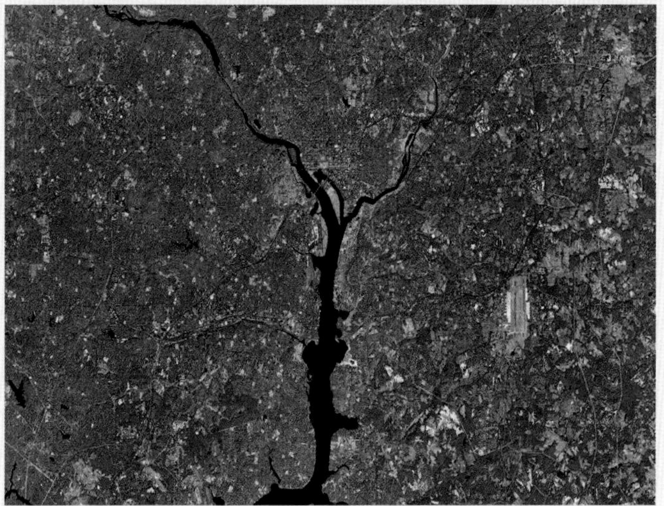

WASHINGTON, D.C.
Potomac River

Population:	582,000
Area:	68 square miles
Settlement:	1790

Washington, D.C. is located on the Potomac River downstream of the fall line that marks the boundary between the tidal and non-tidal portions of the river. The Potomac estuary forms one of the major tributaries of The Chesapeake Bay. The most severe flooding in Washington and the Virginia shore of the Potomac has been from riverine floods, the largest of which occurred in 1889 and 1936. The largest storm surge in the Potomac occurred in September 2003 from Hurricane Isabel.

In colonial times, the Potomac waterfront was viewed as a "malarial swamp," a perception which persisted at least through Washington's first century as the nation's capitol. Water quality issues have long played an important role in the public perception of the Potomac waterfront. The severely degraded water quality of the "Nation's River" in the 1960s lead President Johnson to champion environmental legislation that produced the Clean Water Act in the 1970s. Major advances in Potomac water quality have lead to the reestablishment of significant recreational fishing along the waterfront in the metro region, and the return of anadromous fish species, including shad, that had long been absent from the river. Development of the Potomac waterfront is linked to long standing legal issues concerning "ownership" of the river—extending back to George Washington's 1760s surveys of the headwaters of the river to adjudicate the competing claims of Lord Baltimore of Maryland and Lord Fairfax of Virginia. Waterfront development in the Washington metropolitan region, like development of the New York Harbor waterfront region, has been heavily influenced by transportation infrastructure along the Potomac River. The "highway-parkland" mode of development is prominent on both banks. Large airports are prominent features of the waterfront, both visually and "acoustically." A major waterfront redevelopment effort is underway along the Annacostia River, a tributary of the Potomac passing through low-income areas of eastern Washington, D.C.

Landsat satellite aerial of Washington, D.C. at 40 kilometer elevation

Aerial view of the Potomac River, Washington, D.C.

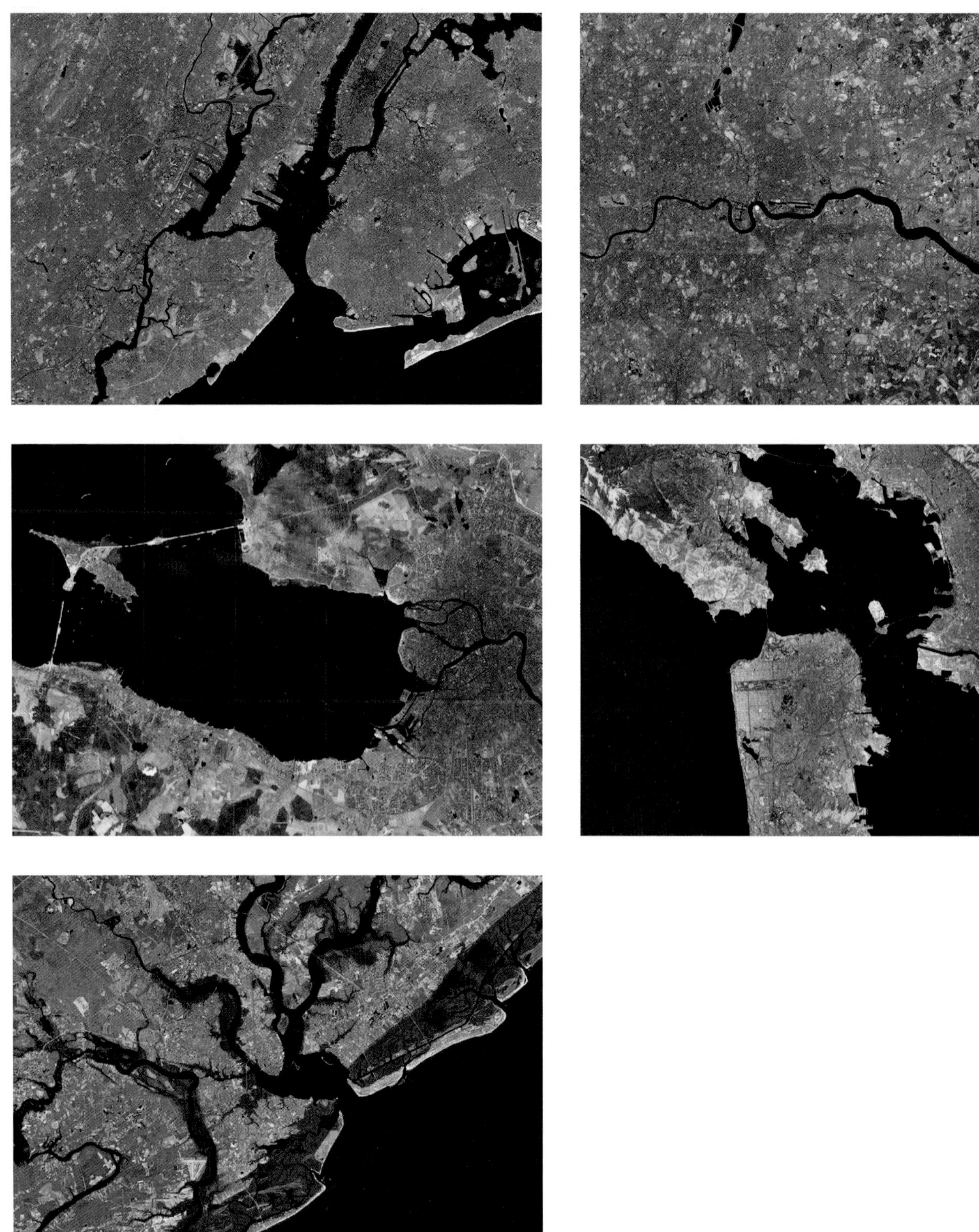

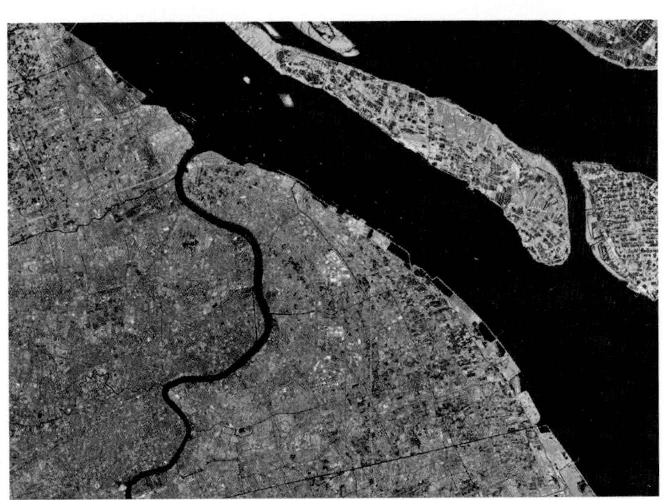

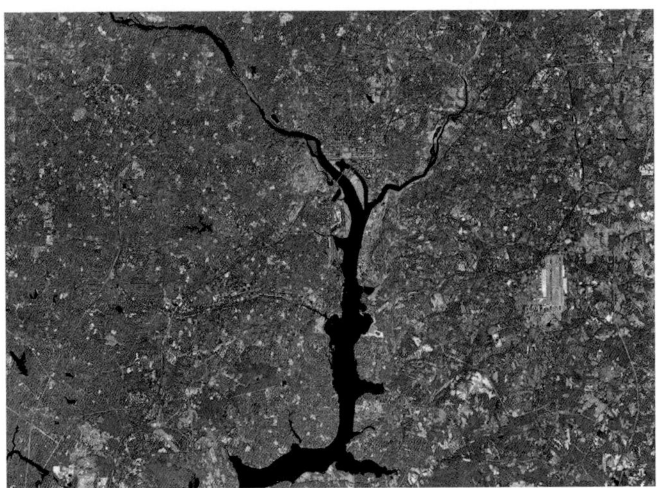

Landsat satellite images at 40 kilometer elevation of selected major urban estuaries at risk from rising sea level and storm surge inundation

from top left, across:
New York City
London
Venice
New Orleans
St. Petersburg
San Francisco
Shanghai
Rotterdam
Charleston
Washington, D.C.

ANALYSIS

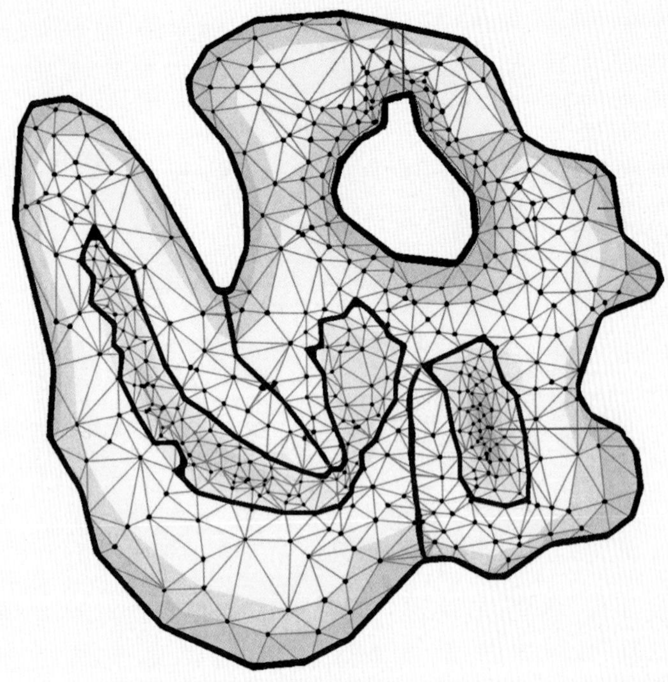

Triangular Irregular Network (TIN) Surface

Previous pages
View of flood extents and elevations in the Upper Bay generated with DEM representation

GIS AND HAZUS ANALYSES

Models were created to understand the consequences of flooding and its potential impact on our infrastructure, ecosystems, and coastal communities. These models incorporate information about water depth and land elevation in the New York–New Jersey metropolitan area and have been collected and analyzed in order to predict both water level during storm events and potential consequences on the environment, infrastructure, transportation systems, and people in the region. Elevation data was initially collected and combined with the use of GIS to form a land and harbor bathymetric model referenced to a single datum. These models were then analyzed with the HAZUS (Hazards US) risk assessment methodology to determine potential impacts and consequences from flooding events.

USING GIS

Geographic Information Systems (GIS) technology was used to collect, store, combine, analyze, and overlay large amounts of information and data related to a common location. GIS technology initially enabled the team to develop geographically based databases and map them in relation to one another. This tool has allowed us to relate different types of information in a spatial context and to reach a conclusion about these relationships. For example, using data about elevations and the location, height, and value of buildings, we were able to relate the intensity of inundated flood areas to every building in the region, and estimate an aggregate of what losses might result. Moreover, we were able to forecast how floodwater profiles generated by likely scenario events would be experienced by different buildings within a region.

Elevation data, for both land and harbor bathymetry, is key to this study. One type of feature which represents elevation information is a digital elevation model (DEM). A DEM is a digital representation of ground surface topography and terrain; it is typically represented as a raster (a grid of squares with values) or as a triangular irregular network (TIN).

Information about water depths and land elevations in the New York–New Jersey metropolitan area was necessary in order to make the best possible predictions of water level during storm events. With GIS models, we were able to highlight areas of interest and view, understand, question, interpret, and visualize the data.

DATA COLLECTION

Data sets utilized in this study include sea level observations, meteorological data, historic shoreline, and sounding depth data, US Geological Survey 7.5 feet (and higher resolution) Digital Elevation

AERIAL IMAGERY
QUARTER-QUADRANGLE DIGITAL ORTHOPHOTO

This image is an assembly of bands of digital orthophoto quarter-quadrangles from the US Geological Survey (2007). A lot of information can be taken from this aerial imagery. The density of development becomes quite clear and parks and open space can be picked out from the built surface of the land. The change in color at the tip of Lower Manhattan indicates a difference in the heights of buildings as the ground becomes more or less shadowy. Perhaps the most interesting aspect of these photos, however, is the waterborne traffic visible in the harbor-scale image. The widest distance across the Upper Bay is about four miles and the total area bounded by the Verrazano Bridge, the Bayonne Bridge, the Holland Tunnel and the Mahattan Bridge covers 20 square miles.

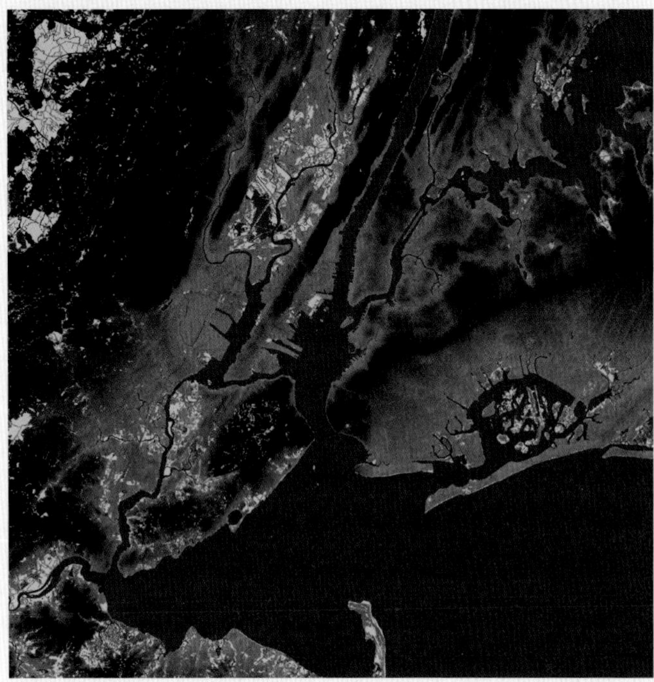

GIS generated map of regional wetlands, 2007

Models and aerial photos. Maps derived from GIS data show topography, population density, household income levels, and housing values overlaid with sea level and flood data.

PROJECTIONS AND DATUMS

In surveying and geodesy, a datum is a reference point on the earth's surface against which position measurements are made and associated in a model of the earth for computing positions. Horizontal datums are used for describing a point on the earth's surface in terms of latitude and longitude. Vertical datums measure elevations or underwater depths and they are either tidal, based on sea levels, or geodetic.

This study uses The North American Datum of 1983 (NAD 83) New York East State Plane Projection in feet as its horizontal datum and the The North American Vertical Datum of 1988 (NAVD 88) in feet as its vertical datum. NAD 83 is the horizontal control datum for the United States, Canada, Mexico, and Central America, based on a geocentric origin and the Geodetic Reference System 1980. It is based on the adjustment of 250,000 points including 600 satellite Doppler stations which constrain the system to a geocentric origin. NAD 83 may be considered a local referencing system.

NAVD 88 is the vertical control datum established for surveying in the United States based upon the General Adjustment of the North American Datum of 1988. Both the topographic and hydrographic data are converted to a horizontal datum of NAD 83 so no additional horizontal datum manipulation was needed. However, thirty different vertical datums were used to collect the land and water elevation data. Manipulation was required to adjust the data sets to a common datum. The USGS topographic data is reported with respect to NGVD 29, a vertical datum defined in 1929, which approximates mean sea level in the US.

Mean sea level for North America was recalculated in 1988 using more stations, resulting in a new zero level known as NAVD 88. This new datum corrects many of the problems encountered in NGVD 29 and accounts for changes due to glacial rebound, tectonic activity and ground-water withdrawal. While NAVD 88 was meant to replace NGVD 29, many workers in the New York–New Jersey metropolitan area (including the real-time tide gauges deployed by USGS) continue to use NGVD 29 rather than NAVD 88. The mean offset between NGVD 29 and NAVD 88 in the New York–New Jersey metropolitan area is about 0.3 meters. In other words, zero meters in NAVD 88 is 0.3 meters above zero meters NGVD 29. In relating information, recorded over different time periods and with different frames of reference, it was crucial for this work to relate information with consistency.

LANDCOVER

Compiled by the United States Environmental Protection Agency as part of the Multi-Resolution Land Characteristics Consortium, the National Land Cover Data set shows the extent of development around the Upper Harbor. In this data set, the color red represents developed land, variations in this color marking different intensities of development. The darkest red, occupying a majority of the land area around the harbor, indicates "high intensity" development. Lighter reds indicate medium and low-intensity development, while light pink, seen in a few large spots represents developed open space. These areas include Liberty State Park, Prospect Park, and Greenwood Cemetery. Green, covering only a small fraction of the land area around the harbor and for the most part confined to Staten Island, represents forested land.

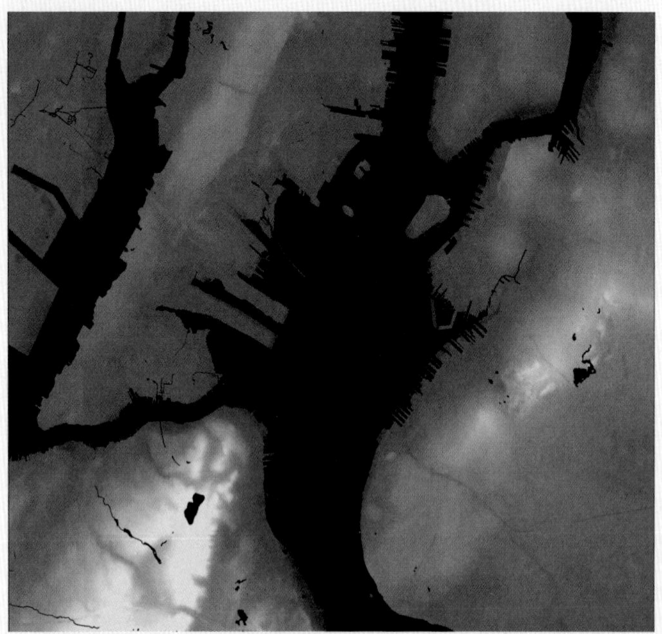

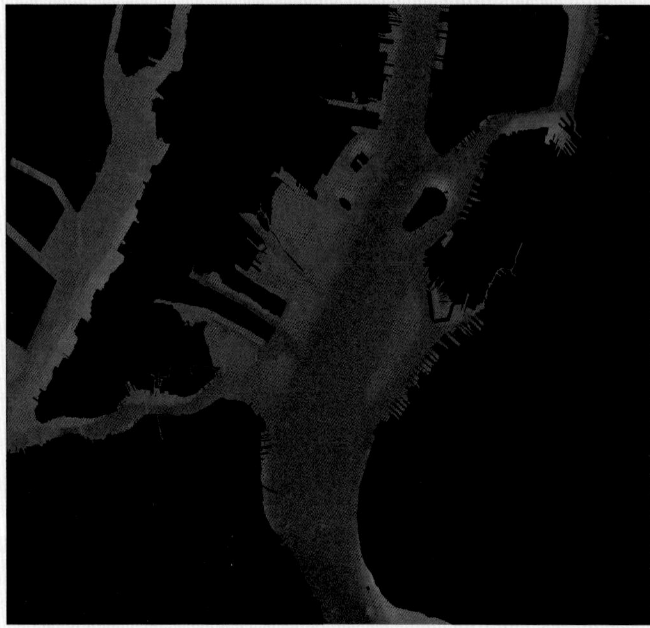

New York metropolitan region, GIS generated map of topography, 2007

Upper Bay and surrounding waters, GIS generated map of bathymetry, 2007

LAND: ELEVATION DATA

Topographic data is derived from USGS digital topographic map files. The USGS National Elevation Data set (NED) has been developed by merging the highest resolution elevation data available across the US into a seamless raster format. Digital elevation data at 1/3 arc-second (about 10 meters) or 1 arc-second (about 30 meters) resolution were compiled in USGS Digital Elevation Model (ASCII DEM) format. The horizontal and vertical datums of these files are NAD 27 and the NGVD 29.

The land in our study area reaches from sea level to an elevation of 400 feet atop Todt Hill in Staten Island. To the east, the east-west ridge of Long Island ends in Prospect Park in Brooklyn. To the west, Bergen Hill, the southern tip of the Palisades, separates the Hackensack-Passaic Rivers estuary from the Hudson River estuary. The remaining land is comprised of lowlands in Manhattan and former tidal wetlands in New Jersey and Brooklyn.

WATER: NAUTICAL DATA

The source of bathymetric data is The National Ocean Service Hydrographic Survey Data Base (NOSHDB) as published by the NOAA National Geophysical Data Center (NGDC). This resource contains the primary bathymetric data as measured by the National Ocean Survey (NOS) during hydrographic surveys since about 1930. The GIS software translates the horizontal datum of the surveys to NAD83, and the vertical datum is either Mean Low Water (MLW) for surveys prior to about 1980 or Mean Lower Low Water (MLLW) for more recent surveys. Generally, zero elevation for land data is about mean sea level, while zero elevation for water data is generally the low tide level.

The bathymetry of the Upper Bay tells a history of its lifetime. The deep floor of the Verrazano Narrows about one hundred feet below sea level, the shallow Jersey Flats and the Bay Ridge Flats near Gowanus Creek, and the meandering thalweg in the East River all hint at the geological processes that shaped this estuary long before human settlement. The straight, dredged lines through the flats reveals the deformations made for the benefit of the maritime industry.

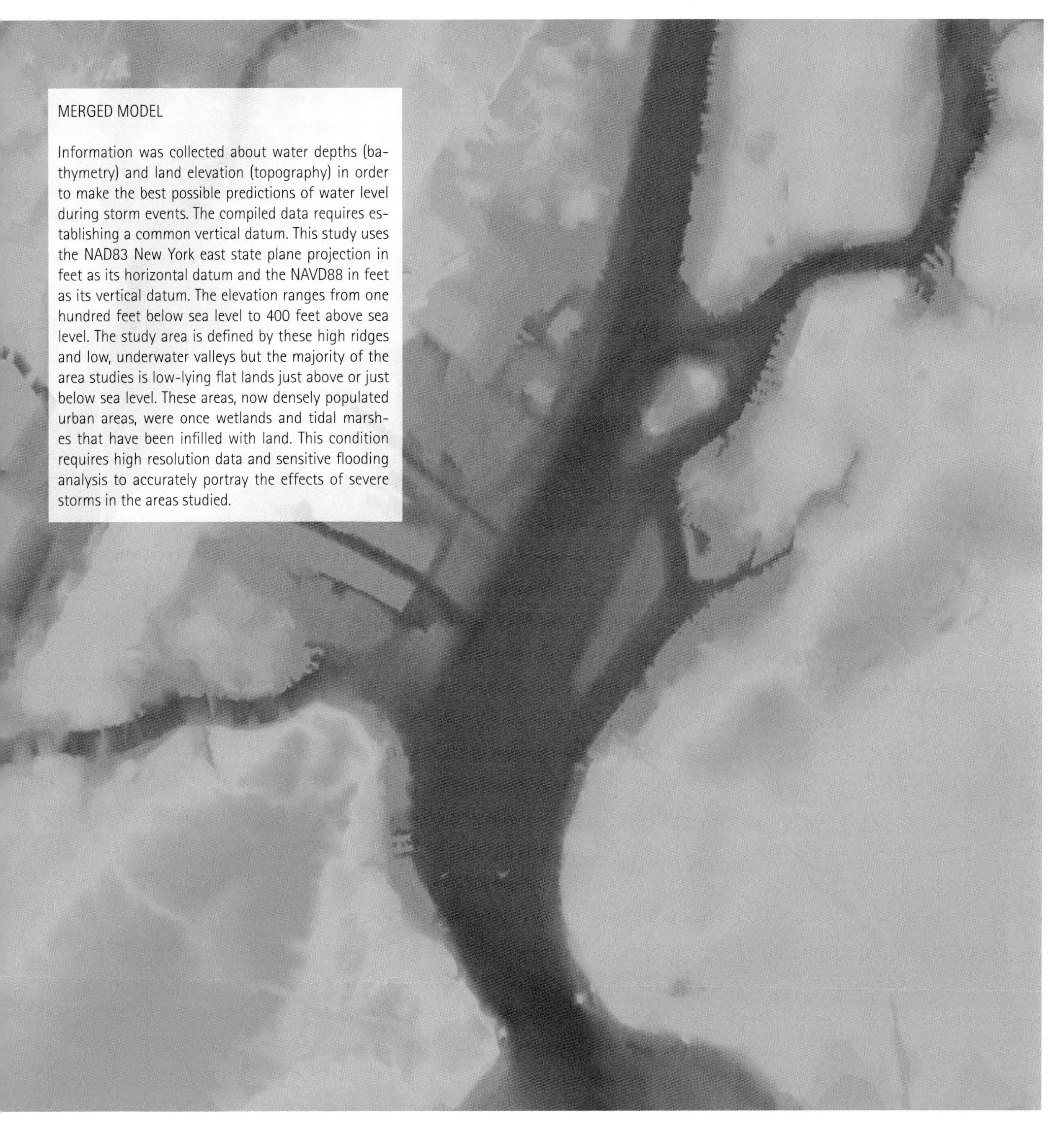

MERGED MODEL

Information was collected about water depths (bathymetry) and land elevation (topography) in order to make the best possible predictions of water level during storm events. The compiled data requires establishing a common vertical datum. This study uses the NAD83 New York east state plane projection in feet as its horizontal datum and the NAVD88 in feet as its vertical datum. The elevation ranges from one hundred feet below sea level to 400 feet above sea level. The study area is defined by these high ridges and low, underwater valleys but the majority of the area studies is low-lying flat lands just above or just below sea level. These areas, now densely populated urban areas, were once wetlands and tidal marshes that have been infilled with land. This condition requires high resolution data and sensitive flooding analysis to accurately portray the effects of severe storms in the areas studied.

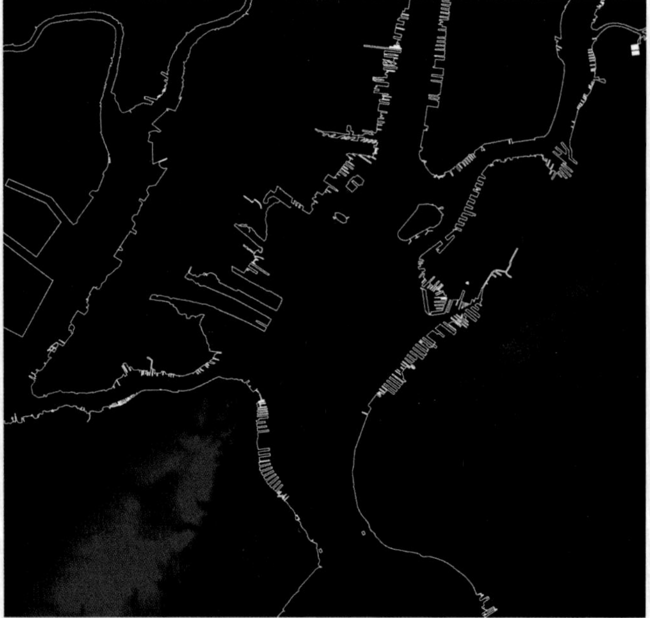

GIS generated map of existing transportation, New York metropolitan region, 2007

GIS generated map of New York New Jersey Upper Bay shoreline, 2007. Constructed shoreline is shown with a white line while the earthen shoreline is shown with a yellow line.

INFRASTRUCTURE

An important requirement for estimating losses from floods is the identification and valuation of the building stock, infrastructure, and population exposed to flood hazard; i.e., an inventory. Inventory data was developed using allocation of census block data via statistical analysis, tax assessor data, and other information about building values, flood vulnerabilities, contents, and occupancies. While tax assessor and census data provide information for the development of the residential structures data, Dun & Bradstreet (D&B) also provided data for non-residential structures at the census block level. Additionally, our model contains data for essential facilities, and selected transportation and lifeline systems, demographics, agriculture, and vehicles.

The geographical size of the region is 124 square miles (eighty-five on land and twenty on water) and contains 624 census tracts. There are over 810,000 households in the region with a total population of 2,038,000 people (2000 Census Bureau data). There are an estimated 540,500 buildings in the region with a total building replacement value (excluding contents) of 22.7 billion dollars (2002). Approximately 88.52 percent of the buildings (and 72.62 percent of the building value) are associated with residential housing. For essential facilities, there are twenty hospitals in the region with a total bed capacity of 10,040 beds. There are 279 schools, sixteen fire stations, twenty-nine police stations, and two emergency operation centers.

BUILDINGS AND TRANSPORTATION INVENTORY

The New York-New Jersey Upper Harbor lies at the center of an intricate network of highly traveled transportation pathways, much of which is at risk to damage and disruption in any storm surge scenario. Higher category storm surges would cause even flooding of the subway system, especially in Manhattan, and inundate more roadways throughout the study area. Most of the region's low-elevation transportation infrastructure will be at risk to flooding in the twenty-first century. For two-thirds of facilities with elevations at or below 10 feet above sea level, flooding may occur at least once every decade, and at some facilities it will occur every few years by the end of this century. It is estimated that losses to transportation systems could be one to two times that of losses to buildings in a severe event.

INUNDATION
SLOSH

SLOSH (Sea, Lake, and Overland Surges from Hurricanes) zones are determined by modeling worst case scenarios for Category 1-4 hurricanes as their surges slam into coastlines. Category 4 hurricane storm surge—with heights approaching 30 feet above sea level—are shown in red and storm surges for hurricanes Category 1-3 are shown receding toward the baseline coastline. The areas most susceptible to these floods are the low-lying former tidal wetlands of New Jersey and Gowanus which also happen to be important centers of maritime commerce. Jersey City and Lower Manhattan are also at high risk. Because of its low-lying lands and proximity to the deep ocean waters, southern Long Island (the area around Jamaica Bay), is the zone most vulnerable in a hurricane storm surge scenario.

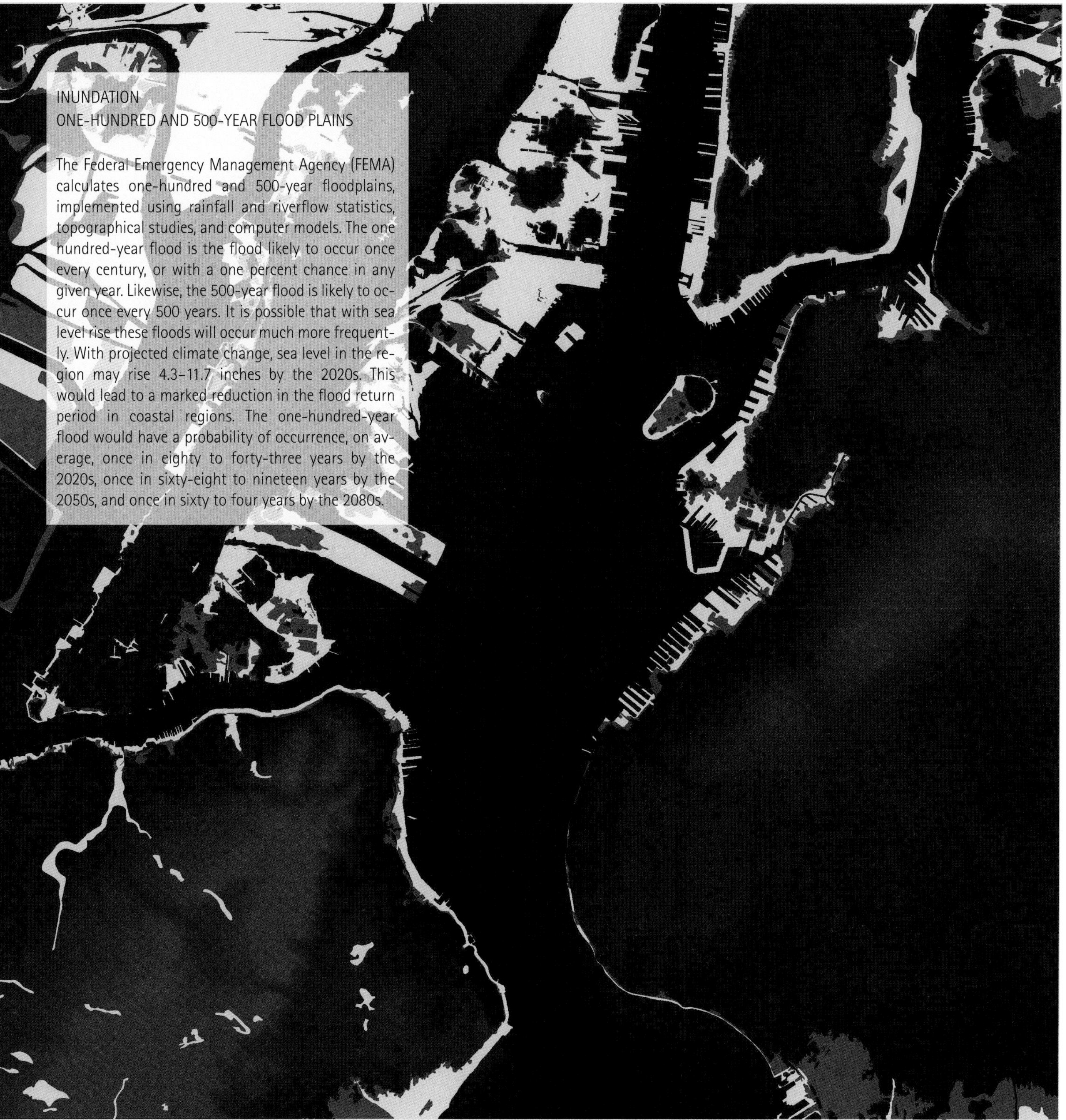

INUNDATION
ONE-HUNDRED AND 500-YEAR FLOOD PLAINS

The Federal Emergency Management Agency (FEMA) calculates one-hundred and 500-year floodplains, implemented using rainfall and riverflow statistics, topographical studies, and computer models. The one hundred-year flood is the flood likely to occur once every century, or with a one percent chance in any given year. Likewise, the 500-year flood is likely to occur once every 500 years. It is possible that with sea level rise these floods will occur much more frequently. With projected climate change, sea level in the region may rise 4.3–11.7 inches by the 2020s. This would lead to a marked reduction in the flood return period in coastal regions. The one-hundred-year flood would have a probability of occurrence, on average, once in eighty to forty-three years by the 2020s, once in sixty-eight to nineteen years by the 2050s, and once in sixty to four years by the 2080s.

HAZUS INPUT

REGIONAL MODEL (LAND AND WATER)

FLOOD ANALYSIS (WATER DEPTH OR RETURN PERIOD)

INVENTORIES

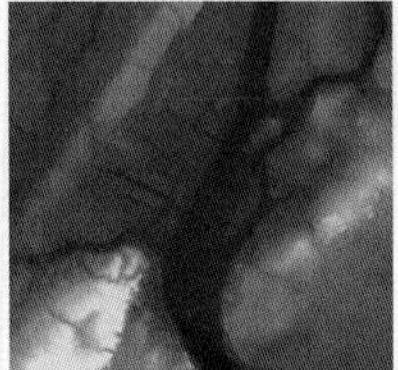

ELEVATION DATA

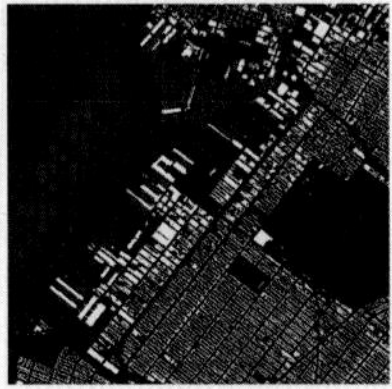

BUILDINGS AND INFRASTRUCTURE

DEMOGRAPHIC DATA

=

HAZUS OUTPUT

INUNDATION AREA

DIRECT AND INDIRECT ECONOMIC IMPACT

CASUALTIES AND SHELTER DEMAND

HAZUS: RISK ASSESSMENT

HAZUS-MH is a natural hazards loss estimation software. The purpose of HAZUS is to quantify the human, property, financial, and social damage of natural hazards such as earthquake, wind, and flood under existing conditions and given a number of possible mitigation measures. Flood hazard is defined by a relation between depth of flooding and the annual chance of inundation greater than that depth. The flood loss estimation methodology consists of two modules that analyze specific processes: flood hazard analysis and flood loss estimation analysis. The flood hazard analysis module uses characteristics such as frequency, discharge, and ground elevation to estimate flood depth, flood elevation, and flow velocity. The flood loss estimation method calculates physical damage and economic loss from the results of the hazard analysis.

Coastal flood hazards are determined by two methods. Both provide a 1-in-100 or 0.01 annual probability of exceedance with a flood surface that serves as the basis for estimating other return period floods using elevation ratios. The first method uses existing data, and is implemented by providing specific ground surface elevations, mapped flood hazard zones, and BFEs. The second method calculates wave crest elevations along shore-perpendicular transects. Required parameters for this analysis include a ground surface, the 0.01 annual probability of exceedance for stillwater elevation, the wave setup at the shoreline, and the initial wave height at the shoreline.

When assessing consequences from flooding, the HAZUS Flood Model uses estimates of flood depth along with depth-damage functions to compute the possible damage to buildings and infrastructure that may result from flooding. Depth-damage functions are plots of floodwater depth versus percent damage, plotted for a variety of building types and occupancies. The extent and severity of damage to structural components and contents are estimated from the depth of flooding and the application of the assigned depth-damage curve.

Scenarios studied included flooding events with current ten-, fifty-, one-hundred-, 200-, and 500-year return periods for the harbor view region. The analysis represents these base-value consequences and losses in terms of equivalent sea level rise changes near Battery Park in Manhattan and as equivalent changes in the current return period events by 2020, 2050, and 2090 as a result of sea level rise.

BUILDING DAMAGE

Flood damage functions are in the form of depth-damage curves, relating depth of flooding (in feet), as measured from the top of the first finished floor, to damage expressed as a percent of replacement cost.

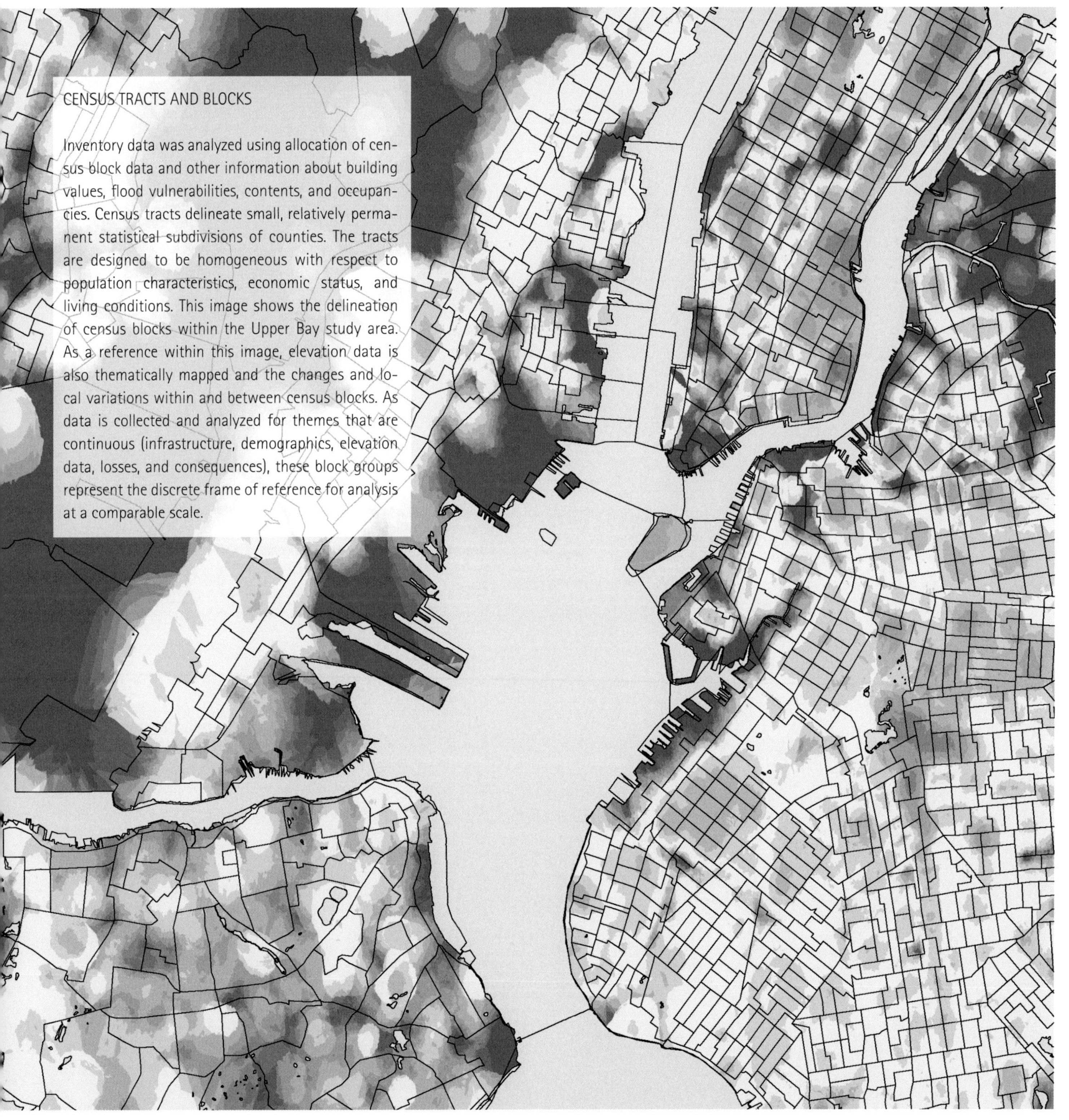

CENSUS TRACTS AND BLOCKS

Inventory data was analyzed using allocation of census block data and other information about building values, flood vulnerabilities, contents, and occupancies. Census tracts delineate small, relatively permanent statistical subdivisions of counties. The tracts are designed to be homogeneous with respect to population characteristics, economic status, and living conditions. This image shows the delineation of census blocks within the Upper Bay study area. As a reference within this image, elevation data is also thematically mapped and the changes and local variations within and between census blocks. As data is collected and analyzed for themes that are continuous (infrastructure, demographics, elevation data, losses, and consequences), these block groups represent the discrete frame of reference for analysis at a comparable scale.

Return Period (years) and predicted with changes					
Today	10	50	100	200	500
by 2020	7	33	65	130	325
by 2050	4	20	40	80	200
by 2060	3	15	30	60	150
Equivalent rise in water (ft, approximate above NGVD 28 at Battery Park)					
	7.45	9	9.7	10.4	13.2
Buildings					
Moderately Damaged	1,612	2,559	2,750	3,172	9,966
Completely Damaged	432	602	640	896	5,129
Debris					
Total (tons)	88,158	213,959	266,262	322,049	660,581
Finishes (%)	94.4	60.8	54.4	52.8	67.2
Structural (%)	1.9	8.9	15.2	15.7	16.2
Other (%)	3.7	30.3	30.4	31.5	16.6
Truckloads (@ 25 tons/truckload)	3,526	8,558	10,650	12,882	26,423
Shelter					
Households Displaced	9,467	11,901	12,246	13,404	34,963
People that require accommodation	26,137	33,080	34,249	37,495	99,671
Economic loss (in thousands of dollars excluding Transportation Systems)					
Building-Related	3,529	11,305	31,099	65,831	165,711
Content	3,332	10,173	27,934	37,748	75,533
Business Interruption	2,674	7,124	19,103	31,704	59,608
Total	9,535	28,601	78,136	135,284	300,852
Percentage of total replacement value (excluding contents)	0.04%	0.13%	0.34%	0.60%	1.33%

This table summarizes the potential flood hazards and consequences within the New York–New Jersey Upper Bay study area as predicted using the HAZUS model, a land and harbor elevation model including bathymetric data and improved building inventory data. The table compares consequences from ten-, fifty-, one-hundred-, 200-, and 500-year return period events relative to equivalent rises in water level. The table also shows estimates for building damage, debris generated, shelter requirements, and economic losses.

Opposite
The top figure shows the relative flood hazard exposure within the New York–New Jersey Upper Bay study area by thematically mapping the distribution of the total replacement value of building infrastructure mapped by census block. The bottom figure shows one aspect of the social exposure by mapping the relative distribution of population density.

Depth-damage functions are provided separately for buildings and for contents. For flood loss analyses, buildings are defined to include both the structural (load-bearing) system, as well as architectural, mechanical, and electrical components, and building finishes. Damage is estimated in percent and is weighted by the area of inundation at a given depth for a given census block. The entire composition of the general building stock within a given census block is assumed to be evenly distributed throughout the block. HAZUS estimates that for a one-hundred-year event, about 2,750 buildings will be at least moderately damaged. For the same event, there are an estimated 640 buildings that will be completely destroyed. A current 500-year event could result in five times as many moderates and ten times as many complete.

The buildings with the greatest risk in our study area in a Category 1 hurricane storm surge are the industrial warehouses, factories, and plants that line the shores of lower Hudson County, New Jersey, and Brooklyn. Generally located in low-lying areas close to the water, these facilities—and thus the money and materials invested in them, and the jobs they provide—are at high risk. Similarly, the economic real estate centered in the Financial District of Lower Manhattan could be devastated by flooding in a hurricane, as would businesses in Jersey City. Neighborhoods throughout the study area—such as Red Hook, Sunset Park, Williamsburg, and Greenpoint in Brooklyn; Greenwich Village and the Lower East Side in Lower Manhattan; Jersey City; and even parts of Staten Island—would be endangered in a hurricane.

DEBRIS GENERATION

HAZUS estimates the amount of debris that will be generated by the flood. The model breaks debris into three general categories: finishes (dry wall, insulation, etc.); structural (wood, brick, etc.); and foundations (concrete slab, concrete block, rebar, etc.). This distinction is made because of the different types of equipment required to handle the debris. For the benchmark one-hundred-year event, the model estimates that a total of 226,000 tons of debris will be generated. Of the total amount, finishes comprises 54.4 percent of the total, while structure comprises 15.2 percent of the total. If the debris tonnage is converted into an estimated number of truckloads, it will require 10,650 truckloads (at twenty-five tons/truck) to remove the debris generated by the flood. Similar estimates are provided for other events.

SOCIAL IMPACT

Shelter Requirements HAZUS estimates the number of households that are expected to be displaced from their homes due to the flood and the associated potential evacuation. Additionally HAZUS also

estimates the number of displaced people that will require accommodation in temporary public shelters. For the benchmark one-hundred-year event, the model estimates 12,246 households will be displaced due to the flood. Displacement includes households evacuated from within or very near to the inundated area. Of these, 34,249 people will seek temporary shelter in public shelters

ECONOMIC LOSS

For the benchmark one-hundred-year event, the total economic loss estimated for the flood is 78.1 million dollars, which represents 34 percent of the total replacement value of the study case buildings. A current 500-year event could result in four times this loss. The building losses are broken into two categories: direct building losses and business interruption losses. The direct building losses are the estimated costs to repair or replace the damage caused to the building and its contents. The business interruption losses are the losses associated with inability to operate a business because of damages sustained during the flood. Business interruption losses also include the temporary living expenses for those people displaced from their homes because of the flood. For a current one-hundred-year event, the total building-related losses were 31 million dollars. An additional 19 million dollars of the estimated losses were related to the business interruption of the region.

FUTURE ANALYSIS

The discussed HAZUS studies and their results are based on static analyses of flooding scenarios. Additionally, this research has implemented advanced models to capture the dynamic nature of flooding and their interactions within the region. These dynamic analyses and robust simulations need to be incorporated within a HAZUS analysis to better understand the significance of their effects.

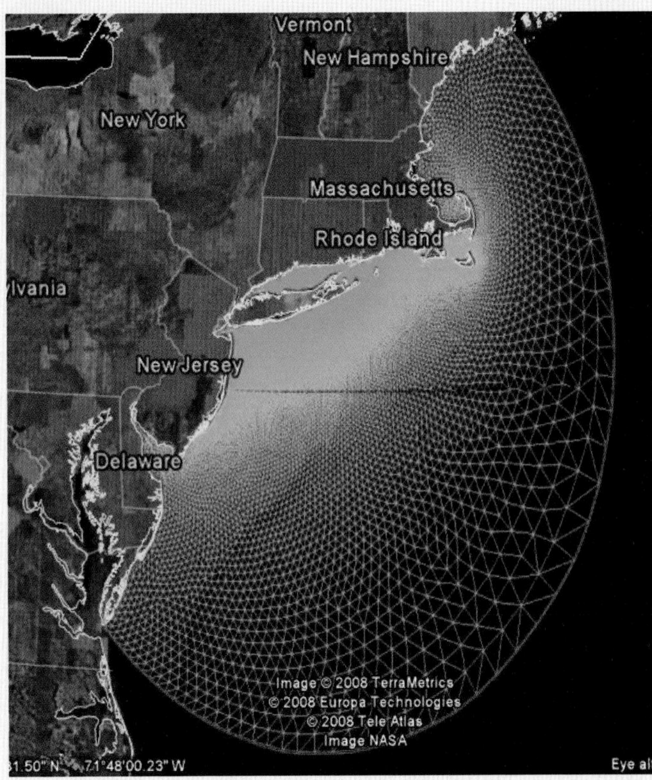

ADCIRC modeling domain used for New York Harbor storm surge simulation

Opposite
Modeling domain in the New York Harbor region, (detail) of ADCIRC modeling domain
The color scale represents the bathymetry. Computational nodes are shown as black dots.

FLUID DYNAMIC ANALYSIS

The modeling system developed for hurricane storm surge in the New York Harbor region consists of an atmospheric model for simulating the near-surface wind and pressure fields and a hydrodynamic model for simulating the storm surge response to meteorological forcing. The model domain extends well into open ocean over the Atlantic with a detailed representation of storm surge in the New York Harbor region. The modeling system is similar to the one developed by SUNY Stony Brook and benefits from modeling resources provided by the Stony Brook team.

OVERVIEW

Hurricanes with tracks that pass over the New York Harbor region are exceedingly rare, but they are a part of the region's history. The "Long Island Express" of 1938 made landfall in central Long Island as a Category 3 hurricane and caused extensive damage on Long Island and throughout New England. Geography of the East Coast of the US from North Carolina to Long Island plays an important role in determining hazards from storm surge over the eastern US. On a large scale, the eastward extension of Cape Hatteras into the Atlantic creates a hot spot for hurricane landfall, and the associated dissipation of hurricane intensity. On a local scale, the geography of the New York Harbor region dictates the storm tracks that can produce the most severe storm surge.

To examine hurricane impacts in the New York Harbor region through the coupled modeling system, we have used Hurricane Isabel as a model storm system. Hurricane Isabel caused extensive storm surge damage in the Chesapeake Bay region on September 18, 2003. The storm had a southeast to northwest oriented track, characteristic of storm motion that could produce severe storm surge in the New York Harbor region. The track of Hurricane Isabel was displaced northward to provide a model system for hurricane-induced storm surge in the New York–New Jersey Bay.

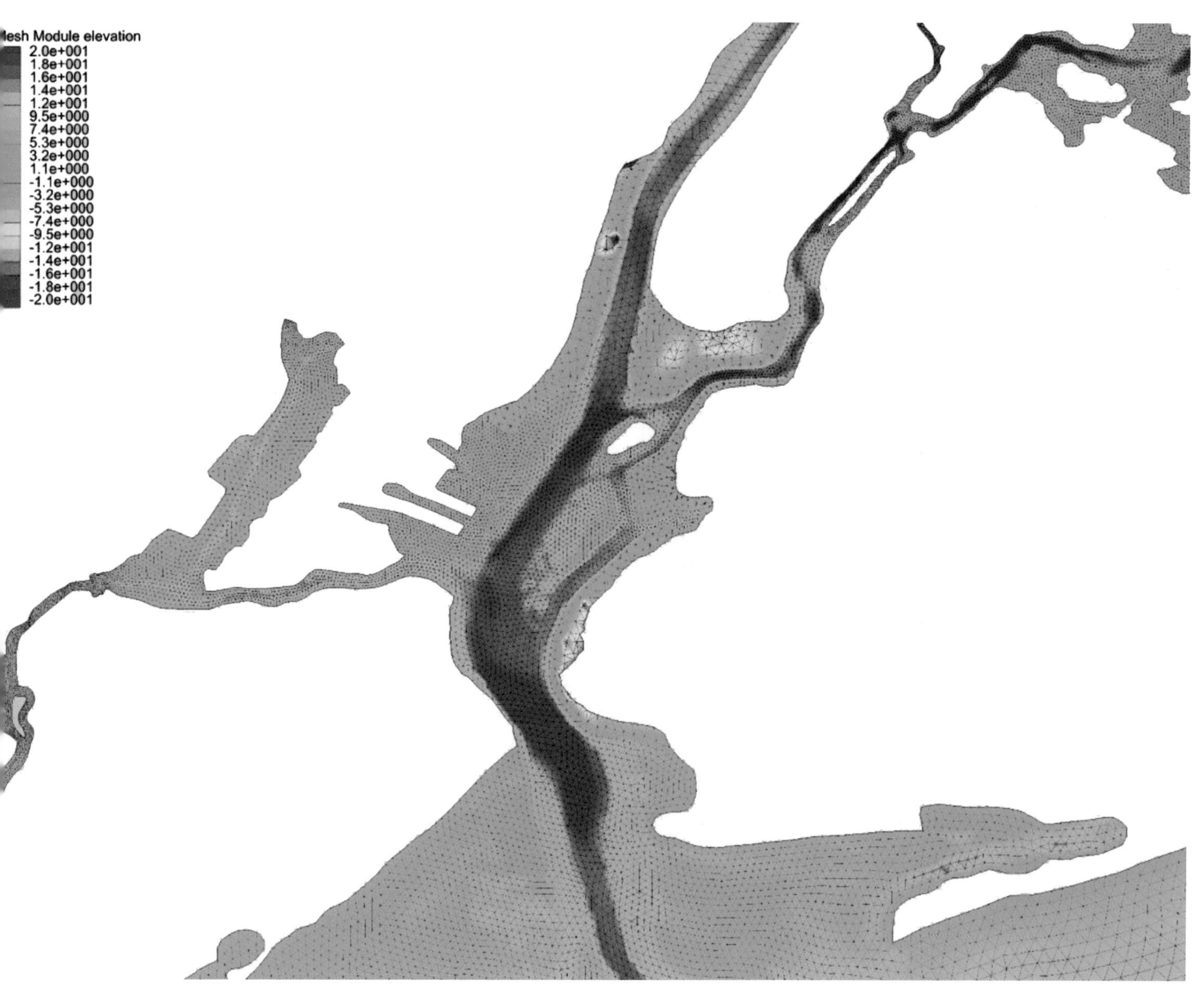
lesh Module elevation
2.0e+001
1.8e+001
1.6e+001
1.4e+001
1.2e+001
9.5e+000
7.4e+000
5.3e+000
3.2e+000
1.1e+000
-1.1e+000
-3.2e+000
-5.3e+000
-7.4e+000
-9.5e+000
-1.2e+001
-1.4e+001
-1.6e+001
-1.8e+001
-2.0e+001

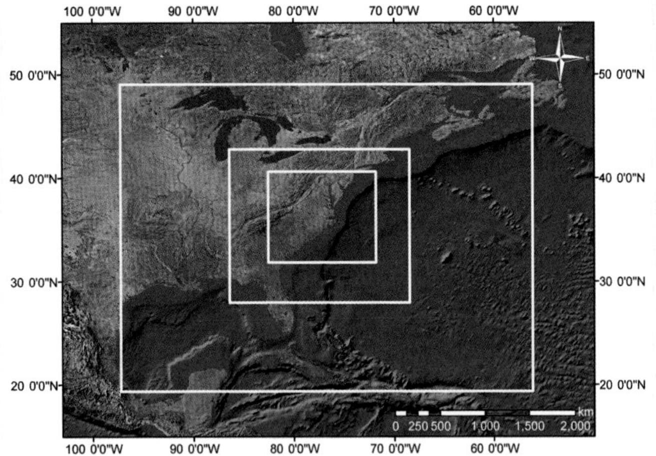

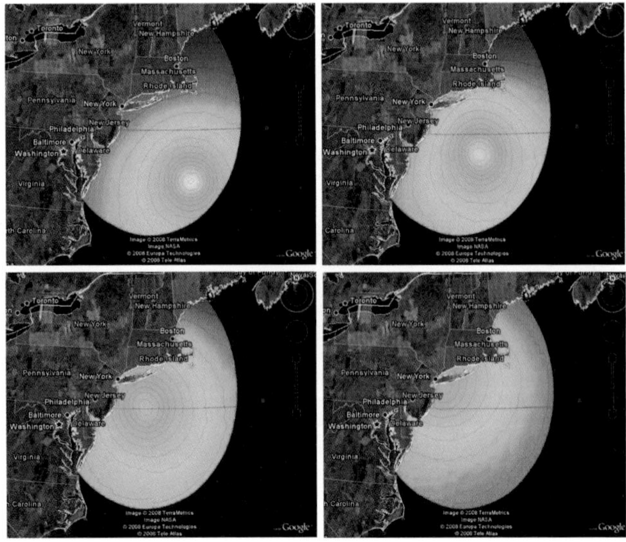

Model domains for WRF simulations of Hurricane Isabel. The inner domain 3 has grid resolution of 1.33 kilometers.

Illustration of the GFDL hurricane initialization at 0000 UTC on September 18, 2003 for Hurricane Isabel. The color scale represents the surface wind speed.

Opposite
Simulated pressure fields from WRF used for ADCIRC simulations. The simulations represent "displaced" Hurricane Isabel.

HURRICANE MODEL

The Weather Research and Forecasting (WRF) model is a state-of-the-art atmospheric modeling system that is widely used for weather forecasting and analysis. WRF has been implemented on the Princeton University supercomputer system and used as the centerpiece of the modeling system for hurricane simulations.

To simulate Hurricane Isabel, the model domain consisted of three "nested" regions with grid resolution of 12 kilometers in the outer domain, which covers much of the eastern US and western Atlantic. The inner domains have grid resolutions of 4 kilometers and 1.33 kilometers respectively, with the innermost domain covering the area of the eastern US most heavily influenced by Hurricane Isabel. Implementation of the model requires "initial conditions" that specify model states throughout the simulation domain at the beginning of the simulation period. Implementation also requires "boundary conditions" that specify state variables along the outer boundary of the model domain at each time step. Initial conditions were developed by the Hurricane Modeling Group of the Geophysical Fluid Dynamics Laboratory (GFDL). Boundary conditions were obtained from the Global Forecasting System (GFS) modeling system and applied to the boundary of the outer domain.

WRF simulations of Hurricane Isabel captured the storm track, intensity changes of the storm and magnitude of the surface wind field. An extensive model validation study has been carried out based on observations from coastal meteorological stations. Sensitivity studies have been carried out to examine the impacts of initial conditions and boundary on properties of the model simulations. Storm intensity at landfall is strongly dependent on initial conditions and the GFDL analyses used to develop initial conditions are a critical element of the modeling system. Boundary conditions play an important role in storm track and intensity changes. Using boundary conditions from GFS resulted in significant improvements in the storm track, relative to simulations using other standard sources for model boundary conditions.

WRF has been implemented for model domains and can be used for storm simulations in the New York–New Jersey region. Future work will examine idealized hurricane simulations for the New York Harbor region. A limitation of the "displaced" Hurricane Isabel analyses is that the impacts of the distinctive geography of the New York–New Jersey region are not reflected in simulated wind fields as the storm nears the coast.

Hurricane Isabel

Init: 2003-09-18_00:00:00
Valid: 2003-09-18_00:00:00

Surface Temperature (C)
Sea Level Pressure (hPa)
Surface Wind Speed (m/s)

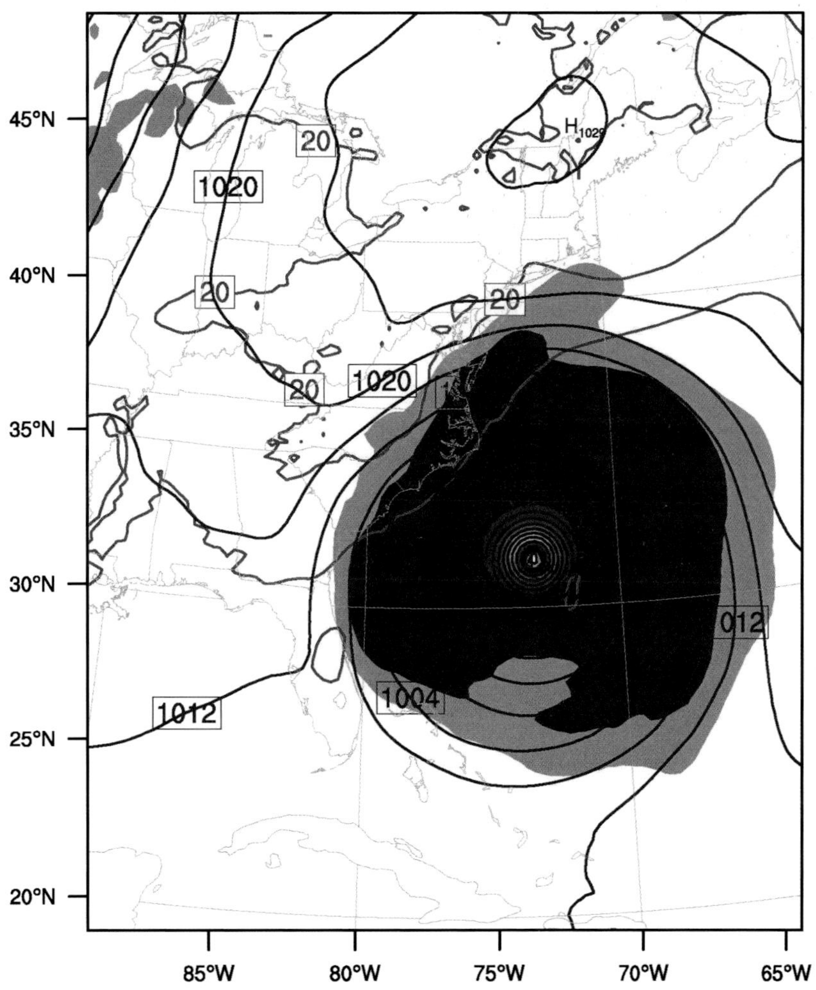

Sea Level Pressure Contours: 900 to 1100 by 4

Surface Temperature Contours: 0 to 45 by 5

Surface Wind Speed (m/s)

10 15 20 25 30 35 40 45 50 55 60 65 70 75 80

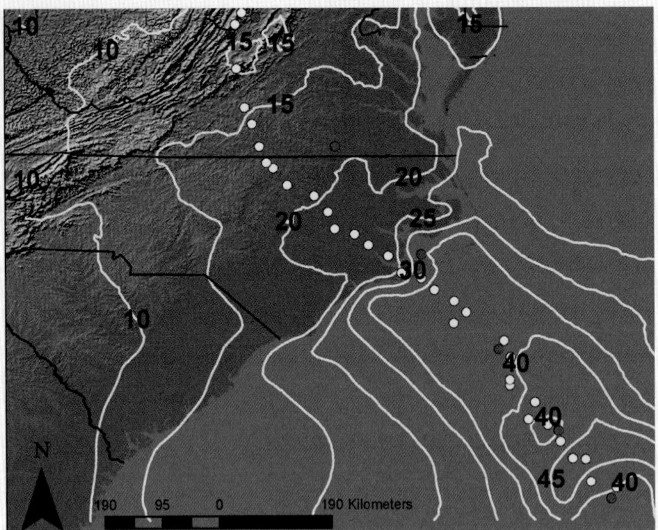

Simulated maximum wind speed (contours in m/s) and storm track (yellow circles) for Hurricane Isabel. National Hurricane Center "best track" data are shown as red circles.

Opposite
ADCIRC time series of simulated water surface elevation (top) and depth-averaged velocity (bottom) for "Point 19." Pink lines are for the control Isabel simulation. Blue lines reflect alterations associated with island configuration.

HYDRODYNAMIC MODEL

The Advanced Circulation model (ADCIRC) is a two-dimensional, depth-integrated, hydrodynamic circulation model that is used to examine dynamics of storm surge and tidal forcings. ADCIRC has been applied to a computational domain extending from deep ocean to the estuarine systems of the New York Harbor region. ADCIRC provides water surface elevations and depth-averaged velocities for each node of the computational domain. ADCIRC solves the "shallow water equations" on a "finite element mesh" based on tidal forcing and atmospheric forcing represented through the surface pressure and near surface wind field. The atmospheric fields of surface pressure and wind that are required as input for ADCIRC are obtained as the output of the WRF model simulations. The coupling between WRF and ADCIRC is through the atmospheric boundary conditions needed by ADCIRC and provided by WRF.

The Surface Water Modeling (SMS) system was used in mesh preparation for ADCIRC. The SUNY Stony Brook modeling group provided a large-scale mesh. SMS was used to extend the mesh to cover a broader area of New York Harbor region. SMS was also used to alter the mesh and topography of the model domain to reflect the impacts of alterations associated with design elements that are being examined as part of the project.

Validation of ADCIRC simulations have been carried out for the New York Harbor region under standard tidal forcings. A mesh has also been implemented for the Chesapeake Bay region and storm surge validation has been carried out for Hurricane Isabel. These analyses (results not shown) provide strong support for application of the coupled modeling system to examine storm surge in the New York Harbor region.

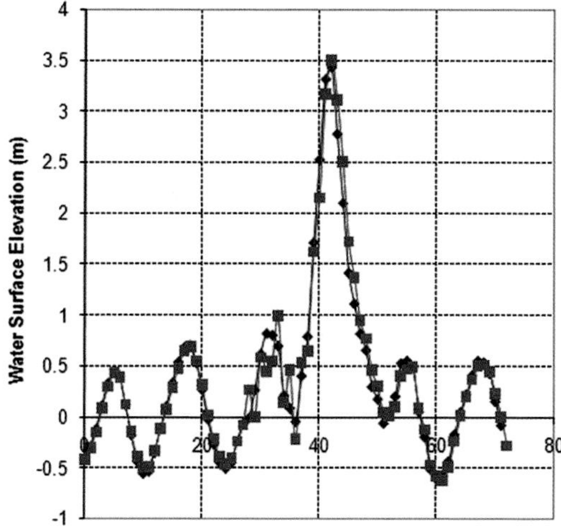

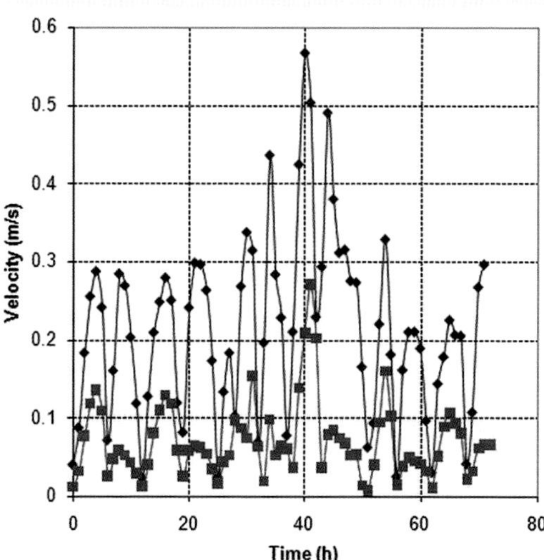

CONCLUSIONS

Hurricane storm surge simulations for the New York Harbor region have been carried out using the WRF model analyses for Hurricane Isabel. Simulations reflect the dynamics of the atmospheric fields associated with the hurricane and of the storm surge response. The displaced Hurricane Isabel used in the ADCIRC simulations passes directly over the New York Harbor region.

ADCIRC simulations result in inundation of portions of Lower Manhattan, as well as other low-lying areas of the New York Harbor region. ADCIRC provides the capability to examine sensitivity of storm surge response to a variety of key elements of the atmospheric environment of the hurricane and coastal hydrodynamics. In addition to hurricane intensity, translation speed of the hurricane and dimension of the area of maximum winds are key elements of the hurricane that affect storm surge. Timing of the hurricane passage relative to the tidal cycle is a key element of the coastal hydrodynamics.

ADCIRC provides a useful tool for examining the impacts of new design elements on storm surge. The effects of constructed islands on storm surge was examined by altering the mesh to represent a series of islands distributed throughout the harbor region. SMS was used for editing the mesh to represent the alterations associated with islands, as well as other design elements.

Sensitivity studies were carried out with ADCIRC to examine the impacts of distributed islands on hurricane storm surge. Simulations were carried out both for the altered mesh and for the existing conditions mesh used to produce the results shown in the charts at left.

A general conclusion of the sensitivity studies is that design alterations have marginal impacts on peak water surface elevations, but they have significant impact on the velocity field. These conclusions point to the utility of design elements that are strategically structured to lower velocities in selected areas of the harbor region, along with "soft" design of the harbor margin.

New York City Watershed model

Chesapeake Bay water model

Opposite
Mississippi Basin water model

FORMAL ANALYSIS

As a counterpoint to the fluid dynamic modeling done with AdCirc software at the Princeton University School of Engineering, an empirical physical model was used as a design tool, observing the resultant currents, flows, and eddies formed by obstructions with water.

BACKGROUND

Scale models of watersheds, river basins, and bays were commonly used in the twentieth century to accurately predict flooding and test flood control barriers. Perhaps one of the earliest was built in 1937, commissioned by the New York City Board of Water Supply for the 1939 World's Fair. It was constructed by the Cartographic Survey Force of the Works Progress Administration (WPA) as a display model, and represented the New York City watershed in relief—tracing the water supply system from the upstream tributaries of the Delaware River to sea level, and identifying aqueducts, tunnels, and drainage basins feeding the city's water supply.

Another WPA-era model is the Mississippi Basin model, a 1:2,000 scale model representing the entire 1,250,000-square-mile basin area. The model covers 800 acres on a rural site outside of Jackson, Mississippi. It was built by the US Army Corps of Engineers to model the flood characteristics of the river and was literally flooded with water to aid in the placement of locks, dams, and flood control structures. Construction began in 1943 with the leveling of the model's huge outdoor site, and the model itself was completed in 1966. It is the largest hydraulic model in the world. While it is now abandoned, the model was used to accurately simulate the conditions of the 1952 and 1973 floods.

Housed in a former World War II warehouse in Sausalito, California, the San Francisco Bay/Sacramento River Delta model is a 1:1,000 scale model of the largest estuary on the West Coast. It measures 320 by 400 feet, approximately the size of two football fields. The vertical scale is exaggerated ten times (1:100), and this exaggeration is compensated by hundreds of thousands of copper tags embedded in the basin to slow down the speed of the water. It was begun in 1956 by the US Army Corps of Engineers to test the Reber Plan, an engineering proposal to fill in much of San Francisco Bay and deepen ship channels for defense purposes.

The model was later enlarged to cover the Sacramento River Delta. The water in the model was given correct salinity properties, with fresh water for the rivers, and ocean water that was maintained at thirty-three parts per thousand. In addition to studying sediment movement and flood control, saltwater intrusion could also be tested. No longer used by the USACE, the model is still partly functional and is maintained as a tourist attraction and for educational purposes.

Above and opposite
Water table experiment testing the effect of boomerang island shape in various orientations to current

The Chesapeake Bay hydraulic model was a 1:1,000 scale model covering eight acres contained indoors in a large warehouse in Matapeake, Maryland. It simulated the largest and most complex estuary in the country. The hand-sculpted model was begun in 1973 and continued until 1977. It was operational for only three years, 1978 to 1981. As in the San Francisco Bay model, ocean salinity was controlled accurately, the vertical scale was exaggerated by a factor of ten but carefully adjusted for flow. 450,000 gallons of water flowed through the model while operational. After it was abandoned in 1982 the model's surface gradually began to buckle and disintegrate, and was completely destroyed in 2005 for a commercial development.

WATER TABLE STUDIES

The Palisade Bay water studies began simply enough in a bathtub with plasticine islands and green dye. Simple studies of circular island formations and the eddy forms produced by a rapid currents yielded compelling sequential images, if not scientific results. In this first simple experiment, two different array formations of islands were tested. The first was a four island array in a grid, and the second a staggered grid with a five island array (one island at the center of a four square grid). The team concluded that the staggered, or offset grid, of island formations was preferable, as the effect of the intermediary offset island row was to slow the flow of the water, creating multiple smaller eddies. By contrast, the flow of water across the four island gridded array, while slowed by eddying, moved quickly between the islands and was propelled forward through this unobstructed channel.

The team subsequently obtained access to a water table developed at the University of Michigan by the late Professor Willard Oberdick with technical staff members Ted Austin and Mark Krecic. The water table has been operational at the University of Michigan for over twenty years, used to study wind and water currents, and with it we began to create more complex patterns of islands, as well as study the effects multiple of current directions. By examining a current passing a smooth sea wall versus a fringe of finger piers, we found the effects of current on the projecting piers creates a zone of protected still water between the bulkhead line and the pier head line.

These studies do not reflect the bathymetry of the Upper Bay since the water table has a flat surface with a skim coat of water moving across it. Yet the surface speed and currents observed in the model were useful in generating a design logic of island formation.

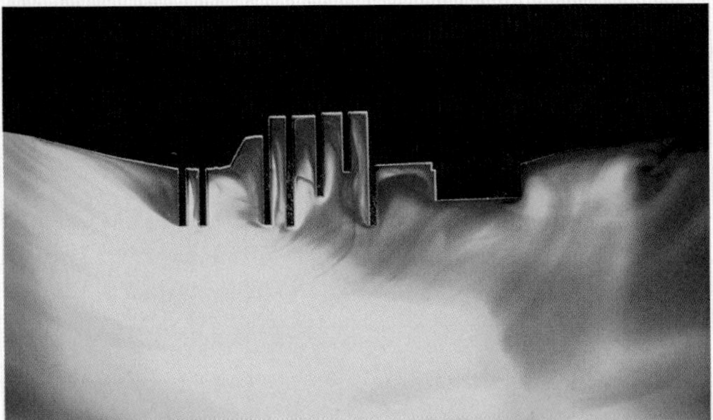

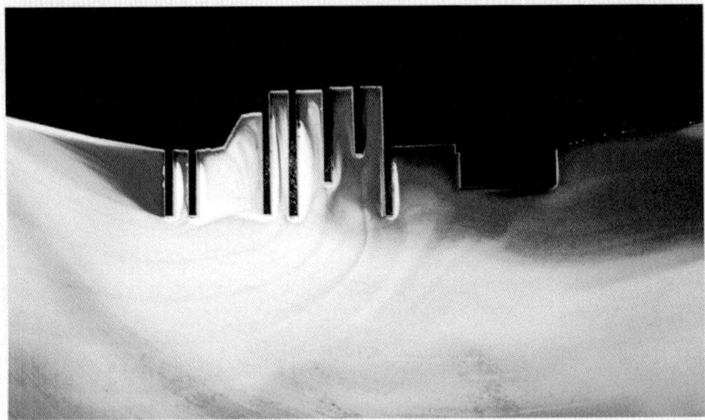

Above and opposite
Water table experiment testing the effect of piers of various lengths

Following pages
Time-lapse sequence showing the effects of two different island shapes

METHODS AND ASSUMPTIONS

The primary challenge of determining the shapes of new barrier islands is the complexity of water flow within the Upper Bay. Within a single day, water current directions in the Hudson River can change from upstream to downstream, stratifying the river mass with both salt and fresh water layers moving in opposite directions. Similarly, current velocities within the East River vary dramatically both daily and seasonally. These dynamic bodies of water converge at the south tip of Manhattan resulting in a torrent portion of the estuary. Our design approach for the barrier islands was driven by two main parameters:

Optimal forms and patterns that would effectively mediate surge flow from variable directions.

Linear formations that are conducive to the geotextile container (recycled dredge tubes, see Zone 0 section method of construction.

Earlier archipelago studies spawned from ideas of extending the city grid into the bay as a means of organizing the island array. This strategy fortified the relationship between the islands and the city, with the islands becoming an extended feathered zone between wet and dry. Having a direct relationship with the city grid would allow for more logical means of inhabiting certain islands as public space. These concepts and parameters lead to island patterns that formalize an intersection of both the city grid and storm surge trajectories.

CONCLUSION

The water table tests primarily demonstrate the impact that the islands have on water flow and current. These tests demonstrate the effectiveness of the island formations to mitigate flow from multiple directions. Trailing eddies, wakes, and vortexes that the islands create provide elements of friction within the body of water prior to its impact with the coastline. Though these experiments negate other variables such as depth and sedimentation, they vividly illustrate and validate the fundamental strategy of the archipelago.

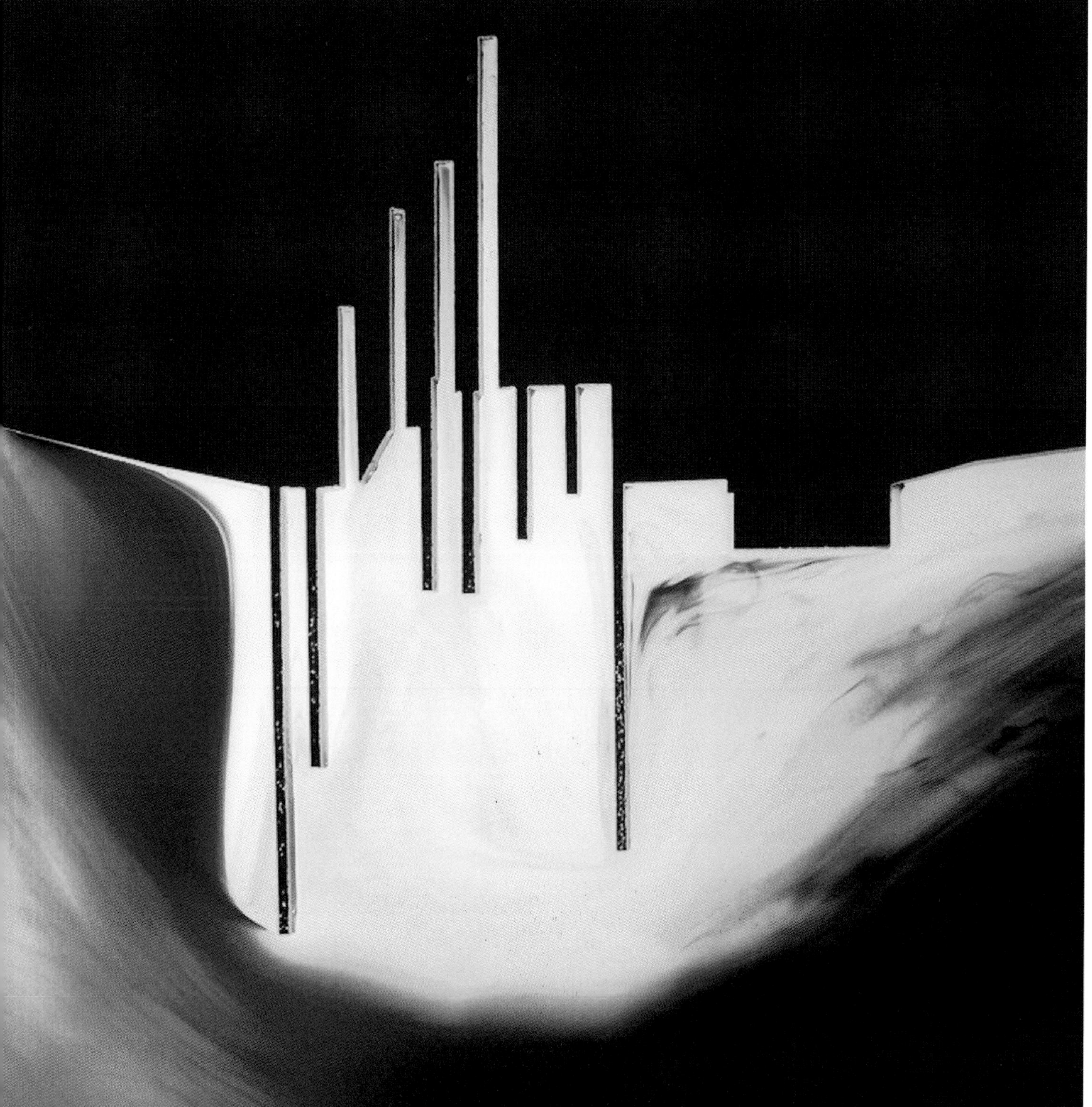

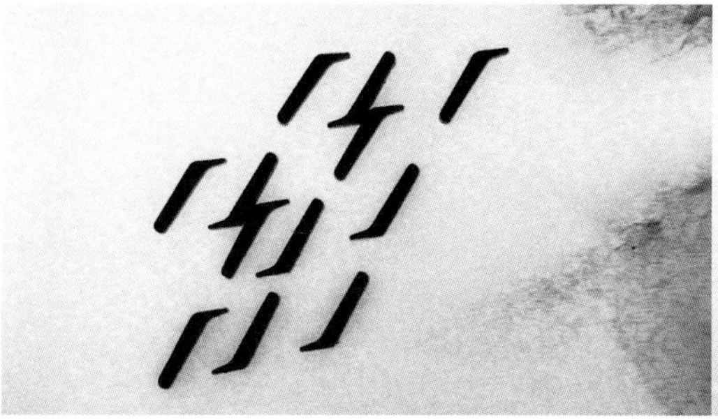

00:00 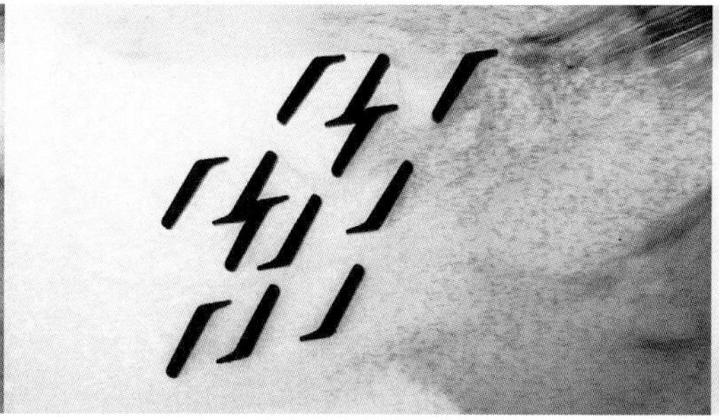 00:02 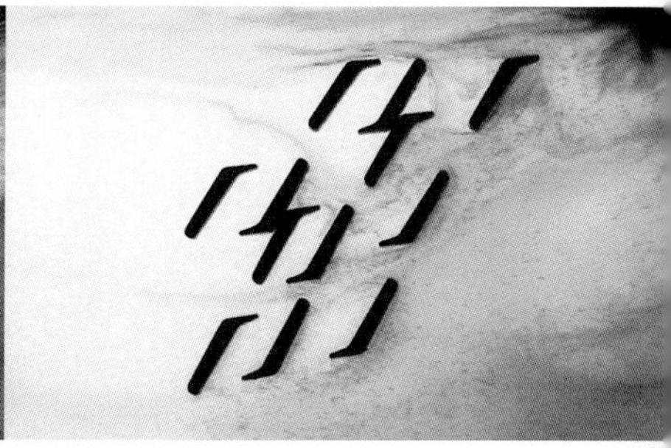 00

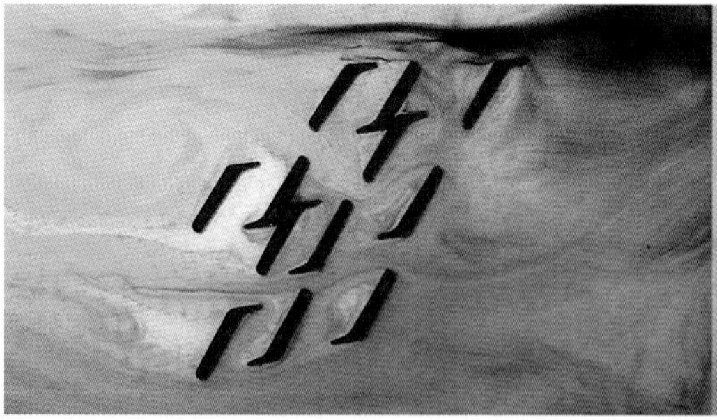

00:12 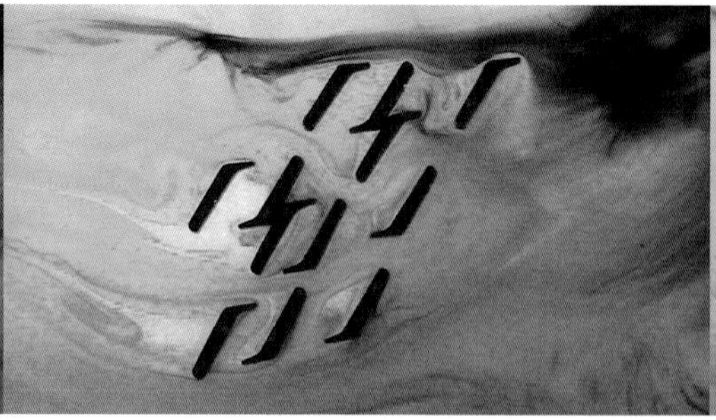 00:14 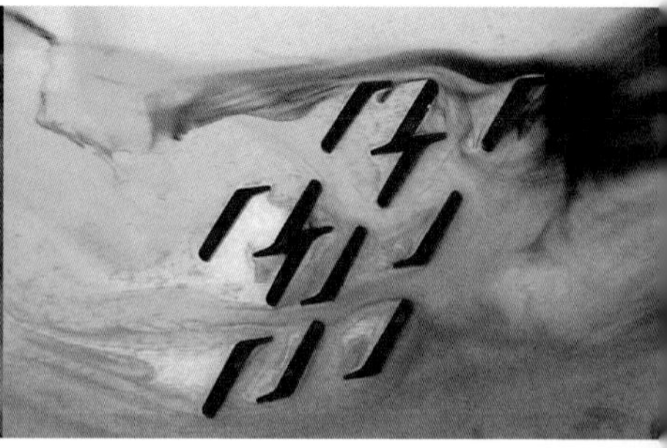 00

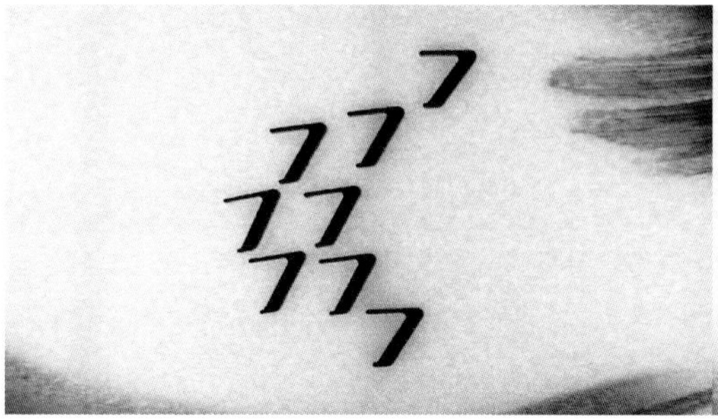

00:00 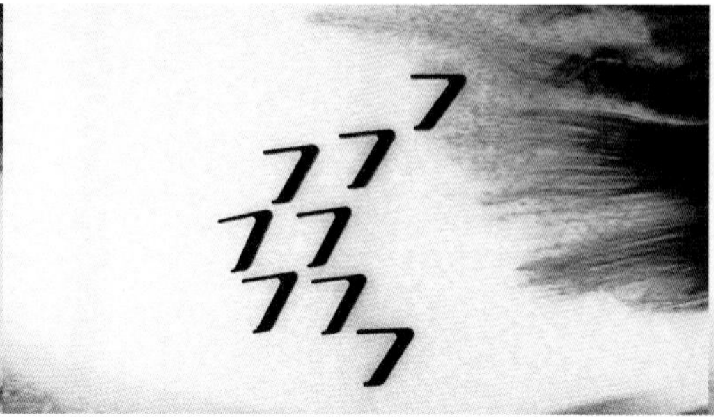 00:02 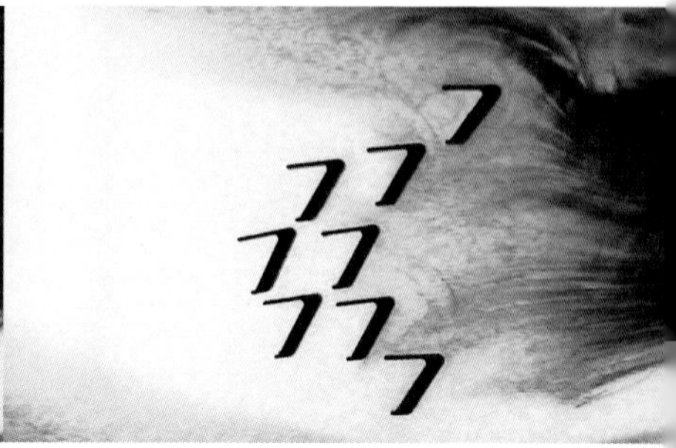 00

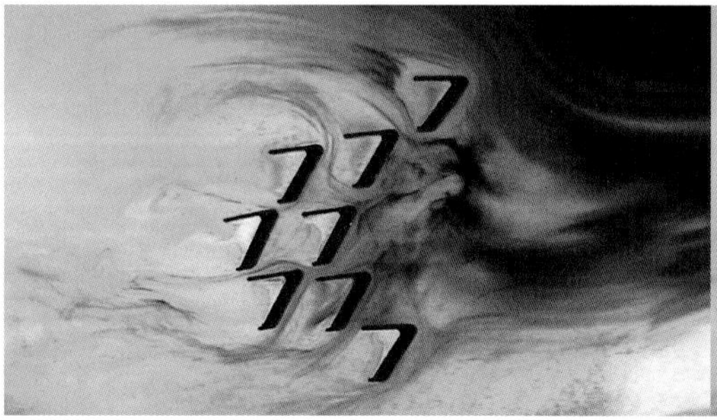

00:12 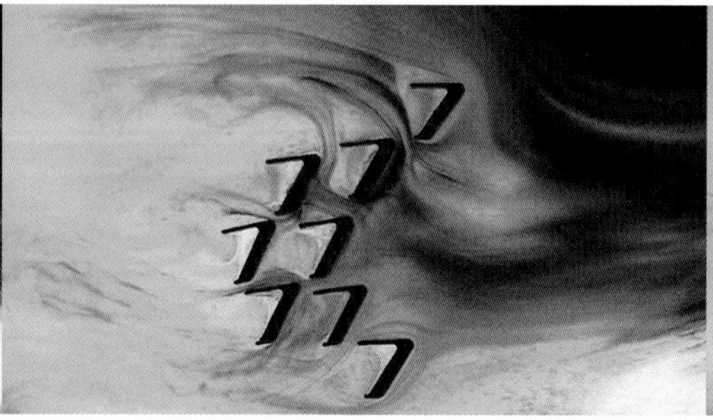 00:14 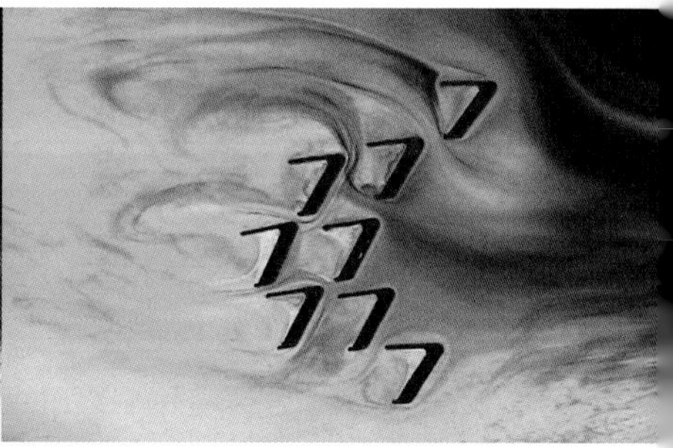 00

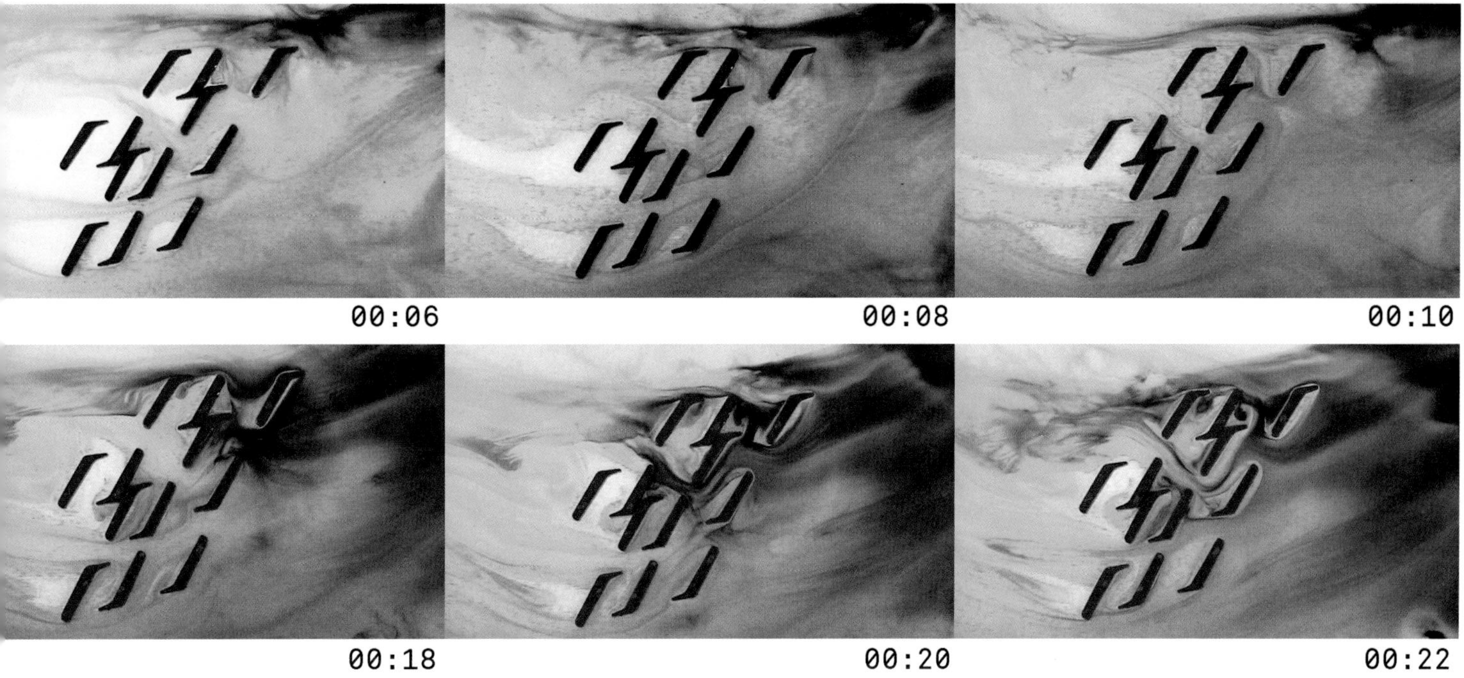

00:06

00:08

00:10

00:18

00:20

00:22

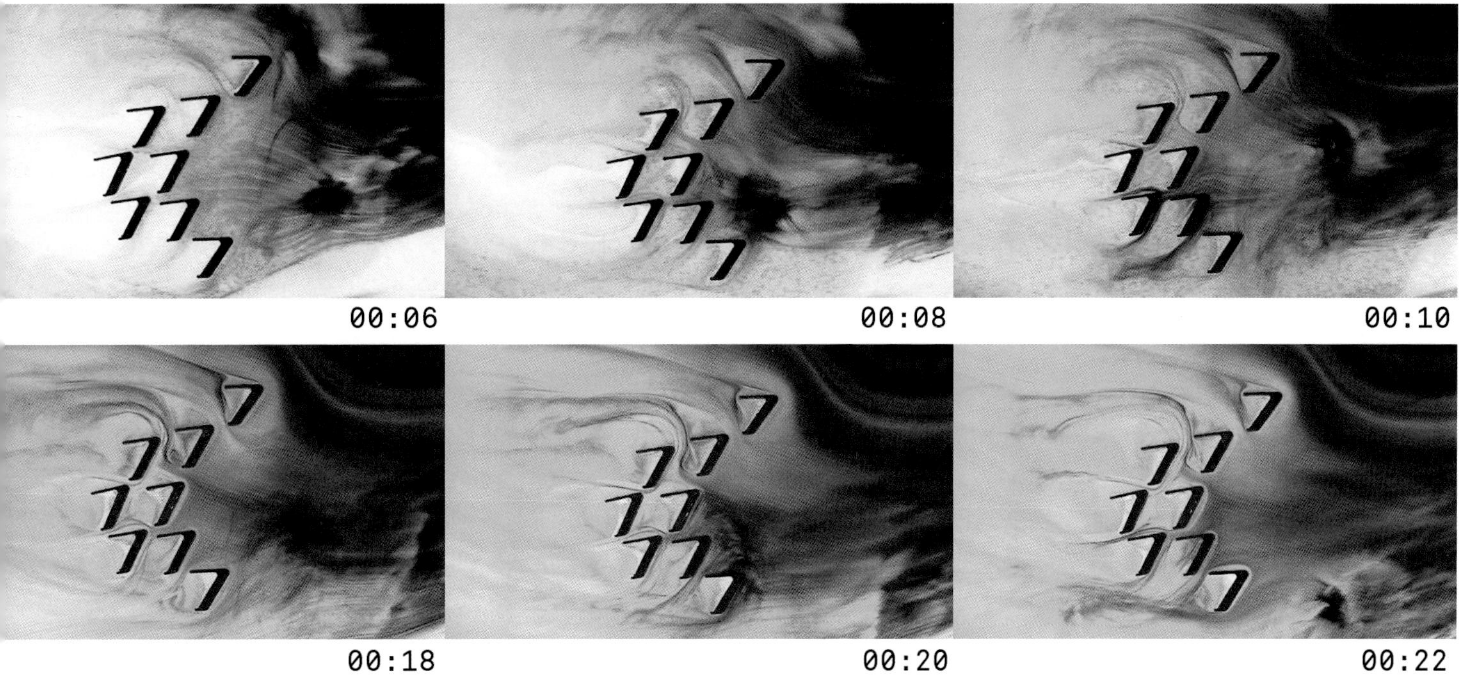

00:06

00:08

00:10

00:18

00:20

00:22

DESIGN STRATEGIES

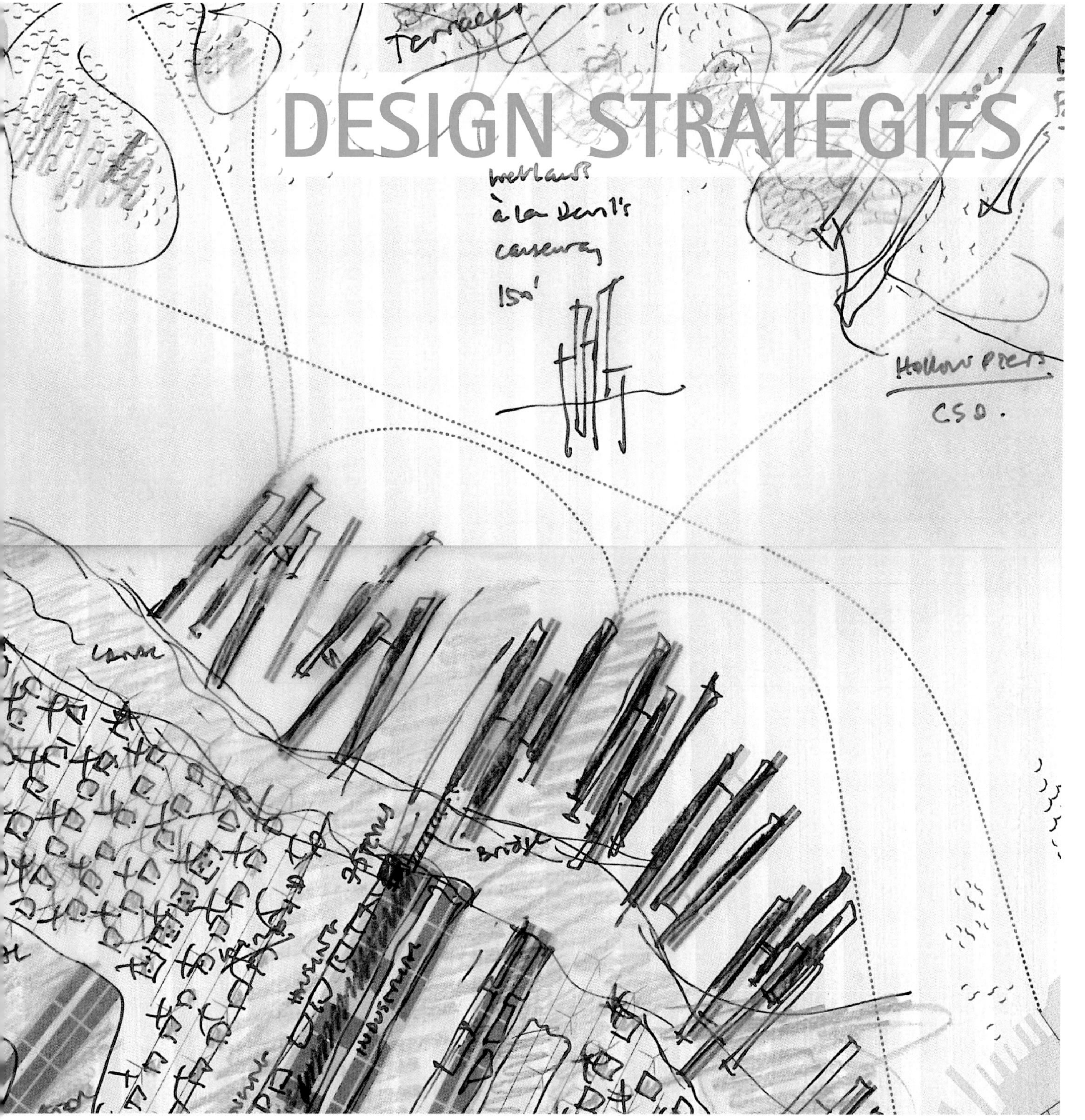

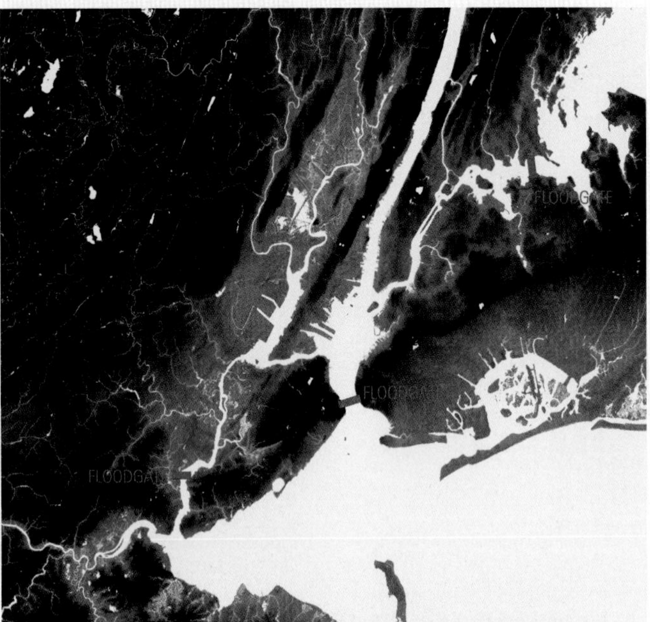

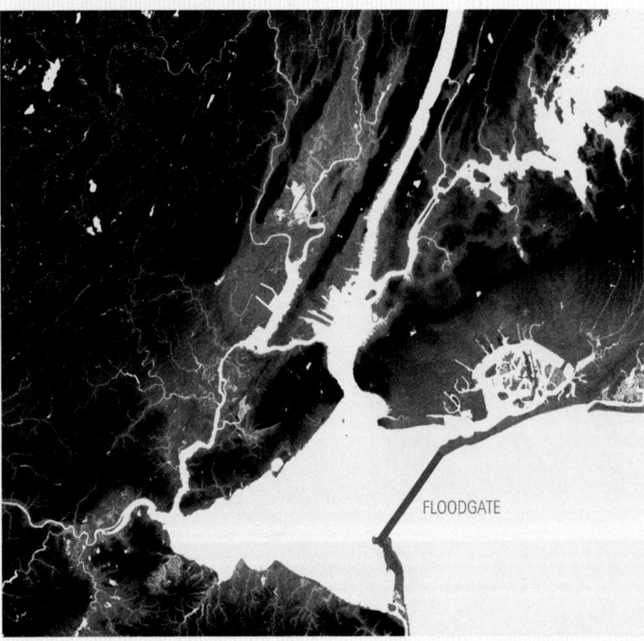

Two possible locations for storm surge barriers

Opposite
Historical North Atlantic Hurricane Tracks

PALISADE BAY

The Palisade Bay proposal reinvents the Upper Bay as the central gathering place for the region. The proposal implements a series of "soft infrastructure" strategies to alternatively buffer or absorb flooding, while also creating a new destination on the water.

RESILIENCE

Approaching the design for the Upper Bay requires an overall strategy which satisfies both the need to protect the region from storm surge and also introduces a new program within the harbor and along its edge. Considering this two-fold criteria led to a new kind of infrastructure—soft infrastructure—that is dispersed throughout the region and implemented by combining natural and artificial landscape elements to provide new ground to eroded areas, remediation to polluted areas, and protection to areas at high risk of storm surge damage. By using the techniques of landscape design, instead of building fortified edges, we can layer programs such as housing and parks, or fresh water storage and urban farms to create activities and destinations within the revitalized harbor zone. A comprehensive harbor transportation system is necessary to facilitate mobility between these new destinations and define this harbor as the center of the New York/New Jersey urban region.

The notion of building a single, massive structure to prevent storm surge—such as in London, Venice (forthcoming), and Rotterdam—is an obvious solution for mitigating storm damage. Malcolm C. Bowman and his colleagues have proposed such a system of storm surge gates to handle the expected consequences of climate change in the Upper Bay. These barriers would be located in three strategic places: at the Narrows, the mouth of the Arthur Kill, and at the upper end of the East River where it meets the Long Island Sound. However, there are unanswered questions regarding the effectiveness of such structures, the degree of flooding on the weather-side of the structures, and the protection provided by partial blockage barriers at certain locations. In theory, the barriers would be closed for just a few hours during hurricane surges, and for several days during high tides in the case of a nor'easter event.[18] A similar solution would be to build a storm gate outside of the harbor along the New York Bight, which is the gulf formed by the geographical indentation of New Jersey and Long Island along the Eastern Seaboard. Placing a flood gate here would prevent surge from severe storms just off the coast from entering the harbor region.

Simply cutting off the flow of water into the bay when such a gate is closed is appealing in some respects because the water basin is controlled to a specific design capacity. While massive storm blockades are invariably expensive to build, they are also manageable construction projects with clear boundaries and extents. The risk of such an

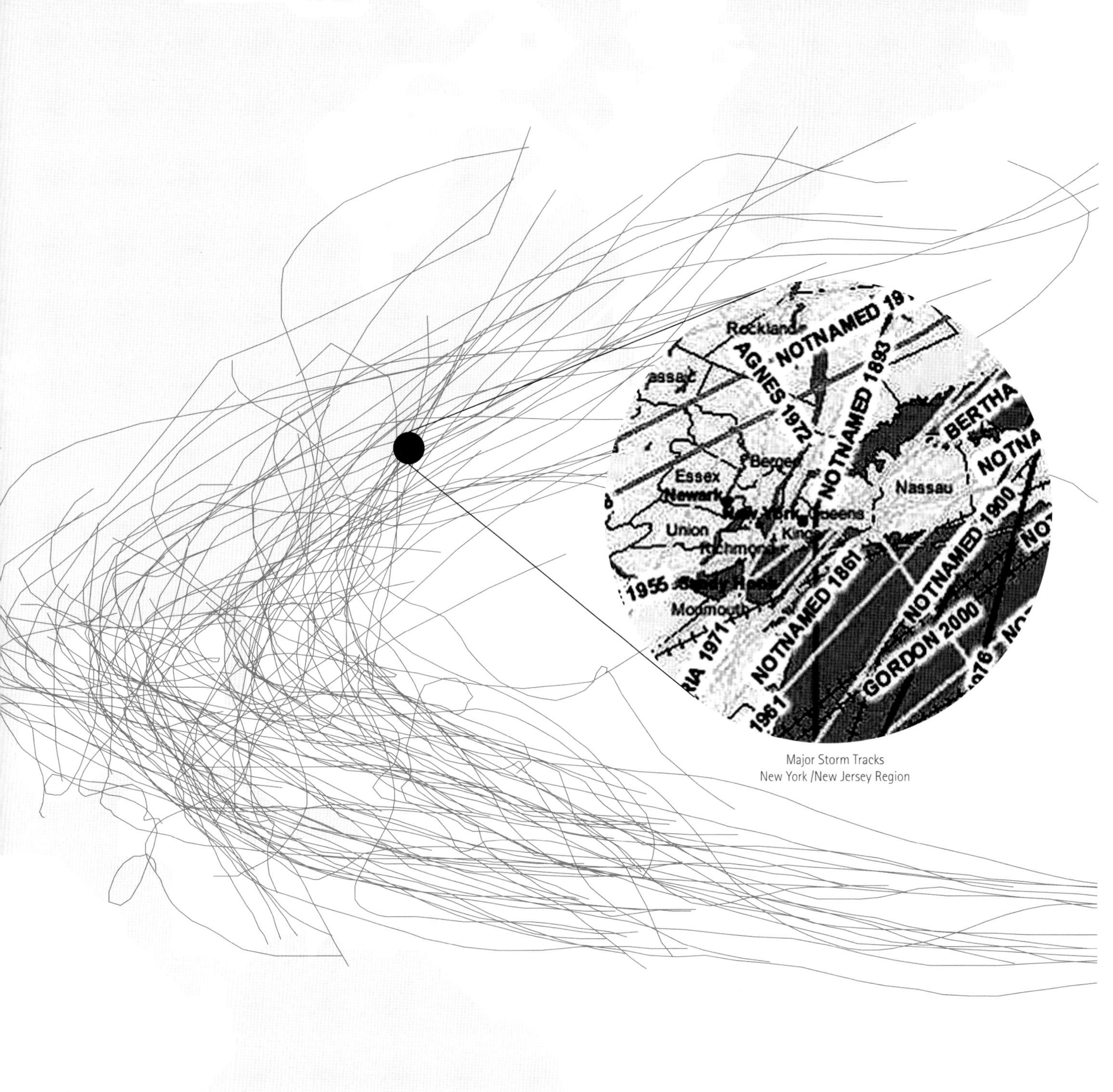

Major Storm Tracks
New York /New Jersey Region

Waterborne shipping traffic routes through the Upper Bay

Shoals and flats in the Upper Bay

Opposite
Exploded axonomentric showing elevation relationships between new design components and existing topography and bathymentry

approach is the unpredictable disturbance a massive infrastructure might have upon the existing estuarine ecosystems both locally and regionally. It is also a great risk to rely on a single defense system to prevent damage from a natural disaster; the failure of the levees in New Orleans after Hurricane Katrina is clear evidence of the devastation which can result from positioning a city against nature in this way.

By implementing a defense strategy that consists of soft infrastructure, the city becomes a place that is resilient to, rather than fortified against, the impact of natural disasters. The components of this soft infrastructure are clusters of constructed islands within the harbor, restored piers in addition to new elongated piers along the southeast and southwest coasts, and constructed wetlands along the harbor perimeter. By combining these elements throughout the harbor in various ways to suit the distinct urban and geographical conditions of a particular site, new places for wildlife, recreation, and industry emerge from the existing harbor area.

MOVEMENT CORRIDORS AND CONSTRAINTS

Maritime traffic in the Upper Bay includes recreational sailboats, the Staten Island Ferry, and industrial container ships. While container shipping has predominantly been relocated from the piers of the Upper Bay to the Port Elizabeth Marine Terminal, massive container ships still need to travel through The Narrows and along the Kill Van Kull to reach these ports. Other ports in Red Hook, Brooklyn are the destination of large cruise ships, as well as container ships operated by American Stevedoring Incorporated. Thus, it is necessary to maintain deep channels in the harbor to accommodate the passage of large ships along specific pathways. These paths are maintained by a dredging process executed by the Army Corps of Engineers.

Adjacent to these corridors are zones of shallow shoals and flats. These areas have not been dredged and thus could be built up with artificial islands, reefs, and wetlands. Roughening these shoals with additive landforms would contribute to curbing the force of storm surge in the harbor.

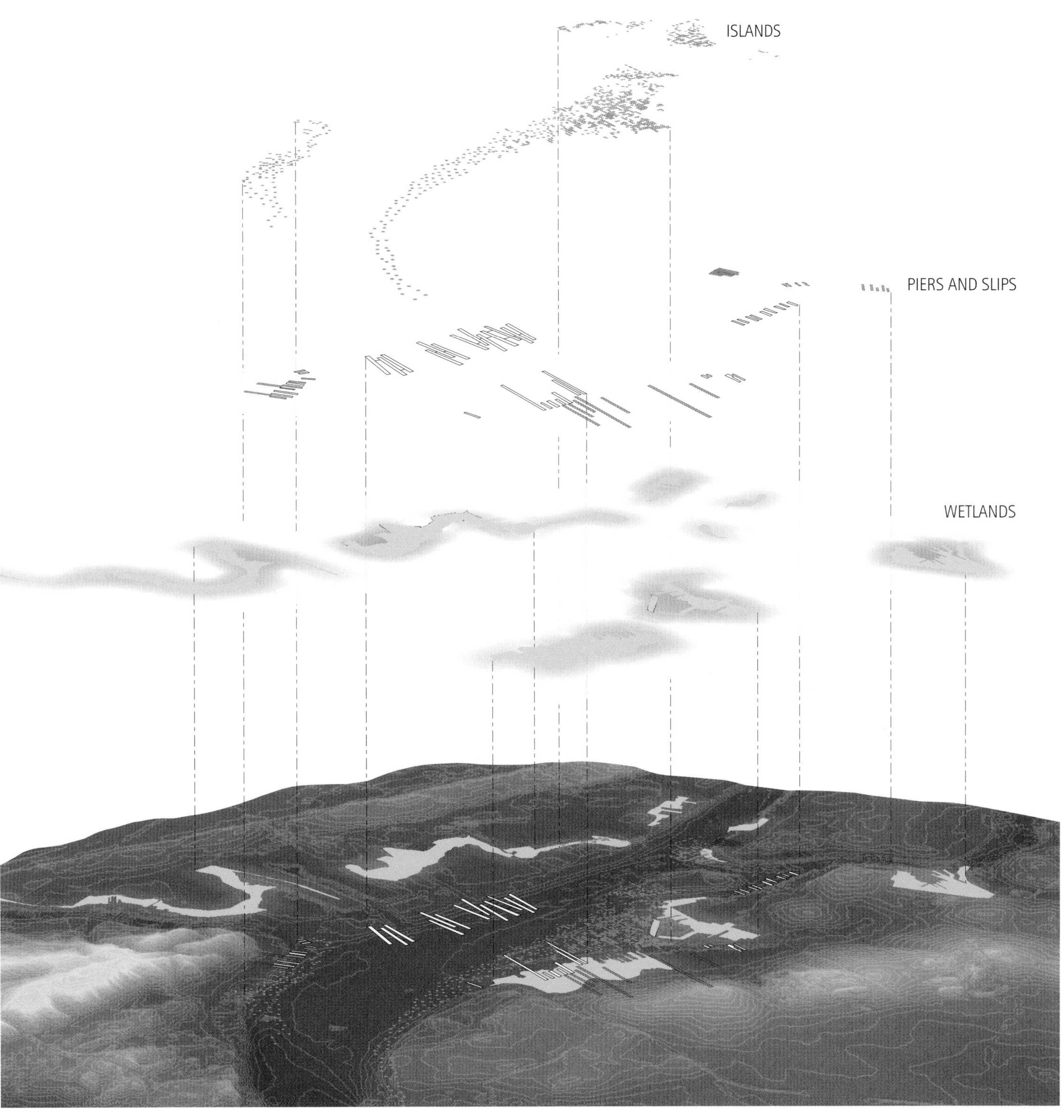
ISLANDS
PIERS AND SLIPS
WETLANDS

HERITAGE OF THE HARBOR

Transformation of the waterfront edge of the New York–New Jersey Harbor has occurred continually over hundreds of years. After the founding of the city in 1626, the edge was first altered by human intervention to accommodate landing ships. As the shipping industry developed, long piers extended along more and more edges to create a characteristic fingered waterfront edge. Over hundreds of years, the ecosystem of the harbor has come to coexist with the pier/slip typology—the shade provided below the piers, in fact, has become a valuable habitat for certain species of spawning fish and other benthic plants and animals. After the peak of the shipping industry in the New York Harbor this infrastructure has gone into disuse, but still contributes to local habitats by providing protected areas of still water and ecological refuge away from the dynamic current conditions in the harbor's tributaries. As the city has grown to incorporate all of the landmasses surrounding the harbor, nearly the entire coastline has been fortified by a sea wall backfilled with earth. The edge is no longer a natural shoreline but rather a border zone of artificial lands which have been filled into the bay.

STRATEGIES FOR THE UPPER BAY

This project proposes a new infrastructural system for the Upper Bay with three main design elements: wetlands; piers and slips; and islands. These elements act alone and in conjunction with one another, and with a series of more isolated and smaller-scale interventions such as oyster beds and offshore windmills, to generate habitat, energy, and a sense of place that is the Upper Bay.

Sunset Park, Brooklyn, existing condition 2006

Sunset Park, Brooklyn, a proposed future transformation

Opposite
Palisade Bay Master Plan

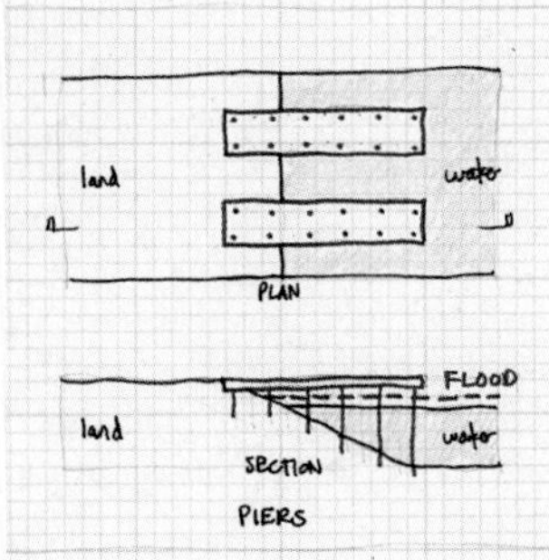

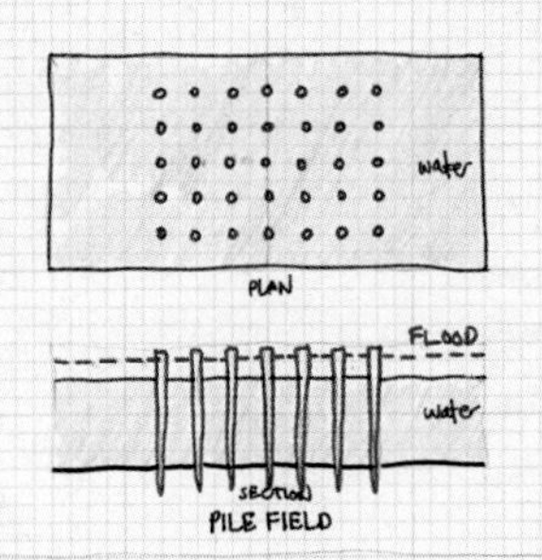

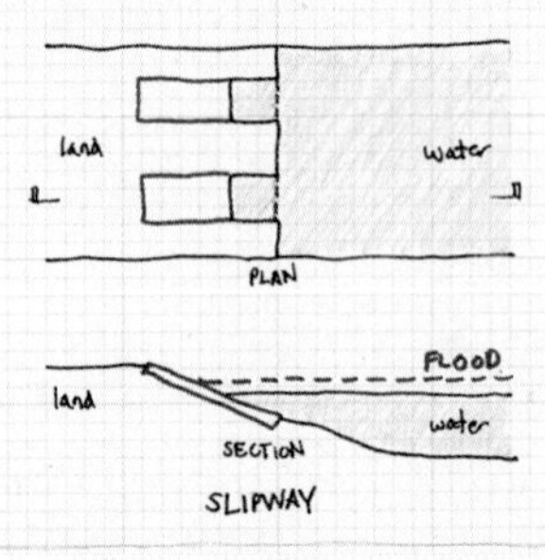

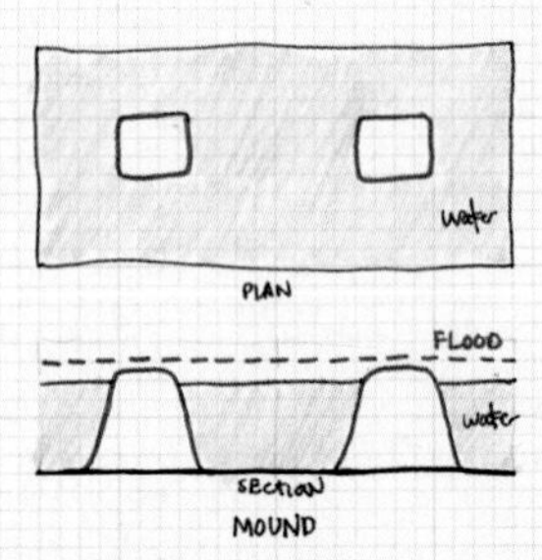

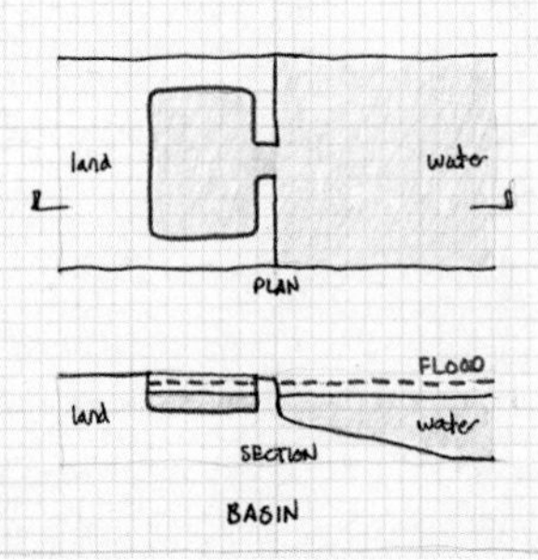

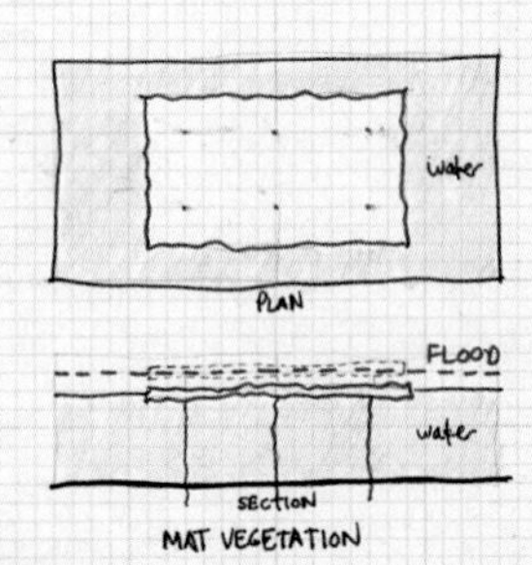

Catalogue of design strategies for the edges (left column) and the flats (right column)

Opposite
Palisade Bay, key to elements used in the masterplan

STRATEGY FOR THE EDGES AND THE FLATS

We see a potential design and planning strategy for the Upper Bay that would serve to remediate the harbor region ecologically; provide the potential for transit links and recreation; and mitigate both the effects of global warming induced flooding, as well as the forces of storm surges due to hurricanes and nor'easters. These design strategies would be implemented within two broad strategic categories, defined here as the edge and the flats. Various design strategies have been catalogued for possible interventions within each zone.

The Edges

The image of the Upper Bay found at the beginning of the Edge Atlas is a temporal overlay of a century of fluctuation along the water's edge, reflecting both the movement of the shoreline in and out, as well as the filling and dredging of the shallow-water flats. The edge is considered to be not just a line dividing water from land, but a zone of varying width. This edge surface expands and contracts between four abstract lines that historically circumscribe the entire Upper Bay: the pier-head line, the bulk-head line, the former coastline, and the extent of former wetland marsh. Our catalog of intervention strategies at the water's edge works with both additive and subtractive methodologies within that zone. The shoreline strategies presented here are deployed either perpendicular or parallel to the edge. Most of the perpendicular strategies have evolved from the shipping language of access—wharves, piers, and slips—whereas the parallel strategies tend to reflect protective natural or man-made conditions such as wetlands, mangroves, and reefs.

The Flats

The flats, sometimes called beds, middle ground shoals, or anchorages, are areas where the bathymetry of the underwater surface approaches the surface of the water. These shallow zones have historically been the site of shellfish beds and ship anchorages, and are often the foundations for landfill. This may be seen with Governors Island, Liberty State Park, and Ellis and Liberty Islands. In some areas, particularly the flats to the southwest of Red Hook and the mouth of the Gowanus Canal, the shoal has been accentuated due to the dredging of shipping channels around its perimeter. The catalog of intervention strategies at the flats examines various possibilities of the creation of "islands" at the surface or transformations of the underwater bathymetry. In both cases these strategies aim to serve as anchorages for the establishment of a new natural growth and habitat, as well as acting to absorb and mitigate wave energy within the bay.

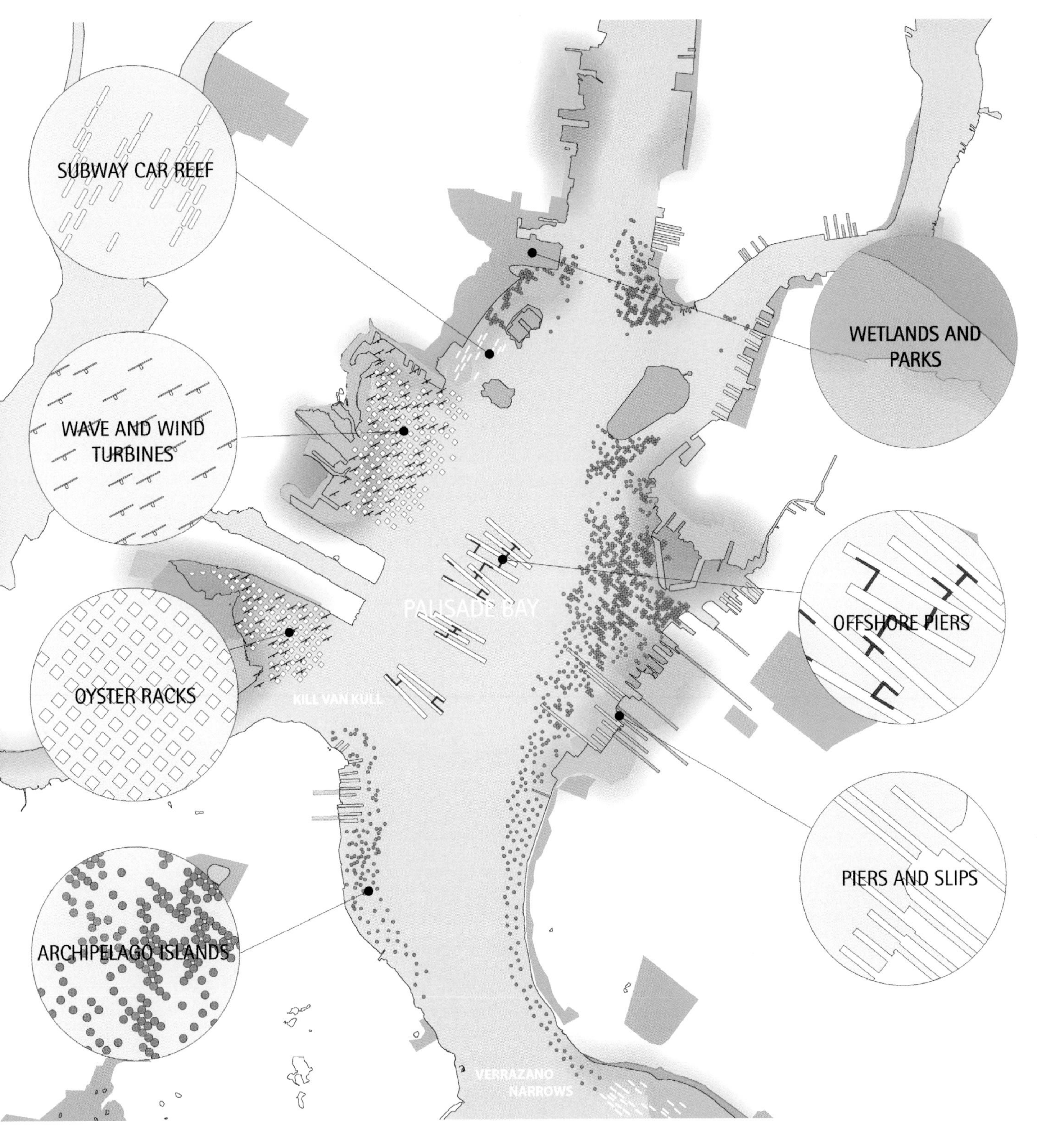

SUBWAY CAR REEF
WETLANDS AND PARKS
WAVE AND WIND TURBINES
OFFSHORE PIERS
PALISADE BAY
OYSTER RACKS
KILL VAN KULL
PIERS AND SLIPS
ARCHIPELAGO ISLANDS
VERRAZANO NARROWS

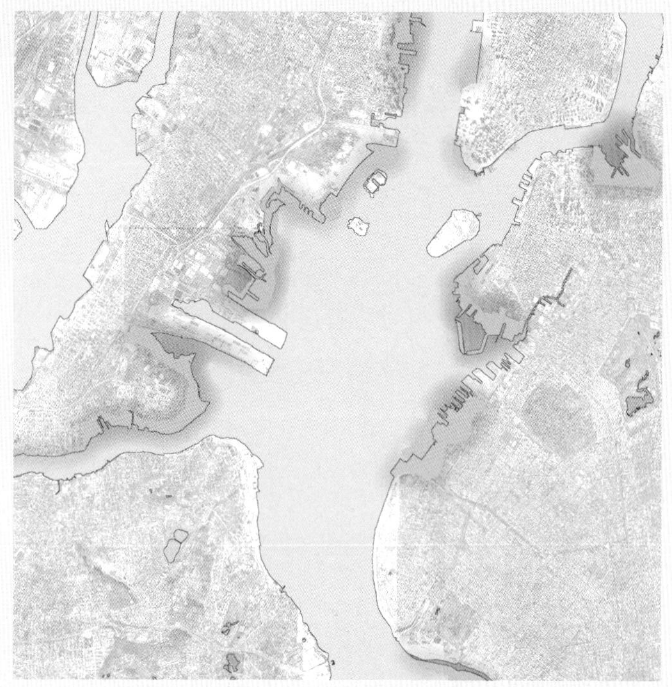

WETLANDS

Natural saltwater wetlands were once extensive along the waterfronts of Bayonne and Jersey City in New Jersey and Red Hook, Gowanus Canal, and Sunset Park in Brooklyn. As well as supporting the diverse habitat of the estuarine ecosystem, these wetlands also acted as biofilters, removing sediments from the water. Constructed wetlands are designed to emulate these natural features, by treating storm water runoff, wastewater, and pollutants. The use of constructed wetlands as an ecological infrastructure within the Upper Bay addresses several issues. These wetlands provide habitat to a diverse range of organisms; they provide visual interest and public space for leisure and recreation; and they act to filter polluted waters and remediate polluted lands.

ZONE OF IMPLEMENTATION

We propose an extensive implementation of constructed wetlands along the New Jersey and Brooklyn waterfronts, generally in locations which are most susceptible to flooding and sea level rise, and which were once the site of marshlands. The strategy of implementing wetlands along the edge of the Upper Bay creates a broad, soft fringe where city grid abuts the watery void, revealing tidal variations to the region's inhabitants. Blurring this land/water interface with the texture, plant life, and depth of the wetlands also provides a natural buffer that adjusts fluidly to flood events and sea level rise.

Proposed wetlands in Palisade Bay occupy the lands within the FEMA-designated one-hundred-year flood zone.

Opposite
Mapping of original shoreline and marshes of Red Hook and the Gowanus Canal, overlaid on the existing street grid, 1875

View of Liberty State Park Nature Center, Jersey City, NJ, 2008

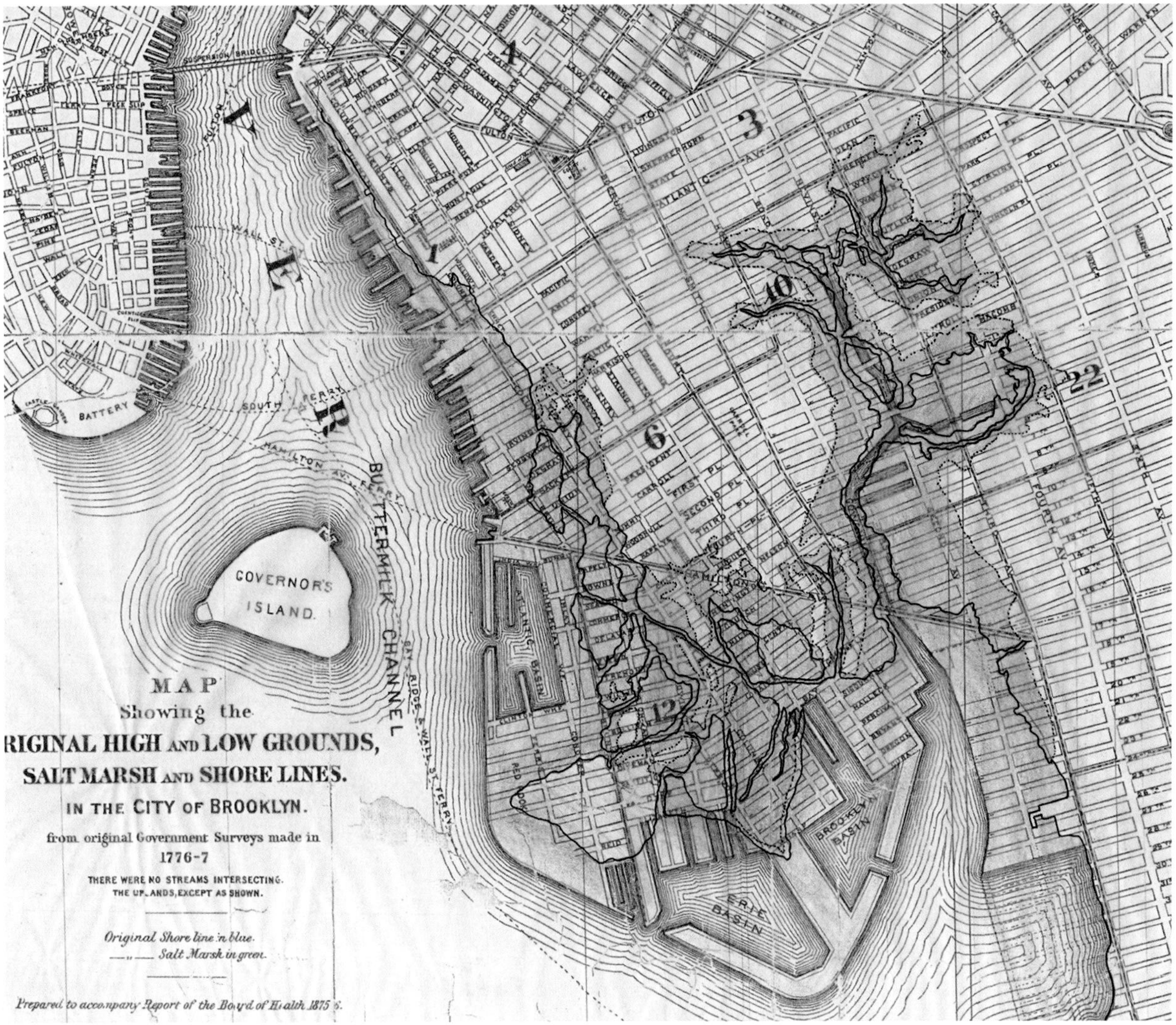

MAP
Showing the
RIGINAL HIGH AND LOW GROUNDS,
SALT MARSH AND SHORE LINES.
IN THE CITY OF BROOKLYN.
from original Government Surveys made in
1776-7
THERE WERE NO STREAMS INTERSECTING.
THE UPLANDS, EXCEPT AS SHOWN.
Original Shore line in blue.
Salt Marsh in green.
Prepared to accompany Report of the Board of Health 1875 6.
COVERNOR'S
ISLAND.
BATTERY
BUTTERMILK CHANNEL
ERIE
BASIN
BROOKLYN
BASIN
ATLANTIC BASIN
SOUTH FERRY
HAMILTON AV. FERRY
SUSPENSION BRIDGE
3
4
6
10
12
22

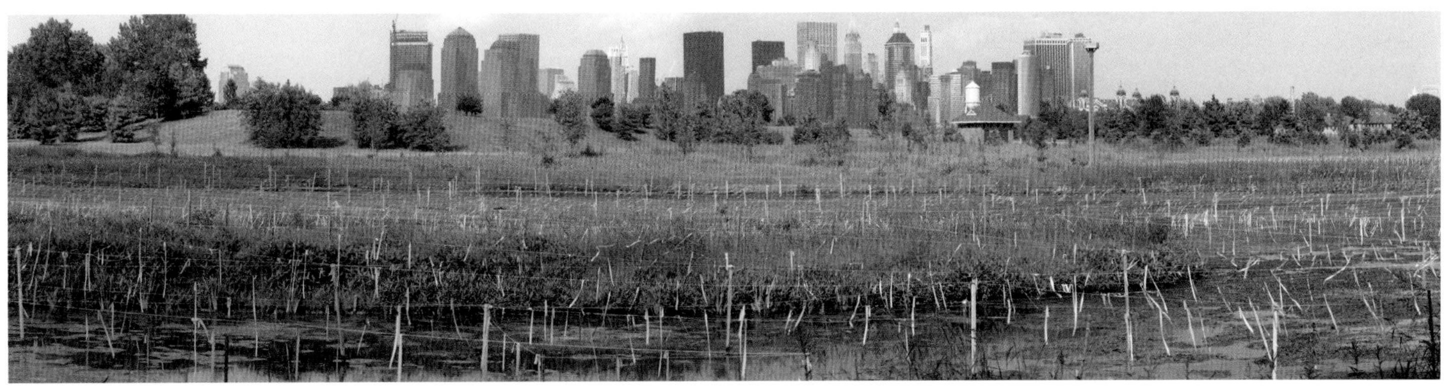

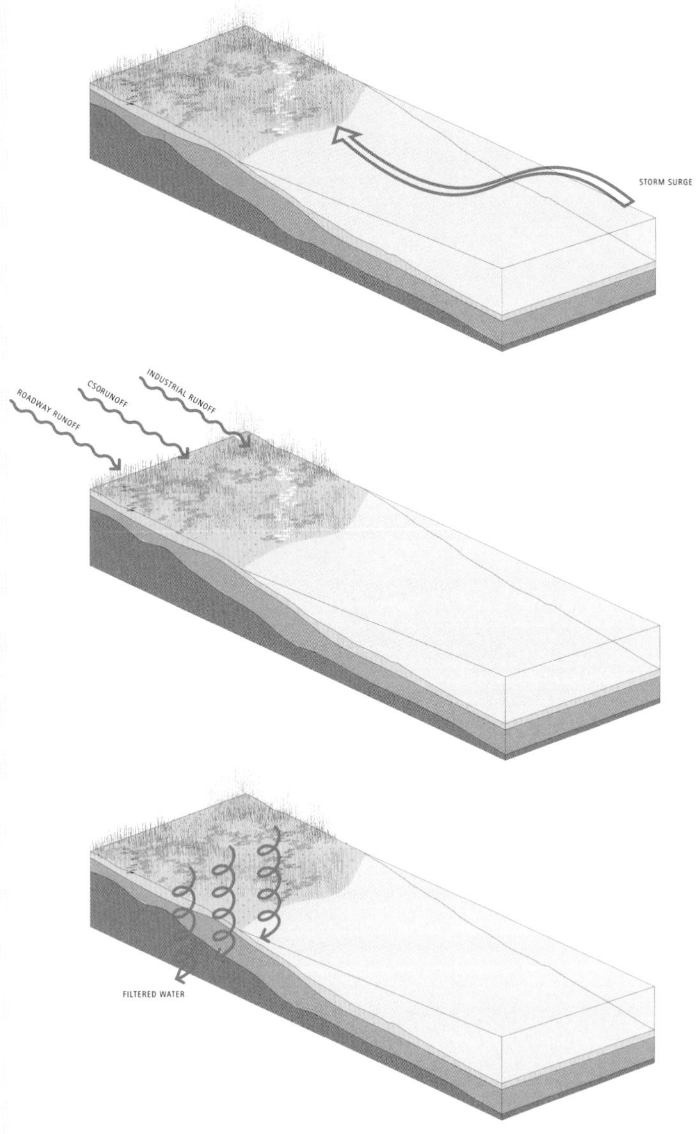

Wetlands serve to dampen storm surge, prevent polluted run-off water from contaminating harbor waters, and filter clean water to be reused as grey water.

Opposite
Hundreds of combined sewer outlets currently line the harbor edge (red circles). Only three major water treatment locations service the area (yellow circles).

FILTERING

The federal Clean Water Act of 1972 authorized the Environmental Protection Agency to begin a National Estuary Program to protect, preserve, and restore American estuaries. This radically transformed the New York-New Jersey Bay, as the Clean Water Act stipulated that sewage must be treated, and the water quality in the bay has since greatly improved. Before the Clean Water Act, the dumping of raw sewage into the bay had been unregulated and resulted in widespread illnesses such as typhoid as well as the loss of native wetlands.

Despite this legislative progress, the city's combined sewer infrastructure, which collects both raw sewage wastewater and storm water in the same pipes, is easily overwhelmed by storm water during moderate rains. As little as one-tenth of an inch of rainfall can trigger combined sewage overflow (CSO) outfalls, discharging raw sewage directly into the Upper Bay at 450 outlets along the shoreline.

New York City's PlaNYC 2030 has addressed the issue of combined sewage overflow outfalls through a "best management practice" strategy. This would harness natural strategies such as the implementation of permeable surfaces, bioswales, and green roofs that would help prevent stormwater from overwhelming the sewage system, by retaining, detaining, or cleansing the water.

But even more radical interventions at a much larger, infrastructural scale are necessary to return the estuary to a state of ecological health. A chain of constructed wetlands in the areas adjacent to the CSO outlets would filter contaminated water before it enters the main current of the harbor.

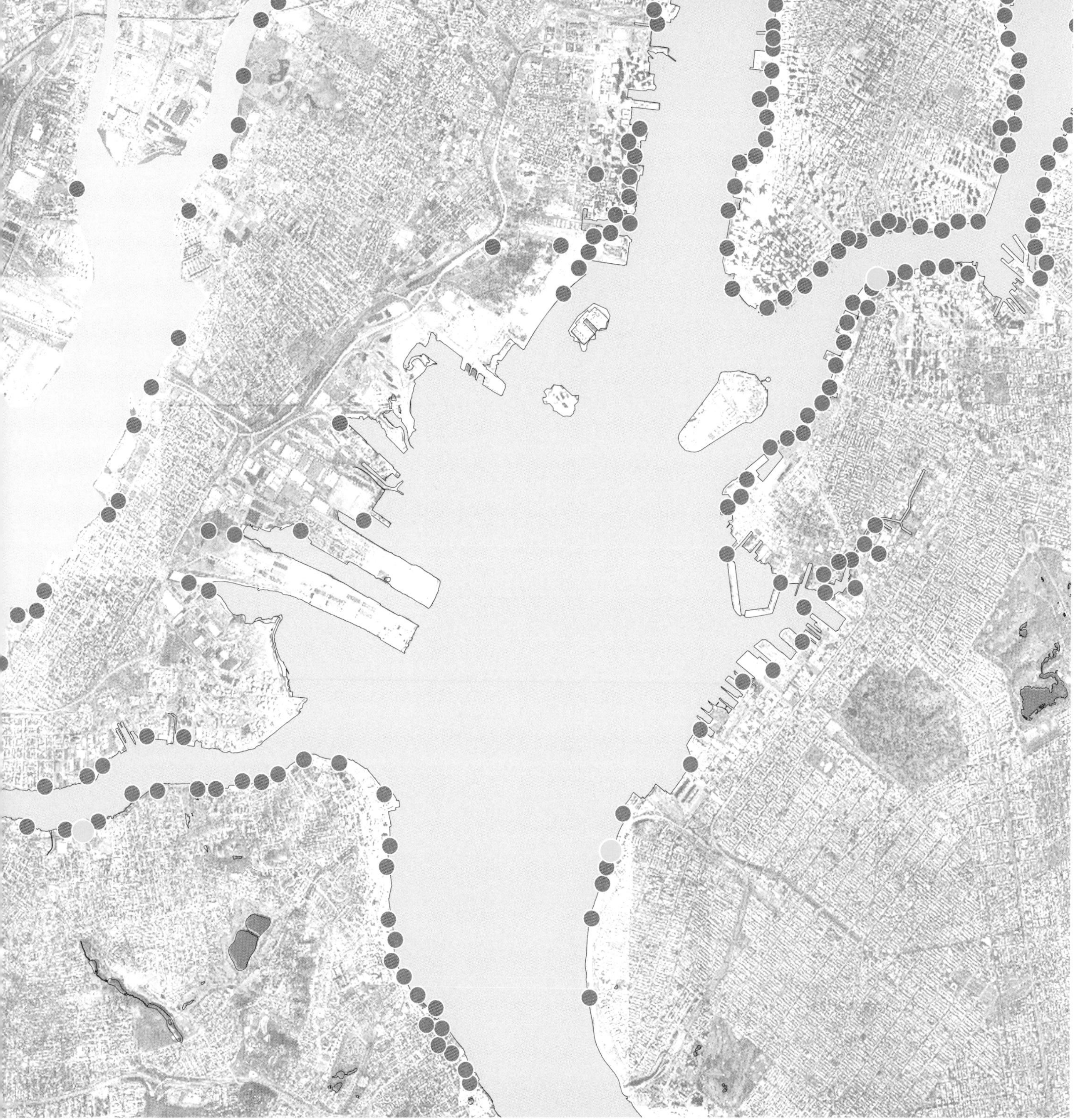

In the Palisade Bay Plan, historic piers are restored, new piers are added, and a series of parallel jetties are constructed on the edge of the shoals and between designated boat anchorages.

Opposite
Hudson and East Rivers from West 67th Street to Blackwells Island, New York, 1906 (detail)

PIERS AND SLIPS

A pier is a raised walkway over water, supported by widely spread piles or pillars. This light structure allows tides and currents to flow almost unhindered below the pier. The solid foundations of a quay and closely-spaced piles of a wharf create the effect of a breakwater, more liable to silting but tending to reduce the intensity of wave action. Piers can range in size and complexity, from a simple lightweight wooden structure, to major structures extending over a mile out to sea. Finger piers extending perpendicular to the shoreline essentially maximize the available length of shoreline for ships to berth, allowing ships to dock and unload perpendicular to the shore. With the development of container shipping in the 1960s, finger piers became relatively obsolete for the handling of bulk cargo ships. A slip, sometimes called a slipway, is the conceptual inverse of a pier. It is an extraction into the land, a ramped sectional channel, rather than an extension outward from it. Slips are used to move ships or boats from the land to the water. Historically slips would be used as the location for building and repairing boats as well as launching newly constructed ships.

Transformation of the shoreline edge of the New York–New Jersey Upper Bay has occurred continually over hundreds of years. Since Henry Hudson sailed beyond the Narrows and up the Hudson River in 1609, the approach to the island of Manhattan and its surrounding landmasses has always been by way of the sea. After the founding of the city in 1626, the edge was first transformed to accommodate the landing of ships. It was transformed again to ward off both unwanted intruders and the encroachment of rising tides. This duality between accessibility and protection led to a sophisticated range of strategies that both mimic and suppress naturally existing conditions. An examination of the chronology of Manhattan's waterfront development reveals the long history of the region's characteristic fingered waterfront edge—the language of piers and slips.

WATERFRONT CHRONOLOGY

At the time of the 1624 purchase by Peter Minuit, the boundaries of Manhattan were defined as the perimeter of the high-water mark circumscribing the island. But with the 1686 Dongen Charter, which transferred ownership of the land from the British Crown to the City of New York, the city limits were extended from the high-water mark to the low-water mark. The city could thus fill and develop these tidal waterfront parcels, which were generally sold to private individuals. The owners were required to improve the street and wharf along the property's waterfront edge. Owners often expanded their land holdings outward with ship ballast, dredge spoils, and even garbage. Finger piers were extended at the ends of the perpendicular streets, and these docks were built out farther, steadily reducing the width of the

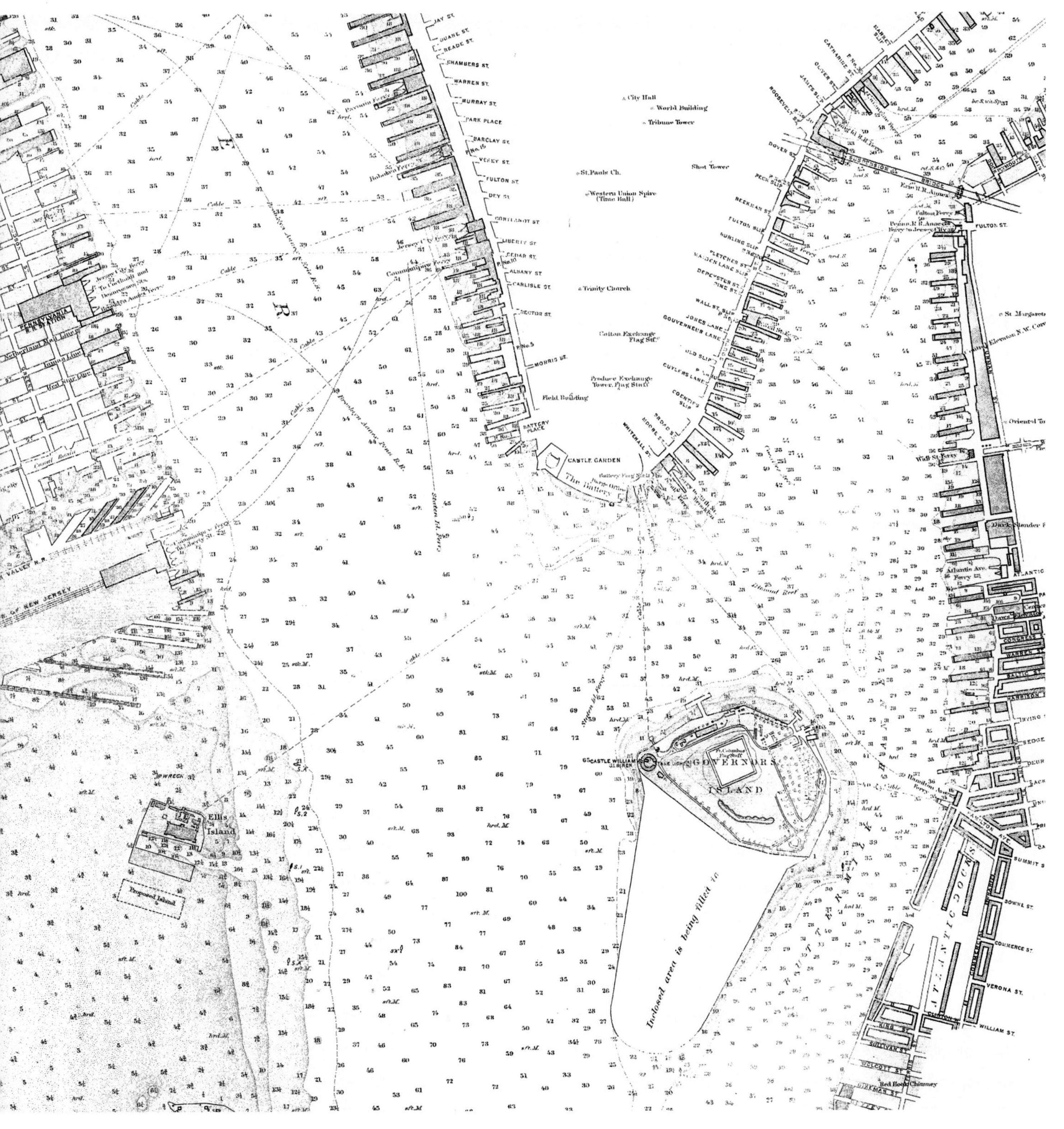
JAY ST.
DUANE ST.
READE ST.
CHAMBERS ST.
WARREN ST.
MURRAY ST.
PARK PLACE
BARCLAY ST.
VESEY ST.
FULTON ST.
DEY ST.
CORTLANDT ST.
LIBERTY ST.
CEDAR ST.
ALBANY ST.
CARLISLE ST.
RECTOR ST.
MORRIS ST.
BATTERY PLACE
CASTLE GARDEN
The Battery
City Hall
World Building
Tribune Tower
St. Pauls Ch.
Western Union Spire (Time Ball)
Shot Tower
Trinity Church
Cotton Exchange Flag Staff
Produce Exchange Tower, Flag Staff
Field Building
WHITEHALL ST.
BROAD ST.
COENTIES SLIP
CUYLERS LANE
OLD SLIP
GOUVERNEUR LANE
JONES LANE
WALL ST. SLIP
PINE ST.
DEPEYSTER ST.
MAIDEN LANE SLIP
FLETCHER ST.
BURLING SLIP
FULTON SLIP
BEEKMAN ST.
PECK SLIP
DOVER ST.
ROOSEVELT ST.
JAMES ST.
OLIVER ST.
CATHARINE ST.
MARKET SLIP
SUSPENSION BRIDGE
Fulton Ferry
FULTON ST.
Wall St. Ferry
Atlantic Ave. Ferry
ATLANTIC
CONGRESS ST.
WARREN ST.
BALTIC ST.
HARRISON
Hamilton Ave. Ferry
HAMILTON AVE.
SUMMIT ST.
ATLANTIC DOCKS
BOWNE ST.
COMMERCE ST.
VERONA ST.
WILLIAM ST.
KING ST.
SULLIVAN ST.
WOLCOTT ST.
Red Hook Chimney
BUTTERMILK CHANNEL
CASTLE WILLIAM
GOVERNORS ISLAND
Inclosed area is being filled in
Ellis Island
Proposed Island
PENNSYLVANIA R.R. STATION
Netherland Mail Line
Inman Line
Red Star Line
Canal Basin
VALLEY R.R.
OF NEW JERSEY
Pavonia Ferry
Hoboken Ferry
Jersey City Ferry
Communipaw Ferry
Brooklyn Annex Penn. R.R.
Staten Id. Ferry
Cable
St. Margarets

waterways. By 1856 the New York Harbor Commission recommended permanent pier and bulkhead lines, to be regulated by the State.

In 1870, the city established the Department of Docks, a municipal agency with exclusive control of all waterfront property—piers, slips, bulkheads, and pier sheds. Private ownership along the waterfront was effectively terminated. General George McClellan, who had lost his presidential bid in 1864 to Abraham Lincoln, was appointed chief engineer of the department. McClellan executed sanitary improvements as well as port facility improvements. At that time, piers were constructed on solid cribwork foundations, or with the block-and-bridge technique, creating a virtually solid rectangular barrier extending perpendicularly to the bulkhead. This led to still water zones between piers, gathering both sediment and raw sewage, emptying from the new duct outlets located at the ends of the city's east-west sewer lines. McClellan recommended the adoption of an open piling system of pier construction, consisting of supporting columns anchored several feet apart, driven into the river bottom and topped with a concrete or wood deck. This allowed the river currents and tides to pick up the sewer debris and sediment, push it through the pilings, and carry it out to the open sea.

Another significant transformation begun by McClellan was his plan to extend a new bulkhead line and establish a wider waterfront street at Manhattan's perimeter. The bulkhead was to be defined by a continuous solid precast concrete retaining wall faced in granite, rising six feet above the high-water line and descending twenty feet below. Beyond the bulkhead line, sixty to one hundred foot long piers were to be constructed to a newly established pier head line. This project for a continuous bulkhead was executed over an extended period, and substantially completed by 1879 under a subsequent chief engineer, George Greene Jr. In 1888, the Federal Rivers and Harbors Act was passed by Congress, establishing the United States Army Corps of Engineers as the agency with jurisdiction over pier head and bulkhead lines. Manhattan's bulkhead construction continued—by 1916, almost half of the island's entire waterfront perimeter was corseted by a massive seawall, extending over 100,000 linear feet.

Construction of Pier 58, Chelsea Pier, North River, Manhattan, 1908

Aerial photograph of Red Hook, Brooklyn, ca. 1935

Opposite
Proposed wharfage, piers, and improved harbor front for the City of New York, plate from *Knights New Mechanical Dictionary*, 1884

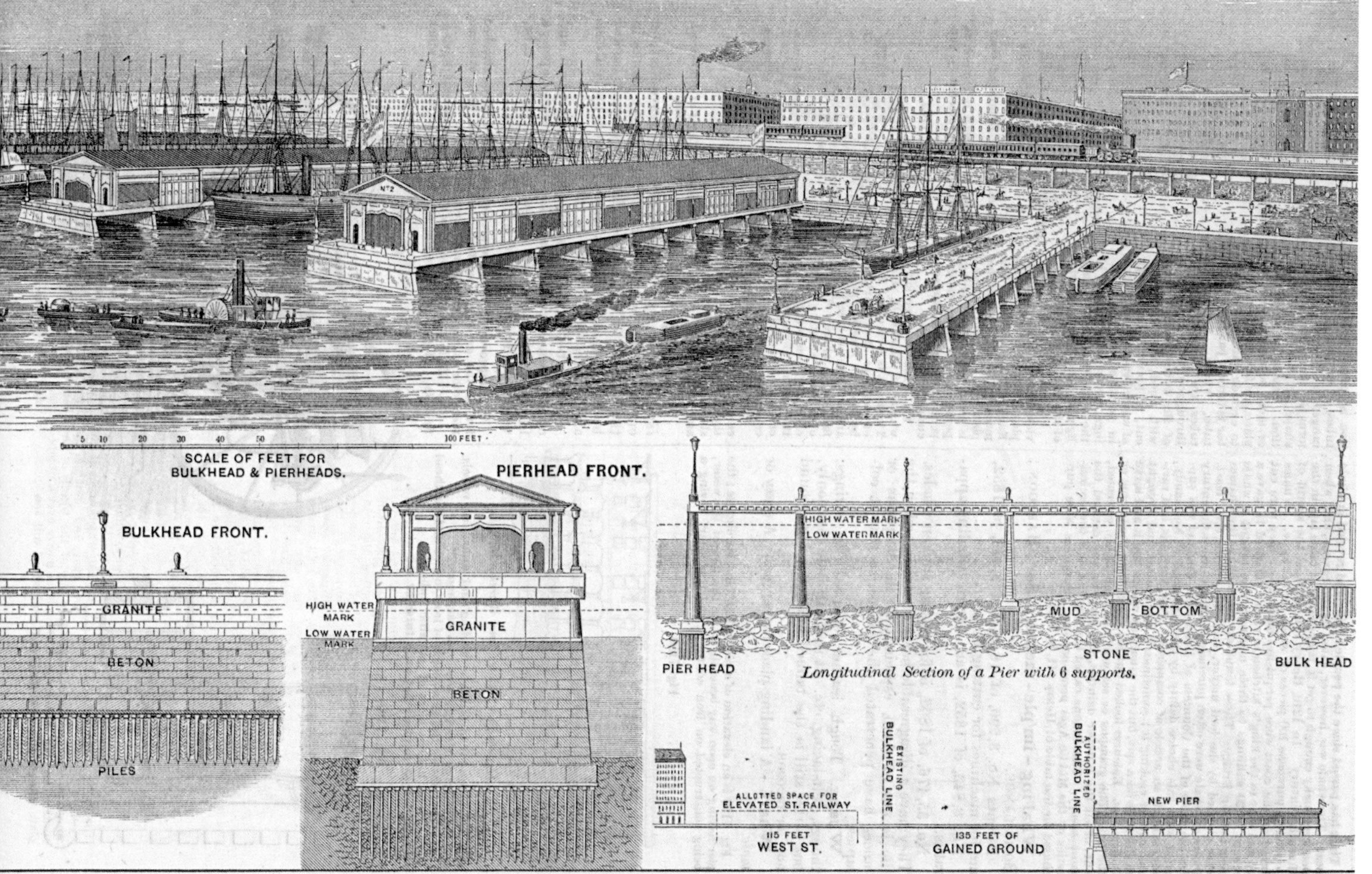

PLATE LXXV. PROPOSED WHARFAGE, PIERS, AND IMPROVED HARBOR-FRONT FOR THE CITY OF NEW YORK. See page 2761.

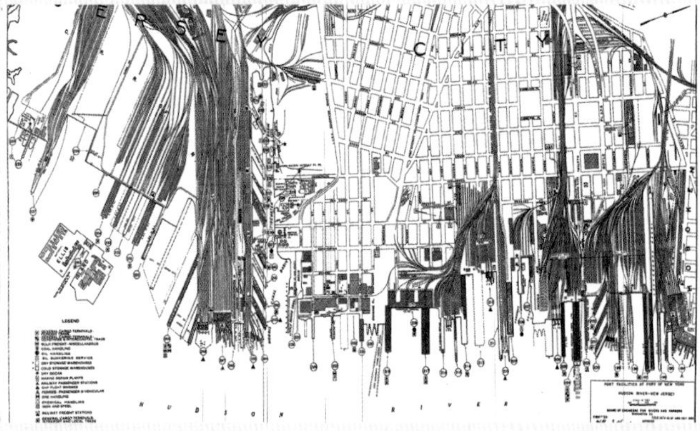

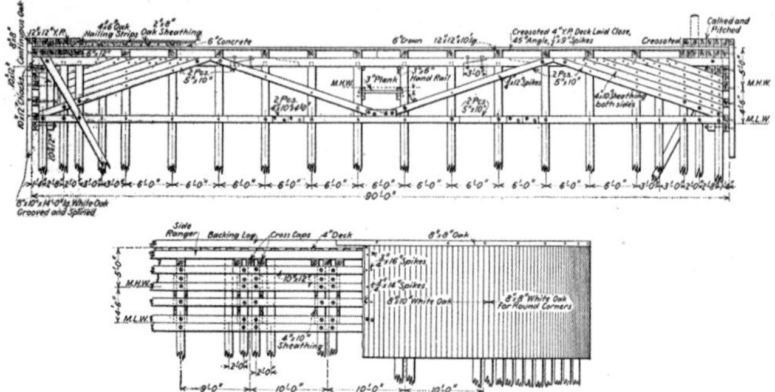
Fig. 66. Cross Section of Heavy Wooden Piers, and Elevation of Outer Corner, North German Lloyd Co., Hoboken. N. J.

ZONE OF IMPLEMENTATION

As the city grew into the twentieth century, another form of shoreline transformation began, the strategy of further extension through landfill. The waterfront edge zone, between the bulkhead line and the pier head line, was often designated as an area for landfill and development. By contrast, our proposal for the Upper Bay returns to the feathered edge of fingers and slips, transforming the edge with the re-implementation of a fringe of piers. Our proposal implements these piers along the shorelines of Lower Manhattan, Brooklyn's Sunset Park, and Staten Island. This fringe will serve to disperse wave energy from storms as well as create a protective zone at the water's edge. By cutting slips back into the land, we address the issue of stormwater runoff, filtering this water with bioswales and permeable surfaces. We suggest potentially harvesting and reusing this filtered fresh water before letting it run into the saline bay; thus treating storm water as a resource, not a liability. Detached piers are also proposed along the anchorages offshore of the Jersey Flats, and we are investigating the potential of developing housing along these piers.

DETACHED PIERS

The detached piers that are proposed for the central region of the harbor are constructed from recycled and dredged earthen materials on a shallow shoal. These piers are oriented perpendicularly to the direction of waves as to diminish wave velocities that accelerate through the narrows, dispersing this energy within the basin before the waves impact the harbor edge. While the elongated form of the detached piers is essential to mitigating storm impact, these piers are intended to replicate the scale and organization of typical New York City blocks. Overlaid on the complex and transformative history of the harbor, it is easy to imagine that the fringed watery gap between the mainland and the detached piers had been gradually erased, leaving the piers a remnant of land. Most of all, the tradition of building places for industry and recreation on the New York piers is also carried forward in a new way.

Plan of the railroad terminus on the Military Ocean Terminal, Bayonne, NJ, 1965 (detail)

North German Lloyd Co., Hoboken, NJ, cross-section of heavy wooden piers and elevation of outer corner, 1917

Opposite
Collage view of a proposed slip in Sunset Park, Brooklyn

KISS & SAIL
PARK & SAIL
BUS TRAFFIC

The islands in the Palisade Bay Master Plan are arrayed in chains along the harbor shoals and flats.

Opposite
Archipelago of New Caledonia, 2001

ISLANDS

The etymology of the word island is rooted in the Old English, for (e)gland, meaning watery land. An island is defined as any emergent piece of land completely surrounded by water at high tide and isolated from other landmasses. An archipelago is a grouping of geographically and geologically related islands.

Many natural islands and reefs are found within the Upper Harbor of New York–New Jersey. Islands include Shooters Island, Ellis Island, Liberty Island, Governors Island, and of course Manhattan Island, all of which have been expanded with landfill. Flats and shoals include the Bay Ridge Flats, the Jersey Flats, the Gowanus Flats, Robbins Reef, and Diamond Reef. Many small islands and shoals that once emerged from the Upper Bay no longer exist, lost over the centuries to the blasting and dredging of navigational channels within the bay. Our proposal for the Upper Bay includes an extensive addition to the existing archipelago and underwater reefs of New York–New Jersey, above, below, and between the tidal fluctuations. In addition to providing an infrastructural field of obstructions to break up the wave energy generated by storm surges, these new artificial islands and reefs will also provide habitat for plants, invertebrates, fish, and birds, enriching the ecosystem, diversity, and health of the harbor.

ZONE OF IMPLEMENTATION

The unit of the archipelago of artificial islands that we are proposing is a circular module of approximately 80 feet in diameter. These will be arrayed in fields, in the shallowest bathymetric zones of the Upper Bay, particularly along the Bay Ridge and Gowanus Flats, along the southern shore of Governors Island, and below the southern tip of Manhattan. Some will also be arrayed along the northern edge of the Jersey Flats. Reef construction using decommissioned subway cars is proposed at the northern Jersey Flats and at Gravesend Bay, southeast of the Narrows.

By examining various arrays and forms for the islands, as well as hypothesizing the effects of current and silting, several construction possibilities for the islands have emerged: floating mesh supporting esturarine grasses, caisson perimeters with solid fill, caisson perimeters with permeable mesh walls, and solid islands versus ring-shaped atoll islands.

We propose to implement this transformation using both cost efficient and environmentally sound and sustainable methods. One potential strategy for achieving the desired bathymetric changes is the use of clean dredge spoils from current and future dredging projects. The Harbor Deepening Project, the largest such undertaking for the Port of New York and New Jersey, will make available an

estimated 40 million cubic yards of dredged material. Habitat restoration and environmental improvement, in conjunction with dredging projects, is a mutually beneficial endeavor.

Costs and feasibility for the use of dredge material in the creation of caisson island fill, mudflats and dredged rock reef construction are promising. Likewise, the use of recycled materials such as decommissioned subway cars to create artificial reefs has proven economical and successful on other waterfronts. Other possibilities for fill material include clean garbage and construction debris, as well as the enormous volume of earth and rock that may be excavated for future subway tunnel construction.

ANCIENT ARTIFICIAL ISLANDS

Artificial islands are formed by humans rather than through natural means. They have a long history, despite the current trend of highly artificial islands created as real estate in the Middle East. Historically, there were two types of artificial islands: wooden or stone structures constructed in shallow waters, and floating structures found in still waters.

In prehistoric Ireland and Scotland, artificial circular islands called crannógs were constructed in lakes, rivers, and estuarine waters. They were between approximately 30 and 200 feet in diameter, defined at their edges by a wooden oak pile palisade enclosure. Thousands of crannóg ruins are found today in Ireland and hundreds in Scotland, now overgrown with trees and shrubs.

Tenochtitlan, the Aztec predecessor to Mexico City, was founded on a small natural island in Lake Texcoco, surrounded by countless artificial chinampa islands. The chinampa is a method of ancient agriculture, almost 1,000 years old, developed in the Valley of Mexico using small rectangular areas of fertile land on the shallow lake beds to grow crops.

On Lake Titicaca on the border of Peru and Bolivia, the pre-Incan Uros people created and still inhabit the floating Uros islands, created with dry bundles of the totora reed. These were anchored with ropes to stakes driven into the lakebed and could be moved if a threat arose. Forty-two of these islands still exist today. Similarly, the Ma'dan, or Marsh Arabs, of Iraq constructed floating islands and houses of dried bundled reeds and mud in the wetland marshes known as Hor in southern Iraq. The Iraqi dictator Saddam Hussein embarked on an extermination campaign against the region's Shiite population in the 1980s and 1990s, draining and mining the marshes where this unique culture had developed for over 5,000 years.

Mad'an Reed House, Iraq, 2008

Opposite
Elevation and section of caisson fortification at Cherbourg, France, 1782–83

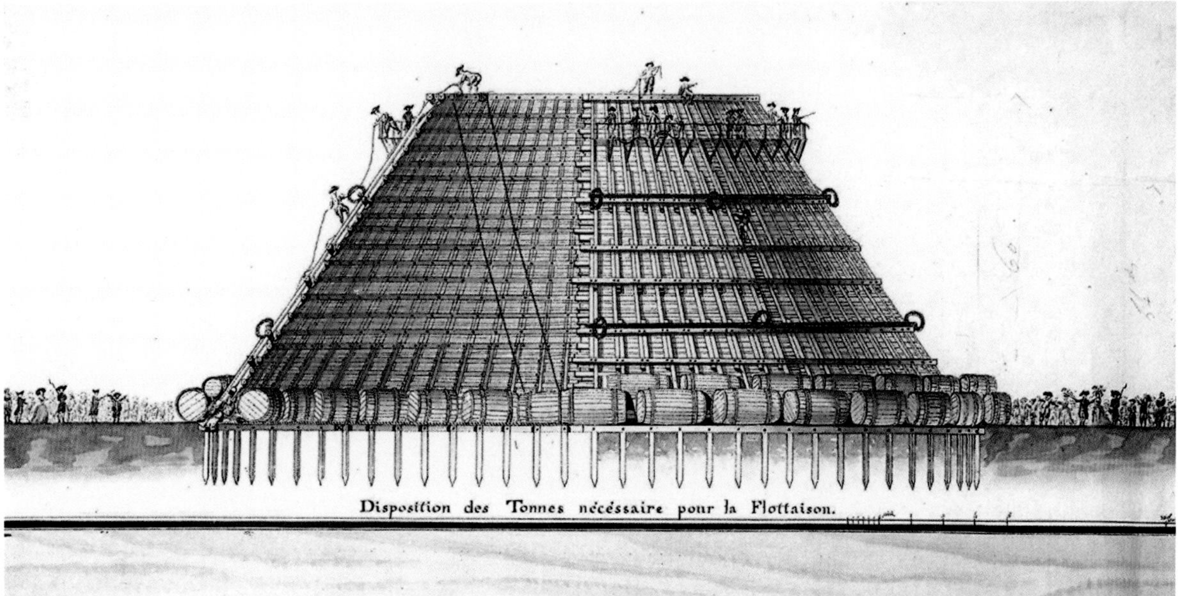

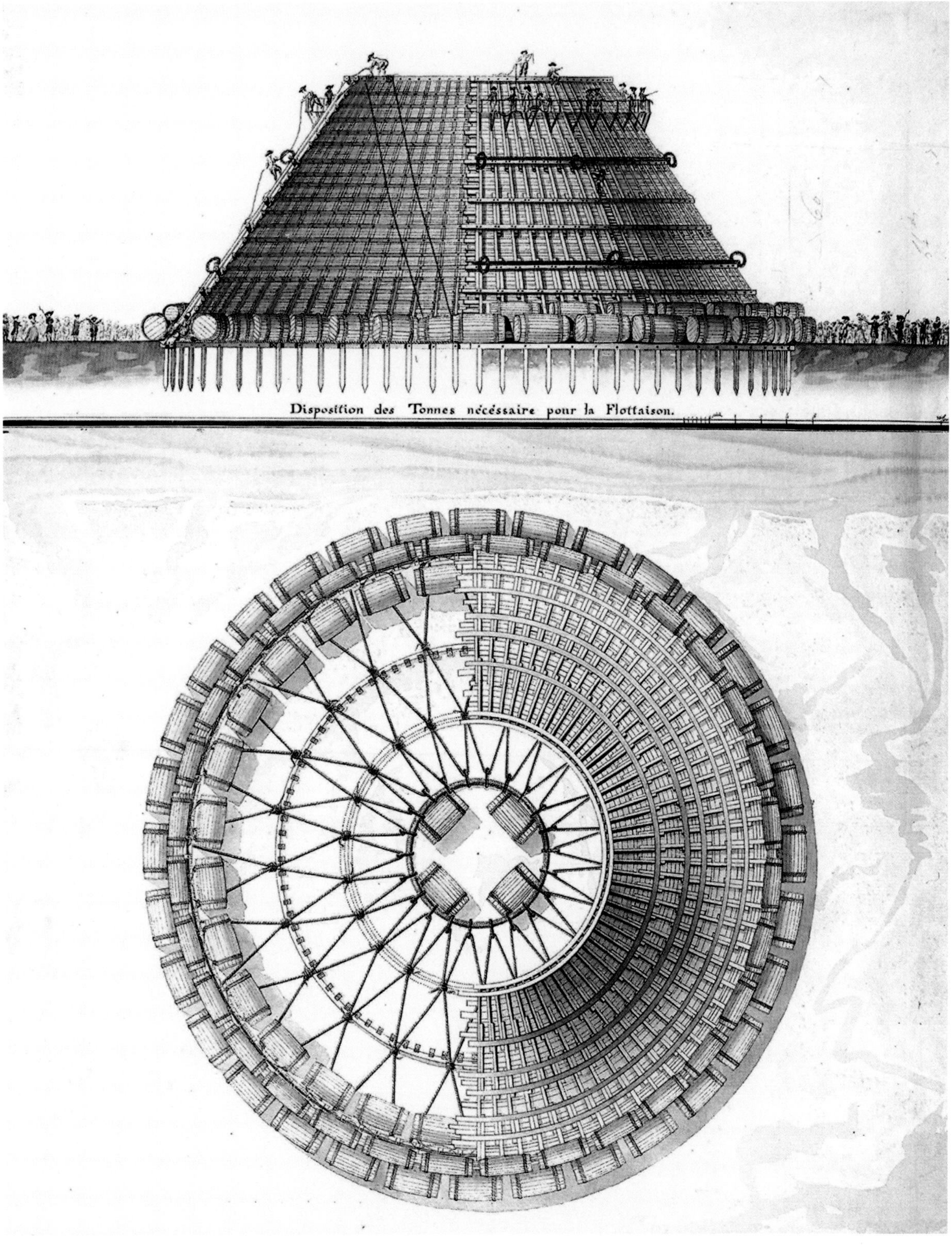

Disposition des Tonnes nécéssaire pour la Flottaison.

ARTIFICIAL ISLANDS OF THE UNITED STATES

NEW YORK
U Thant Island (Belmont Island)

In New York's East River, the U Thant Island (officially Belmont Island, renamed in 1976 for U Thant, the UN Secretary General from 1961-71), is a tiny artificial island measuring 100 by 200 feet and located at the southern end of Roosevelt Island opposite the UN Headquarters. The island was constructed in the 1890s as a byproduct of William Steinway's trolley tunnels, connecting Manhattan to his company town in Queens. This project was later completed as the IRT subway Flushing Line by August Belmont.

NEW YORK
Ellis and Liberty Islands

Ellis Island, first Little Oyster Island, served as the main entry facility for 12 million immigrants to the United States between 1892 and 1954. It is now property of the federal government and is a monument operated by the National Park Service.

Liberty Island is a small uninhabited island offshore of Liberty State Park. Formerly called Bedloe's Island, it has been the site of a private home, a smallpox quarantine station, and a fort following the Revolutionary War. Today the fort, in the shape of an eleven-pointed star, serves as the pedestal for the Statue of Liberty.

SAN FRANCISCO
Treasure Island

In the San Francisco Bay, Treasure Island is a 395-acre artificial island connected by a small isthmus to Yerba Buena Island. It was constructed by the Federal Government in 1936-37 for the Golden Gate International Exposition, and built of imported fill upon existing shoals. After the exposition the island was to have become a military airport, but this was constructed at an alternate site and the island instead served as a naval base during World War II. Although still owned by the navy, it was decommissioned and opened to the public in 1996; approximately 1,500 people currently live on the island.

Liberty Island and Ellis Island in the New York-New Jersey Upper Bay, 2008

Opposite
The city of New York, with Castle Williams and Governors Island on the bottom right, and Battery Park and Castle Clinton in the center, Cheltnam, 1855

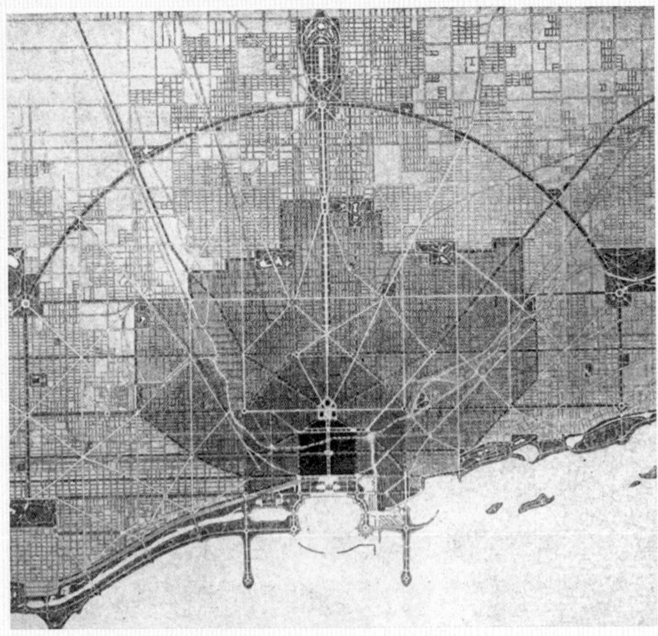

Daniel Burnham, Chicago, Plan of the City, showing the general system of boulevards and parks existing and proposed (includes Northerly Island and others), 1909

Opposite
Star and Venetian Islands, Miami, 2008

CHICAGO
Northerly Island

Northerly Island is a 91-acre artificial island along Chicago's lakefront. It is connected to the mainland via a narrow isthmus. The idea for the island, which began construction in 1920, emerged from Daniel Burnham's 1909 Plan of Chicago, in which he imagined Northerly Island as a lakefront park and one of the northernmost points in a series of five of man-made islands stretching along the waterfront. In 1933-34 the island served as the location of the world's fair. Merrill Meigs recommended converting the island into an airfield in 1935, and in 1946 it became Meigs Field. It was removed in 2003, and the island was converted into a park.

SEATTLE
Harbor Island

Harbor Island is an artificial island in the mouth of Seattle's Duwamish Waterway. It was completed in 1909 and at 350 acres in size, it was at the time the largest man-made island in the world. Since 1912, the island has been used for various commercial and industrial activities. It is currently a Superfund site and is on the Environmental Protection Agency's National Priorities List. Harbor Island was made from 24 million cubic yards of earth removed in the regrading of city streets as well as dredge material taken from the Duwamish River. It was not surpassed as the world's largest artificial island until 1938, with the completion of Treasure Island in the San Francisco Bay.

MIAMI
The Venetian Islands

The Venetian Islands are a chain of artificial islands in Biscayne Bay, linking the Florida mainland to Miami Beach with the scenic Venetian Causeway. The eleven islands, six of which are inhabited, were built by developers during the Florida land boom of the 1920s, adding valuable new real estate to the city. When the stock market crashed in 1929, additional projects were abandoned.

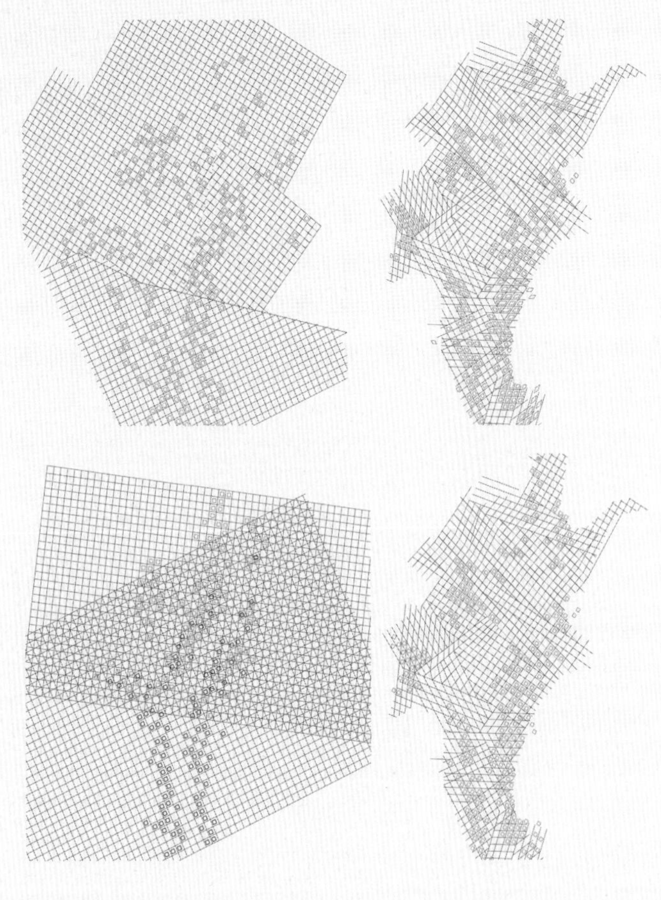

Grids overlayed on the harbor to create different patterns of islands

Following pages
Preliminary studies for island infill in the Upper Bay

ISLAND INFILL

Islands can serve as a porous land infill within the watery void of the harbor. Such constructed land in the harbor would help to diminish the force and impact of storm surge and protect the established neighborhoods and business districts further inland. A formal study of the size, orientation, placement, and density of these islands begins to shape the design by marking the range of programmatic and topological differences within the harbor zone. Our final island arrangement traces both the city grid and the depths of the harbor waters. As a starting point, we can consider infilling the harbor with an alternating grid of generic square islands to yield a new harbor figure which is equally land (figure) and water (ground). These islands are densely packed so that each island is discreet but touches four adjacent islands on its corners.

To accommodate a necessary corridor for shipping routes, swaths of these islands are removed from the central area of the harbor so that four to five discreet island areas are identified. These areas are neither land nor water but rather a transition zone between the edge of the land and the harbor waters. To further articulate these zones, we explored a gradient in island heights; the islands might get taller as they approach established land and then sink below the surface of the water at the extremities.

STRETCHING THE CITY GRID

The following pages document the design studies of how 800 by 800 foot islands can create new land in the harbor waters while relating the edge of the five major urban zones which define the figure of the harbor. These zones include Manhattan, Brooklyn, Staten Island, Bayonne, and Jersey City. The street grid is established differently in each zone and thus orients the city blocks to the harbor in a unique way. These studies extend the array of urban grids into the harbor void and infill its fringes and intersections with islands. The final scheme rotates the orientation of the islands according to an extension of grid lines derived from the Verrazano Bridge, the Gowanus Expressway, Canal Street in Manhattan, and the massive Bayonne piers. This array of islands starts to indicate a new shape to the harbor by diminishing its clear boundaries and establishing land that can accommodate new types of urban landscapes.

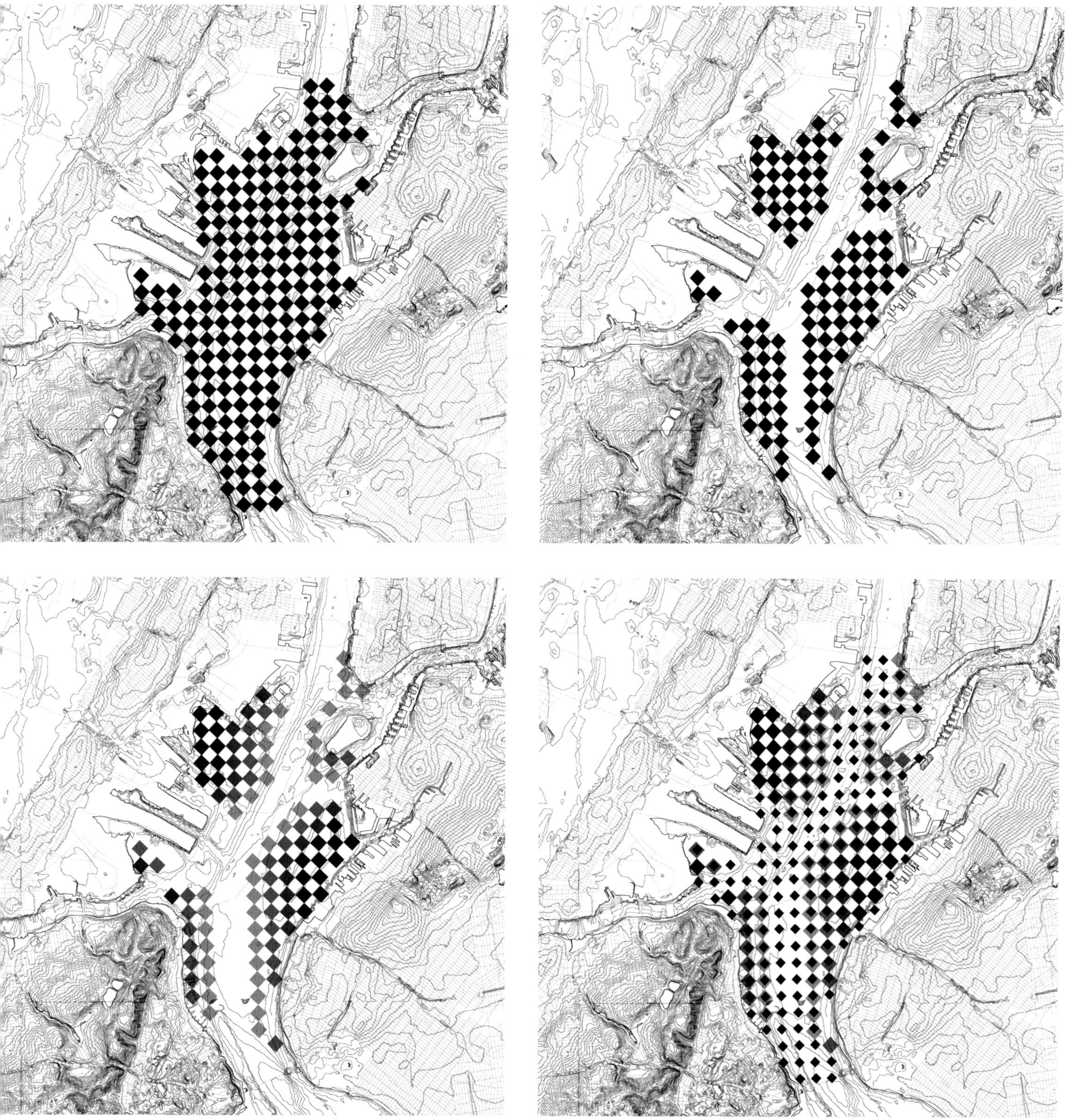

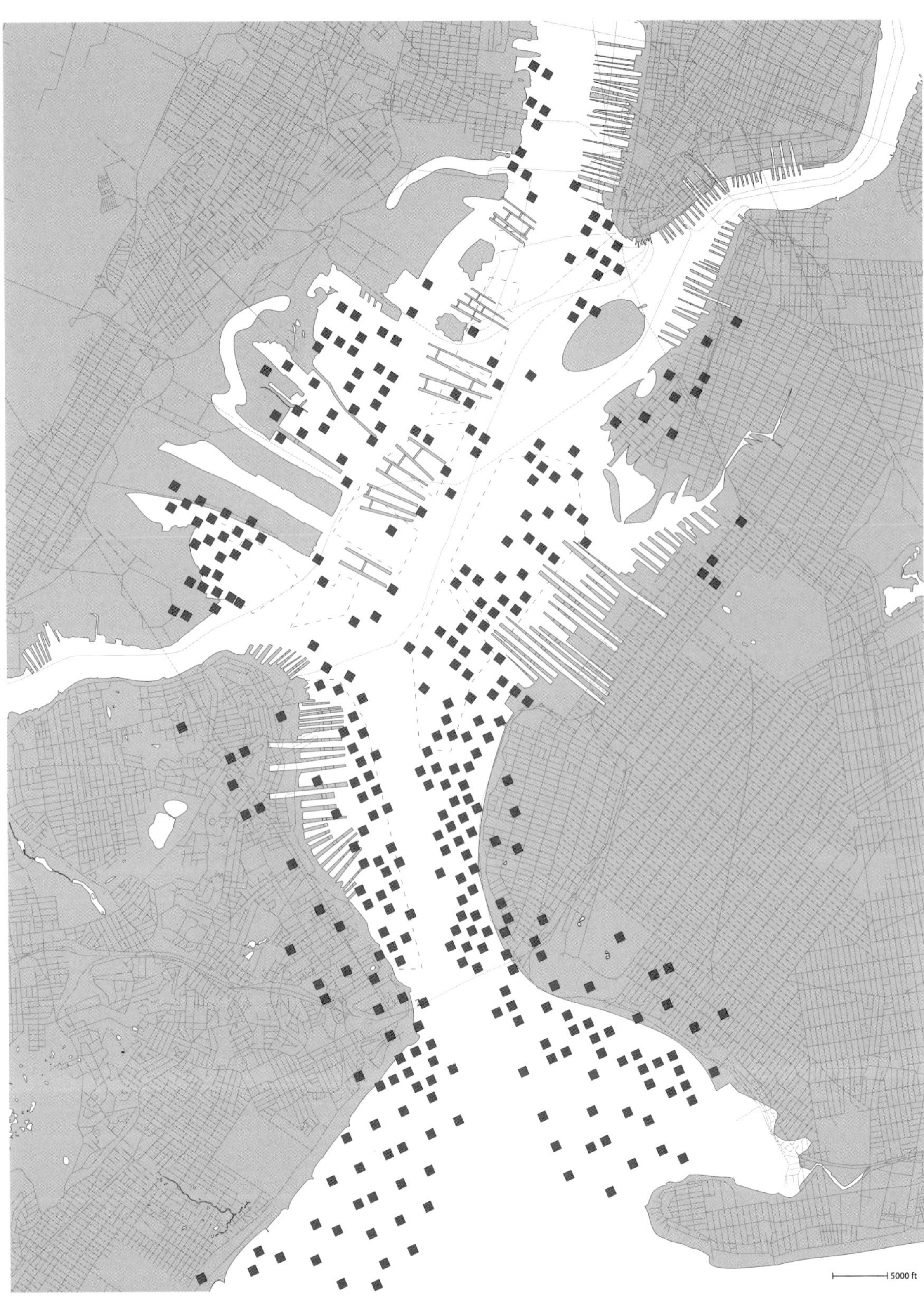
5000 ft

Wetlands and salt marshes create a rich biodiverse habitat.

Opposite
NOAA map of Bayonne piers overlaid on satellite image illustrating the shallow flats that are ideal locations for salt marshes (detail)

GENERATING HABITAT

The word estuary is derived from the Latin aestus, meaning tide. An estuary is a semi-enclosed coastal body of water with one or more rivers flowing into it, with an open connection to the sea. As estuaries are usually located at the tidal mouths of rivers, they are associated with high levels of silt and sedimentation. The mixing of tidal sea water and fresh river water creates a brackish environment with varying levels of salinity. An estuary is often associated with high levels of biodiversity—it is characterized by estuarine-dependent plants, invertebrates, fish, and bird species.

HABITAT: NATURAL AND ARTIFICIAL

Estuaries consist of moving and still waters, and the mixing of fresh, brackish, and salt waters where rivers meet the sea. They are characterized by the existence of mudflats, wetlands, and marshes. These systems are rich in native organisms, resilient species that have high tolerances for the estuary's extremes of temperatures and salinity and thrive on the rich organic environment found here. However it is the seasonal and migratory organisms that enhance the rich diversity of an estuary system. The ecological richness of the New York–New Jersey Harbor is in particular due to its role as a place of transition, a zone of interchange of diverse ecologies and species, each with specific needs.

The habitat of the New York–New Jersey Upper Bay exisits in both the waters and the banks and bottoms of its bays and rivers. Centuries of human activities on its shores, with the consequential effects of industrial pollution, storm and sewage runoff, and even hunting and fishing activities, have massively degraded this fragile habitat. Huge areas of native wetlands, particularly on the New Jersey shores, have been landfilled and destroyed. But as ecological sensitivity has risen, and the region has begun to abate pollution and the adverse effects of industry, the ecosystem of the New York–New Jersey estuary has improved substantially.

With the decline of shipping and other waterfront industries, the ecosystem of the harbor has begun to adapt over time to new artificial habitats. Living organisms have come to coexist with the pier and slip typology at the shoreline. For example, the shade and shadow provided below pile-supported piers has become precious habitat for certain species of spawning fish. These areas of deep shadow and shade provide valuable complexity to the habitat along the shorelines of the bay. This construction technique of open pile structures was specifically adapted for New York's waterfront piers, to allow waste and silt to wash between the piles and flush out to the sea, rather than accumulating and silting between piers. Shipping basins, particularly along the Brooklyn waterfront of the East River, are a remnant of the former shipping industry.

Caven Pt.
TOWER
ELEVATOR
Under construction
MILITARY OCEAN TERMINAL
TANK
TANK
rock pile
HORN
BELL
ROBBINS REEF
Constable Hook
STACK
SILOS
GONG
Baxters Ledge
CONSTABLE HOOK REACH
TOWER

Even the granite and concrete block bulkheads that corset much of the waterfront of Manhattan and Brooklyn provide a reef-like underwater habitat, with firm surfaces and protective crevasses, for mollusks and fish.

Much of what we propose as soft infrastructural design strategies to mitigate storm surge effects—reefs, improved wetlands, archipelago islands, new piers and slips—also serves to improve and strengthen the ecology of the bay. Improving ecology and creating habitat works significantly to protect the uplands from storm surge and flooding damage. Adaptive design strategies addressing the consequences of global warming work handsomely with habitat creation and restoration.

WETLANDS AND PLANTS

Habitat consciousness today is particularly focused on the restoration of wetlands, which are considered to be the richest element within the food web of coastal estuaries. Establishing a plant base is necessary to the development or restoration of wetlands. Although many plants are adapted to coastal habitat, salt spray, and occasional inundation, only two species of land plants can thrive in the salty tidal waters of the east coast of North America. Both belong to the genus Spartina, the perennial deciduous grass which is the fundamental component of a healthy salt marsh. It grows on the peat formed by accumulated sediment and its own rhizomatic biome over time. Spartina patens, commonly known as saltmarsh hay, grows best at higher marsh elevations that are only incrementally flooded by saltwater. It is a short, sturdy, matted grass that was often used as animal feed. At lower elevations that are more affected by regular tidal inundation, Spartina alterniflora thrives. Also known as smooth cordgrass, this species is coarser and taller than Spartina patens, and it is able to spend considerably more time submerged in saltwater. Spartina is unique in its ability to concentrate salt at a cellular level and exclude salt from entering its roots, thus preventing the loss of fresh water and the withering effects of saltwater exposure that other plants experience. A healthy salt marsh is dependent on the presence of these two grasses, which together create a rich nutrient base and a protective habitat to numerous organisms, particularly crustaceans and mollusks, which are then sought as food by fish and birds.

Spartina alterniflora growing in brackish tidal waters

Hauling the largest shad seine in the world on the Potomac River, ca. 1870

Opposite
Collage showing sunken, retired subway cars creating artificial reefs in the shallow waters along the New Jersey coastline

N. N. Kondakov, *American Eel*, 1957, drawing

Opposite
Ospry nests on U Thant Island in the East River, New York, 2007

FISH

Estuaries, as a place where saltwater and freshwater meet, are productive and diverse systems, and as nutrient traps, they are important fish nursery habitats. The great diversity of fish species found in an estuary is due to the presence of fresh water, estuarine, and marine fish that utilize the tidal river and its grassy shoals and wetlands for spawning habitat. The resultant abundance of fish and invertebrates adds to the productivity of the entire system, by providing a forage base of substantial quantity for fish-eating birds. It is these seasonal migratory fish that enhance the rich diversity of an estuary system—diadromous fish migrants that travel between salt and fresh water. Of the diadromous fish, there are two types of migrants. Anadromous (meaning upward running) fish live mostly in the ocean, and breed in fresh water. Catadromous (meaning downward running) fish live in fresh water, and breed in the ocean. In the New York-New Jersey estuary system, striped bass, American shad, and Atlantic sturgeon are some of the anadromous fish that live in the ocean but return every spring to swim up the harbor and the Hudson River to spawn. These fish leave the river soon after spawning in spring, and in autumn their progeny swim back to the ocean in an endless stream, to the delight of migrating birds. Journeying in the opposite direction is the freshwater American eel of the genus Anguilla, whose larvae drift on the open ocean feeding on dissolved nutrients. These larvae develop into glass eels and then young eels, often traveling thousands of miles back to their original streams. Many invertebrates such as shrimp also reproduce in the shelter of the region's wetlands and then move out to the ocean for their adulthood.

BIRDS

The diversity of life in the waters of the estuary supports the feeding habits of wading birds. These birds—glossy ibis, great egrets, snowy egrets, yellow and black-crowned night herons, and green herons—have recently surged in number as the water quality and harbor habitat have improved. They nest in large numbers around the Upper Bay shores but only in particular locations. Some, like Shooters Island, have been acquired by New York City's Department of Parks and Recreation and designated as "forever wild" sites. Interestingly, the various types of wading birds share nesting sites but minimize competition for feeding by specializing in their habits. They carve out separate but overlapping niches by relying on differences in tidal levels, feeding times, salinities, and favored prey. Also, many Neotropical migratory songbirds along the Atlantic flyway stop to feed in the Bay. Both types of birds thrive on the diversity of the estuarine food web. The interdependence of plants, invertebrates, fish, and birds in this rich ecosystem is extremely complex.

LONG

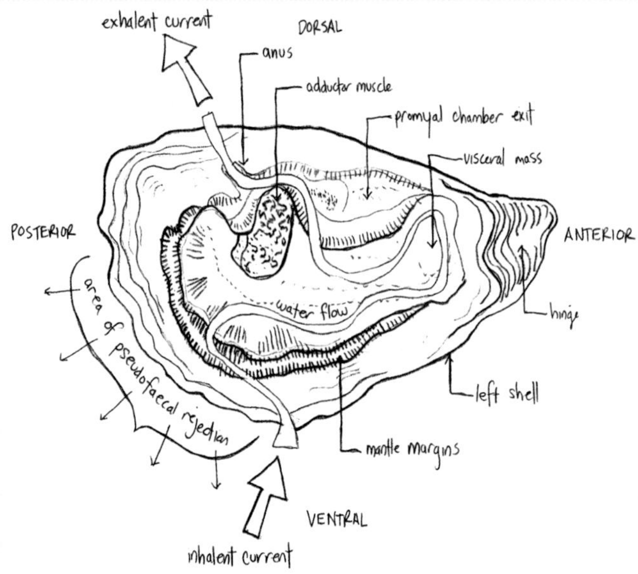

Open oyster at market, 2006

Anatomy of an oyster, 2008, drawing

Opposite
Oyster racks off the north coast of New Zealand, 2007

OYSTERS

The shallow brackish intertidal zones along the edge of the New York Harbor were once home to millions of mollusks, the *Crassostrea virginica*, more commonly known as the eastern oyster. Biologists estimate that in the seventeenth century, the Hudson river estuary held half the world's oyster population. The oyster, a bivalve (two-shelled) filter feeder, inhales sea water, drawing it over its mantle and through its gills, extracts nutrients, and exhales the filtered water. It is believed that in the eigtheenth century, the flourishing oyster beds of the New York Harbor were capable of filtering the bay's entire water volume of excess nutrients every three or four days.

As the population of New York grew, it industrialized rapidly, and polluted extensively. A 1929 study correlating the location of sewage outlets and the location of shellfisheries resulted in a ban on the "drinking" of oysters. This practice held harvested oysters in perforated tanks at the mouths of the freshwater tributaries feeding the bay to rinse them of salt and grit. But these tributaries were carrying raw sewage and waste to the bay. Several typhoid outbreaks in the 1920s were directly connected to the consumption of raw oysters harvested in the bay and, by 1927, governing bodies officially closed all of the harbor's oyster beds in order to control the spread of typhoid and other food-borne diseases. Although oyster harvesting ceased, water pollution did not. Raw sewage continued to be pumped directly into the waters of the bay. As industry grew, industrial waste including heavy metals, toxic PCBs (polychlorinated biphenyls), and even Agent Orange were also dumped into the harbor waters. The oysters could not digest these poisons, and by the 1960s they had completely disappeared.

The restoration of native oyster populations is an important aspect of our constructed wetland strategy. We propose to establish seed beds for oysters along the New Jersey tidal flats, reintroducing *Crassostrea virginica* into the complex food web of marine and terrestrial ecosystems. Oysters consume algae and blooms of phytoplankton that rob the water of oxygen, needed by fish, crabs, and other marine life. Their creviced beds create underwater reefs, consummate habitat for worms, shrimp, crustaceans, and fish.

Crassostrea virginica is an important element of the marine food web, interconnecting multiple food chains in the estuarine community. Their filtering capability would curb pollution and sediment, digesting or shaping this material into small packets that are then deposited onto the seabed, where they are harmless. Seeding the waters with plentiful oysters would cleanse the waters of the bay and may lead to a revival of aquaculture. However these oysters would not be edible until the issues of pollution have been significantly abated.

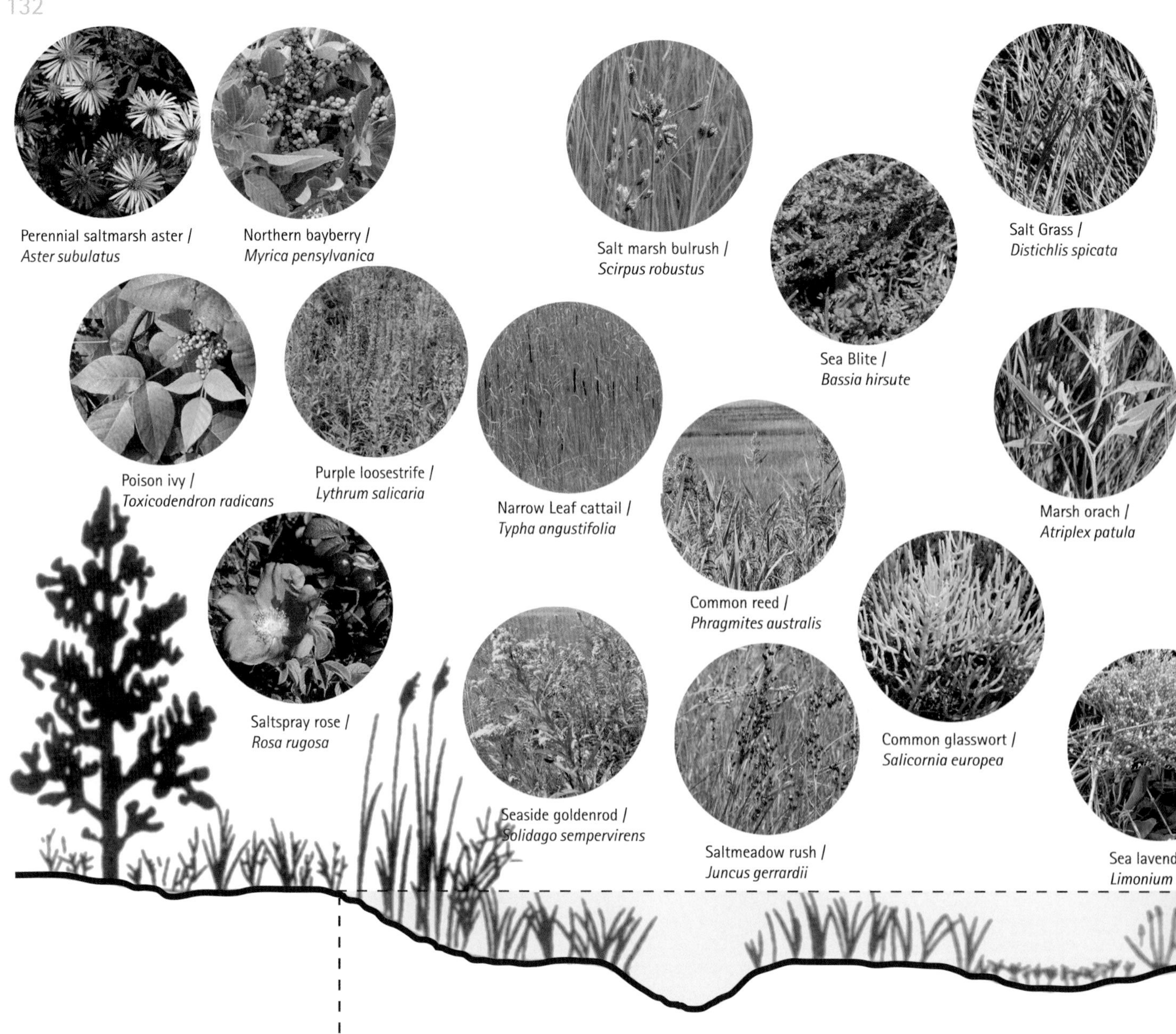
Perennial saltmarsh aster /
Aster subulatus
Northern bayberry /
Myrica pensylvanica
Salt marsh bulrush /
Scirpus robustus
Salt Grass /
Distichlis spicata
Sea Blite /
Bassia hirsute
Poison ivy /
Toxicodendron radicans
Purple loosestrife /
Lythrum salicaria
Narrow Leaf cattail /
Typha angustifolia
Marsh orach /
Atriplex patula
Common reed /
Phragmites australis
Saltspray rose /
Rosa rugosa
Common glasswort /
Salicornia europea
Seaside goldenrod /
Solidago sempervirens
Saltmeadow rush /
Juncus gerrardii
Sea lavende
Limonium n
SUPRALITTORAL ZONE
INTERTIDAL LITTORAL ZONE
irregularly flooded

ESTUARINE HABITAT

MARSH PLANTS

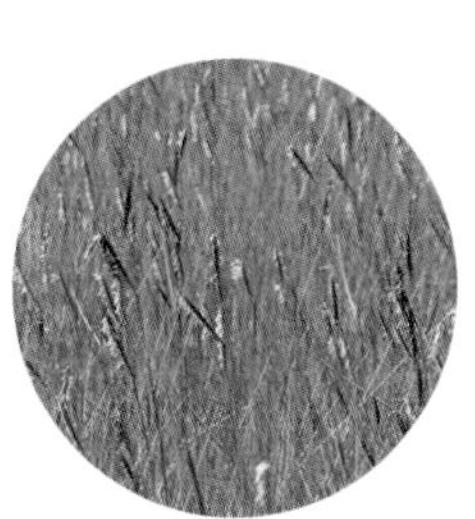

Saltmeadow cordgrass / *Spartina patens*

Bladderwrack / *Fucus vesiculosus*

Smooth cordgrass / *Spartina alterniflora*

Eelgrass / *Zostera marina*

extreme high spring / storm tide

mean high tide

mean low tide

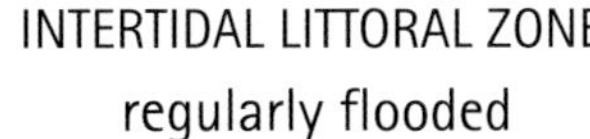

Blue-green algae /
Cyanobacteria

Rough periwinkle /
Littorina saxatilis

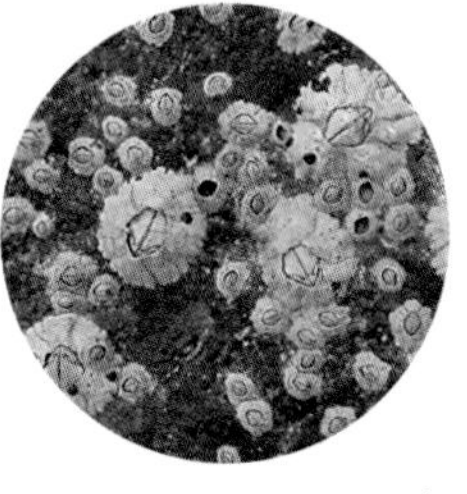

Northern rock barnacle /
Balanus balanoides

Red plumed worm /
Diopatra cuprea

Atlantic horseshoe crab /
Limulus polyphemus

Ghost crab /
Ocypode quadrata

Smooth periwinkle /
Littorina obtusata

Ribbed mussel /
Geukensia demissa

Razor clam /
Ensis directus

Eastern mud snail /
Ilyanassa obsoleta

Beach flea /
Orchestiidae

Soft-shell clam /
Mya arenaria

Quahog clam /
Mercenaria mercenaria

SUPRALITTORAL ZONE

INTERTIDAL LITTORAL ZONE
irregularly flooded

ESTUARINE HABITAT

MOLLUSKS AND INVERTEBRATES

Hydroids / *Hydrozoans*

Eastern oyster / *Crassostrea virginica*

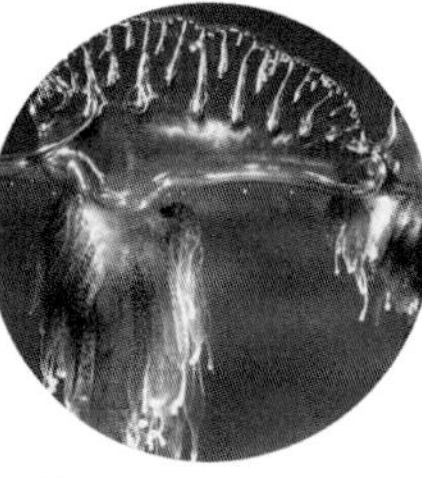

Portuguese man-of-war / *Physalia physalis*

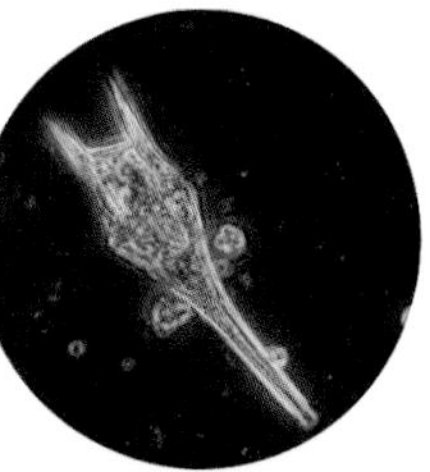

Dinoflagellates

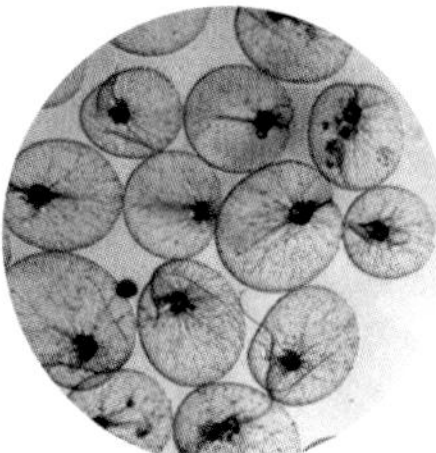

Dinoflagellates

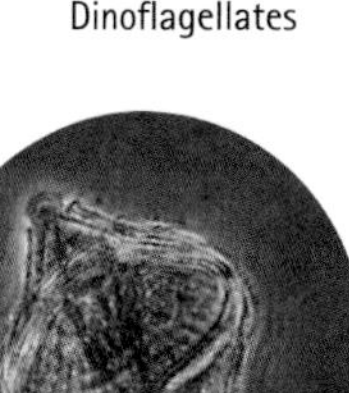

Dinoflagellates

Blue mussel / *Mytilus edilus*

Amphitrite worm / *Amphitrite ornata*

Blue crab / *Callinectes sapidus*

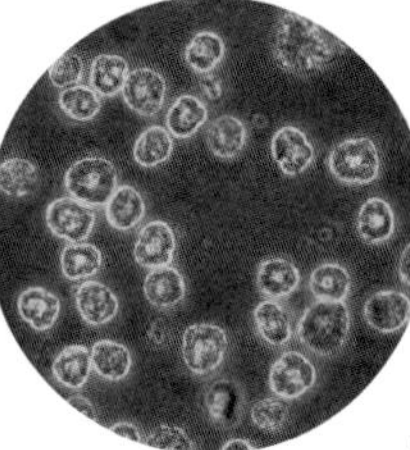

Dinoflagellates

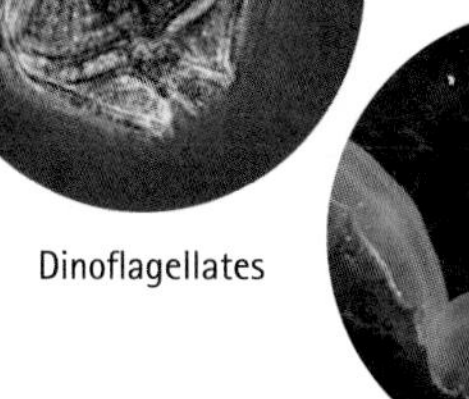

Sand shrimp / *Crangon septemspinosa*

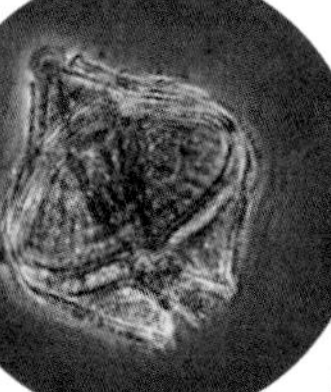

Dinoflagellates

Parchment worm / *Chaetopterus variopedatus*

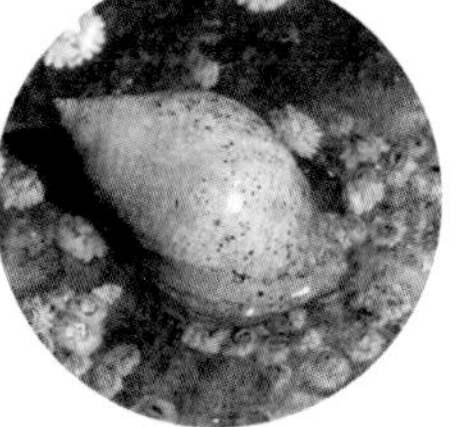

Atlantic dogwinkle / *Nucella lapilus*

Atlantic mole crab / *Emerita analoga*

Lady crab / *Ovalipes ocellatus*

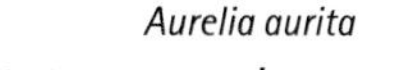

Moon jelly fish / *Aurelia aurita*

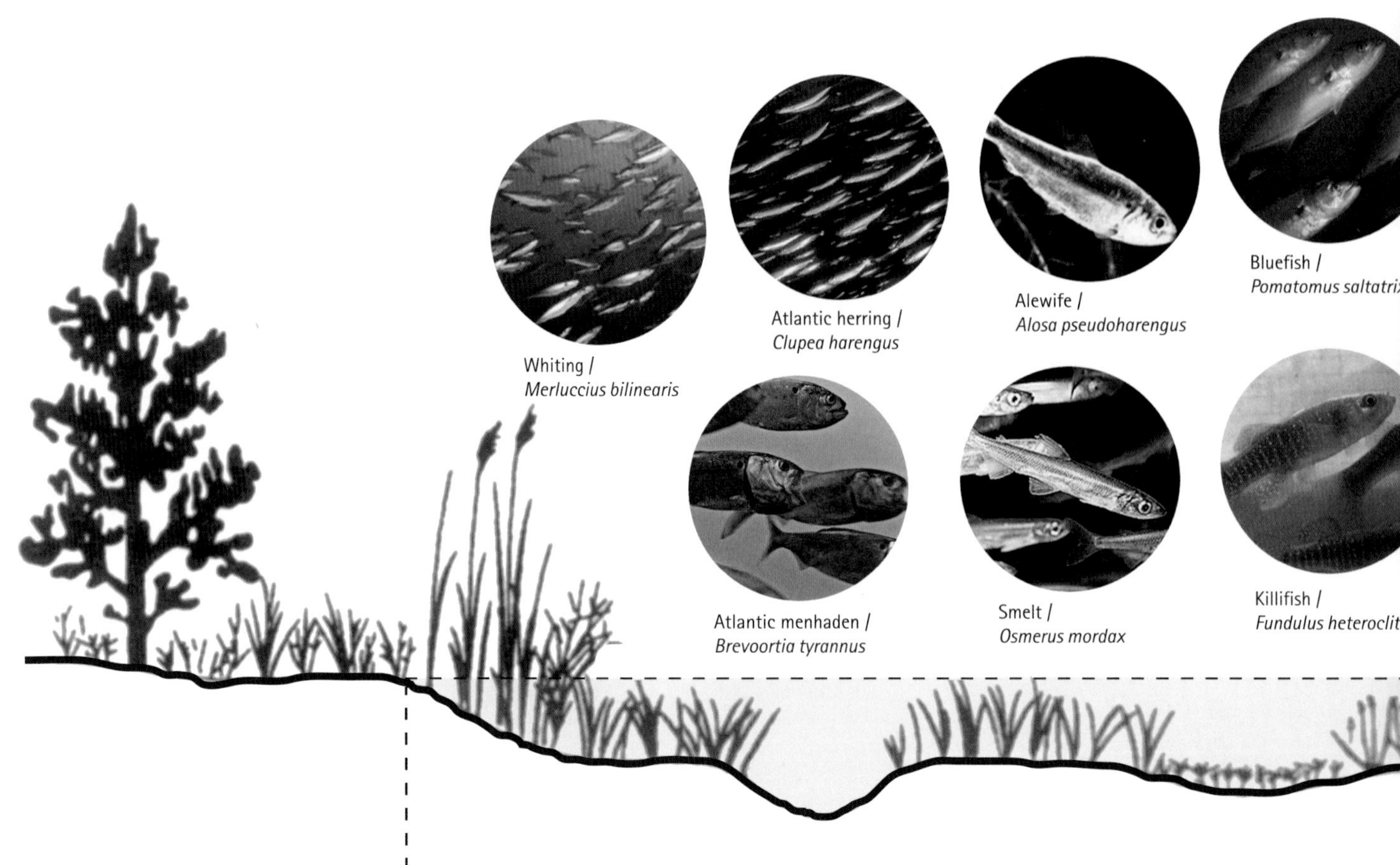
Whiting /
Merluccius bilinearis
Atlantic herring /
Clupea harengus
Alewife /
Alosa pseudoharengus
Bluefish /
Pomatomus saltatrix
Atlantic menhaden /
Brevoortia tyrannus
Smelt /
Osmerus mordax
Killifish /
Fundulus heteroclit
SUPRALITTORAL ZONE
INTERTIDAL LITTORAL ZONE
irregularly flooded

FISH

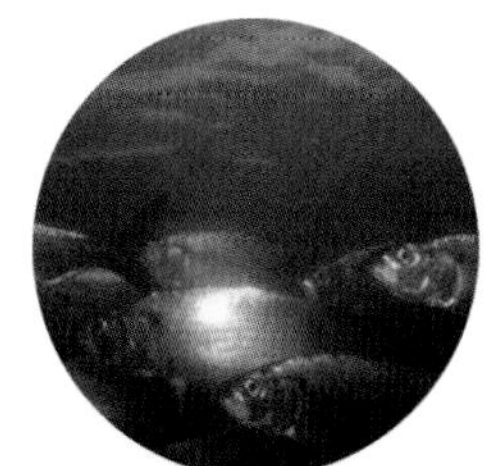

American shad / *Alosa sapidissima*

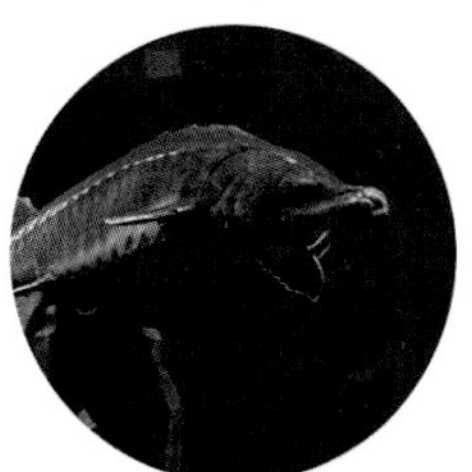

Atlantic sturgeon / *Acipenser oxyrinchus*

gy / *notomus versicolor*

Bluegill / *Lepomis macrochirus*

American eel / *Anguilla rostrata*

Weakfish / *Cynoscion regalis*

Striped bass / *Morone saxatilis*

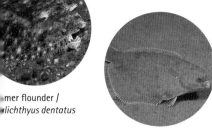

mer flounder / *lichthyus dentatus*

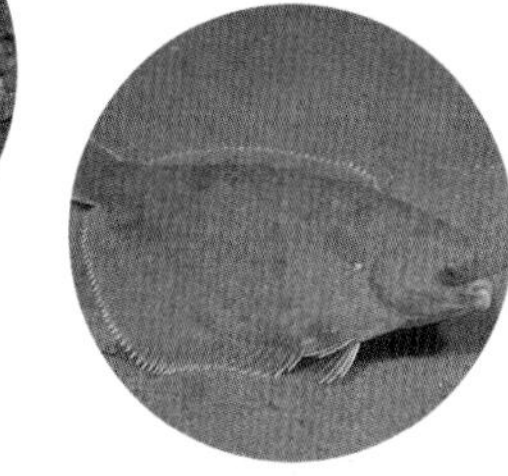

Winter flounder / *Pseudopleuronectes americanus*

Sea lamprey / *Petromyson marinus*

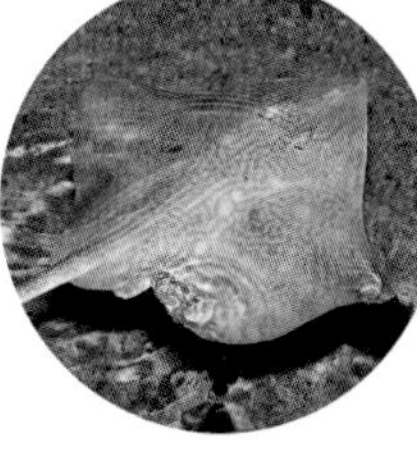

Common skate / *Raja erinacea*

Brown catfish / *Ameiurus nebulosus*

extreme high spring / storm tide

mean high tide

mean low tide

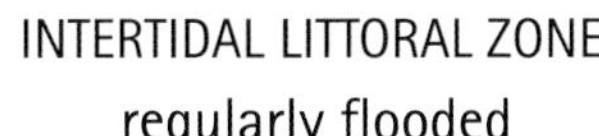

INTERTIDAL LITTORAL ZONE
regularly flooded

SUBLITTORAL ZONE

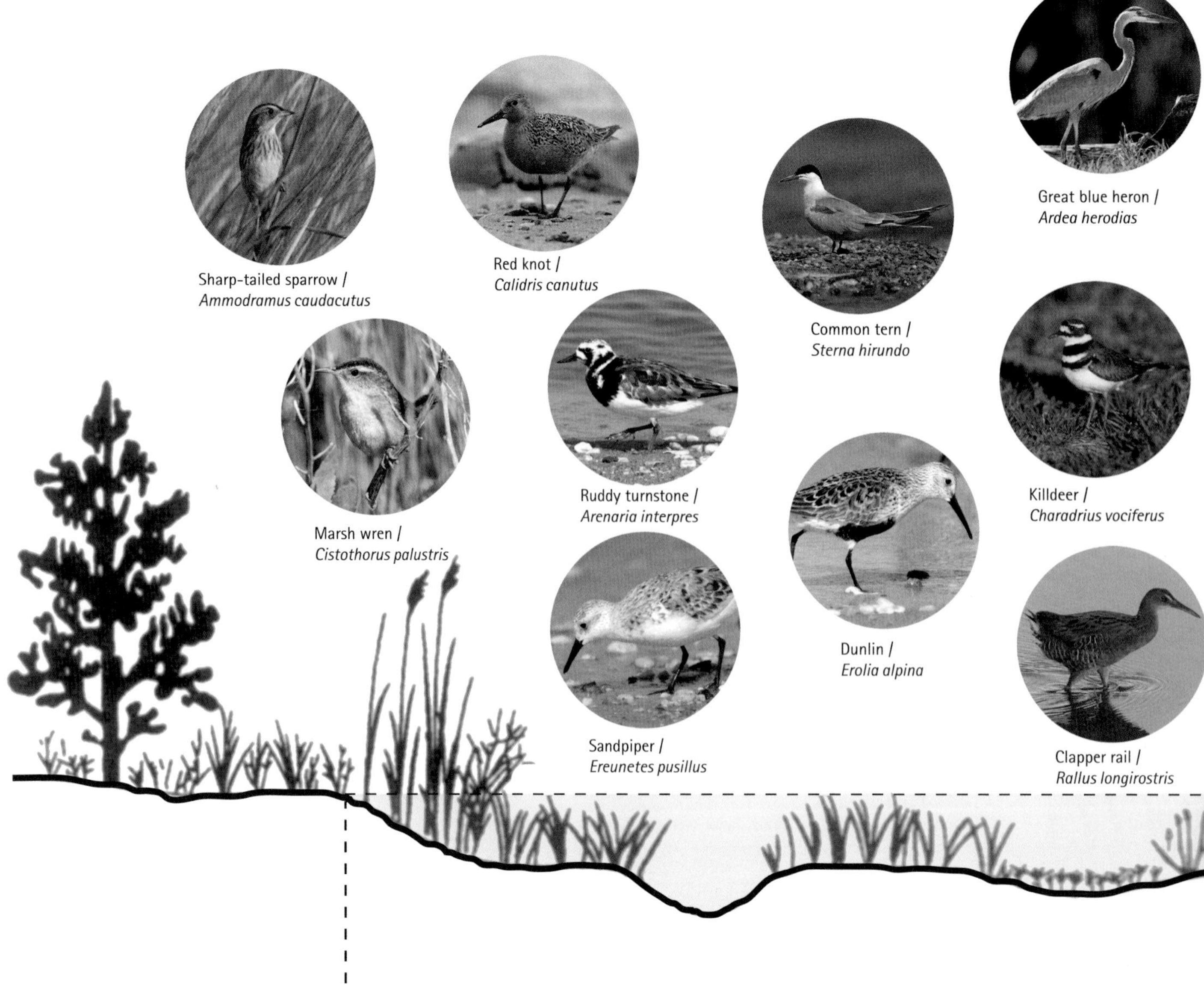
Sharp-tailed sparrow /
Ammodramus caudacutus
Red knot /
Calidris canutus
Common tern /
Sterna hirundo
Great blue heron /
Ardea herodias
Marsh wren /
Cistothorus palustris
Ruddy turnstone /
Arenaria interpres
Killdeer /
Charadrius vociferus
Dunlin /
Erolia alpina
Sandpiper /
Ereunetes pusillus
Clapper rail /
Rallus longirostris
SUPRALITTORAL ZONE
INTERTIDAL LITTORAL ZONE
irregularly flooded

ESTUARINE HABITAT

SHORE BIRDS

Black-crowned night heron / *Nycticorax nycticorax*

Double-crested cormorant / *Phalacrocorax auritus*

Pied-billed grebe / *Podilymbus podiceps*

Herring gull / *Larus argentatus*

Glossy ibis / *Plegadis falcinellus*

Hooded merganser / *Lophodytes cucullatus*

American black duck / *Anas rubripes*

Snowy egret / *Leucophoyx thula*

Little blue heron / *Egretta caerulea*

Canada goose / *Branta canadensis*

Horned grebe / *Podiceps auritus*

extreme high spring / storm tide

mean high tide

mean low tide

INTERTIDAL LITTORAL ZONE
regularly flooded

SUBLITTORAL ZONE

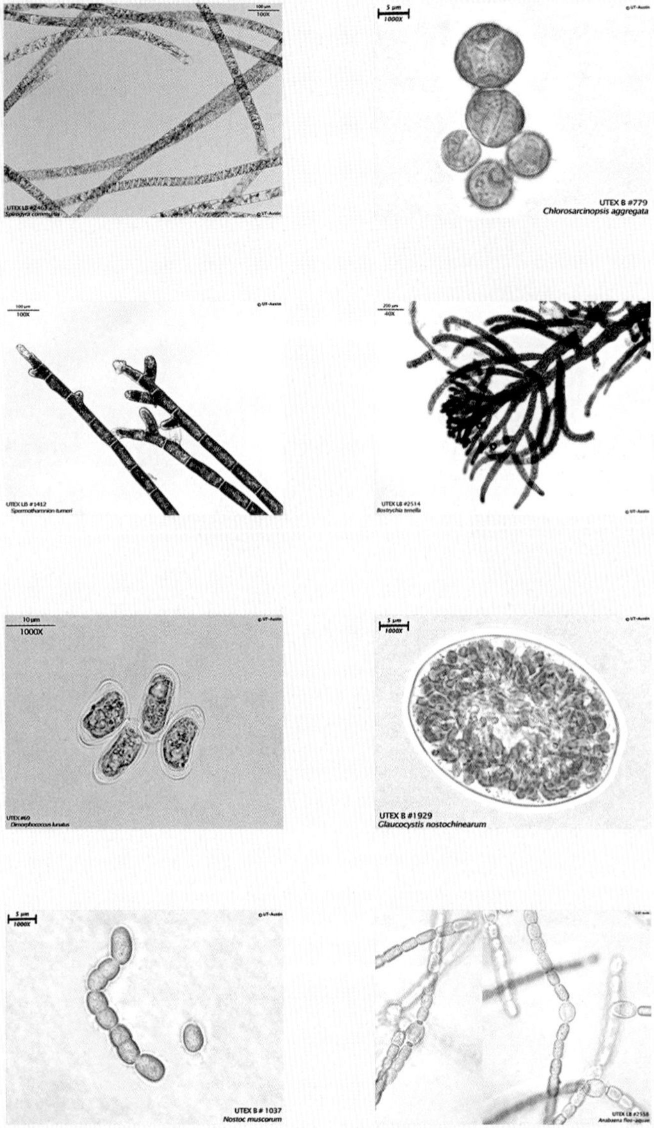

GENERATING ENERGY

WIND AND TIDAL TURBINES

We propose that public space and clean energy production could share the same space. In the wetland flats of New Jersey, we have proposed the implementation of a field of wind turbines, interspersed with oyster beds. This proposal would require an extensive study of the energy potential of wind that could be harvested here. Tidal turbines are also currently being studied in the East River, and we would propose their implementation in the Upper Bay as well, perhaps incorporated into the extended and detatched pier foundations of our masterplan. Environmental impact analyses of the effects of both wind and tidal turbines would be needed to examine the effects on the wetland environment and fish, as well as on the birds passing through the Atlantic flyway (the migration flyway following the shoreline from the coast of Greenland south to Florida, the Caribbean, and South America). We imagine that our proposed ecological transformations to the Upper Bay will create an attractive stopping point for migratory birds travelling along the flyway, similar to the oasis of Central Park.

ALGAE

Harnessing certain algae species is an energy-producing strategy that may also produce positive effects on the health of the estuarine ecosystem. We propose locating algae farms producing biocrude (sometimes called "green crude" which can be refined to make gasoline, diesel, or jet fuel) or ethanol in the new wetland regions of the Upper Bay. Many consider algae to be a better source of fuel than food crops, from which ethanol is derived, as the carbon footprint of energy and emissions required to grow algae is very low. Many algae species are high in oils, which they produce naturally—their predecessors helped make oil many millions of years ago. Carbon dioxide, sunlight, and brackish water, the three key ingredients for an algae farm, are plentiful in the Upper Bay. An added advantage is the fact that algae can also clean up waste, by processing nitrogen from wastewater and carbon dioxide from power plants. However, studies are still needed to examine the ecological consequences of introducing algae, which has the potential to become an invasive species, to this ecosystem.

Algae farms have the potential to generate biocrude to be used for fuel.

Opposite
Palisade Bay, proposed offshore wind turbines among oyster racks

George Hayward, *View in Central Park, Southward from the Arsenal 5th Avenue and 64th Street*, 1858, lithograph

Opposite
Joseph C. Geissler after Pierre Martel, *Martel's New York Central Park, Respectfully Dedicated to the Park Commissioners*, 1864, lithograph

GENERATING PLACE

The Upper Bay has been selected as the site for this proposal because of its potential to create a unified regional place for New York and New Jersey. While it is rarely traversed and primarily serves as a port, this estuarine body of water is the geographic center of the region. We imagine the Upper Bay could be reconceived as a new Central Park for the region by re-centering the city away from Manhattan and towards the boroughs and adjoining New Jersey counties. We envision the bay as a common "ground;" a figure within the mega-city that can be—like the Bacino di San Marco in Venice—a meeting place and cross roads on the water.

CENTRAL PARK

The planning and development of Central Park in Manhattan predated the growth of the city around it. The planners, politicians, and designers of Central Park anticipated this dense development and the plans for Central Park coupled landscape and infrastructure to serve the growing city. Inverting the sequence of city development in the conception of Central Park serves as the metaphor for our contextualization of the Upper Bay today within the development of the New York region. The condition to which this project for the Upper Bay responds is a fully developed urban region which frames a void within itself. In order to develop a resilience to the threats of storms and sea level rise, the region must reinvent its void as the locus for a twenty-first century, ecological infrastructure. This new infrastructure can be contained within the institution of the public park which, as the enormous success and popularity of Central Park demonstrates, is equally vital to the health of the city as any infrastructural public work.

The Greensward Plan by Fredrick Law Olmstead and Calbert Vaux was chosen in a competition for the design of Central Park by the Parks Commissioners on April 28, 1858. The design can be considered an enactment of progressive urban reform: Olmstead and Vaux believed that the use of the park would improve public health across all classes of society. Vaux positioned the project by stating that in a "true and intelligent republicanism," all citizens were entitled to enjoy the comforts and benefits of society's wealth through its public institutions and that a "man of small means may be almost on the same footing as the millionaire."[19] The Parks Commissioners' decision to place Central Park in the center of Manhattan, as well as its vast size—843 acres—supported Vaux's populist revision of the public park. Central Park's enormous reservoir and many fountains served as symbolic elements within the urban landscape. Fed by the new Croton River Aqueduct, each provided a visual testament to the great health achievement of delivering fresh water to New York City from the mountains upstate.

The sectional manipulation in Central Park is particularly sophisticated, sorting several types and modes of transportation into different levels with relatively minimal sectional variation. The section works pragmatically with social programs, as well as ecological and infrastructural programs. For example, vehicular traffic and pedestrian movement are entirely separated throughout the park, and both pathways circulate above and between elaborate waterworks and drainage systems underneath the surface of the park grounds. The various speeds and directions of traffic are directed along various pathways; transverse roadways allow vehicular traffic direct crossing through the park while the looping bridle ways and carriage road allow slow moving traffic to explore the park. Similarly, the Race and the Promenade provide a backdrop for daily fitness while the Ramble allows leisurely pedestrians to wander in the park.

When considering the Upper Bay, the use of section is again critical, albeit in a less obvious way. When wetlands are restored within the intertidal zones along the perimeter of the bay a sectional relationship emerges from layering social and ecological programs; boardwalks might carry pedestrians over tall grasses which retain and filter water to a collection tank below. Landfill piers and constructed islands that cut through the depth of the water create new still water habitats for marine life. In Central Park the imagery tends to be that of a place of a sectional nature, surrounded by a perforated wall with points of entry (the Gates). The surrounding city itself is considered flat and the perceived urban flatness juxtaposes the rolling, pastoral hills in Central Park.

By contrast, the waters of the Upper Bay are perceived as a vast expanse of empty flatness. With our transformation of the bay, and with the reestablishment of thickened intertidal zones at its perimeter, the sectional variation is clearly established at the edges of the void. These zones create both perceptual and literal points of entry through and across the bay. An element of time is introduced as the depth of sections at the edge are hidden and revealed through the daily phases of the tide. Beneath the water, the flats and shoals that describe the harbor bathymetry drive the decisions and formal patterning of the placement of reefs and islands.

Central Park and the Upper Bay plan are both constructed landscapes which are tailored to suit the social and infrastructural needs of the city. By situating this project after the model of Central Park—by accepting the harbor as a found place which is marked by both natural geological processes and hundreds of years of human interaction—the park is inverted.

A. Brown and Co., *South Gate House, New Reservoir, during construction: Viewed from the South—Looking into the Resevoir*, 1862, lithograph

Opposite
Proposed wetlands along the Staten Island coastline in Palisade Bay

View of the Staten Island Ferry

Existing ferry routes through the Upper Bay, 2007

Following pages
Proposed waterborne transportation routes in Palisade Bay for future development

URBAN TRANSPORTATION

Despite the relative proximity of New York City's boroughs and eastern New Jersey, which line the Upper Harbor, the perceived distances between Manhattan, Brooklyn, Staten Island, Jersey City, Newark, and Bayonne is much greater than its measured distance. This is because distance in an urban setting is generally equated with travel time, which is determined by public transportation networks. The extensive travel time required to cross the watery divide and then transfer to a subway or bus thus makes cross-borough destinations cumbersome.

CURRENT TRANSPORTATION NETWORKS

Presently, the Upper Bay is a border and the city's edge is a definite limit which restricts perpendicular movement. This boundary is breached only at key locations, with a series of sunken tunnels and elevated bridges that prohibit interaction with the water itself and a very limited number of ferry routes. In an effort to collapse this perceived distance, and re-envision the bay as shared urban space, our design scheme includes the proposal for a new interborough and interstate water based transportation system—a system that transforms the water from the status of an empty void to the very infrastructure used to facilitate movement.

By surveying the region's existing transportation routes it is evident that the phenomenon of urban transit in New York City has traditionally followed a center-to-edge trajectory, resulting in a lack of connection to the waterfronts and underserved edge territories. By contrast, our scheme identifies an opportunity to re-center the city away from Manhattan to the Upper Bay region which includes with equal emphasis all the boroughs and adjoining NJ cities. Public transit is a vital force for this transformation.

THE VAPORETTO

The Venetian vaporetto-circuit exemplifies an alternative to Manhattan's land bound network of interconnected corridors. Venice's intricate urban pattern denies the possibility of traversing the city in a linear fashion and instead, the principal public routes are pushed outwards, giving new definition to the strict border that exists between land and water. Strung along the city's edge, the Venice circuit is characterized by a system of loops and weaves that trace routes between predetermined points. Moving along a circular course these paths negate the fixed directionality of a transit line with a clear beginning and end, and as a result, the island appears more interconnected with perceived travel distances greatly reduced.

WATERBORNE TRANSPORTATION ROUTES
NY/NJ EXPRESS
CENTRAL LINE
STATUE OF LIBERTY LINE
MANHATTAN LOOP
BROOKLYN LOOP
STATEN ISLAND LOOP
NJ LOOP
NY/NJ WEAVE
MANHATTAN/BROOKLYN WEAVE
BROOKLYN/SI WEAVE
BAY RIDGE - BAYONNE
SUNSET PARK - BAYONNE
SUNSET PARK - PORT LIBERTE
ATLANTIC BASIN - LIBERTY VILLAGE
BROOKLYN PARK - LIBERTY HARBOR
GOVERNORS ISLAND FERRY

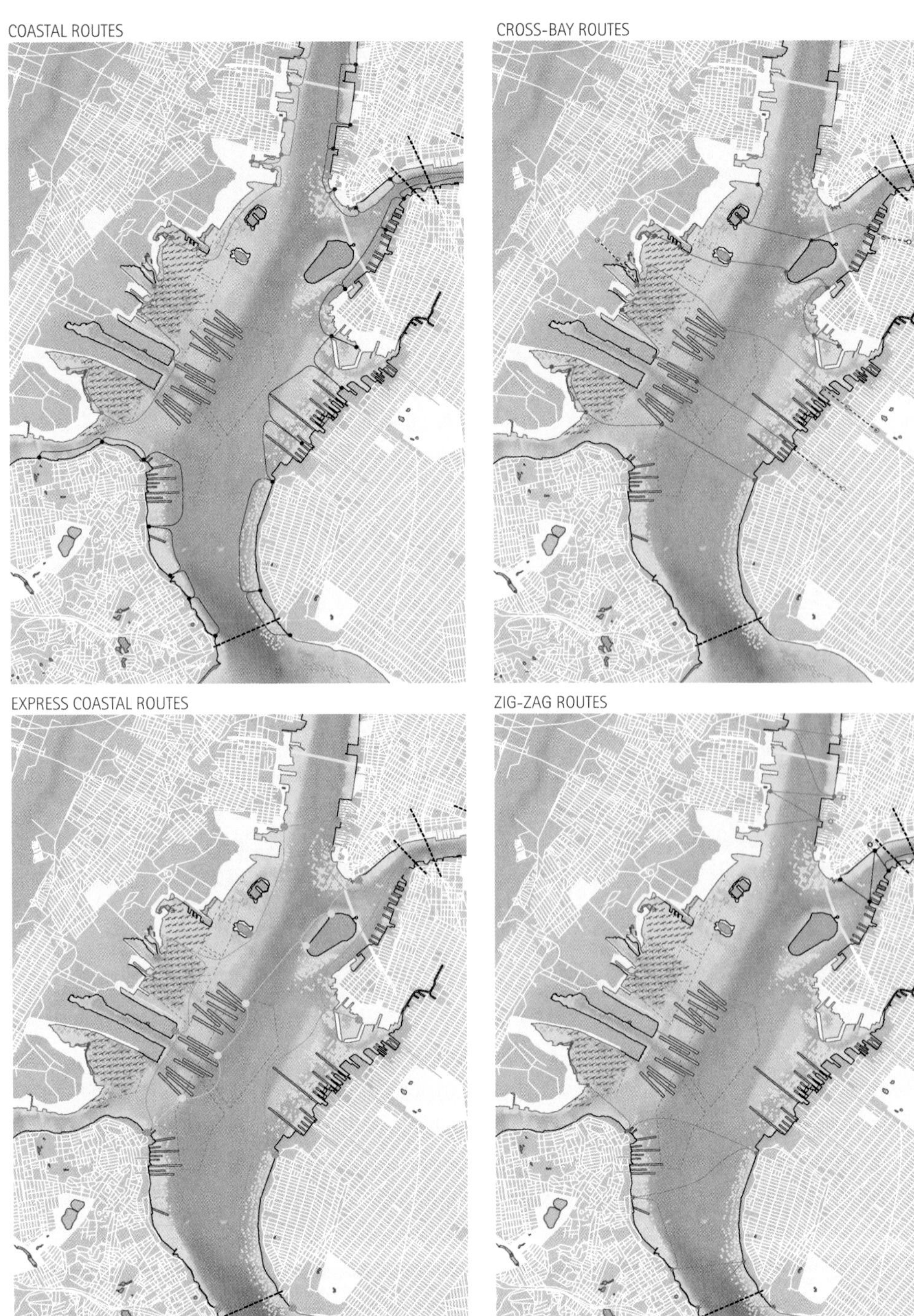

Proposed ferry routes through the Upper Bay

Opposite
Proposed destinations (green) and existing destinations (black) in Palisade Bay

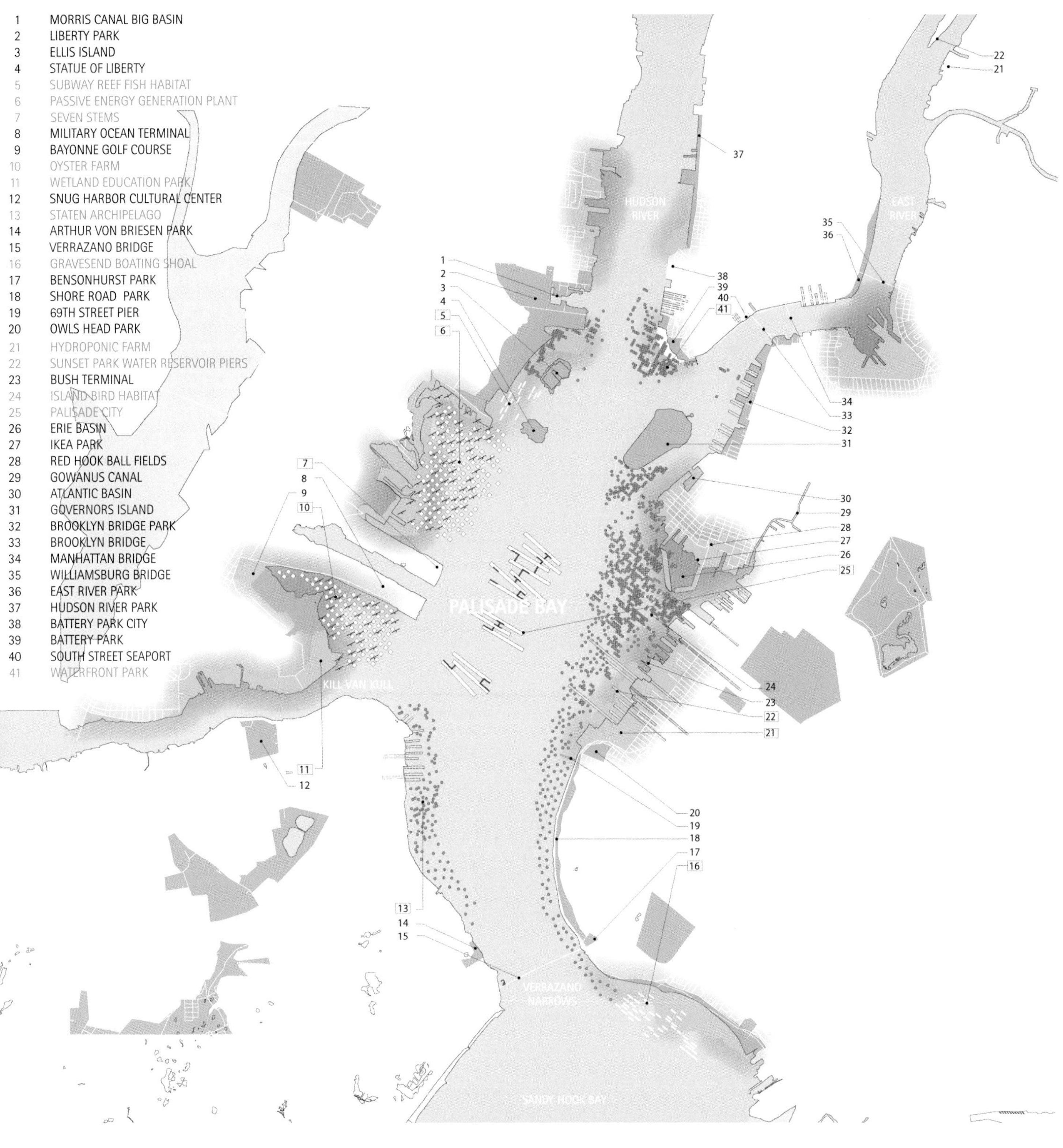
1 MORRIS CANAL BIG BASIN
2 LIBERTY PARK
3 ELLIS ISLAND
4 STATUE OF LIBERTY
5 SUBWAY REEF FISH HABITAT
6 PASSIVE ENERGY GENERATION PLANT
7 SEVEN STEMS
8 MILITARY OCEAN TERMINAL
9 BAYONNE GOLF COURSE
10 OYSTER FARM
11 WETLAND EDUCATION PARK
12 SNUG HARBOR CULTURAL CENTER
13 STATEN ARCHIPELAGO
14 ARTHUR VON BRIESEN PARK
15 VERRAZANO BRIDGE
16 GRAVESEND BOATING SHOAL
17 BENSONHURST PARK
18 SHORE ROAD PARK
19 69TH STREET PIER
20 OWLS HEAD PARK
21 HYDROPONIC FARM
22 SUNSET PARK WATER RESERVOIR PIERS
23 BUSH TERMINAL
24 ISLAND BIRD HABITAT
25 PALISADE CITY
26 ERIE BASIN
27 IKEA PARK
28 RED HOOK BALL FIELDS
29 GOWANUS CANAL
30 ATLANTIC BASIN
31 GOVERNORS ISLAND
32 BROOKLYN BRIDGE PARK
33 BROOKLYN BRIDGE
34 MANHATTAN BRIDGE
35 WILLIAMSBURG BRIDGE
36 EAST RIVER PARK
37 HUDSON RIVER PARK
38 BATTERY PARK CITY
39 BATTERY PARK
40 SOUTH STREET SEAPORT
41 WATERFRONT PARK
HUDSON RIVER
EAST RIVER
PALISADE BAY
KILL VAN KULL
VERRAZANO NARROWS
SANDY HOOK BAY

When Venice's diagram is imposed on the figure of New York's Upper Harbor, these same loops and weaves work to establish new connections and minimize distances both between and within the four distinct land masses. Multiple intermodal hubs are established along the perimeter of the bay connecting the ferry system with the region's existing public infrastructure.

PROGRAM

This intricate new waterborne transportation system for the Upper Bay would serve not only to ease the burden of commuting in the metropolitan area but also to link existing and proposed places of interest on and around the water. Like the Statue of Liberty and Ellis Island, many of the proposed destinations would be accessible only by ferry.

The map on the previous page highlights a selection of these elements of program. New recreational areas would include a Wetland Education Park in Bayonne on a former Superfund site, recreational piers in Sunset Park, Brooklyn, and a new waterfront park at the tip of Manhattan. A boating shoal offshore of Brooklyn below the Verrazano Narrows would be a new element of the Gateway National Recreation Area. An oyster farm near Liberty State Park and hydroponic farming in Brooklyn would bolster local food production for the metropolitan area. Residential development is proposed on detached piers near the center of the Upper Bay.

This new transportation system and the destinations it connects will transform the Upper Bay into a body of water which no longer divides but instead binds the region around it.

View of Venice's Grand Canal where vaporettos provide an alternative to land based transportation, 2008

Opposite
Giovanni Antonio Canal, known as Canaletto, *Bacino di San Marco, Venice*, ca. 1738, Photograph © 2010 Museum of Fine Arts, Boston

HARBOR ZONES

Opposite
Five zones of intervention on Palisade Bay

FIVE ZONES OF INTERVENTION

Five neighborhood zones in and around the periphery of the Upper Bay have been identified, each with its own topographic, historic, and programmatic characteristics. Our goal is to assemble a group of design teams to transform these zones using the general design strategies outlined in the master plan. Architecture Research Office of New York has developed the design for Lower Manhattan, Zone 0.

ZONE 0
Lower Manhattan

Of the waterfront land surrounding the Upper Bay, Lower Manhattan requires the most protection due to its high density of valuable real estate at sea level. Adaptive design strategies deployed here would include increasing the height of the existing sea wall to prevent inundation. Peripheral land may also be reconsidered a wetland zone, and sloped fill may be built up against the seaward side of the seawall. Channels and slips may be extracted from streets that were formerly inlets to allow water to move inland in a controlled way. The shallow areas just south of Lower Manhattan are a potential site for a protective offshore archipelago of artificial islands.

ZONE 1
The Jersey Flats

This zone comprises the northern edge of the Upper Bay along the New Jersey waterfront, and includes the newly developed waterfront of Jersey City. It also includes the historically significant Liberty Island and Ellis Island as well as Liberty State Park. Formerly a shellfish mudflat, this zone would be inundated with a relatively small rise in sea level. Our master plan strategy in this zone is to reestablish much of the former tidal wetlands flats and shellfish habitat. Wetlands would reduce the force of a storm surge and mitigate pollution from surface runoff, as well as promote a more diverse ecology. Active shellfish would improve the bay's health by filtering its waters. This zone is also an ideal area in which to locate offshore artificial reefs to support underwater habitat.

ZONE 2
Bayonne, the Kill Van Kull, and Staten Island

This zone, the Southwest Palisade Bay, includes the Bayonne waterfront, the twin Bayonne Piers, Richmond Terrace, the northern waterfront of Staten Island, and the Kill Van Kull. Here, the New Jersey coastline is very low-lying and vulnerable to sea level rise, while the Staten Island shoreline rises to a ridge. The Kill Van Kull is a major shipping artery and its dredged depth is maintained at 50 feet by the US Army Corps of Engineers. In the shallow offshore

0
1
2
3
4

anchorages to the southeast of the Bayonne piers, we propose a series of detached piers arrayed perpendicular to the shoreline to buffer storm surges moving northward though the Upper Bay. This zone is suitable for various modes of clean energy generation including submerged tidal turbines, a field of wind turbines to harness energy from the prevailing northwest winds as well as the possibility of generating bio-crude oil from algae farms.

ZONE 3
The Verrazano Narrows and Sunset Park, Brooklyn

This zone includes the Verrazano Narrows, the deep mouth of the Upper Bay, and the neighborhoods on each side of the mouth.Given their elevation above sea level, these areas would not be significantly affected by storm surge and rising sea level. However, the water's edge in this area presents an opportunity for both modifying an existing sea wall and adjacent parkway to accommodate access to the waterfront promenades and supporting a more ecologically diverse shoreline. By elevating the Shore Parkway the space under the highway would be opened to new salt marshes. This transformation would decrease the force of an accelerating storm surge. Islands are also deployed parallel to the edge of the land to further promote this wave energy interference.

ZONE 4
Red Hook, the Gowanus Canal, and Governors Island

This zone includes Red Hook, Brooklyn; the Gowanus Canal; Buttermilk Channel; and Governors Island. The industrial waterfront in this area is characterized by long paved piers which are constructed over both landfill and piles extending over the water. Given the low elevation and extensive landfill of this zone, as well as its exposure to strong currents from the Narrows and the East River, extensive inundation would occur with a one foot rise in sea level. Adaptive design strategies deployed in this area include the acceptance of flooding and subsequent rezoning, as well as the reestablishment of wetland edges in the Red Hook neighborhood and along the Gowanus Canal. We are proposing extended piers and extracted slips, and using bioswales to filter storm water runoff. Offshore, in the shallow waters of the Bay Ridge and Gowanus Flats, we propose an archipelago of constructed islands.

Red Hook waterfront, Brooklyn, NY, 2007

Containership anchored in Bayonne, NJ, 2008

Opposite
Bayonne Golf Club on site of former landfill with Old Standard oil refinery beyond, 2007

ZONE 0

ZONE 0: LOWER MANHATTAN

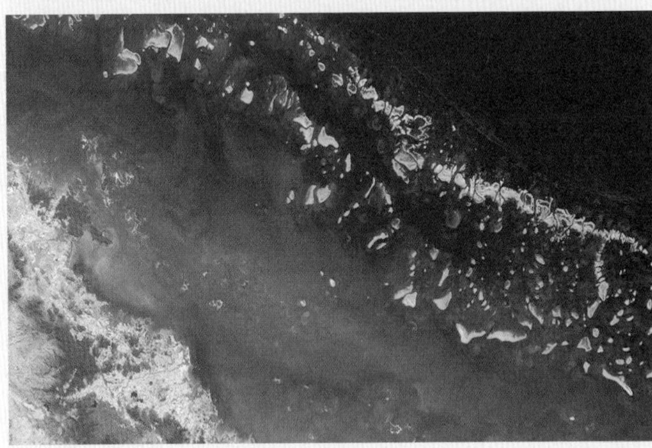

GENERAL DESIGN PRINCIPLES

The dense urban development at the southern tip of Manhattan is proximate to sea level and immediately adjacent to the water's edge, rendering it at risk of inundation due to gradually rising water level and more frequent storm surges. In order to sustain the continued occupation of this part of the city, it is necessary to prevent the harbor from encroaching onto land. Also, it is imperative to blunt the destructive force of waves associated with a storm surge in order to prevent damage to the existing structures. We propose two interrelated strategies, one on land and one in the water, to protect this area.

To prevent flooding due to the incremental rise in the level of the ocean, the coastline is slightly elevated. This is achieved by incorporating the existing vertical seawalls into a new topography that surmounts them. The existing linear fixed boundary between land and water is replaced by a tidal zone that helps to revitalize the wetland ecology indigenous to the Upper Bay area. The exact configuration of the resulting re-contoured waterfront edge is contingent on local conditions. This park-like area also has an ample horizontal dimension that helps absorb the force of destructive waves associated with a storm surge.

To break up waves before they reach land, a matrix of islands made from dredged material is situated in the harbor around the tip of Manhattan,forming a reef-like barrier. The location and pattern of these islands are determined by currents, existing shipping channels, and water depth. Several different shapes, sizes and arrays of islands were evaluated to determine the most effective combination. In contrast to the harbor's dredged channels, the islands slow down the water flow and create shallow, protected places for marine plants, mollusks, crustaceans, and fish. This new marine habitat replaces wetlands lost over centuries as the harbor has been filled, improving water quality and strengthening the productive capacity of the estuary.

Water transportation routes at the tip of Manhattan

Australia's Great Barrier Reef, 2001

Opposite
Lower Manhattan, aerial view

Geotextile by Tencate™

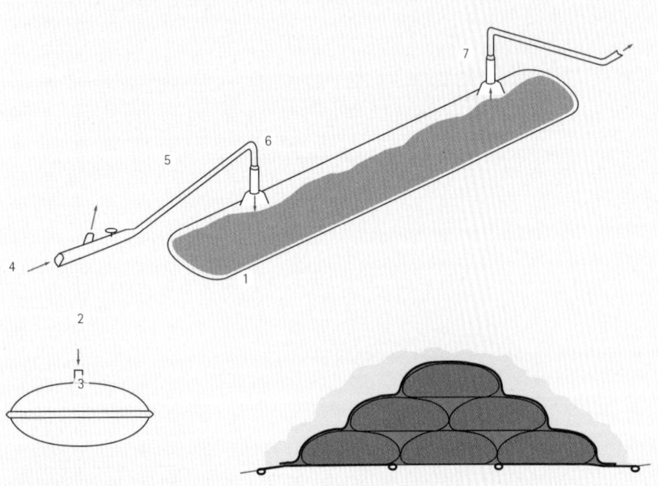

Geotextile tube construction process

① Double seam geotextile tube
② Inlet
③ Two layers of woven geotextile
④ Dredge discharge
⑤ 8" diameter pipe
⑥ Flexible inlet pipe
⑦ Outlet control

ISLANDS: MATERIALS AND METHODS OF CONSTRUCTION

Each year, millions of cubic yards of sediment are dredged from the harbor in order to maintain the depth of the shipping channels. This sediment is contained in runoff that flows into the rivers emptying into the harbor. Additional dredging has occurred periodically to deepen the channels to accommodate larger commercial vessels at the port of New York and New Jersey. If clean, the dredge spoil is often dumped in designated areas far offshore. However, the US Army Corps of Engineers, which is responsible for the waterways, has identified productive uses for this material, such as improving the ecosystem of the harbor by restoring wetlands and making islands.

Employing dredge spoil for reclamation projects requires the participation of numerous stakeholders, detailed assessment of impact upon existing conditions and extensive regulatory approvals. These significant near-term challenges to the implementation of our proposals, must be weighed against the manifold long-term benefits.

We propose to utilize dredge spoil as a building material for the creation of new elevated waterfront edges and islands, through commercially available technology already used in the US and throughout the world. The construction method utilizes geotextile fabric containers (such as Geotubes® manufactured by the Tencate corporation) which are filled with sediment and stacked to create new landforms. The weave of the geotextile cloth retains fine matter and the resultant shapes are massive and stable.

Replacing methods such as gabion walls, rock piling, and precast concrete blocks, this construction strategy has a great economy of means: a small quantity of fabric is needed to create substantial results. Also, the work is performed from the water, with little disruption from human activity. This building technique could also be applied to creating new islands and elevated edges in the outer harbor, offering further protection to adjacent populated areas such as Staten Island and Brooklyn.

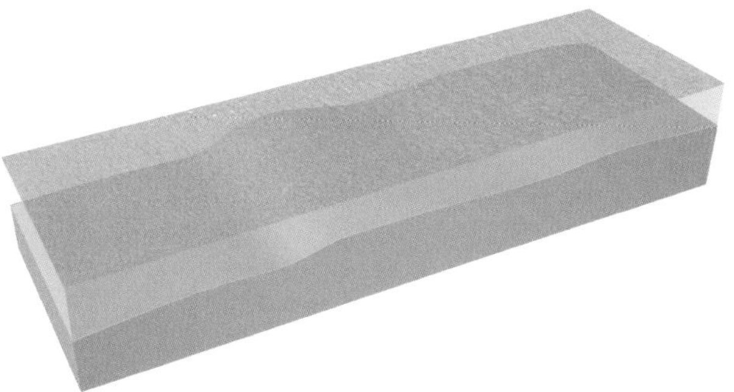

Existing vacant sea bed sites

Positioning of geotextile tubes

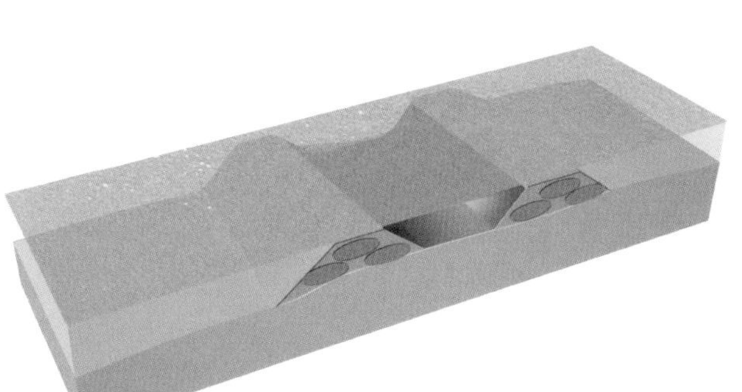

Fill / island formation

Recycled rubble / debris as dry island foundation

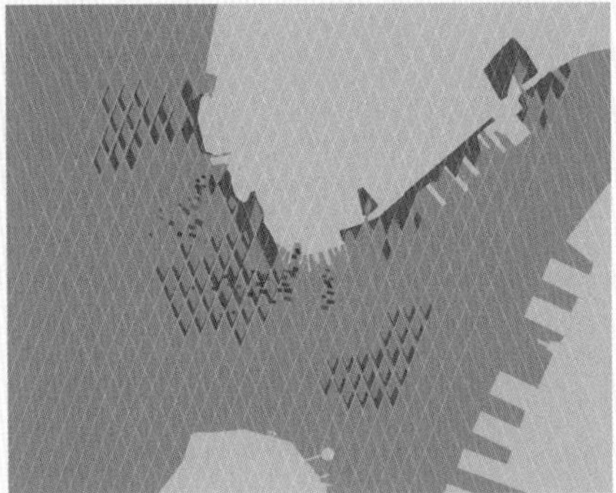

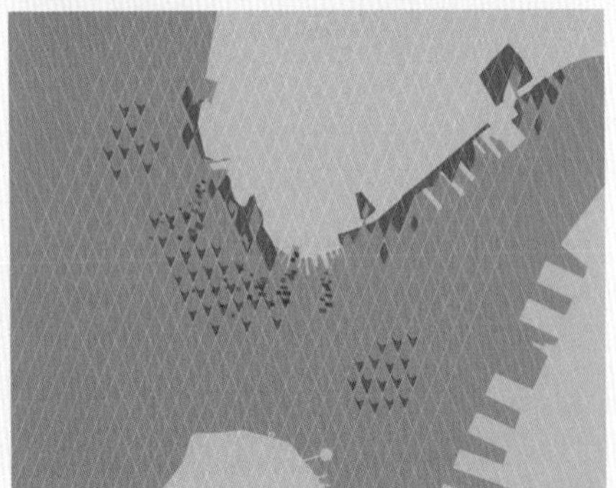

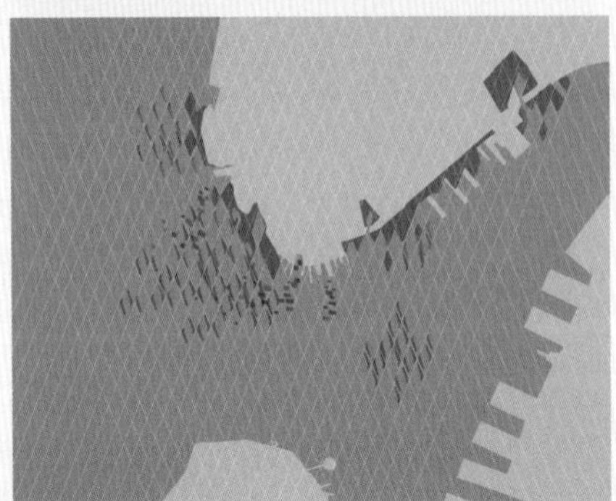

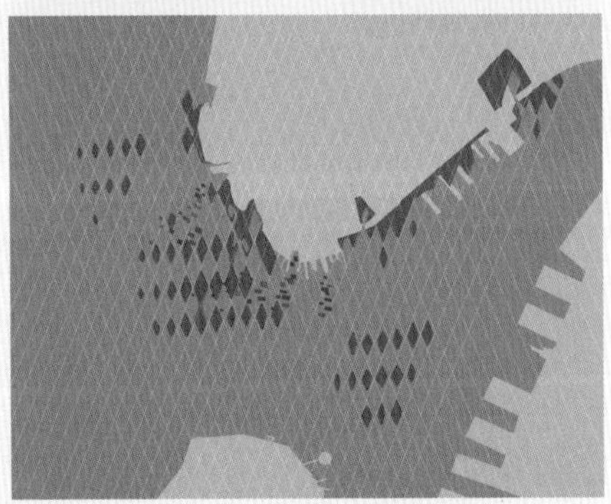

Proposed island formation at the tip of Lower Manhattan

Opposite
Reshaped coastline with barrier islands

BARRIER ISLAND FORM AND ORGANIZATION

As described in the "Formal Analysis: Water Table Experiments" section, the design of the barrier island archipelago is guided by several parameters. The shape and arrangement of islands are optimized to decrease the velocity of currents and waves associated with storm surges, while respecting navigation lanes. Linear islands, which are conducive to being made from stacked tubular geotextile fabric containers, are practical to construct and make efficient use of material. The ultimate extent of the island formation is limited by the available quantity of dredge spoils. However, the proposal depicted uses much less than the available material, so capacity is not presently a decisive parameter.

In addition to addressing these criteria, the configuration of islands mediates between the scale of the existing urban grid and the bathymetry of the harbor. This creates a gradient between the city and the water. The layout of the islands extends the city pattern southward from the tip of Manhattan, to mitigate a storm surge entering the harbor from the southwest through the Verrazano Narrows.

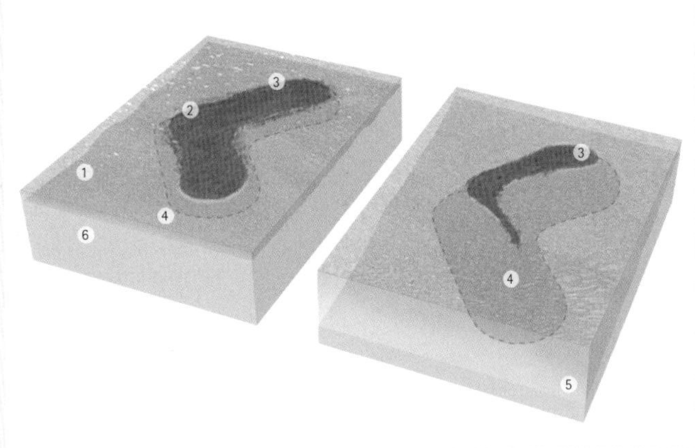

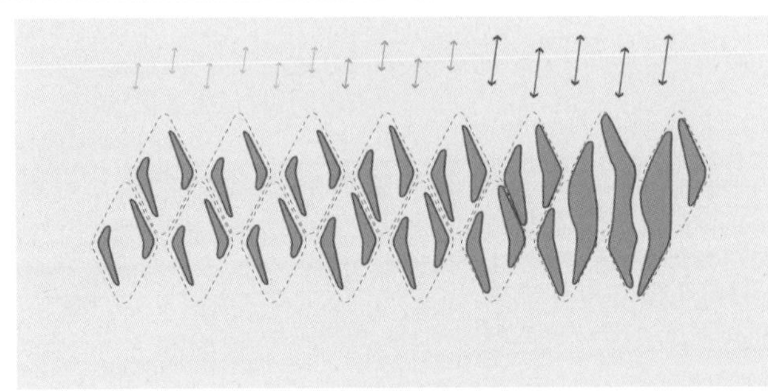

① Greater overall shallow water resistance to storm surge flow
② Larger surface area to buffer high tide storm surges
③ Unique island footprints due to vary bathymetry
④ Recycled dredge geotextile tube construction
⑤ Greater deep water undercurrent resistance to storm water surge flow
⑥ Collective sedimentation

Opposite
Island array pattern and estuary bathymetry

ISLAND ARRAY TECHNIQUE

Variations in the pattern of islands are created in relation to the changing bathymetry of the harbor: in plan, all proposed islands have identical footprints on the seabed, regardless of water depth, tapering in pyramidal stacked formation up toward the surface of the water. This creates bigger islands (more area above the water line) in shallow waters, and smaller islands in deep waters. Larger islands are therefore located near the tip of Manhattan, providing the most surface area for storm surge protection and blending with the coastline. Farther offshore, smaller islands provide deep water resistance—due to greater submerged mass—which slows water flow along the bottom of the harbor. Gradually extended and agglomerated over time by the sediment "wake" formed in its lee, the island pattern is a framework that helps to restore the natural processes of the estuary.

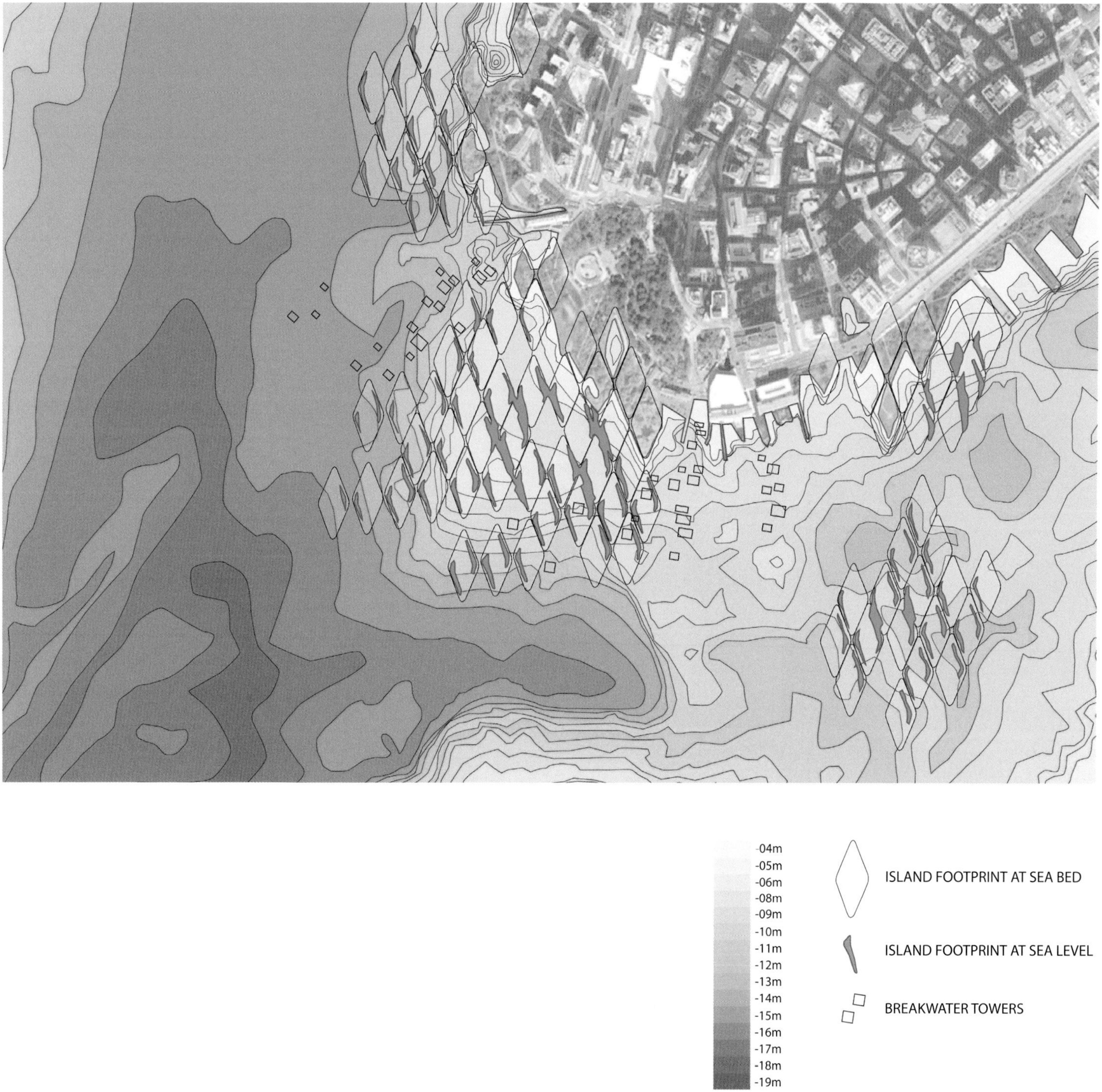

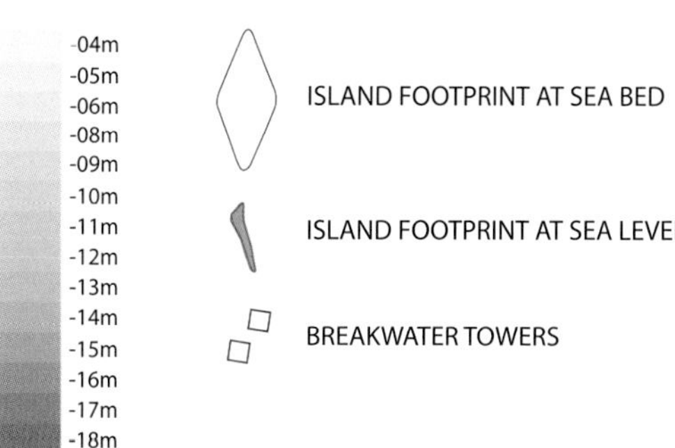
-04m
-05m
-06m
-08m
-09m
-10m
-11m
-12m
-13m
-14m
-15m
-16m
-17m
-18m
-19m
ISLAND FOOTPRINT AT SEA BED
ISLAND FOOTPRINT AT SEA LEVEL
BREAKWATER TOWERS

BREAK WATER TOWERS:
WET/DRY ECOSYSTEMS

In areas adjacent to ferry terminals and alongside navigation lanes, seawall re-shaping and islands are impractical because they conflict with docking requirements and obstruct boat traffic. At these locations, multiple "breakwater towers" are proposed. Fixed in place, these rectilinear pile structures are porous obstructions that break up storm surge waves. Above water, they serve as scaffolds for vegetation and provide refuge for birds. Below water, the breakwater towers provide beneficial shaded cover for marine life. Clusters of these structures echo the inhabited buildings on the land side of the coast.

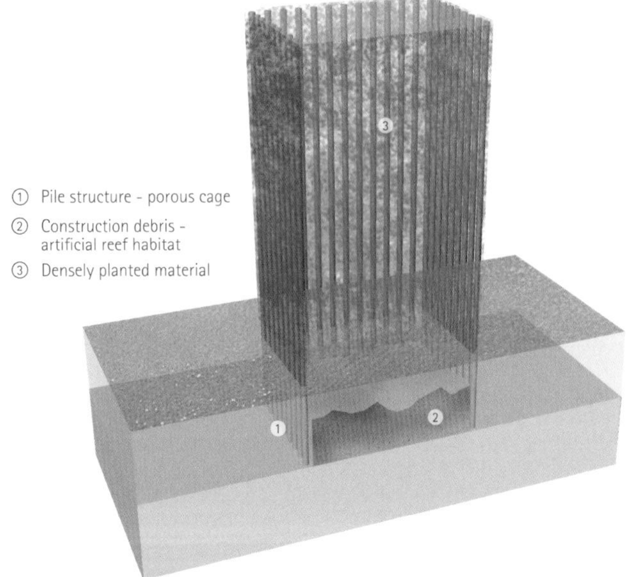

Opposite
Top, rendering of breakwater tower

Bottom left, water distribution

Bottom right, attenuation

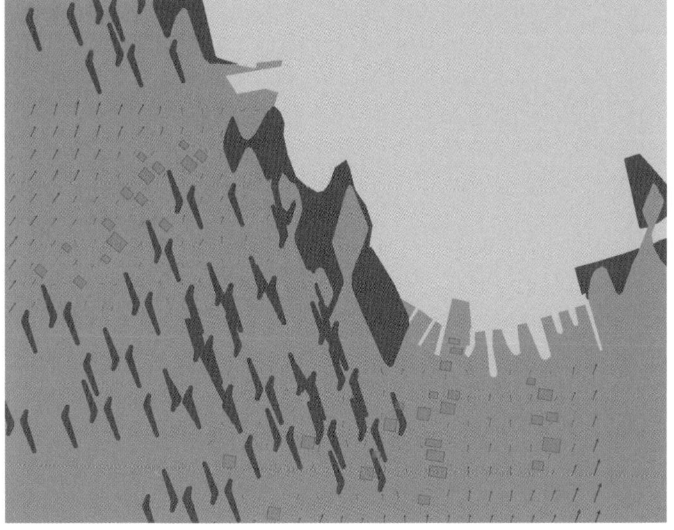

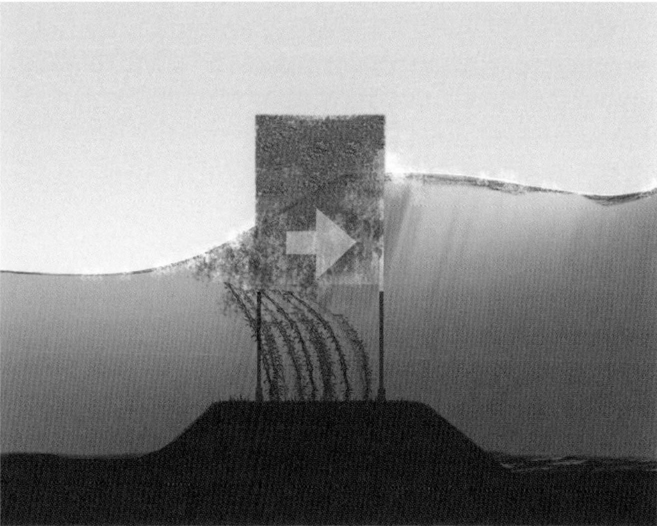

Aerial view of Lower Manhattan, 2008

Battery Park seawall during a hurricane in 1938

Overleaf
Existing and proposed island and coast sectional condition

REBUILDING MANHATTAN'S COASTLINE

The redesign of Manhattan's southern coastline is based upon five distinct urban conditions which presently exist along the water's edge. These inform specific design strategies that preserve the existing urban fabric while raising the effective height of the land around the perimeter, blocking the entry of water from rising sea level. Several of these strategies include wide landscape areas that mitigate the force of storm surge waves, diminishing potential damage to the city. As with the barrier islands, tubular geotextile containers are the principal means of construction. The resultant edges increase public access to the harbor and strengthen the existing greenway around Manhattan. Two seemingly oppositional results are achieved: the actual separation between land and water is strengthened, while the apparent boundary between them is diminished. Viewed in the historical context of Manhattan's development, the rebuilding of the coastline recalls the situation which existed prior to human settlement, before extensive landfill and the construction of the sea wall around the perimeter of the island. Since comparable conditions occur elsewhere in the harbor and in other coastal cities, what follows may also be understood as an emerging typology of design approaches to waterfront edges.

AREA 1: NARROW PARKSCAPE WATERFRONT WITH SMALL BUILDINGS

AREA 2: WIDE PARKSCAPE WATERFRONT

AREA 3: FERRY TERMINALS

AREA 4: ELEVATED HIGHWAY WITH TALL BUILDINGS

AREA 5: ELEVATED HIGHWAY WITH NEW LANDSCAPE

1 NARROW PARKSCAPE WATERFRONT WITH SMALL BUILDINGS

2 WIDE PARKSCAPE WATERFRONT

3 FERRY TERMINAL STRUCTURES TO REMAIN

4 ELEVATED HIGHWAY WITH ADJACENT HIGHRISES TO REMAIN

5 ELEVATED HIGHWAY WITH LOWRISES BEYOD TO BE REDEVELOPED INTO PARKSCAPE

PIER STRUCTURES

HARD EDGE - SEAWALLS / REVETMENTS

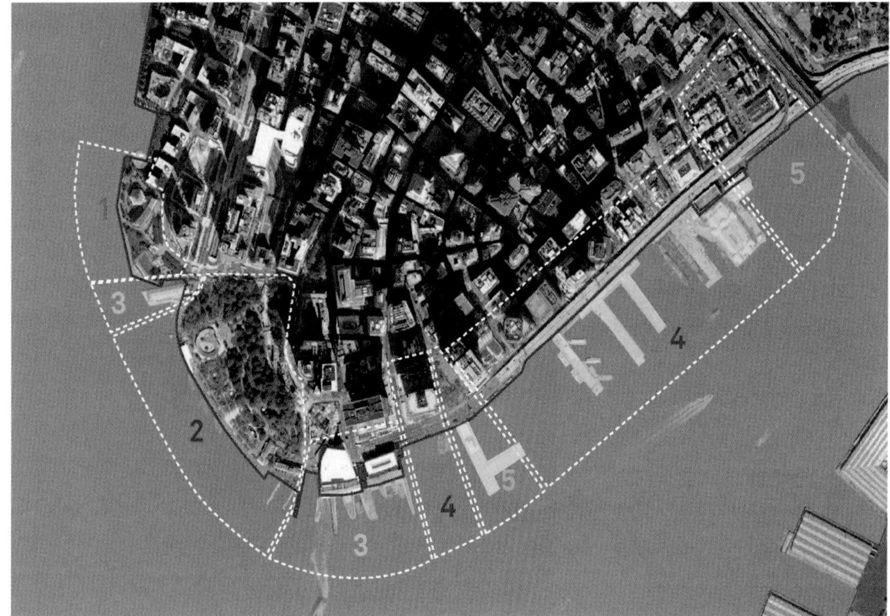

Existing Lower Manhattan Coastline

1 NARROW PARKSCAPE WATERFRONT WITH SMALL BUILDINGS

2 WIDE PARKSCAPE WATERFRONT

3 FERRY TERMINAL STRUCTURES TO REMAIN WITH CAISSON BREAKWATER STRUCTURES

4 ELEVATED HIGHWAY WITH ADJACENT HIGHRISES TO REMAIN

5 ELEVATED HIGHWAY WITH LOWRISES BEYOD TO BE REDEVELOPED INTO PARKSCAPE

PIER STRUCTURES

HARD EDGE - SEAWALLS / REVETMENTS

SOFT EDGE - ORGANIC BARRIERS

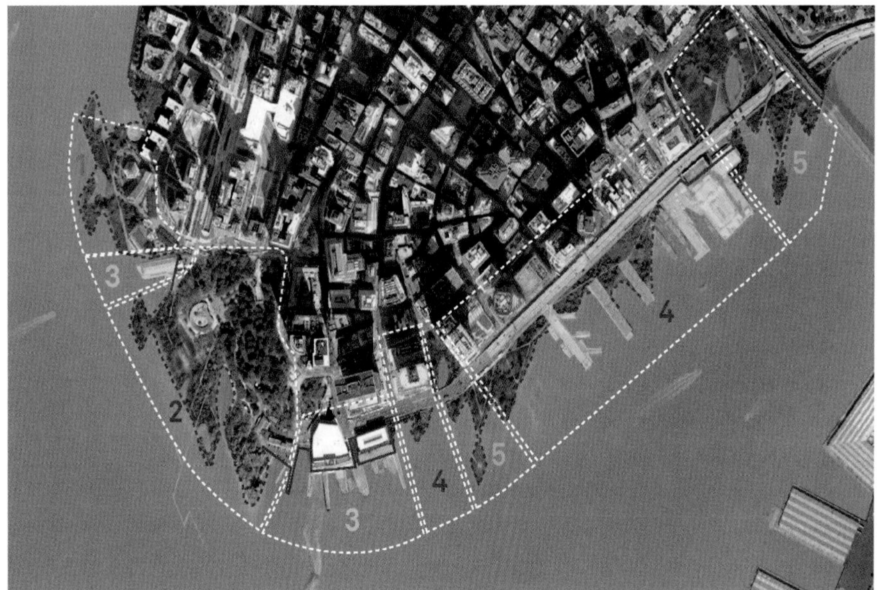

Proposed Lower Manhattan Coastline

Storm Surge Water Line

Mean High Water Line

Mean Low Water Line

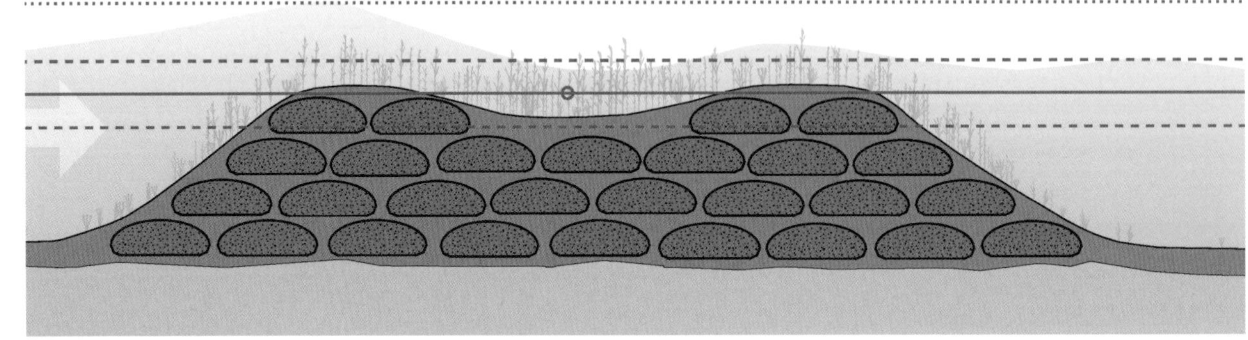

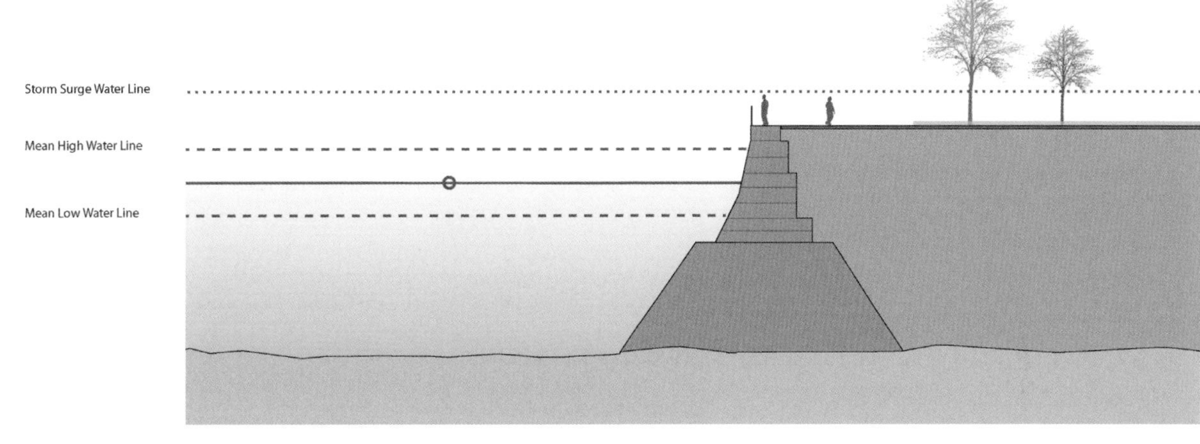

Storm Surge Water Line
Mean High Water Line
Mean Low Water Line

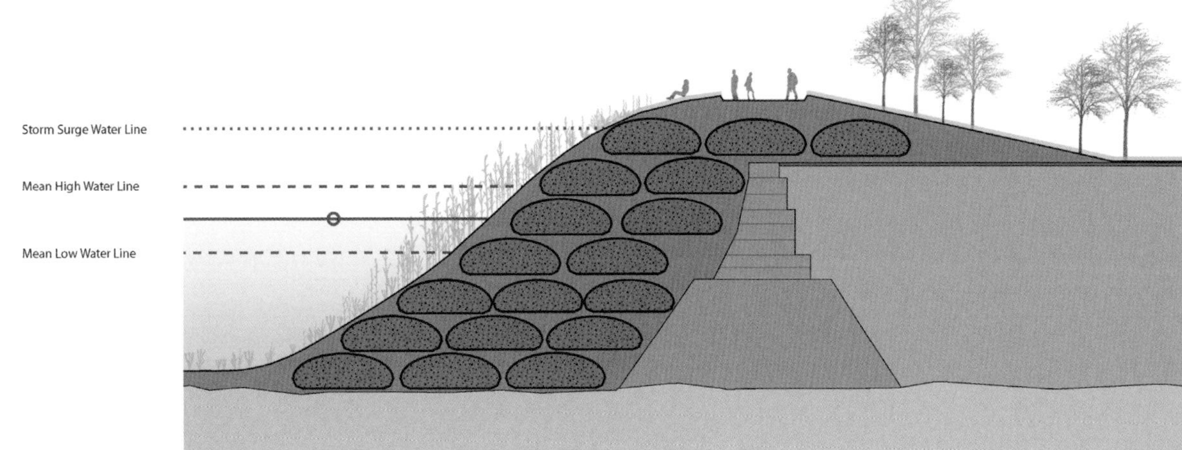

Storm Surge Water Line
Mean High Water Line
Mean Low Water Line

Proposed coastline at low tide 0'

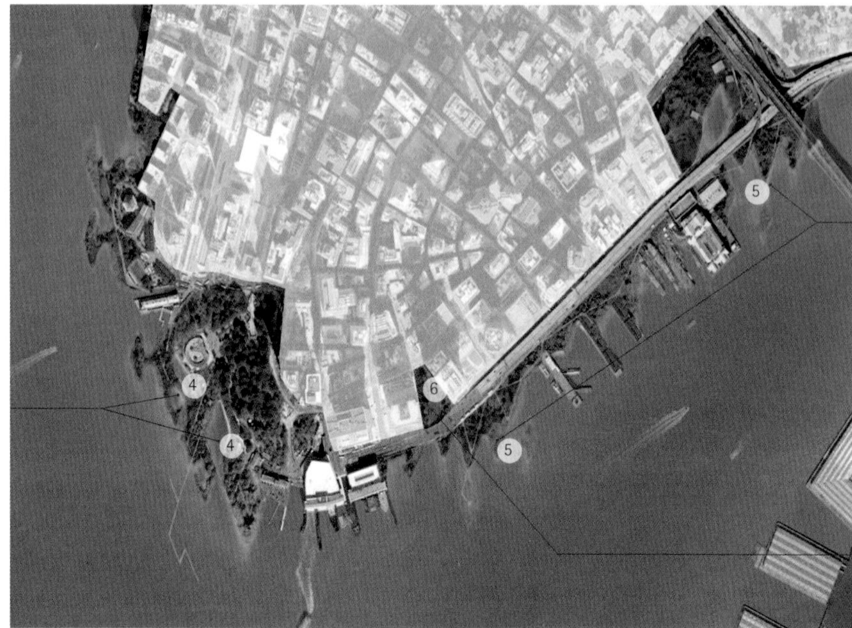

Proposed coastline at high tide +8'

① Isolated tidal pools for recreational use

② Exposed wetlands and park walkways

③ Mostly dry inlet/slipway parkscape

④ Tidal pools flood and merge with upper bay submerging a few walkways creating temporary inaccesible areas of the park by land

⑤ Submerged wetlands and park walkways

⑥ Inlet/slipway park flood with water to create wetland parkscape

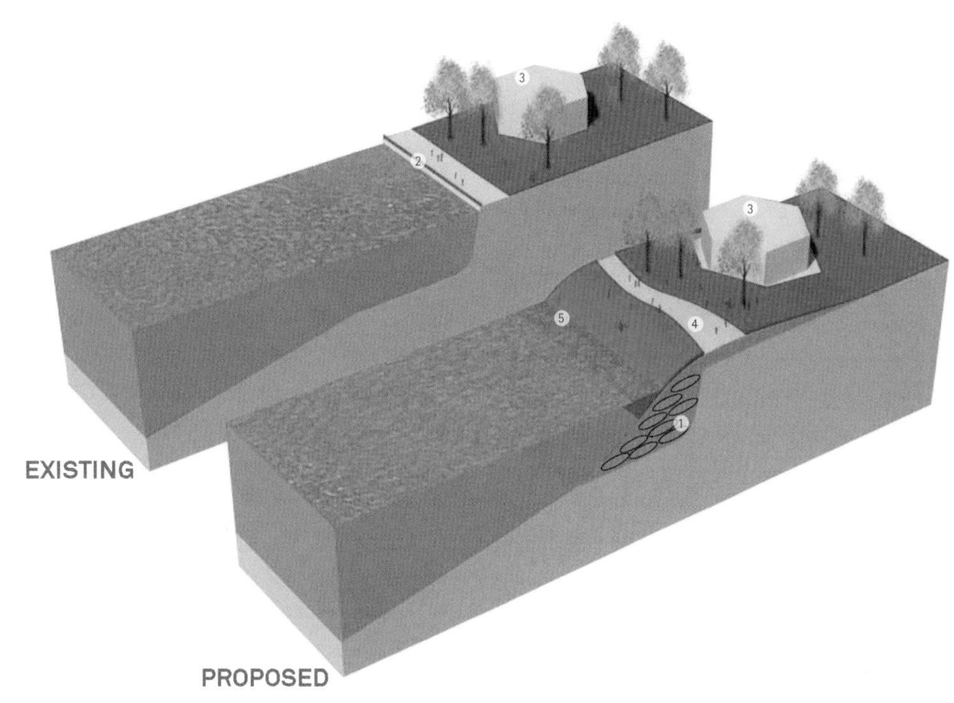

AREA 1: NARROW LANDSCAPE WITH SMALL STRUCTURES

Battery Park City contains a waterfront promenade, with adjacent structures such as the Museum of Jewish Heritage and the pavilions in the Robert F. Wagner Park. The goal is to maintain public circulation along the edge, and to protect adjoining buildings and their programs. The design reshapes the seawall into a gentle berm, with its peak higher than the current seawall elevation, gradually sloping into the river and providing new wetland habitats. Adjacent buildings are integrated into the new topography and the pedestrian promenade is reconstructed at the top of the berm.

① Geotextile tube/recycled dredge material construction
② Existing seawall & boardwalk
③ Existing buildings
④ New elevated pedstrian/bike path
⑤ Tidal wetlands

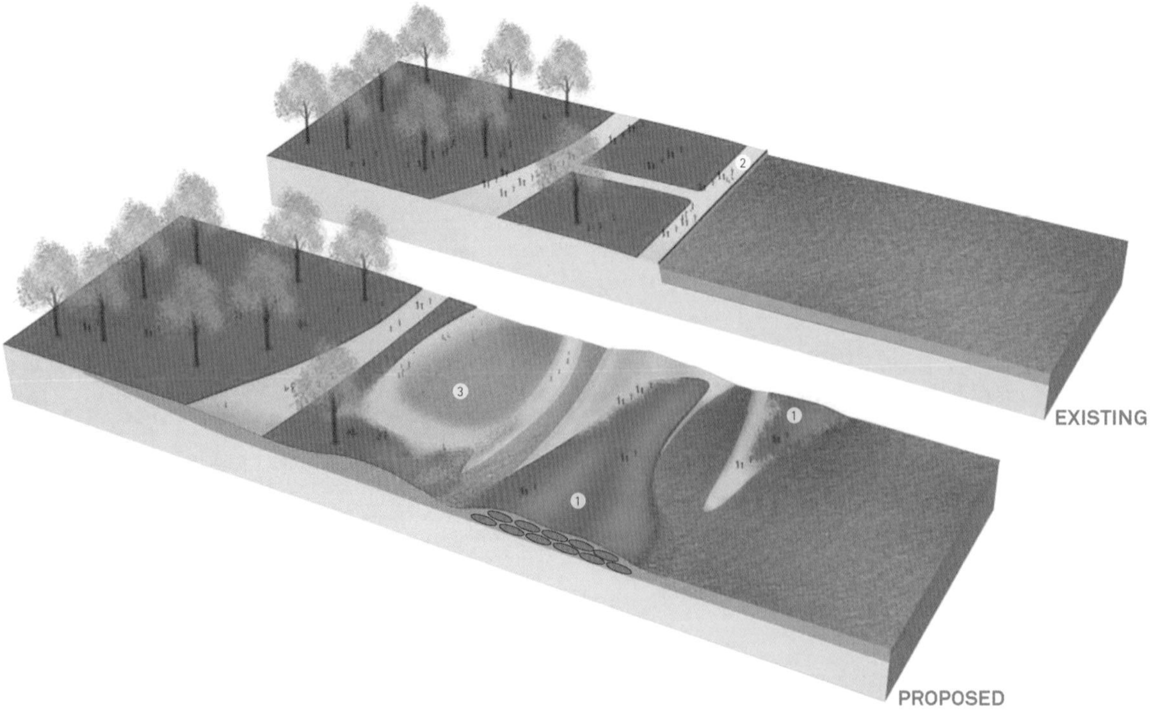

EXISTING

PROPOSED

AREA 2: WIDE LANDSCAPE

Battery Park consists mostly of open space that functions as a buffer between water and land. The augmentation of its existing landscape to include recreational tidal pools and new wetland habitat creates a dynamic edge with the water in place of the existing seawall. Strategically positioned berms act to divert tidal surges. This new landscape extends Battery Park into the harbor and also provides continuity between Hudson River Park and the new East River Park.

① Geotextile tube berm/recycled dredge material construction

② Existing seawall and boardwalk

③ Existing buildings

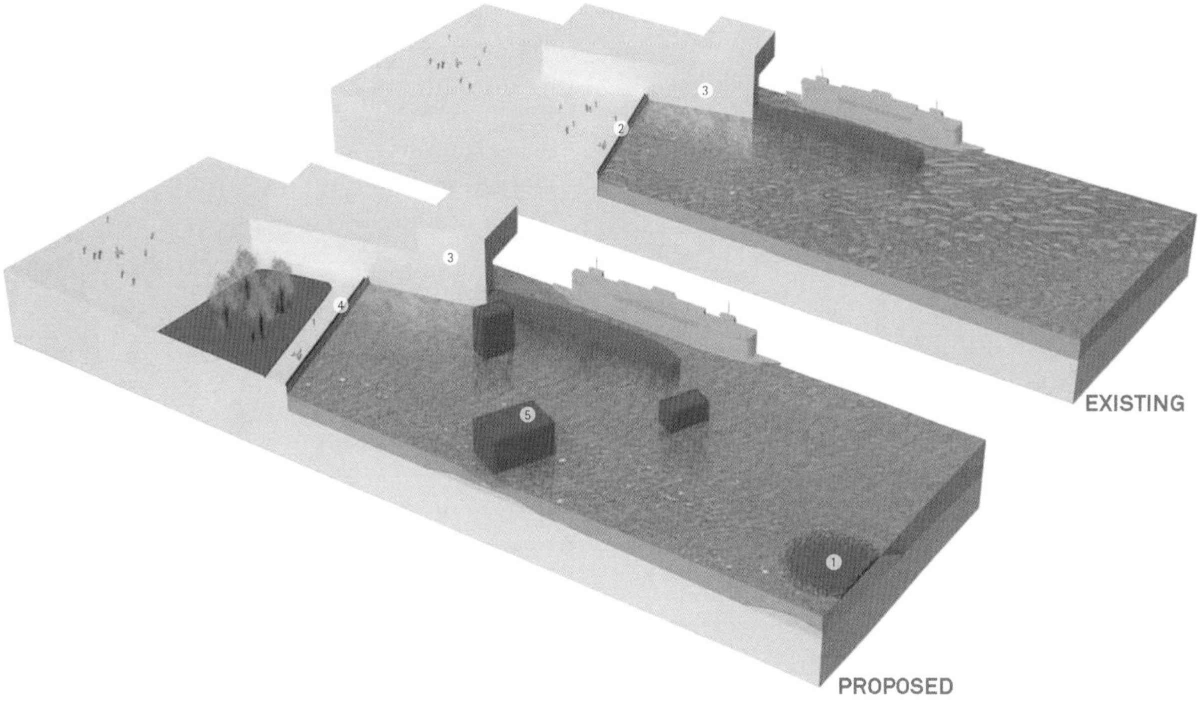

EXISTING

PROPOSED

AREA 3: FERRY TERMINALS

There are currently three major ferry terminals at the southern tip of Manhattan, all of which remain to provide public transportation service as an important part of the larger vision of the harbor. The existing seawalls are raised and clusters of breakwater towers are positioned off-shore to shield existing ferry terminals and adjacent pedestrian paths from a tidal surge. These towers create both marine and avian habitats.

① Geotextile tube/recycled dredge material construction

② Existing seawall and boardwalk

③ Existing ferry terminal to remain

④ Existing seawall to be raised

⑤ Breakwater towers

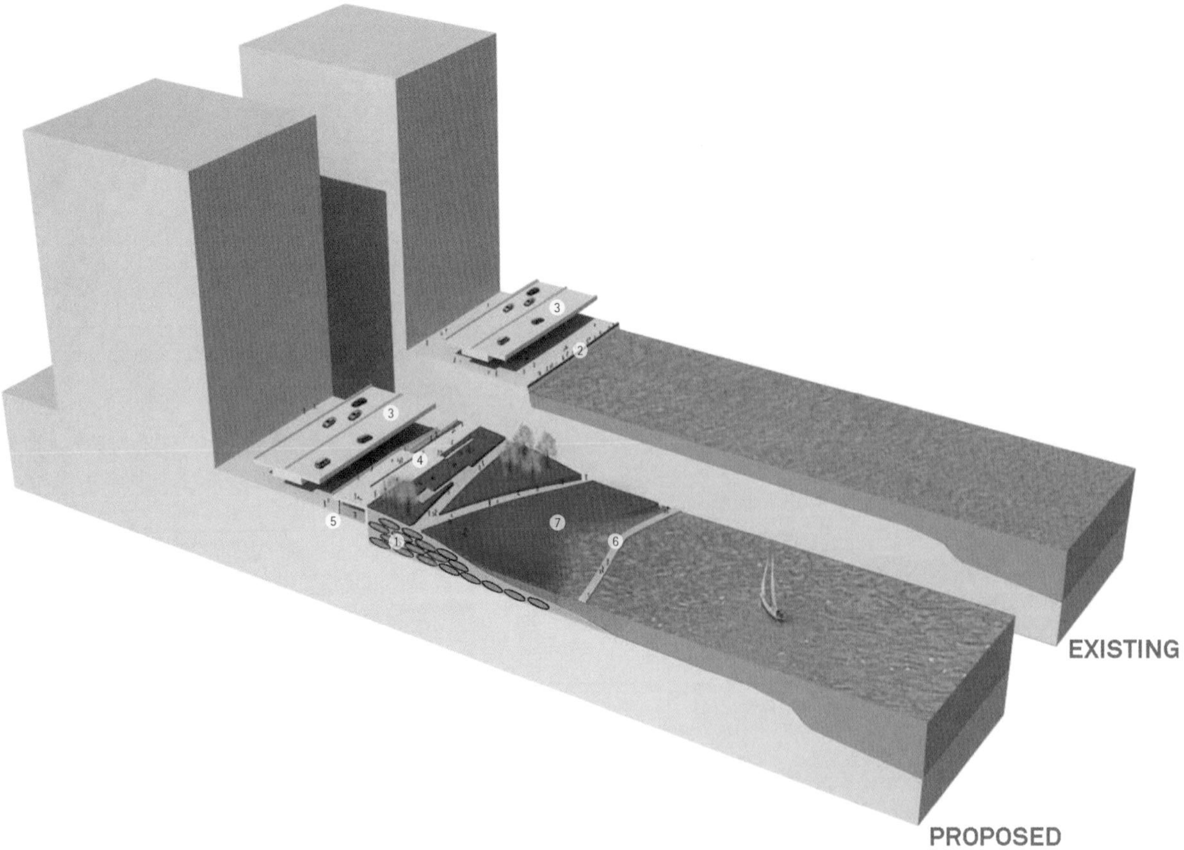

EXISTING

PROPOSED

AREA 4: ELEVATED HIGHWAY WITH TALL BUILDINGS

The elevated Franklin D. Roosevelt East River Drive along the southeast portion of the tip of Manhattan constitutes a narrow linear strip with a seawall/boardwalk on one side, and a row of dense highrises on the other. The seawall adjacent to the Franklin D. Roosevelt East River Drive is elevated as a linear berm with a hard edge facing the city. This interior edge contains commercial space for stores and restaurants, supporting a new elevated boardwalk that feathers into the river as a wetland landscape.

① Geotextile tube/recycled dredge material construction
② Existing seawall boardwalk
③ Existing elevated Franklin D. Roosevelt East River Drive
④ New elevated pedestrian/bike path
⑤ Embedded commercial real estate
⑥ New wetlands boardwalk
⑦ Tidal wetlands

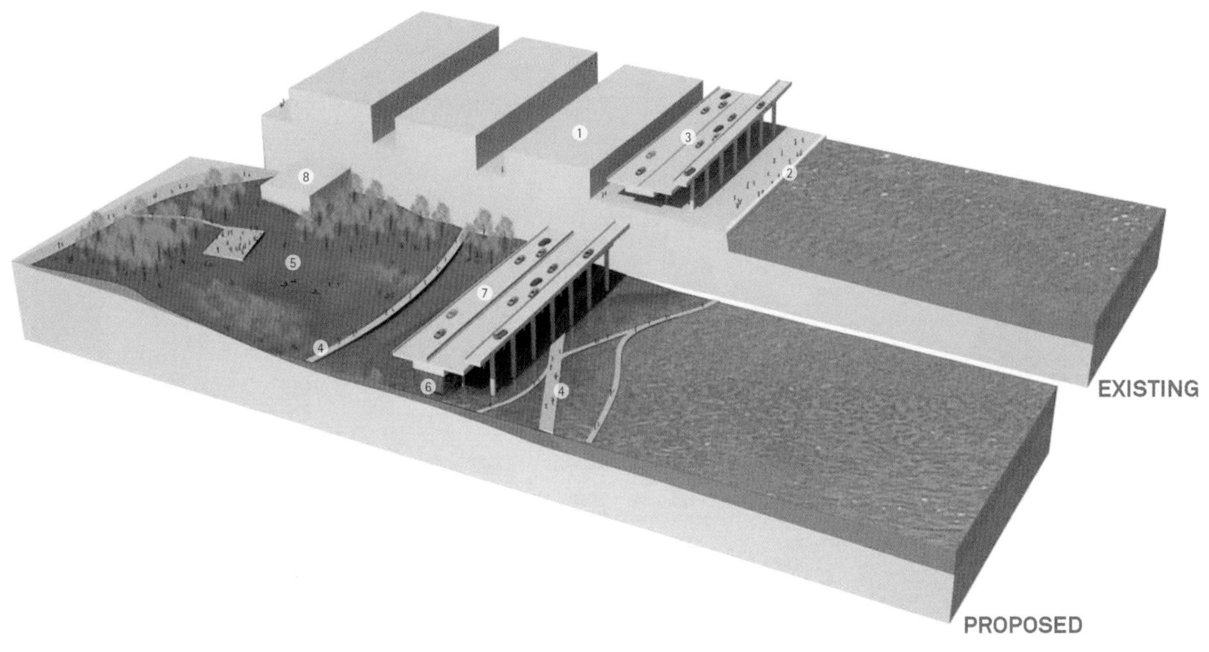

AREA 5: ELEVATED HIGHWAY WITH NEW LANDSCAPE

The area along the East River just south of the Brooklyn Bridge consists of roughly ten acres of two to five story structures. The removal of these buildings allows for an open green space that contains and filters storm water runoff, benefitting the water quality of the harbor. The adjacent historical South Street neighborhood, a mix of commercial and residential buildings, is enriched with more air, light, and the presence of water. The underside of the Franklin D. Roosevelt East River Drive houses breakwater towers, permitting water flow to and from the park, and shields the immediate area from a tidal surge.

① Demolition of selected existing lowrises
② Existing seawall boardwalk
③ Existing elevated Franklin D. Roosevelt East River highway
④ New pedestrian/bike path
⑤ New wetlands parkscape water surge buffer
⑥ Semi-porous green breakwater barrier
⑦ Reinforced elevated Franklin D. Roosevelt East River highway
⑧ New buildings

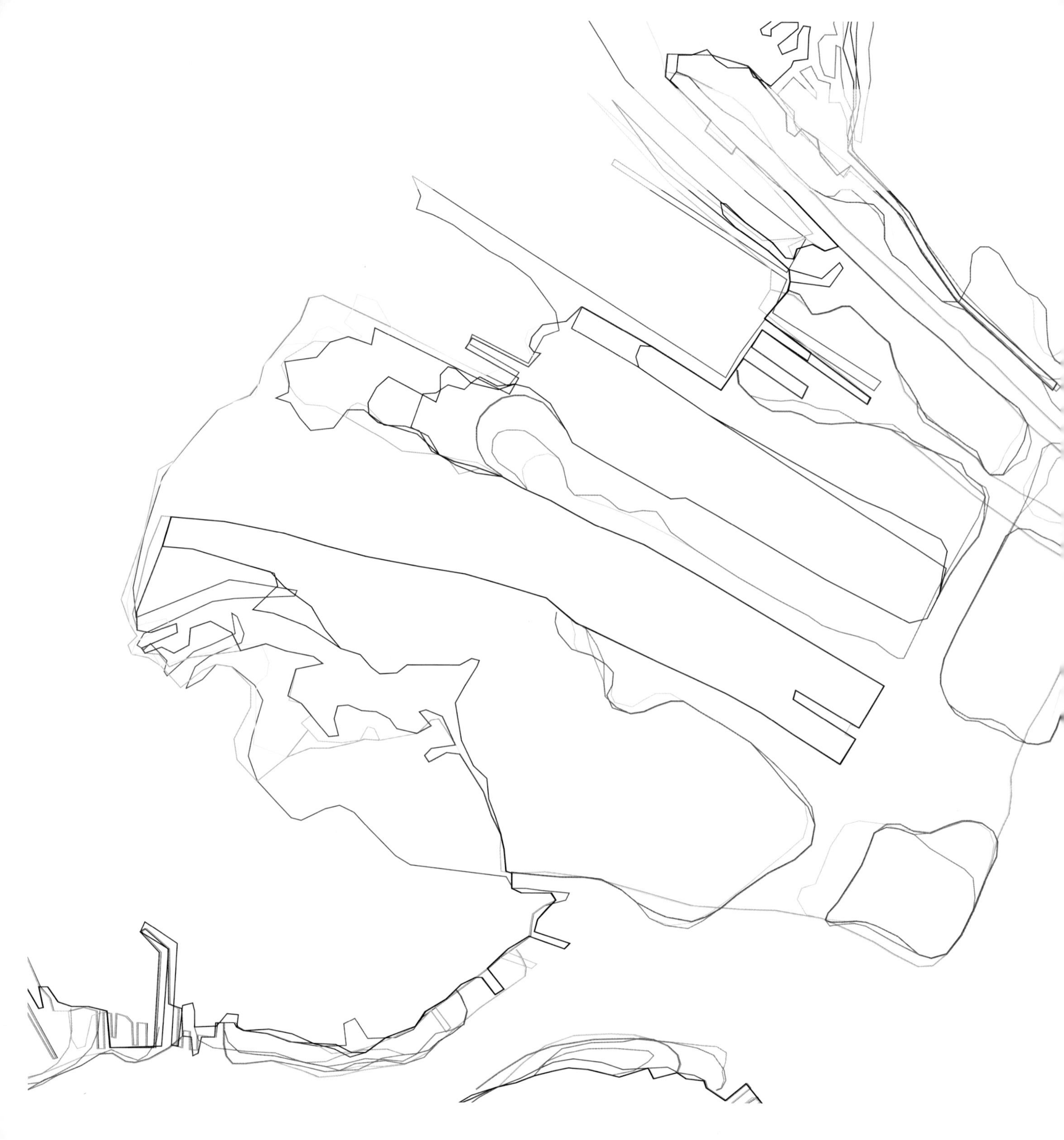

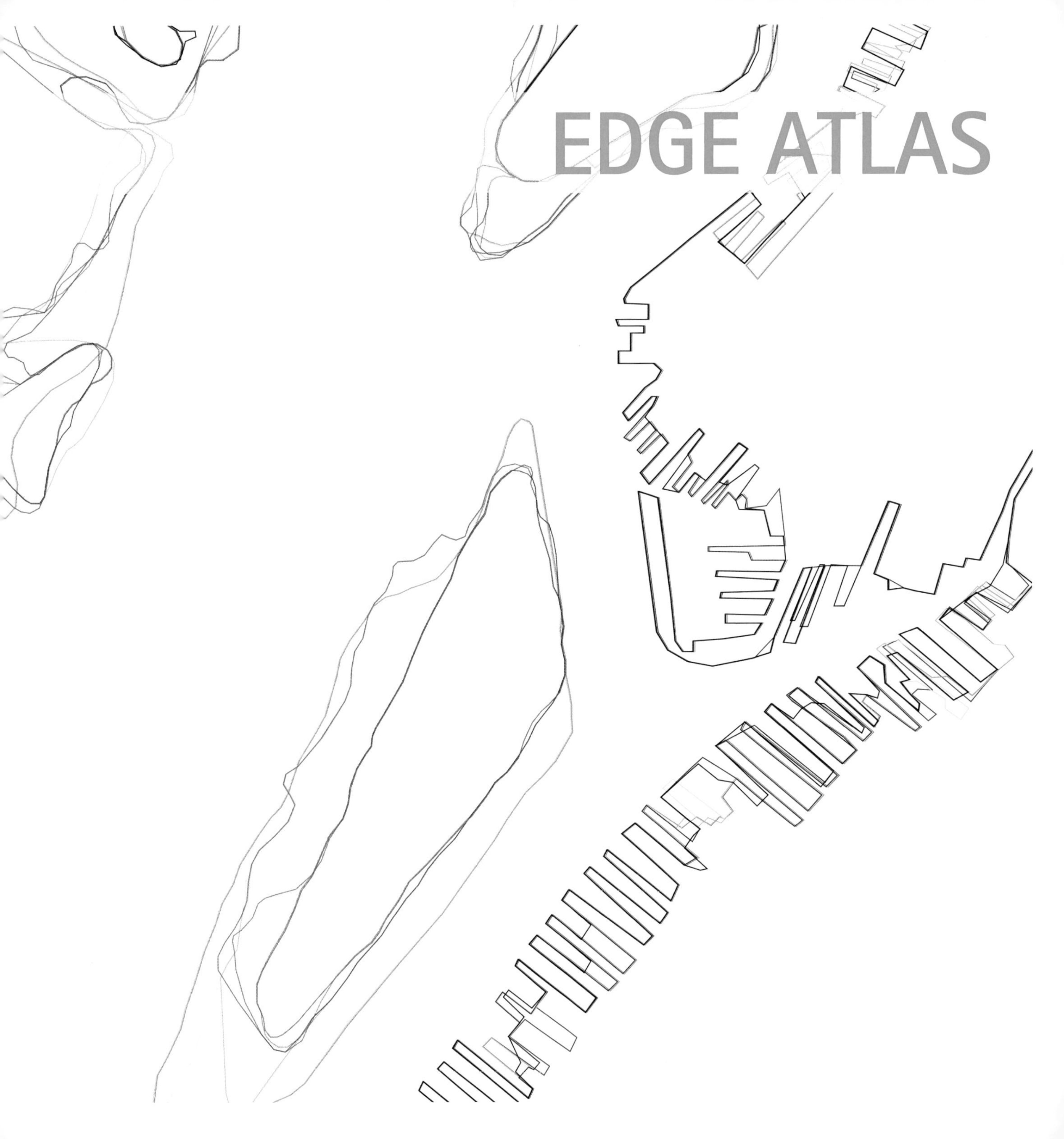
EDGE ATLAS

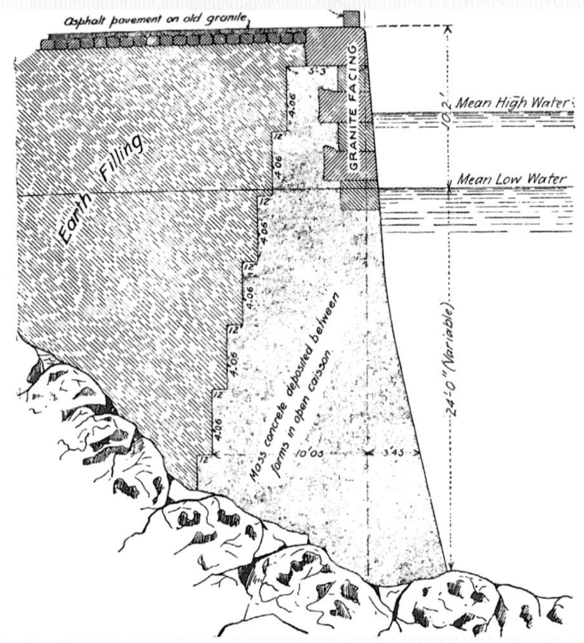

Structured piers along the Hudson River on the west side of Manhattan. These piers lined much of the perimeter of lower and midtown Manhattan with a protective fringe, 1930

A seawall section from the book *Wharves and Piers: Their Design, Construction and Equipment* by Carleton Greene, 1917

Opposite
Upper Bay coastline throughout the twentieth century, traced from nautical charts of the National Oceanic and Atmospheric Administration (NOAA)

Previous pages
Historical nautical charts, Office of Coast Survey, National Ocean Service, National Oceanic and Atmospheric Administration (NOAA)

EDGE ATLAS

Be it at the hand of man or Mother Nature, the coastline of the New York-New Jersey Upper Bay is constantly being redrawn. Its current shape has been in the making for tens of thousands of years. The most legible changes occurred with the settlement and development of New York City and the surrounding metropolitan region. This section details our efforts to understand the transformation of the edge and to document its current state for comprehensive and scientific purposes.

TRACING THE HISTORIC COASTLINE

In the past century or so, once gradual adjustments to the coastline due to geological and climatological processes gave way to more frequent and more dramatic adjustments due to artificial processes. It was during that time that the metropolitan New York region underwent a number of important changes including major growth in its population, the peak and subsequent decline of local industry, shifts in maritime use, and the establishment of the highway system.

With these historical changes to the urban environment, the coastline of the New York–New Jersey Upper Bay was likewise reshaped. The line drawing at right illustrates the state of the coastline and the shallow underwater flats decade by decade throughout the twentieth century. The years between 1918 and 1928 saw extensive construction of piers along the eastern waterfront of Staten Island and elsewhere around the harbor. By 1944 significant filling of land on the New Jersey side had begun, including the development of the Military Ocean Terminal, and harbor shoals and flats were made smaller or eliminated altogether by dredging. Between 1967 and 1977, the maritime industry recentered itself in New Jersey, resulting in the construction of a second large landfill pier in Bayonne and the removal of the piers lining Manhattan. The end of the century saw continued disintegration of piers in Brooklyn and Staten Island.

While the New York waterfront today remains a zone in transition, for our purposes, charting its current shape has been quite informative. But to fully understand the state of the current coastline one must look beyond the shape of the line itself both to its material qualities and its sectional characteristics.

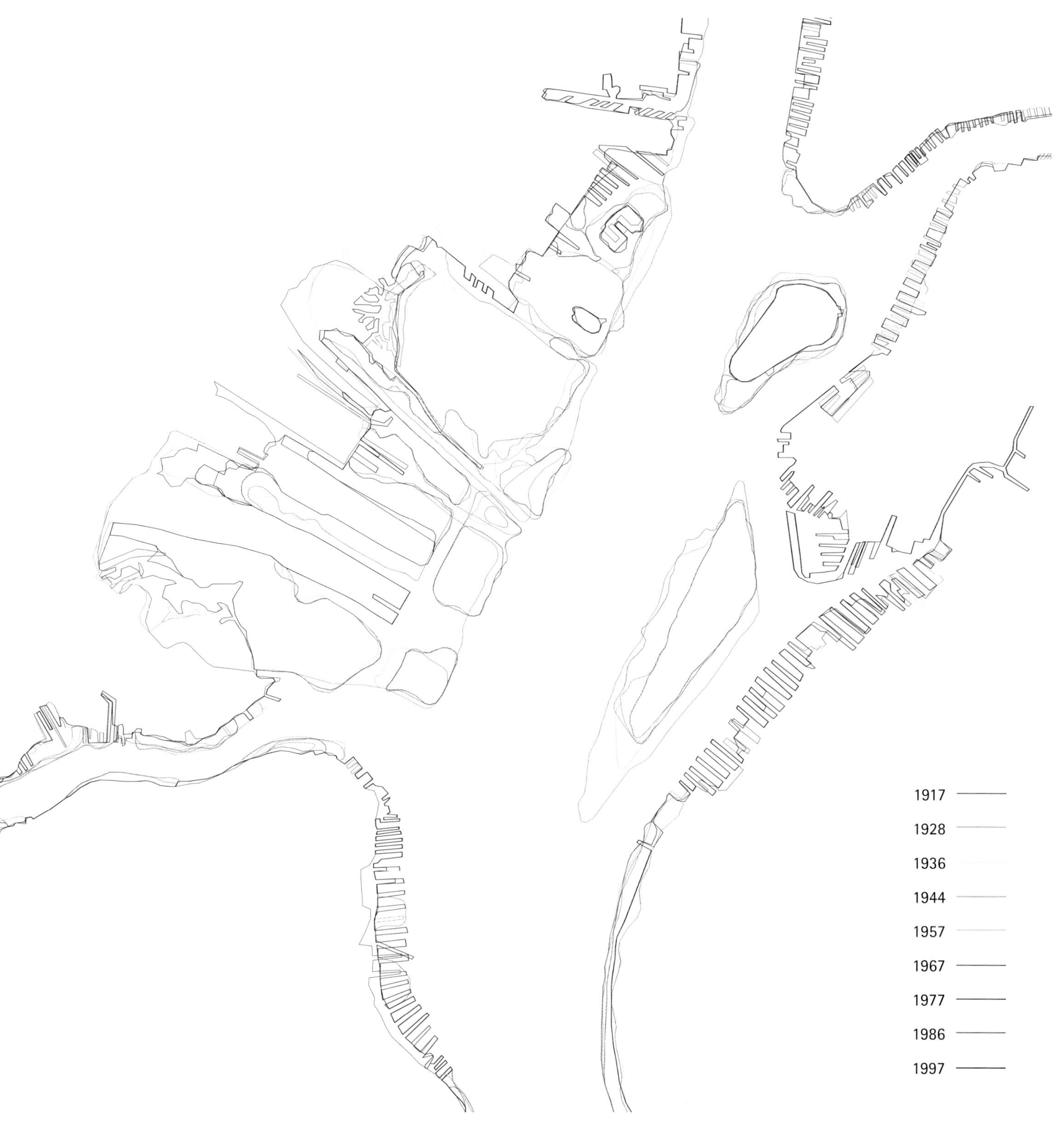

1917
1928
1936
1944
1957
1967
1977
1986
1997

1917

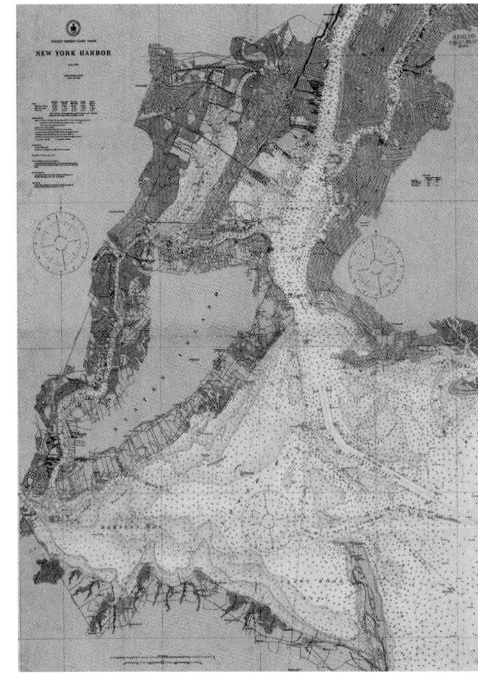

1928

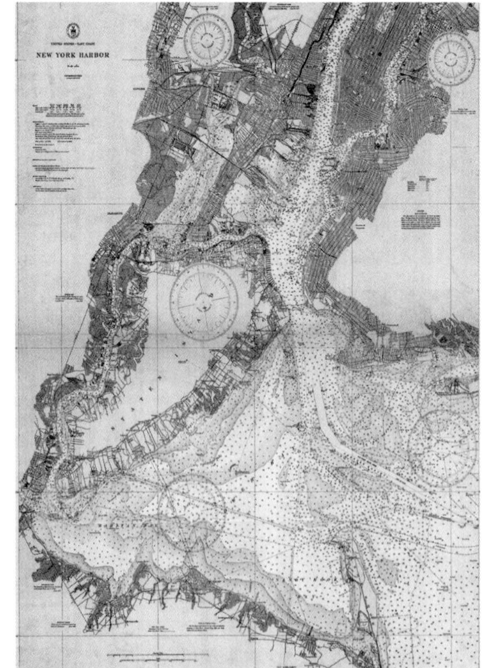

1967

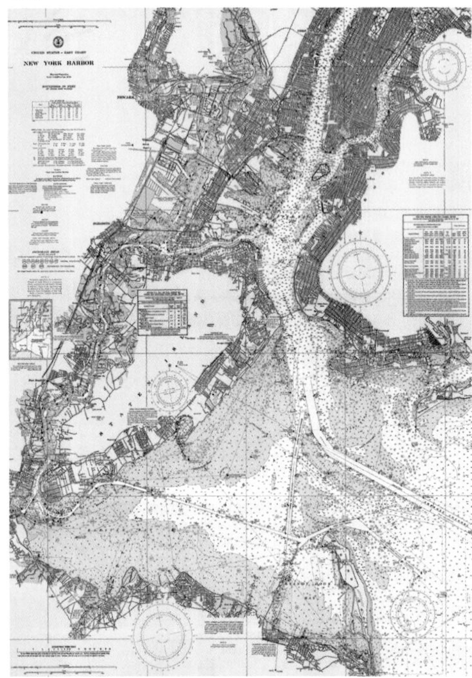

1977

1936

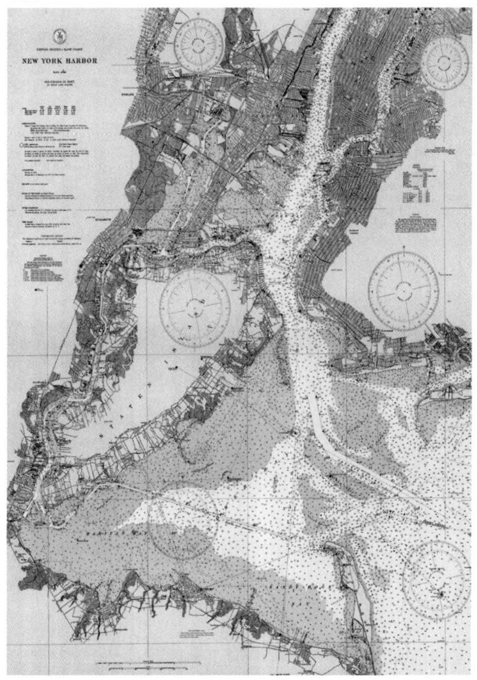

1944

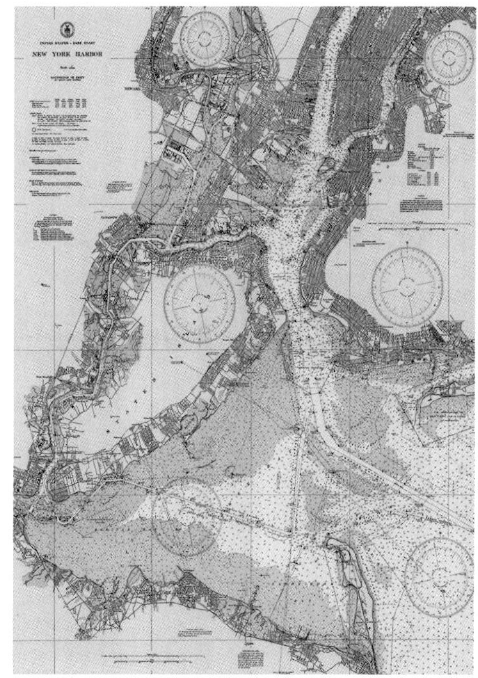

1986

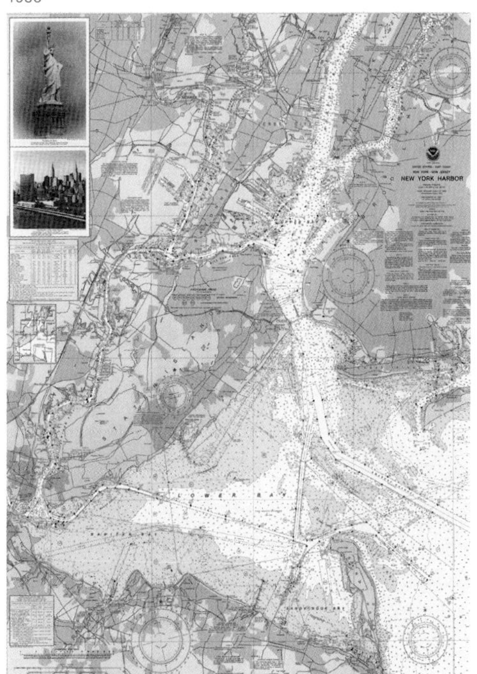

1997

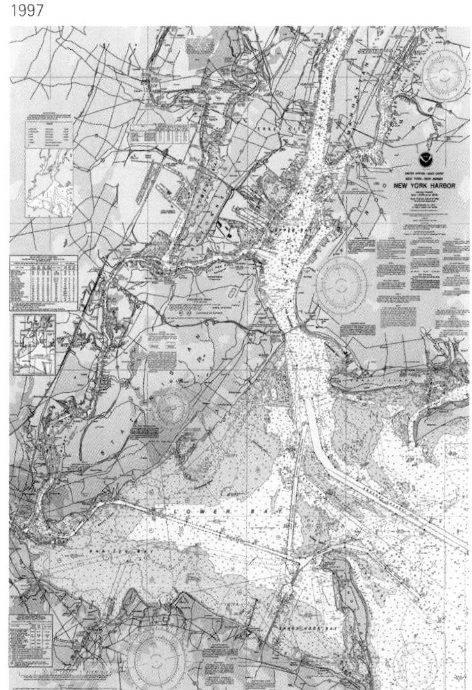

Key of edge conditions

Opposite
Map of edge conditions around the Upper Bay

DESCRIBING THE EDGE

A more qualitative approach to documenting the coastline involved the use of high-resolution, two-dimensional aerial imagery and oblique aerial photography in order to identify various conditions along its length.

This simple analysis examines the edge of the harbor from the land side and the water side and designates areas as two categories, one for each "side." On the water side, a strip of coastline may be marked by a seawall, pier, or breakwater, or left visibly natural. On the land side, a coastline may be paved, blanketed by buildings, covered in mud, used as parkland, or treated as natural wetland.

The most common condition found on the water side of the coastline is the seawall. Pavement and buildings cover the majority of the land mass, especially in Brooklyn and Lower Manhattan.

The edge map shows that the line between water and land is often a fuzzy one. Conditions typically lie somewhere between a hard edge and a soft edge rather than at one end of the spectrum.

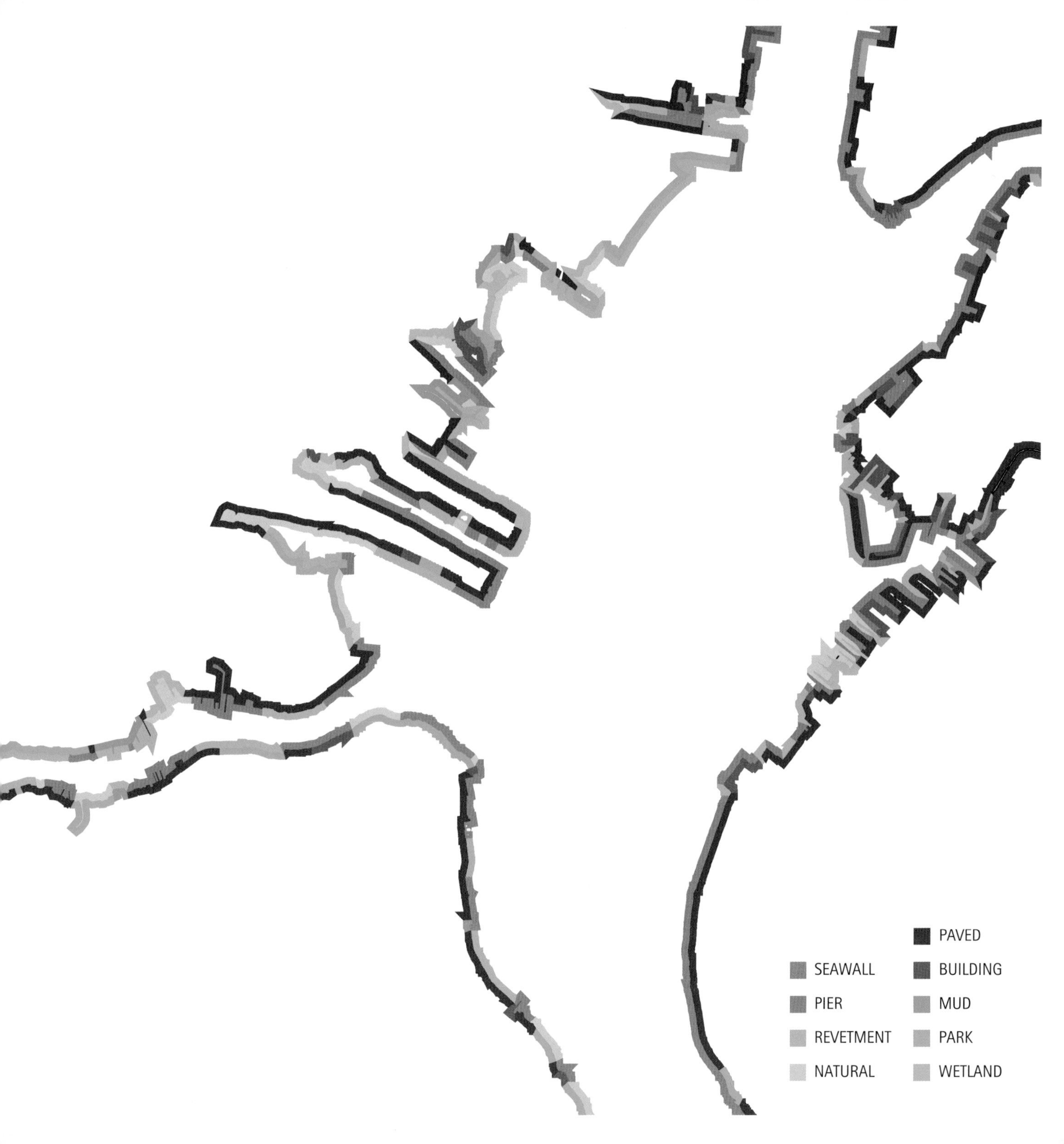

PAVED
SEAWALL
BUILDING
PIER
MUD
REVETMENT
PARK
NATURAL
WETLAND

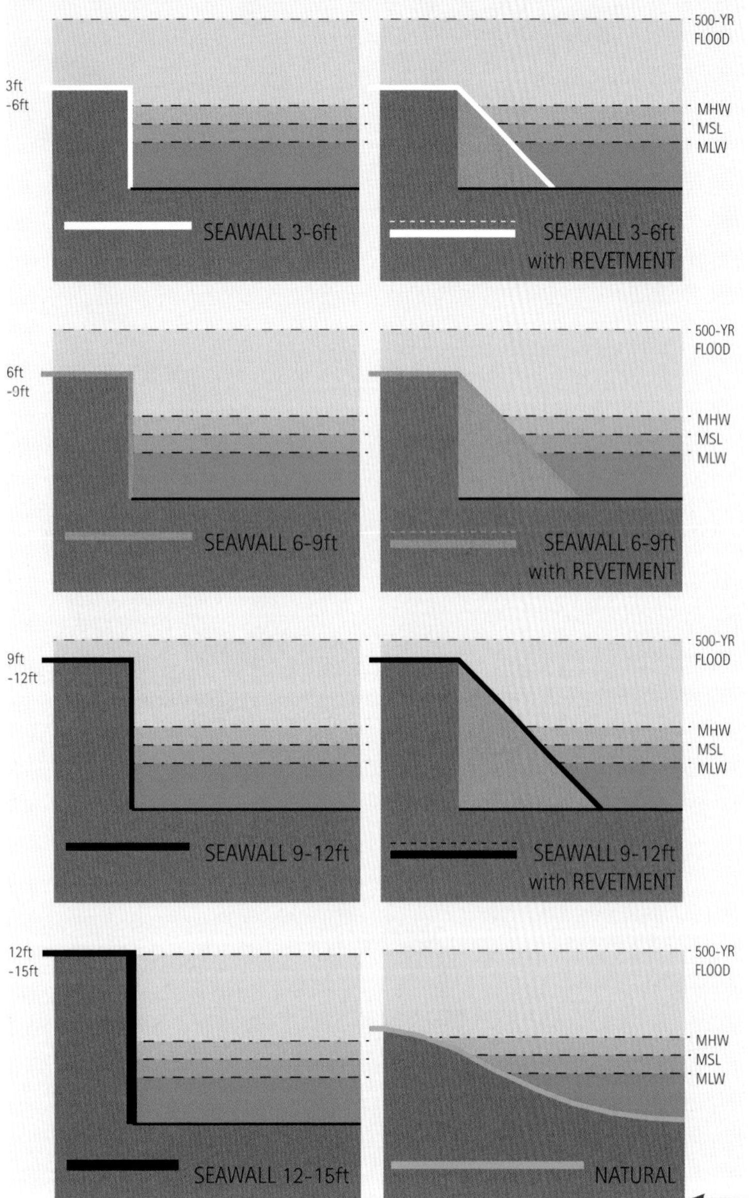

Sectional diagrams showing edge conditions and their vulnerability to flooding, with seawall heights increasing from black to white

Opposite
Explanatory key of Edge Atlas maps

EDGE ATLAS

The following pages document the edge condition and flood risk areas for the entire edge of the New York-New Jersey Upper Bay. To display this information at a legible scale, the map of the harbor was split up on a grid of ten squares by ten squares. Including only those squares containing the water-land edge led to a series of forty-eight individual maps. Each individual map square then represents a swath of the New York-New Jersey Upper Bay coastline and surroundings measuring 5,400 by 5,400 feet, with an area just over one square mile.

Each map contains a key to place the particular square shown in the context of the whole harbor at the top left of the page; an aerial photo of the square for reference at right; and a map with the edge condition line, the mark of the one-hundred-year and 500-year floodplains, and the water.

The sectional diagrams at left illustrate the various edge conditions around the Upper Bay, where white represents a seawall with heights in the three to six foot range, grey represents the six to nine foot range, black represents the nine to twelve foot range, and the heavy black line represents the twelve to fifteen foot range. This thick black line can be found at only one point in the entire harbor, at the Staten Island Ferry terminal at the tip of Manhattan. The green line represents a "natural" edge condition. Finally, a dashed line represents revetment or riprap, rock material built up in a slope along a seawall.

Note that these diagrams are simplified for ease of differentiation and the undersea condition varies throughout all of the categorical conditions. The water levels marked as Mean High Water (MHW), Mean Sea Level (MSL), Mean Low Water (MLW), and the 500-year flood reveal the vulnerability of each seawall height to certain flood levels and hint at the planar registration inherent in each condition.

On the maps, the light orange areas represent predicted inundation during the one-hundred-year flood according to Federal Emergency Management Agency (FEMA) floodplain data. Similarly, light red areas represent inundation during the 500-year flood. Given the effects of future sea level rise and increasing severe storm frequency, these areas can also be understood as the thirty-year and one-hundred-year floodplains of the future.

MAP NUMBER
KEY MAP
100-YEAR FLOODPLAIN
500-YEAR FLOODPLAIN
6
0
500
1,000 ft
WATER
SCALE BAR
EDGE CONDITION

1
2
3
4
5
6
7
8
9
10
11
12
13
14
15
16
17
18
19
20
21
22
23
24
25
26
27
28
29
30
31
32
33
34
35
36
37
38
39
40
41
42
43
44
45
46
47
48

1

0
500
1,000 ft

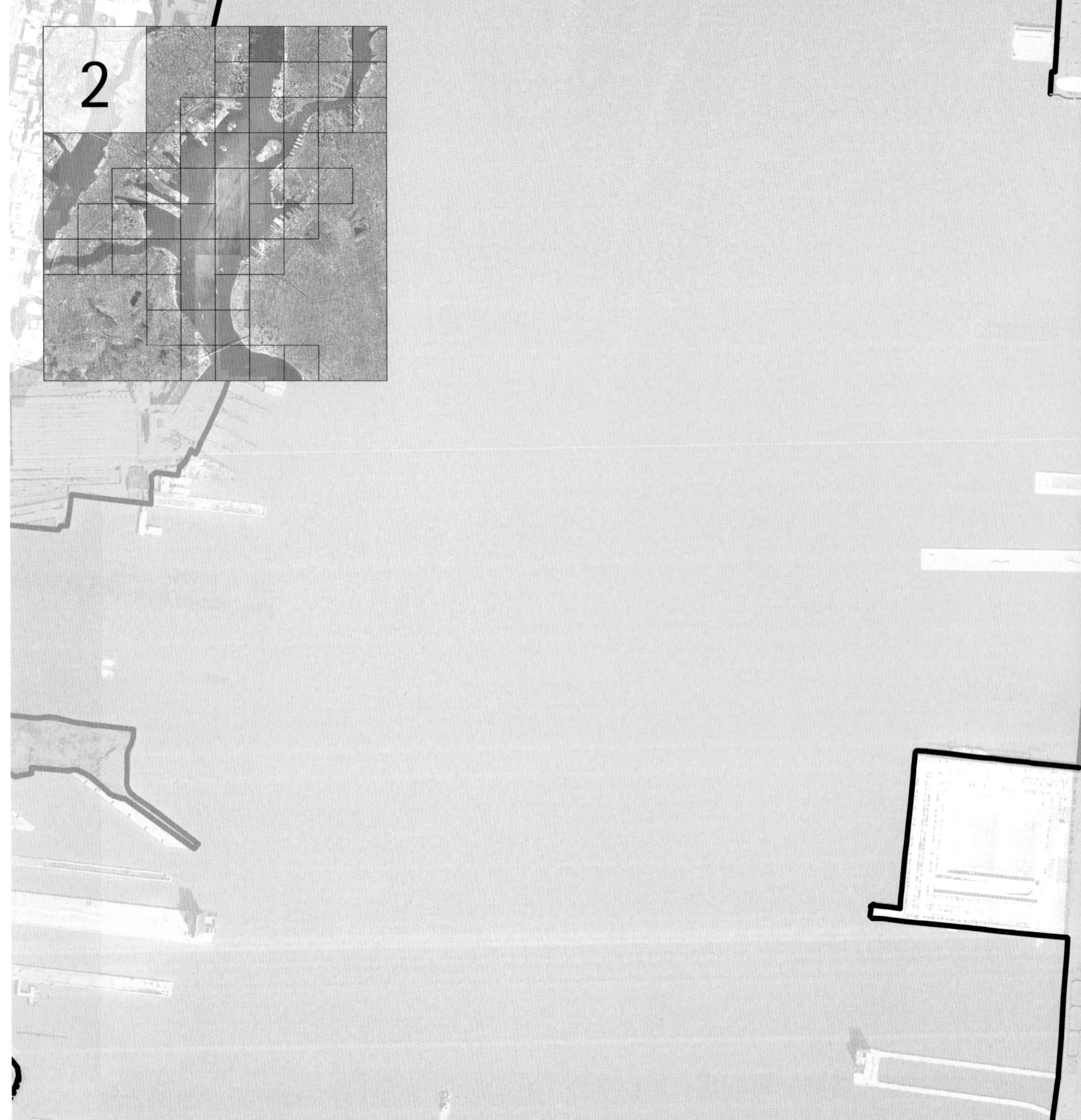
2

0
500
1,000 ft

3

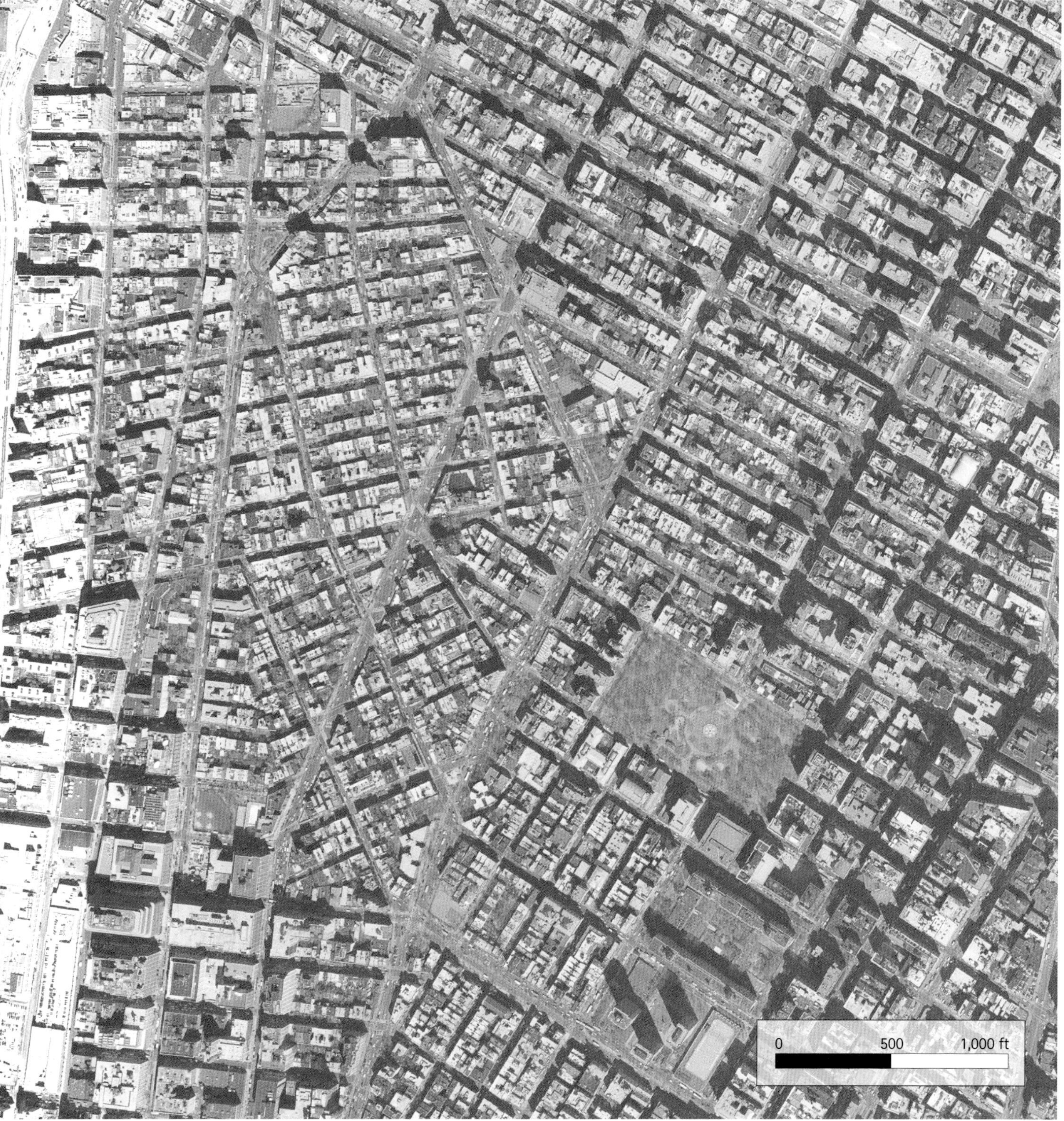
0
500
1,000 ft

4

0
500
1,000 ft

5

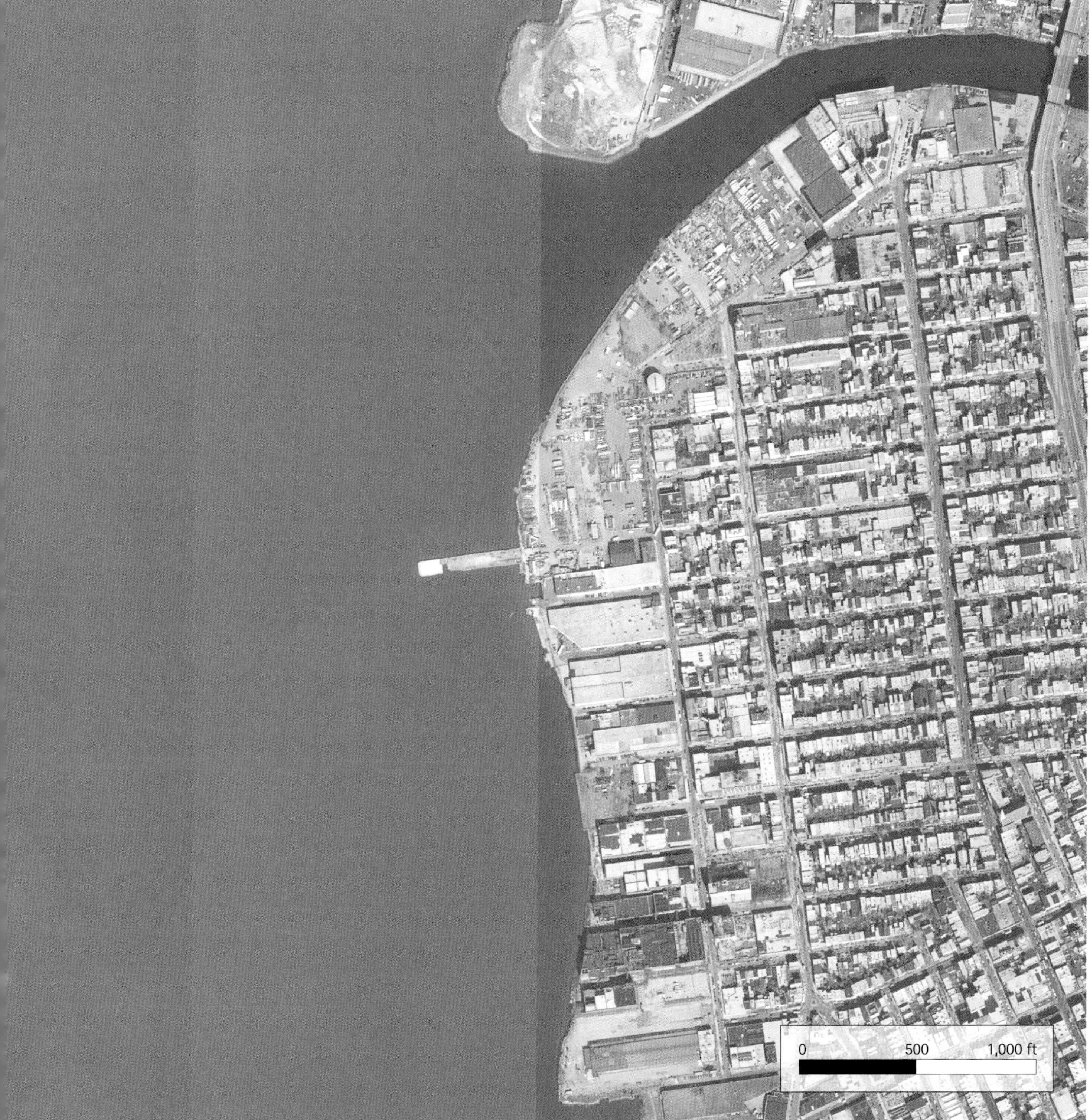
0
500
1,000 ft

6

0
500
1,000 ft

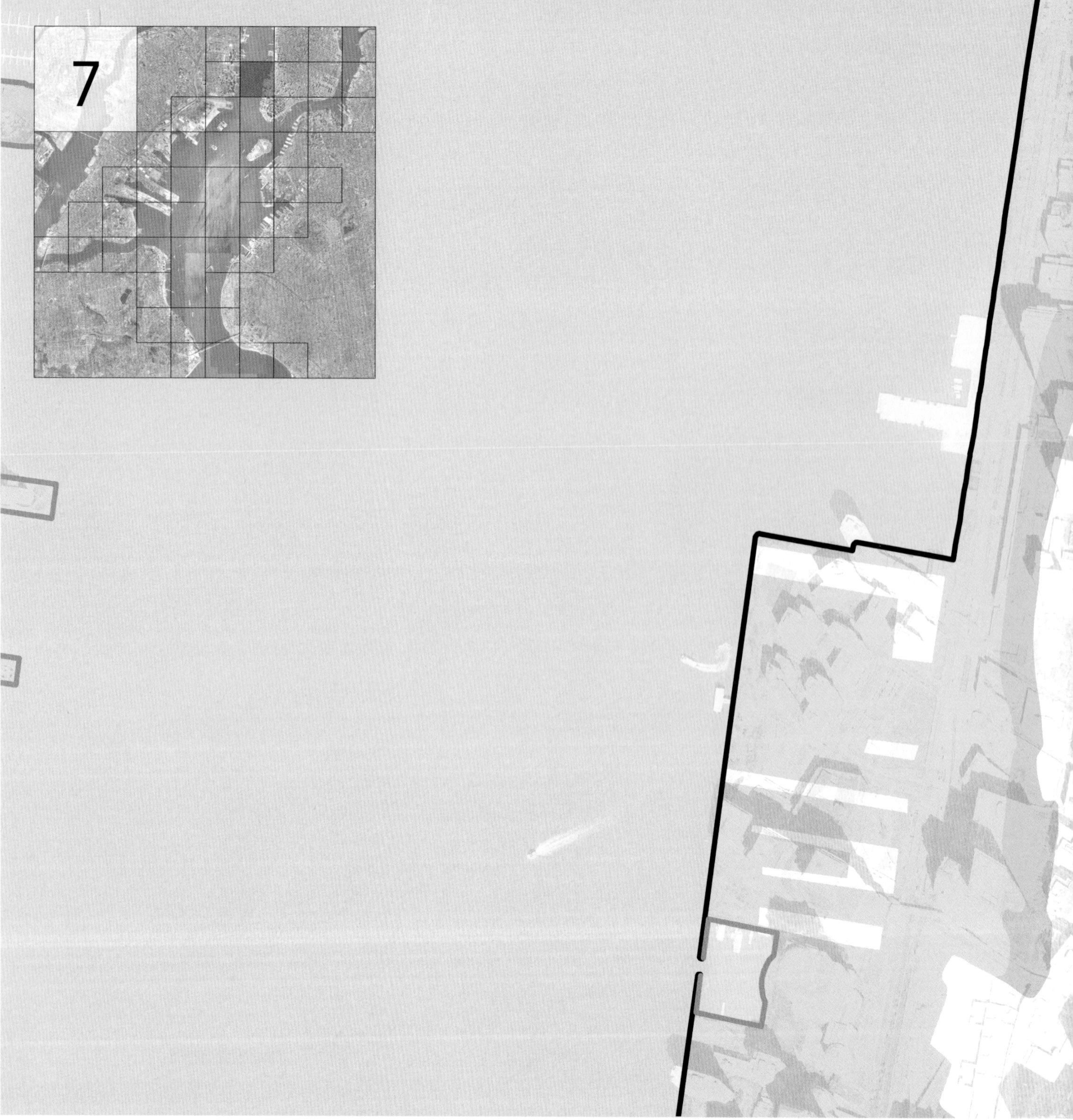
7

0
500
1,000 ft

8

0
500
1,000 ft

9

0
500
1,000 ft

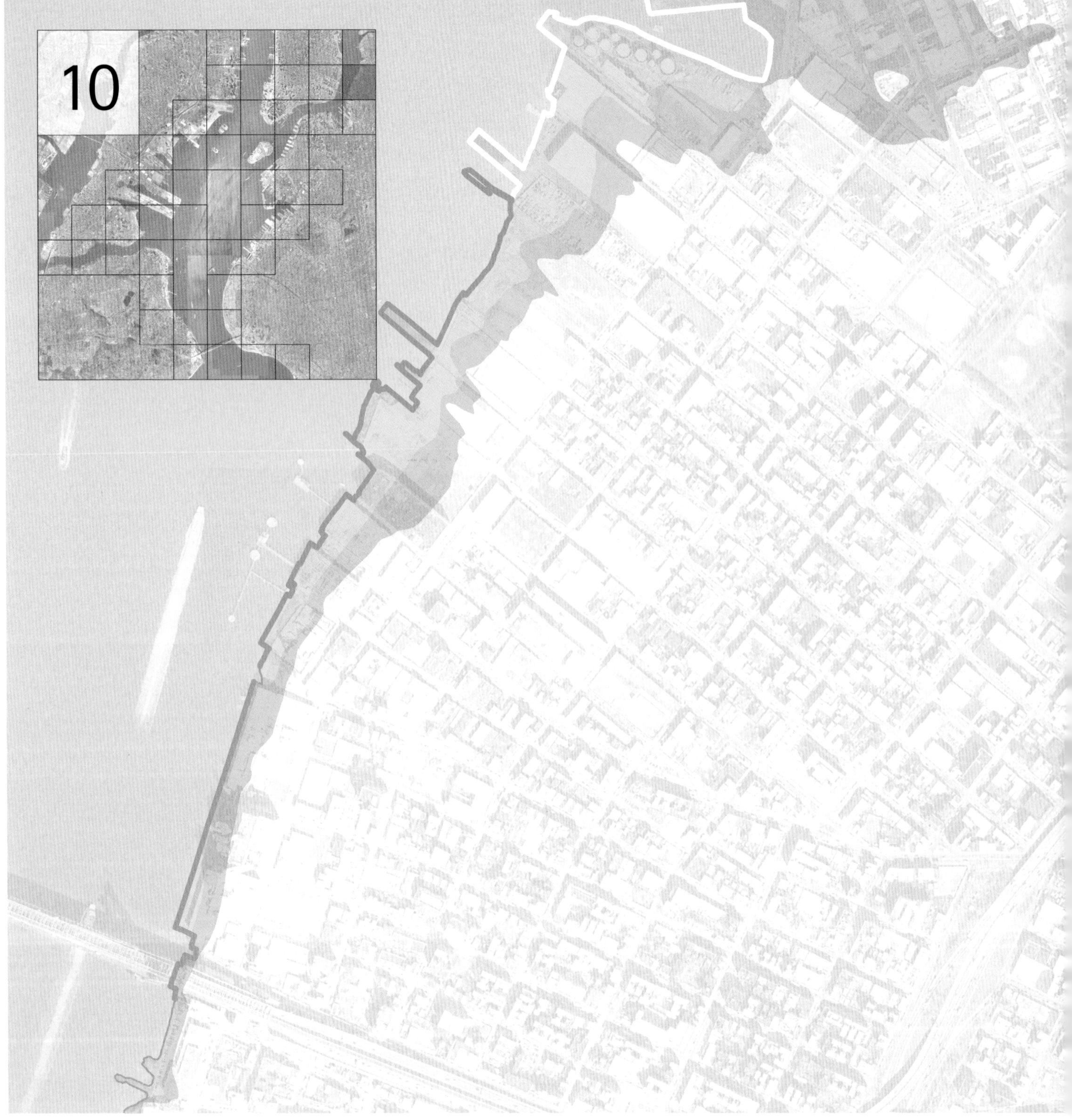
10

0
500
1,000 ft

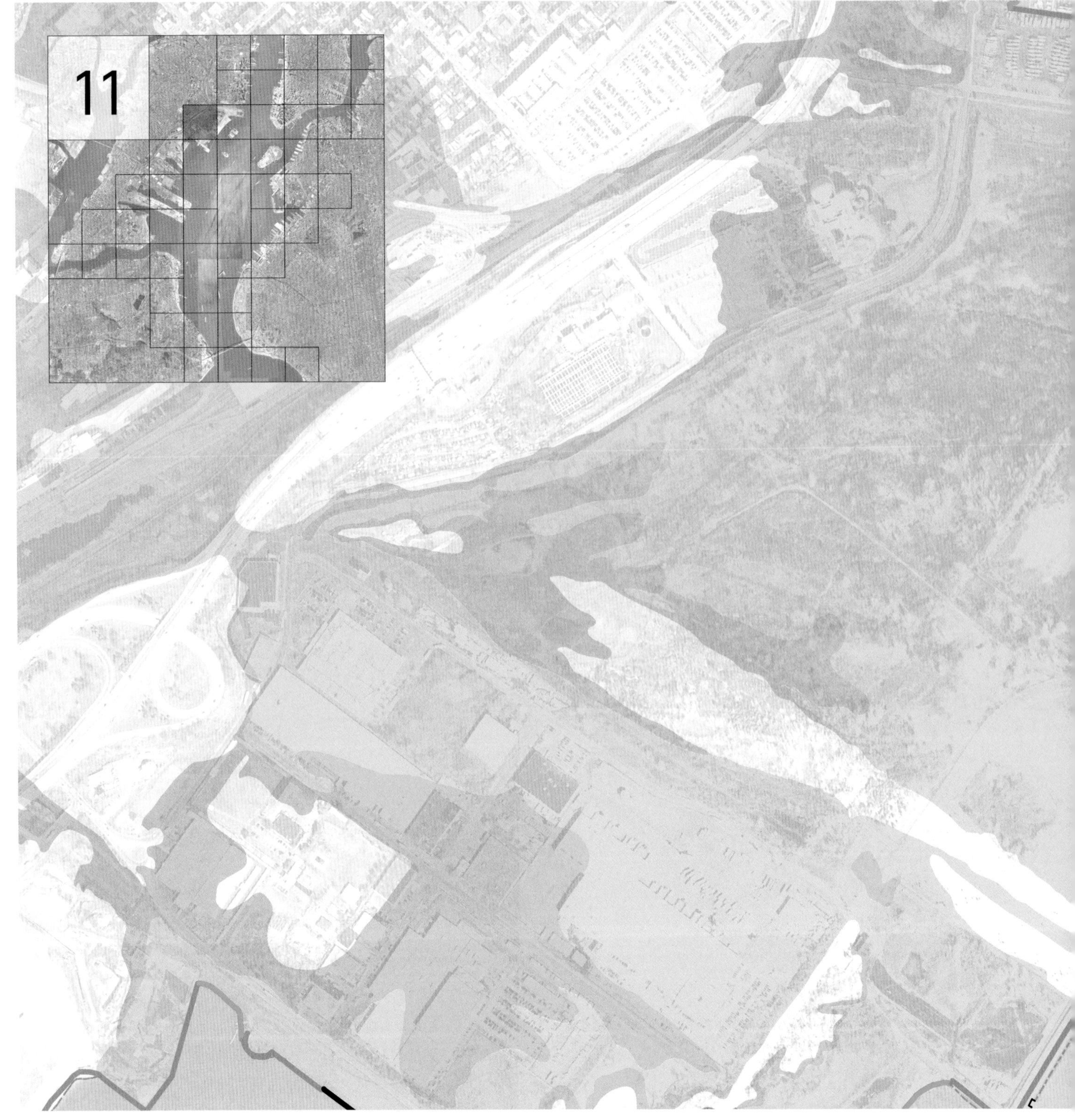
11

0
500
1,000 ft

12

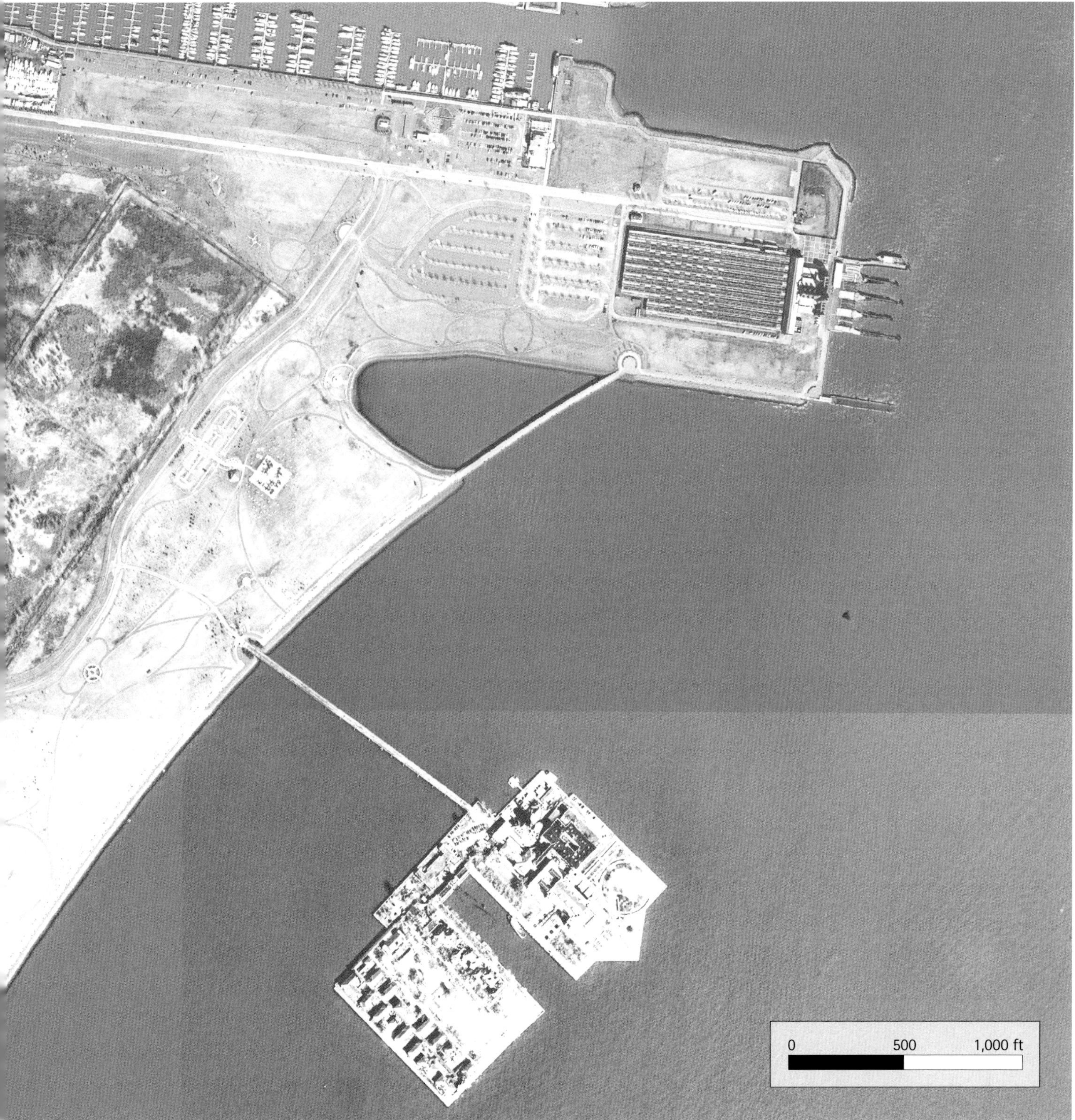
0
500
1,000 ft

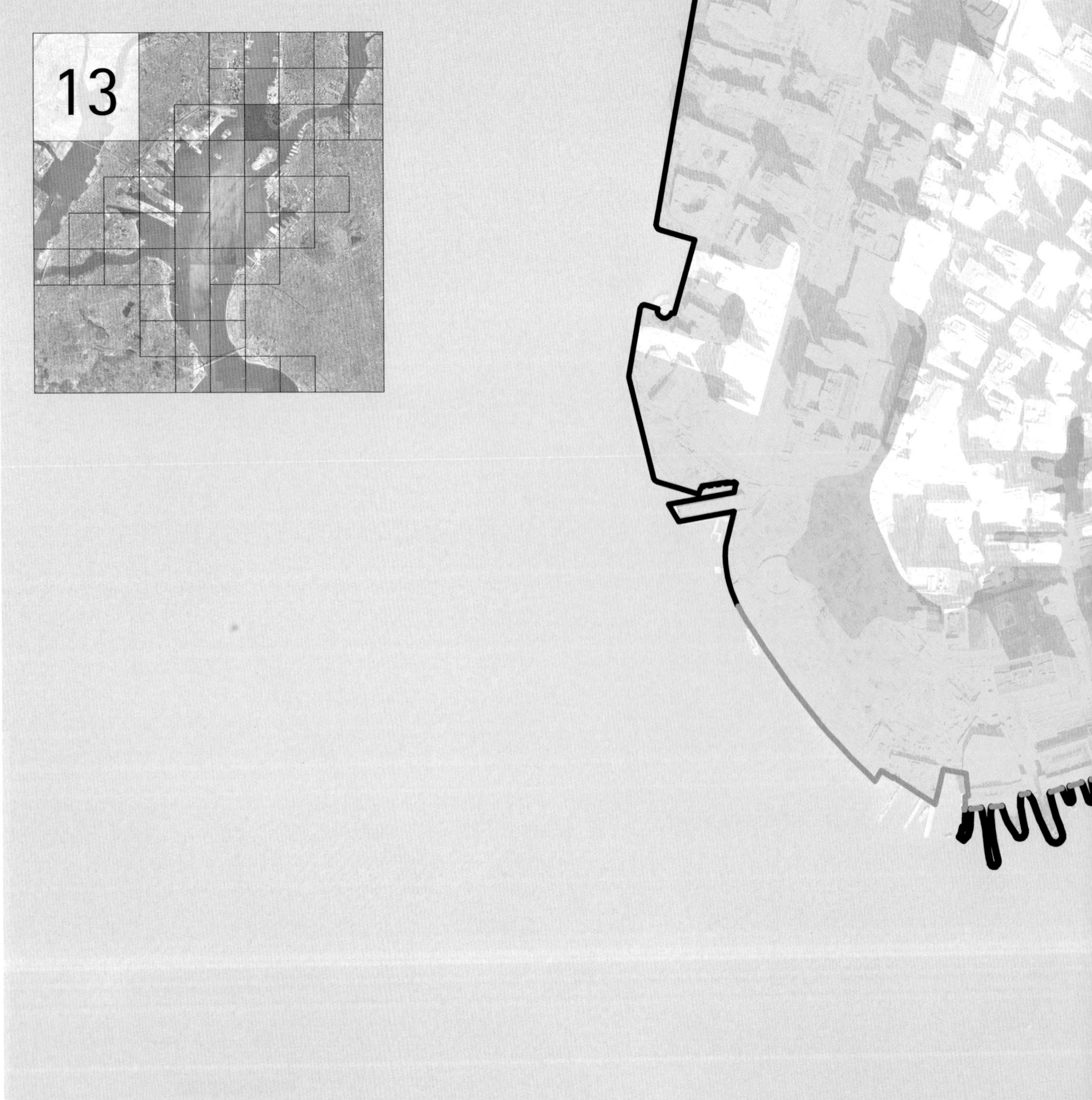
13

0
500
1,000 ft

14

0
500
1,000 ft

15

0
500
1,000 ft

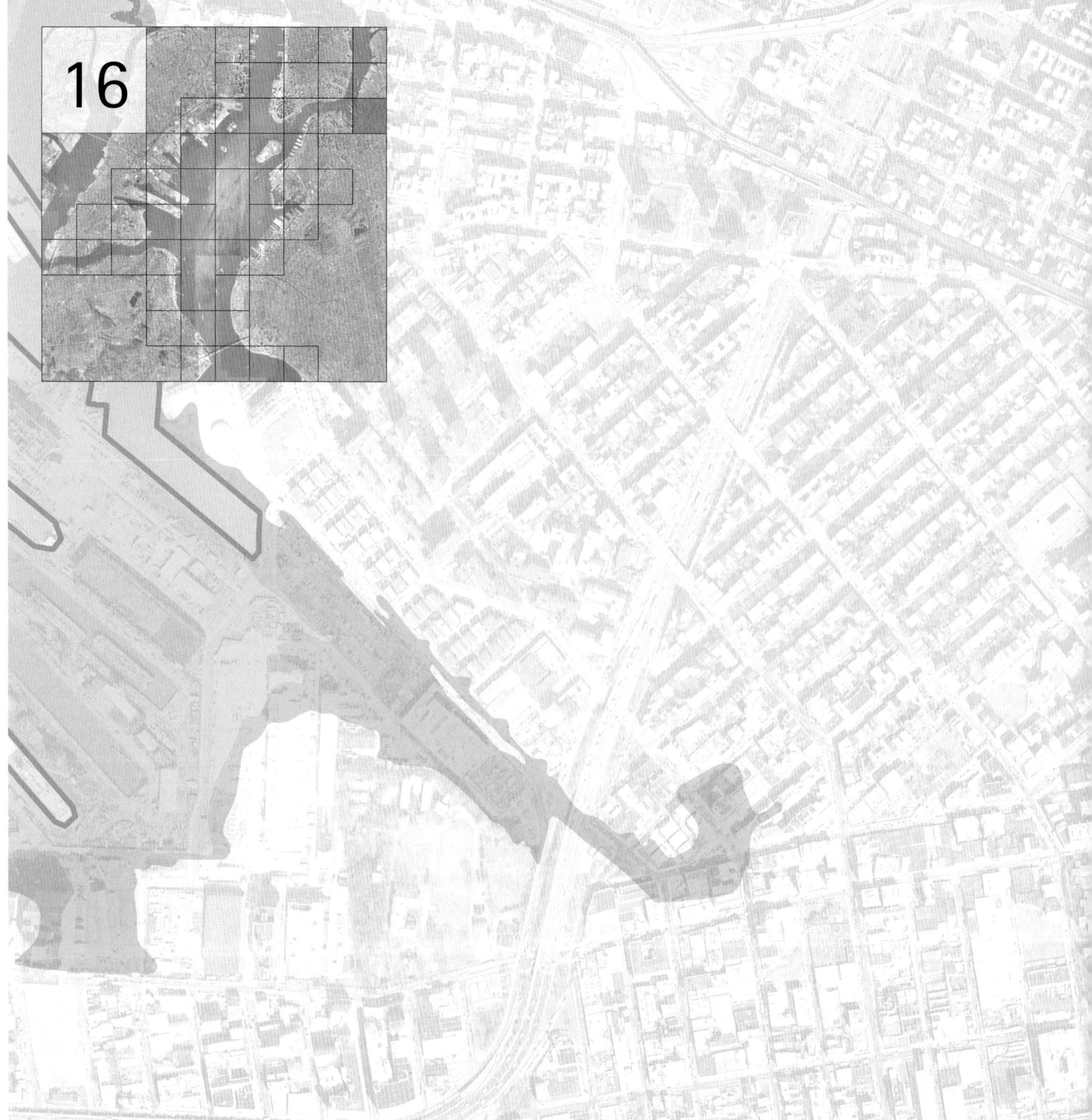
16

0
500
1,000 ft

17

0
500
1,000 ft

18

0
500
1,000 ft

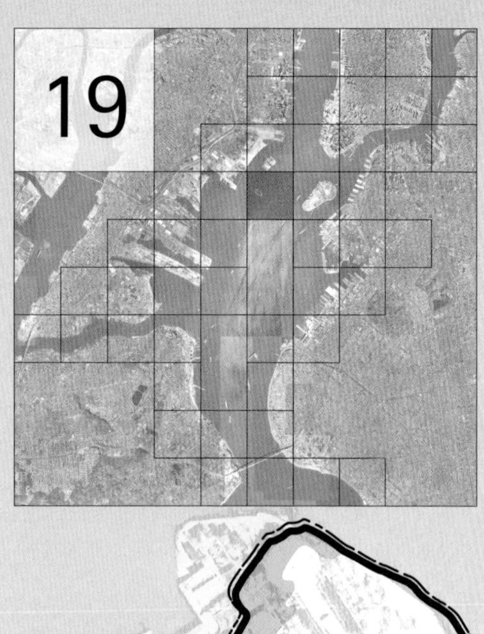
19

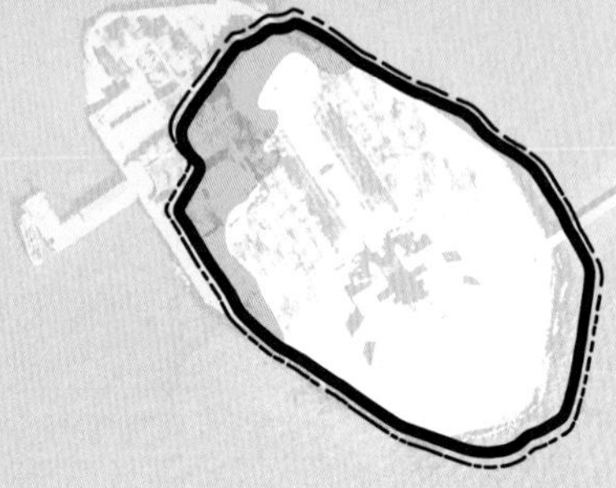

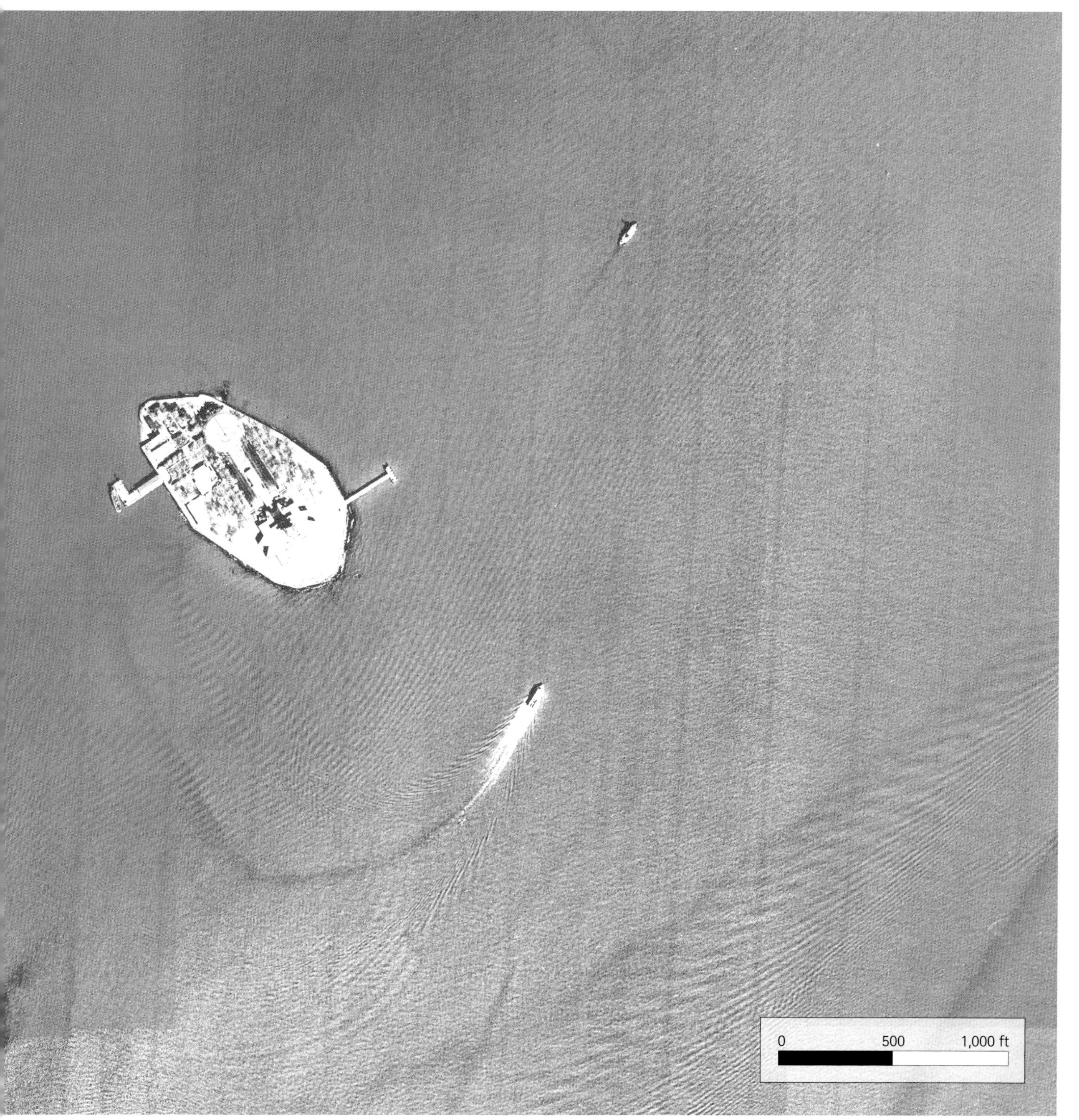
0
500
1,000 ft

20

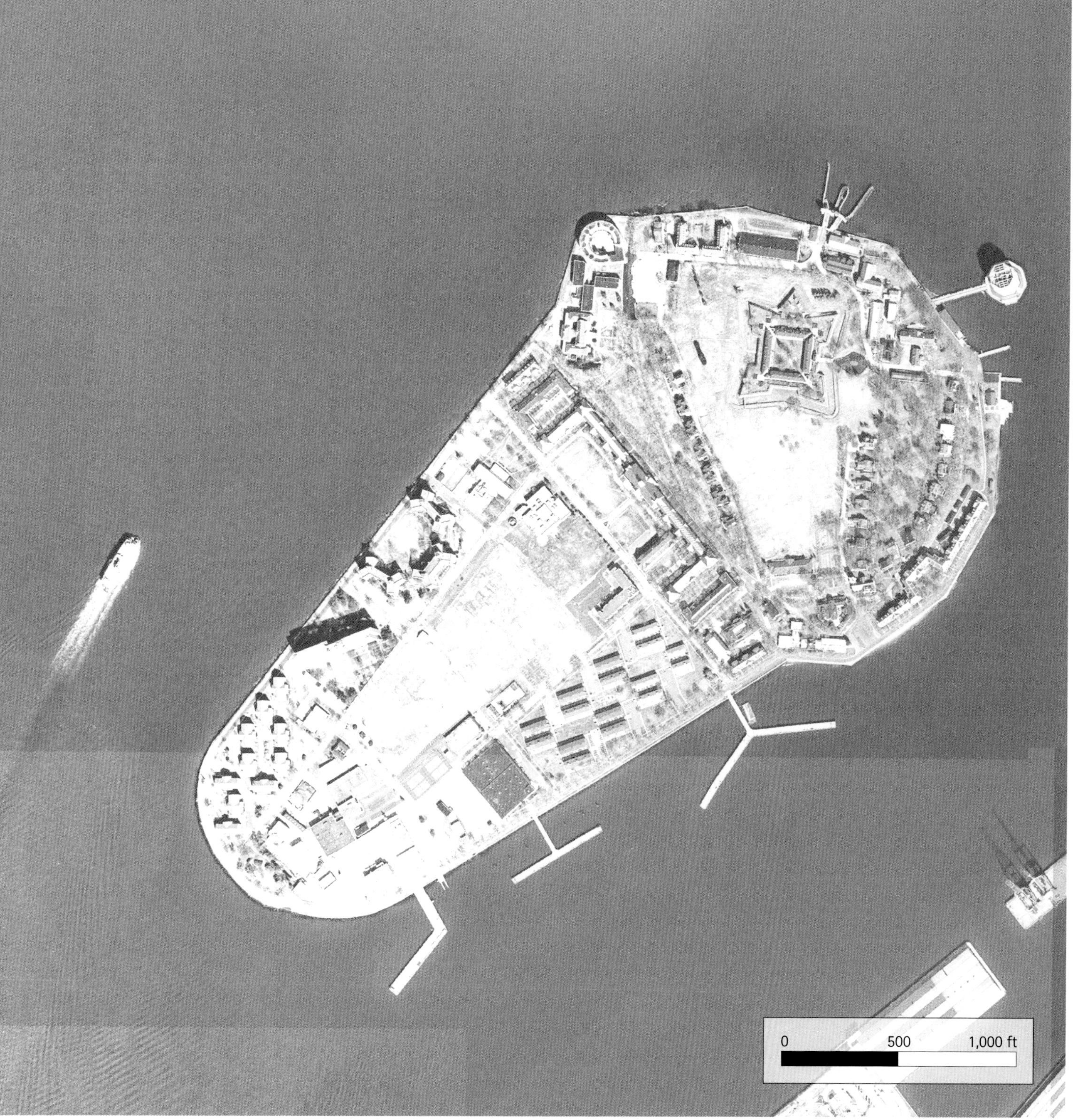
0
500
1,000 ft

21

0
500
1,000 ft

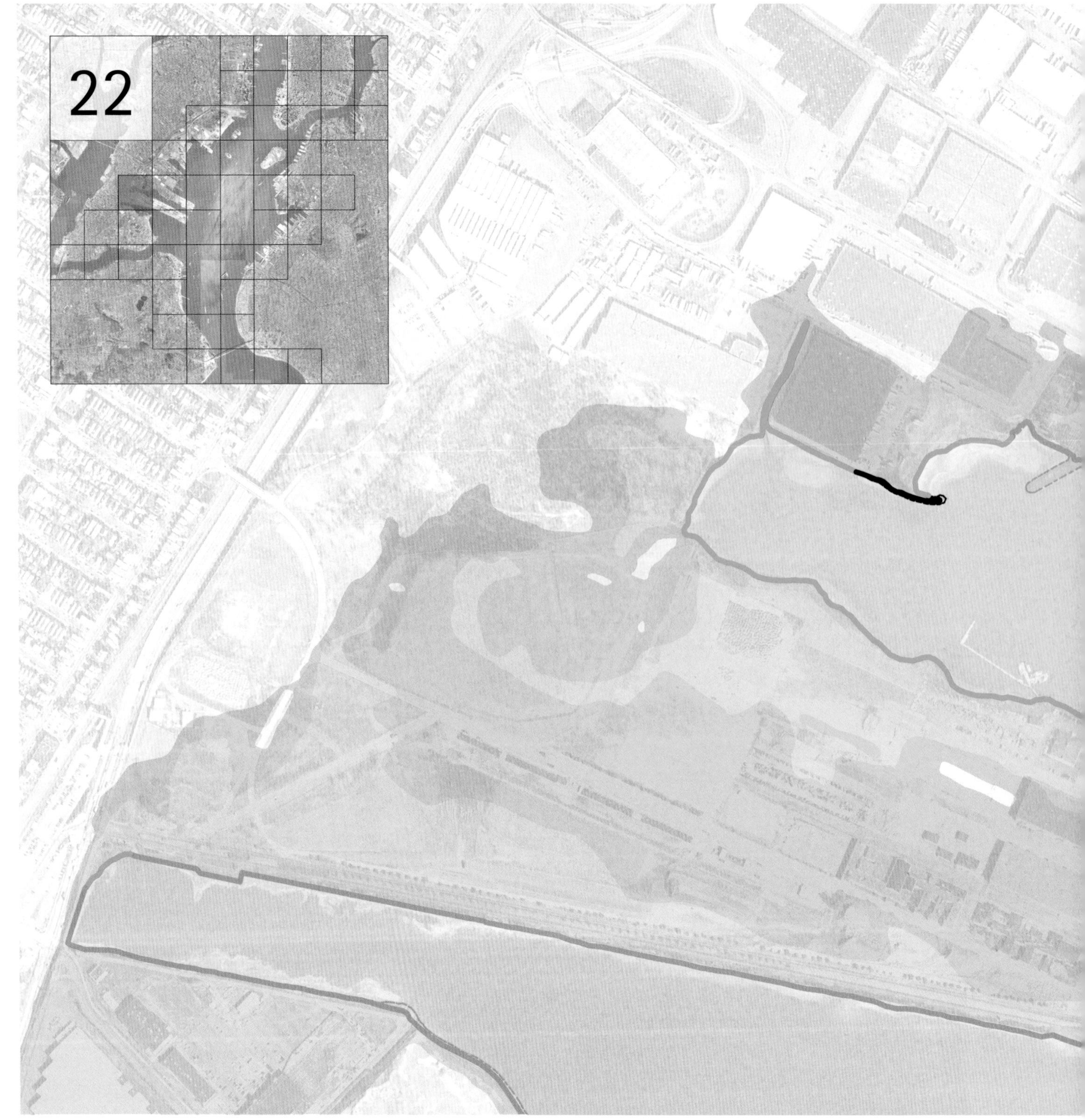
22

0
500
1,000 ft

23

0
500
1,000 ft

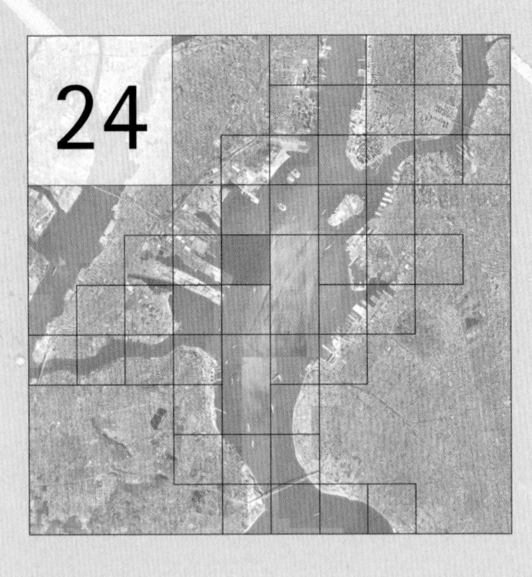
24

0
500
1,000 ft

25

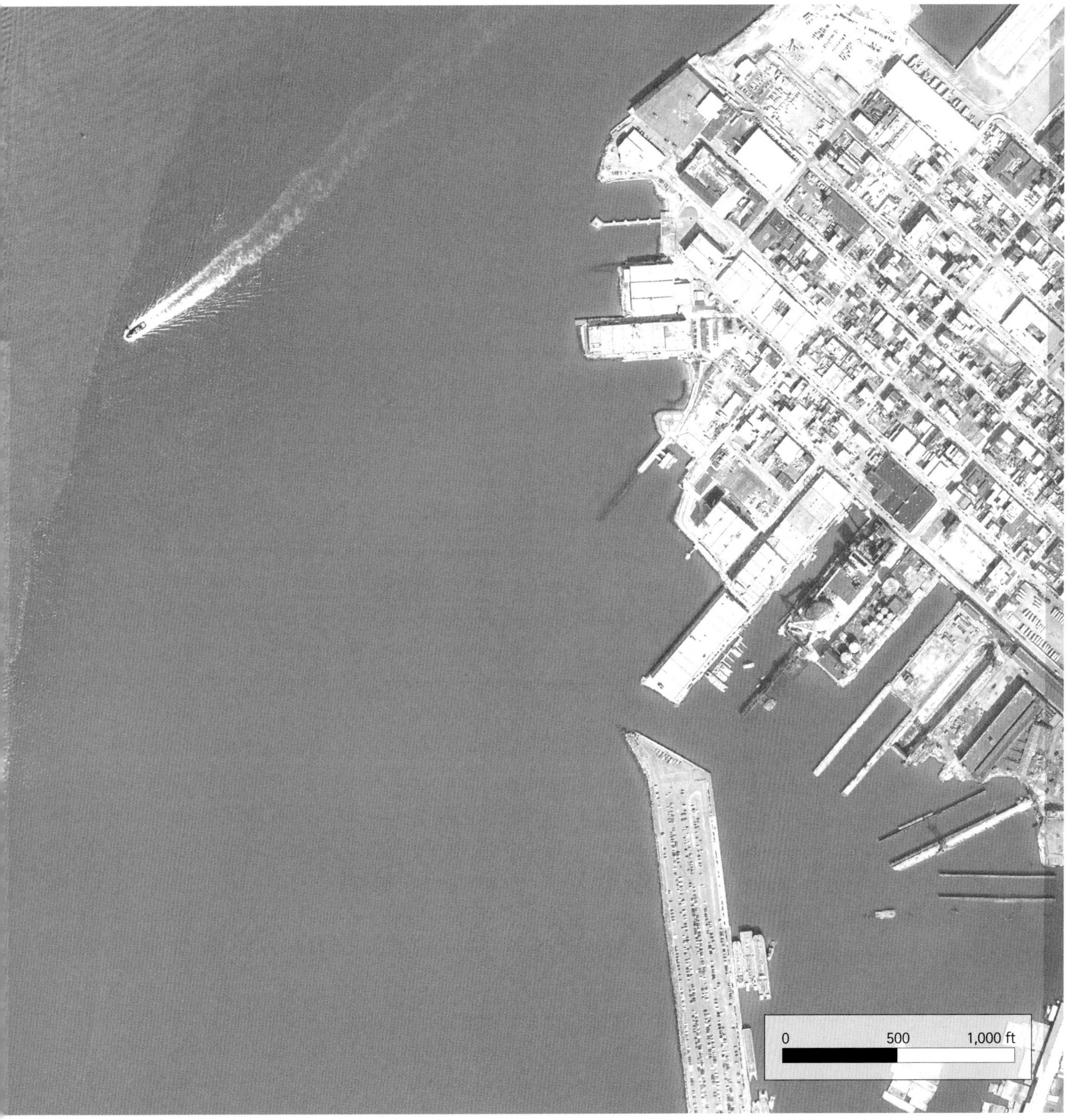
0
500
1,000 ft

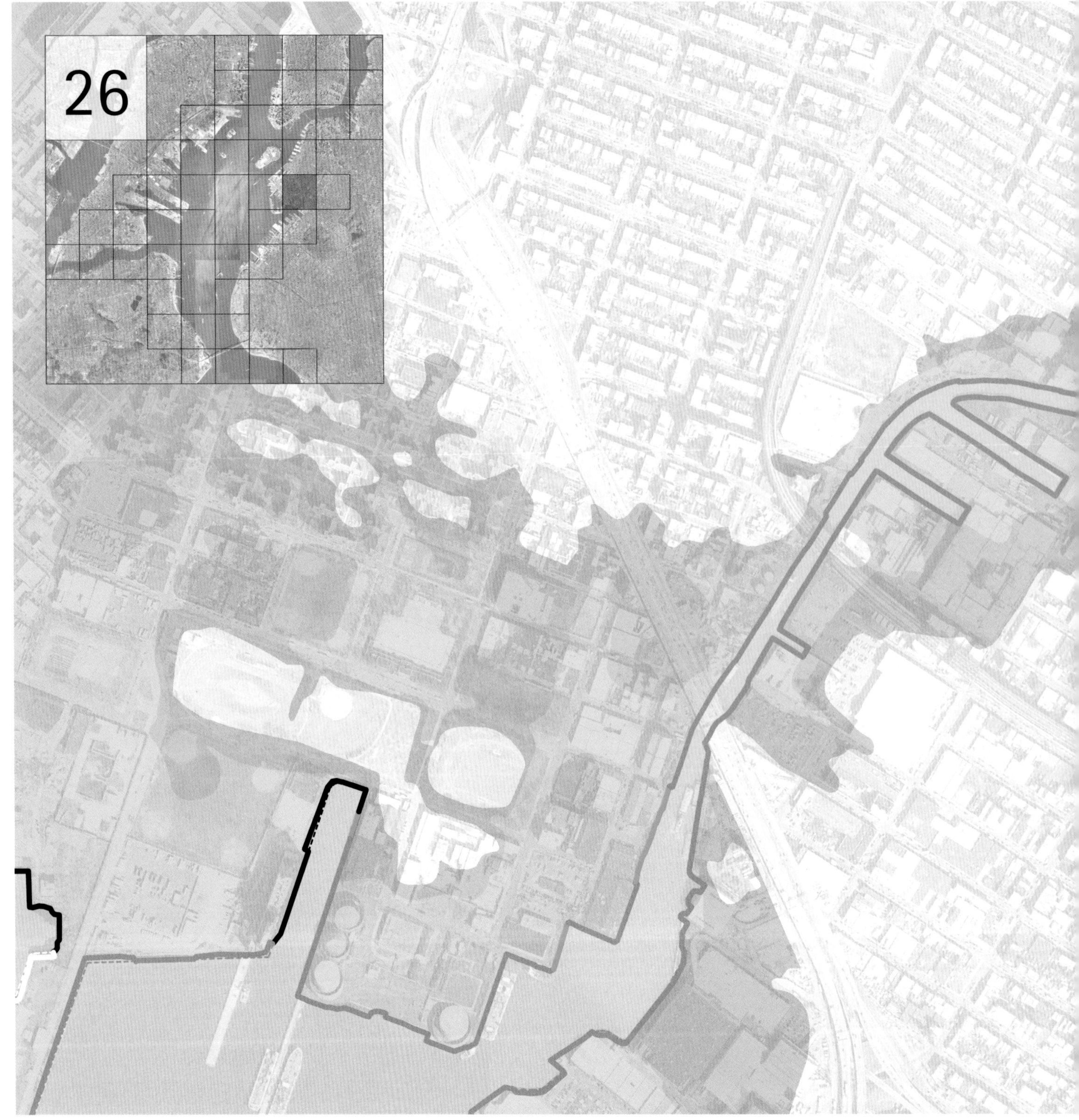
26

0
500
1,000 ft
HESS

27

0
500
1,000 ft

28

0
500
1,000 ft

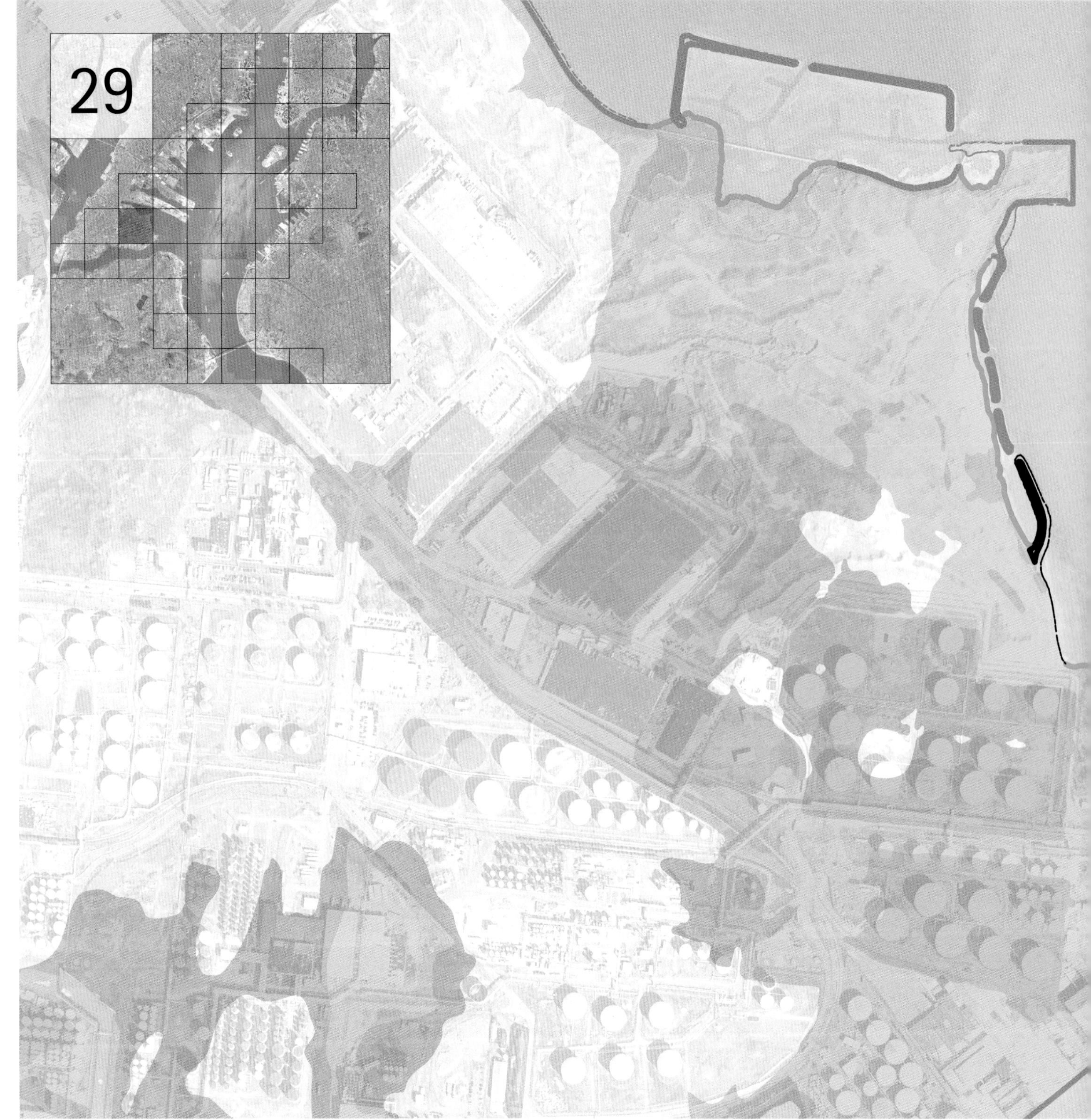
29

0
500
1,000 ft

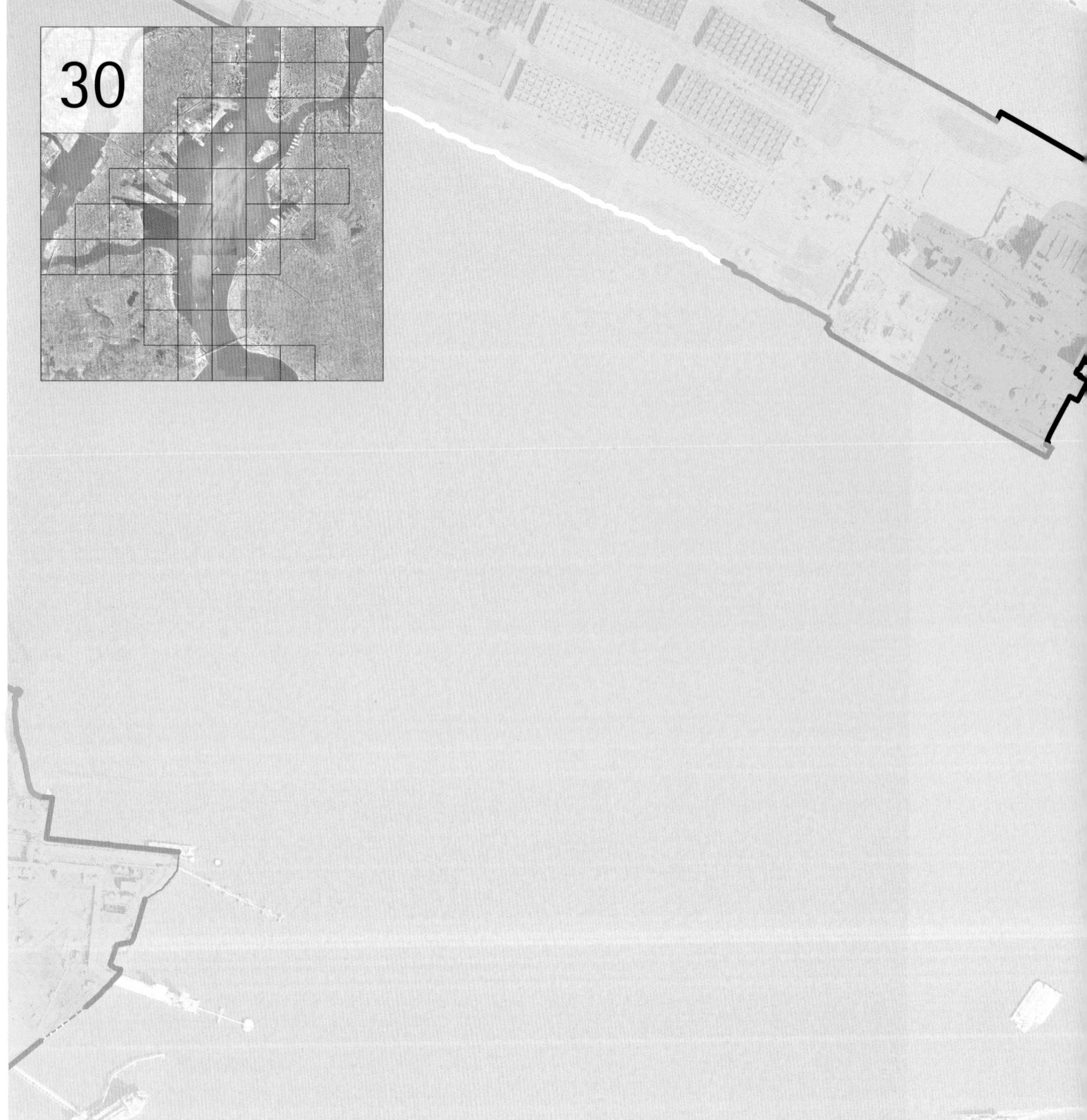
30

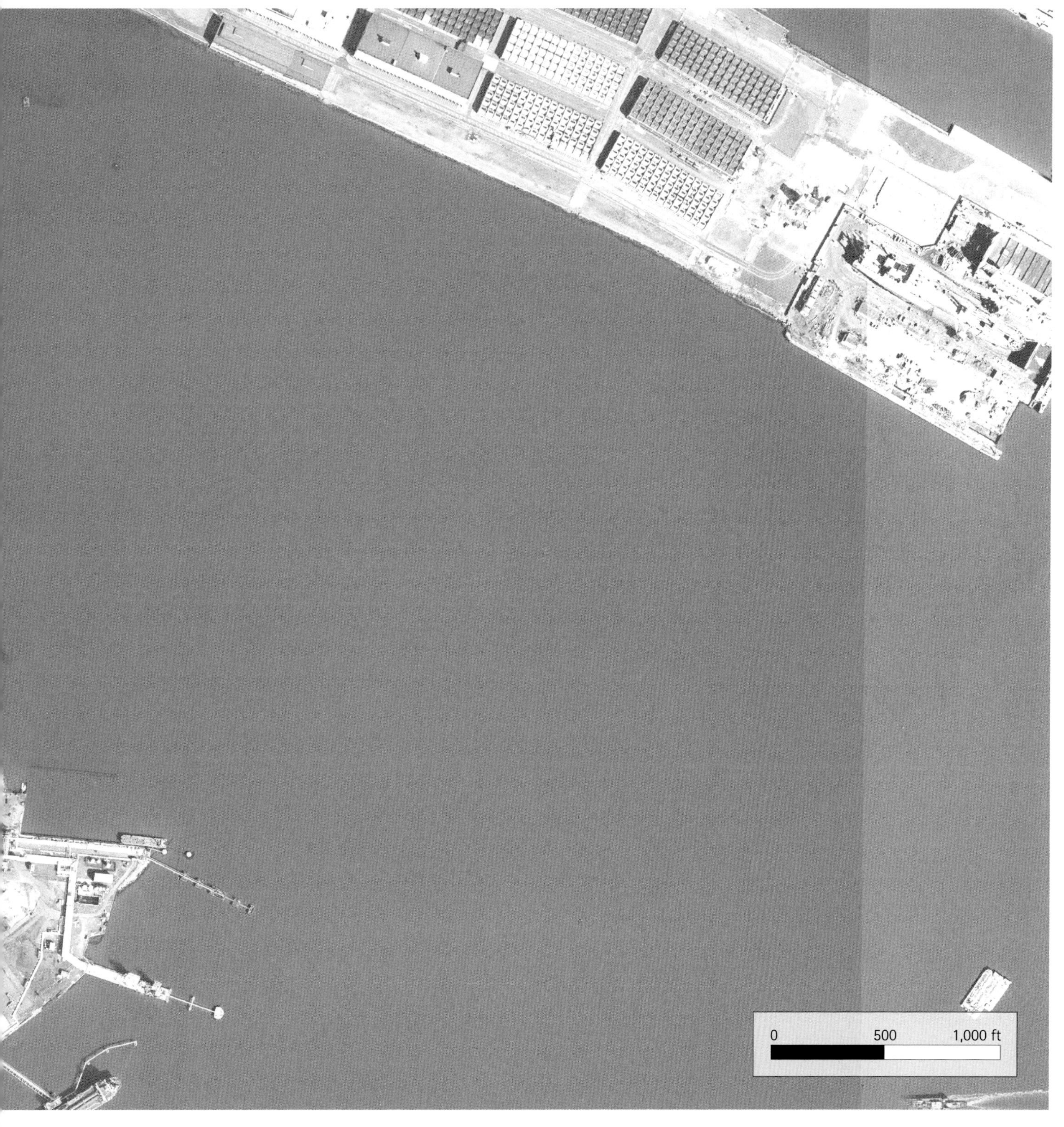
0
500
1,000 ft

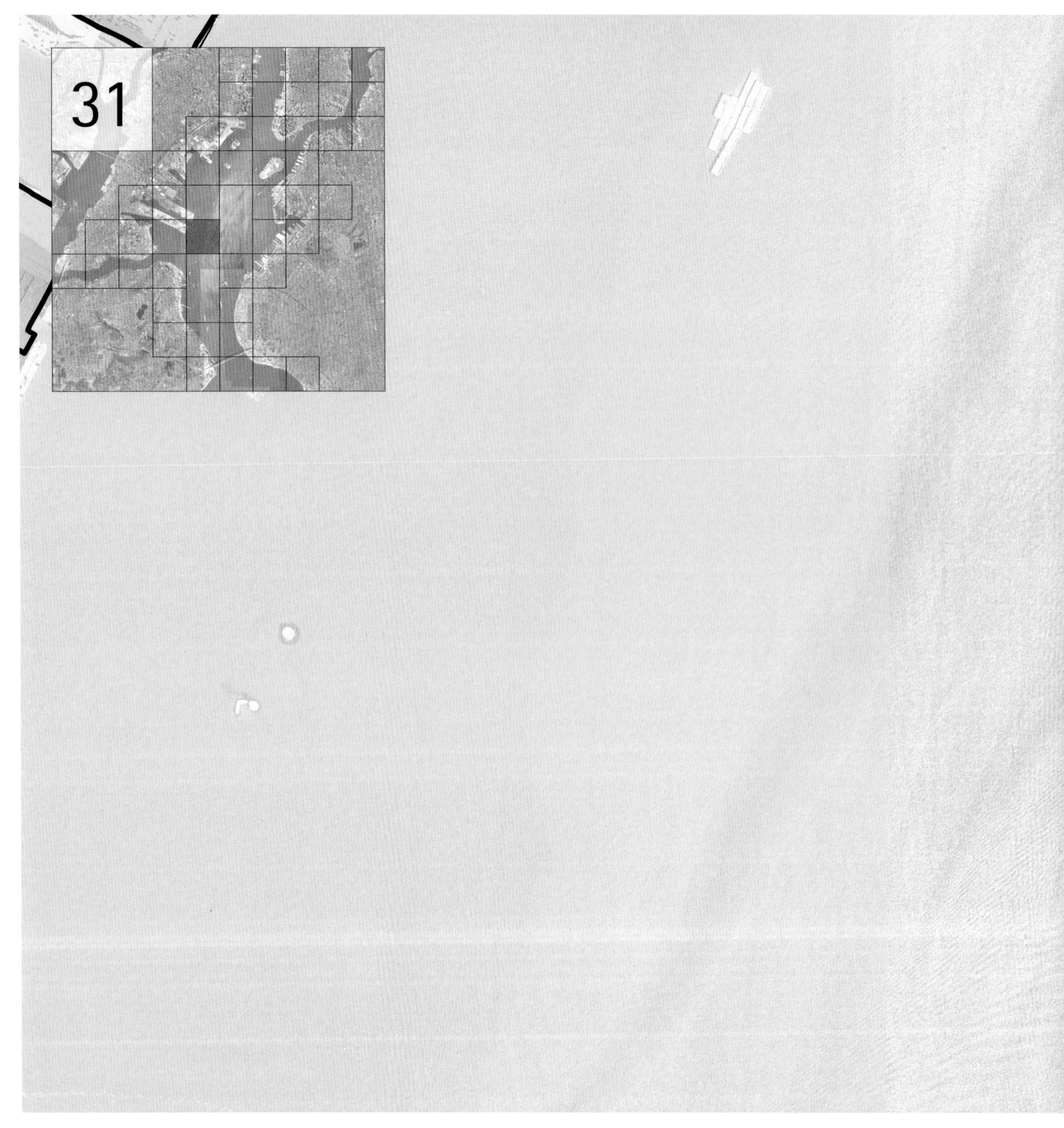
31

0
500
1,000 ft

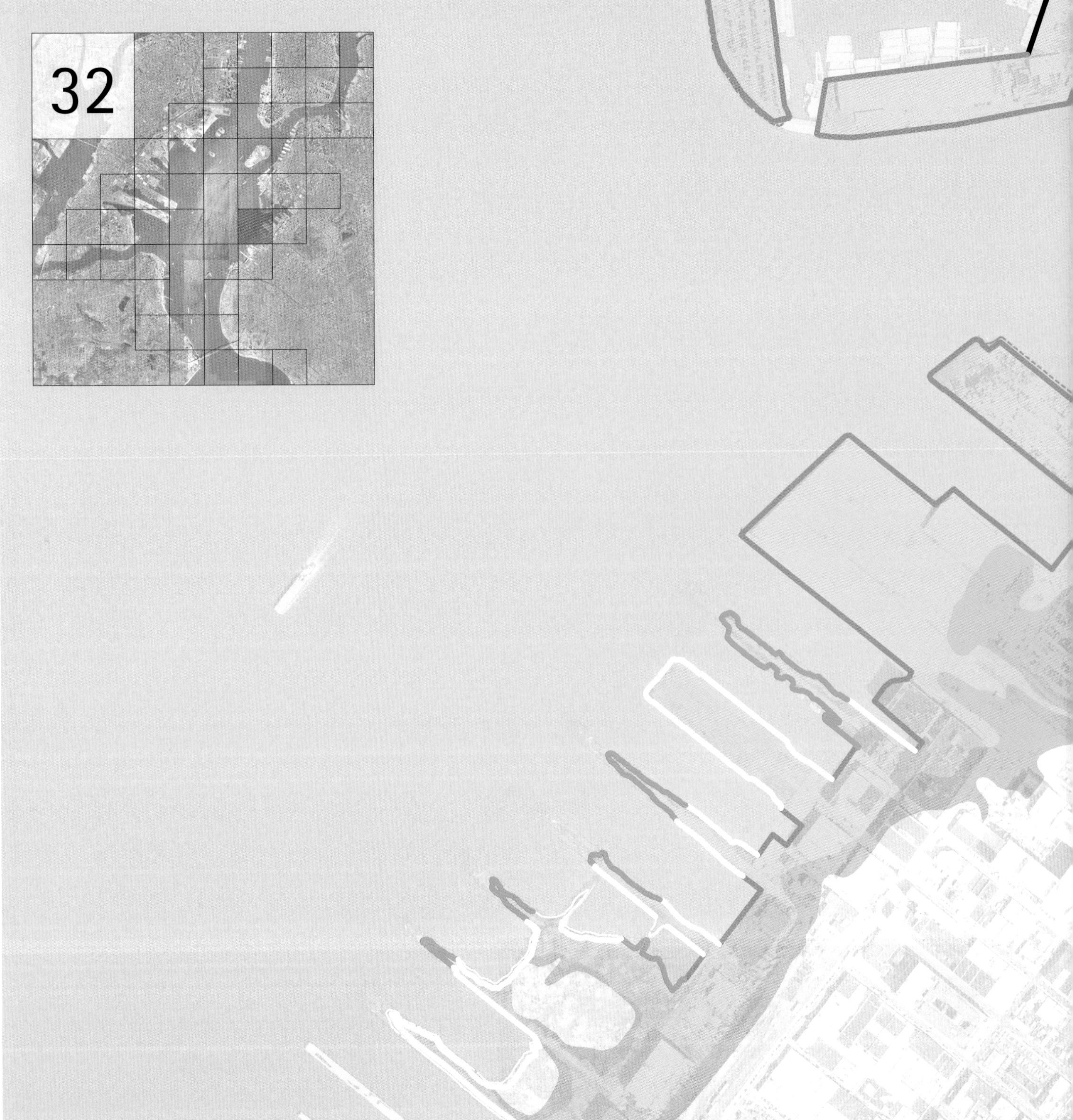
32

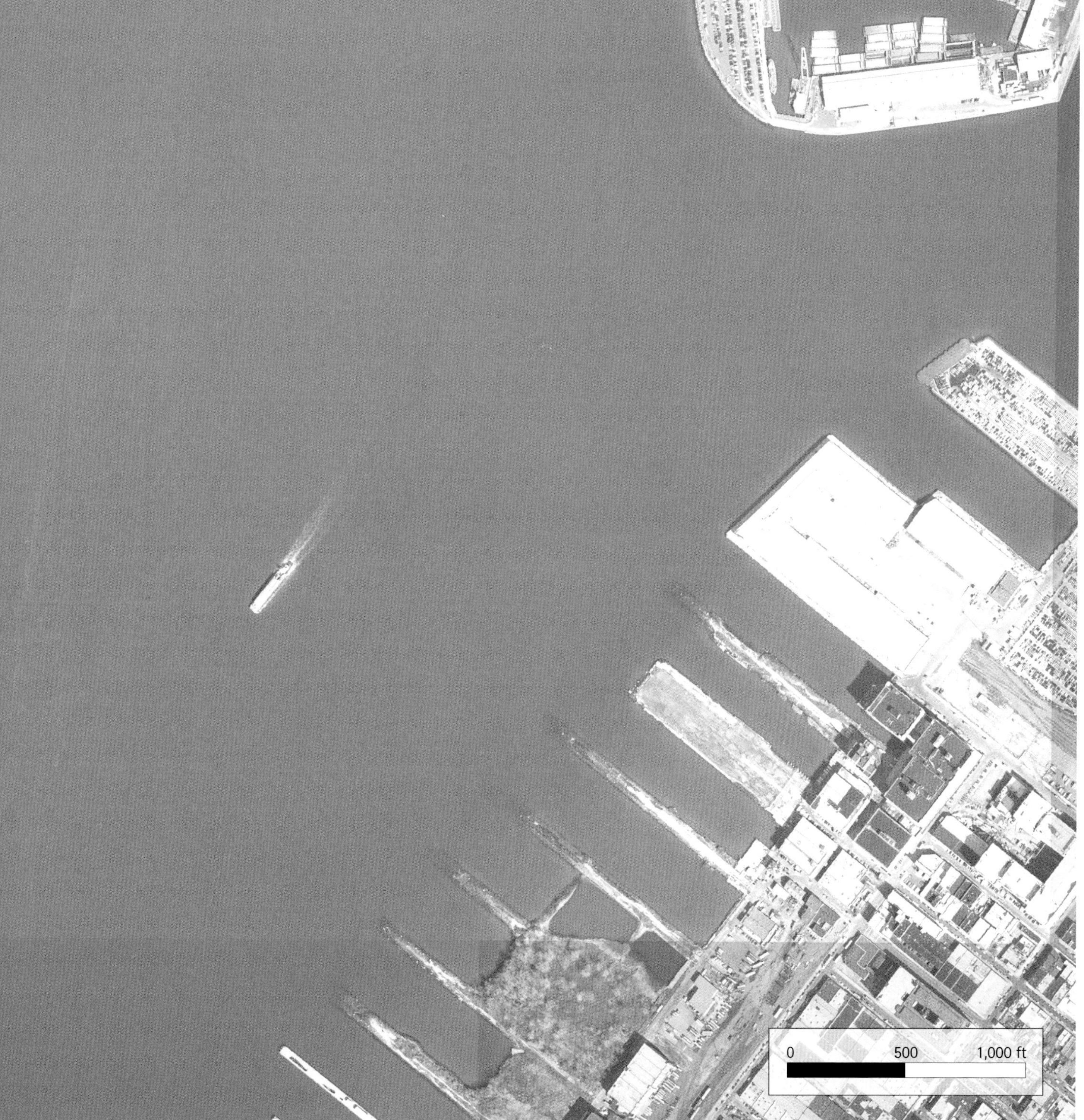
0
500
1,000 ft

33

0
500
1,000 ft

34

0
500
1,000 ft

35

0
500
1,000 ft

36

0
500
1,000 ft

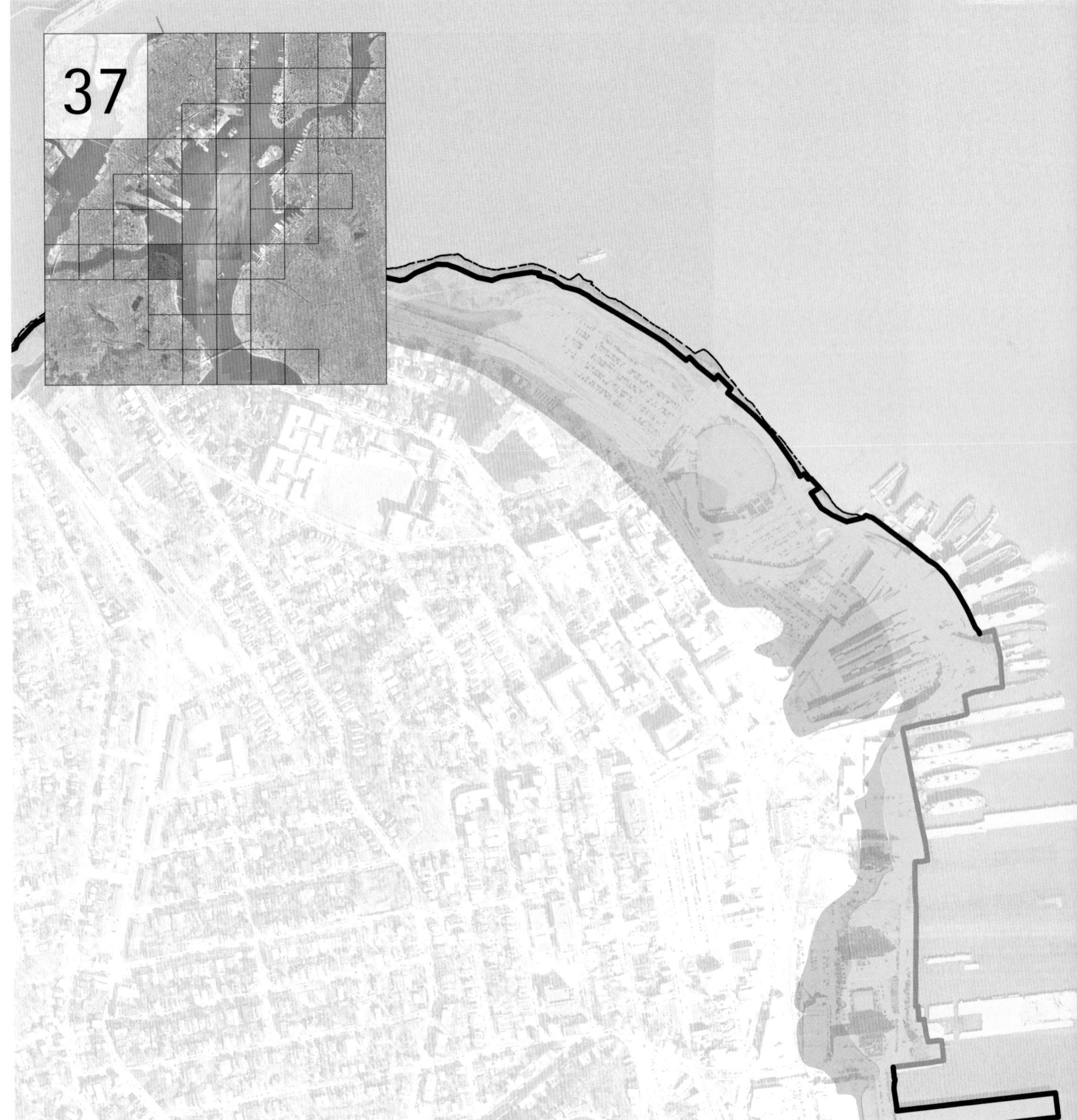

37

0
500
1,000 ft

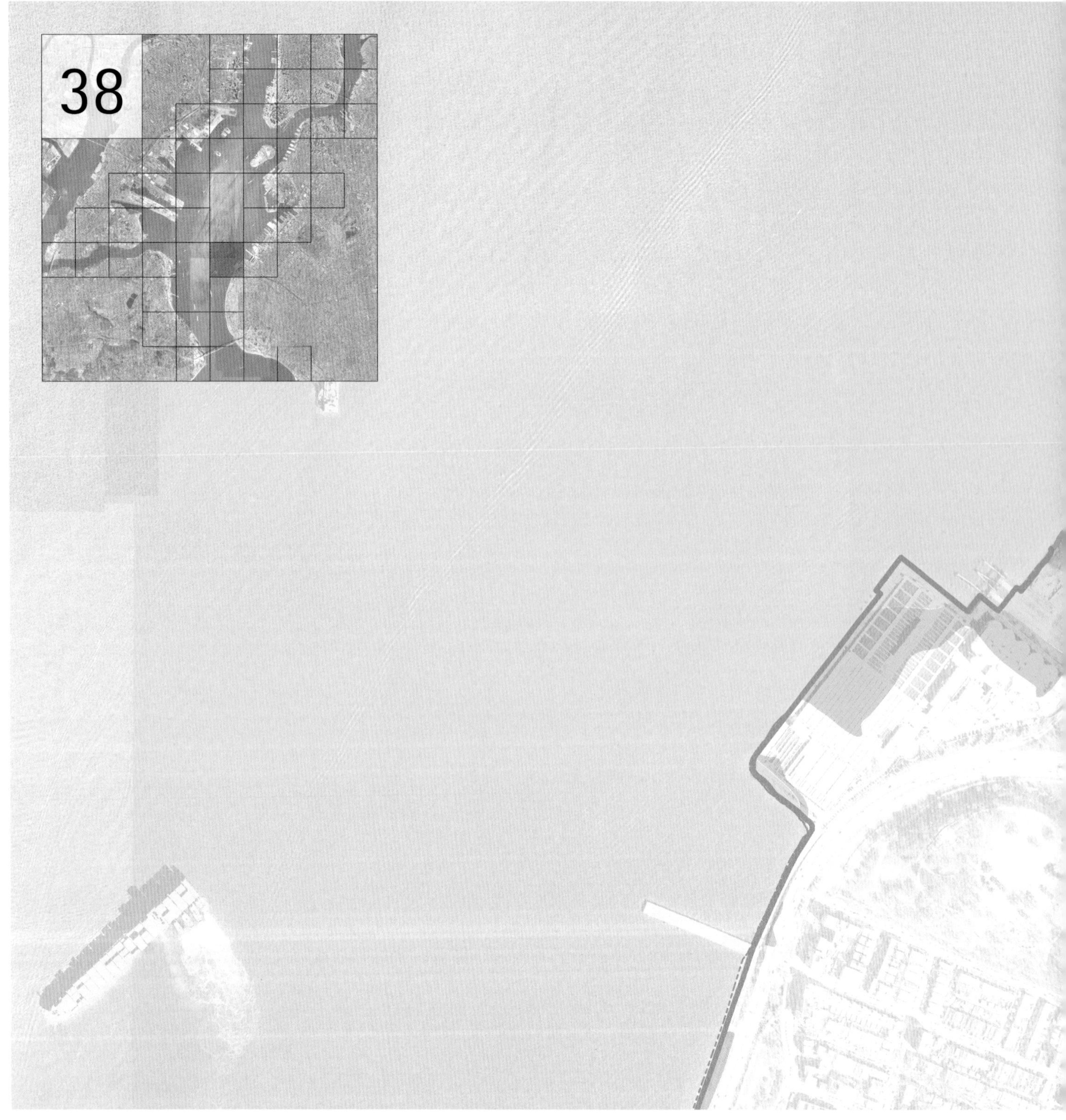
38

0
500
1,000 ft

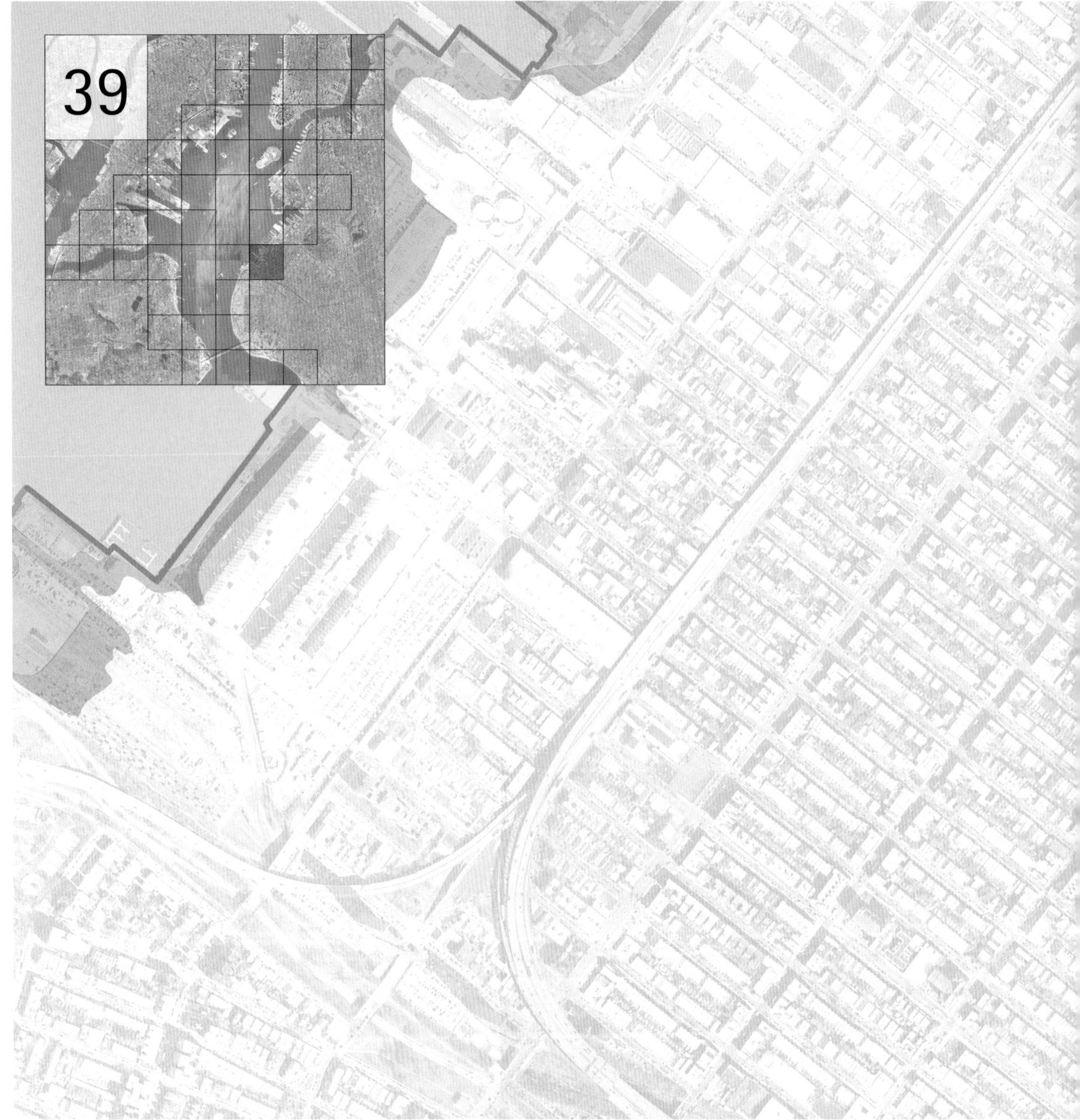
39

0
500
1,000 ft

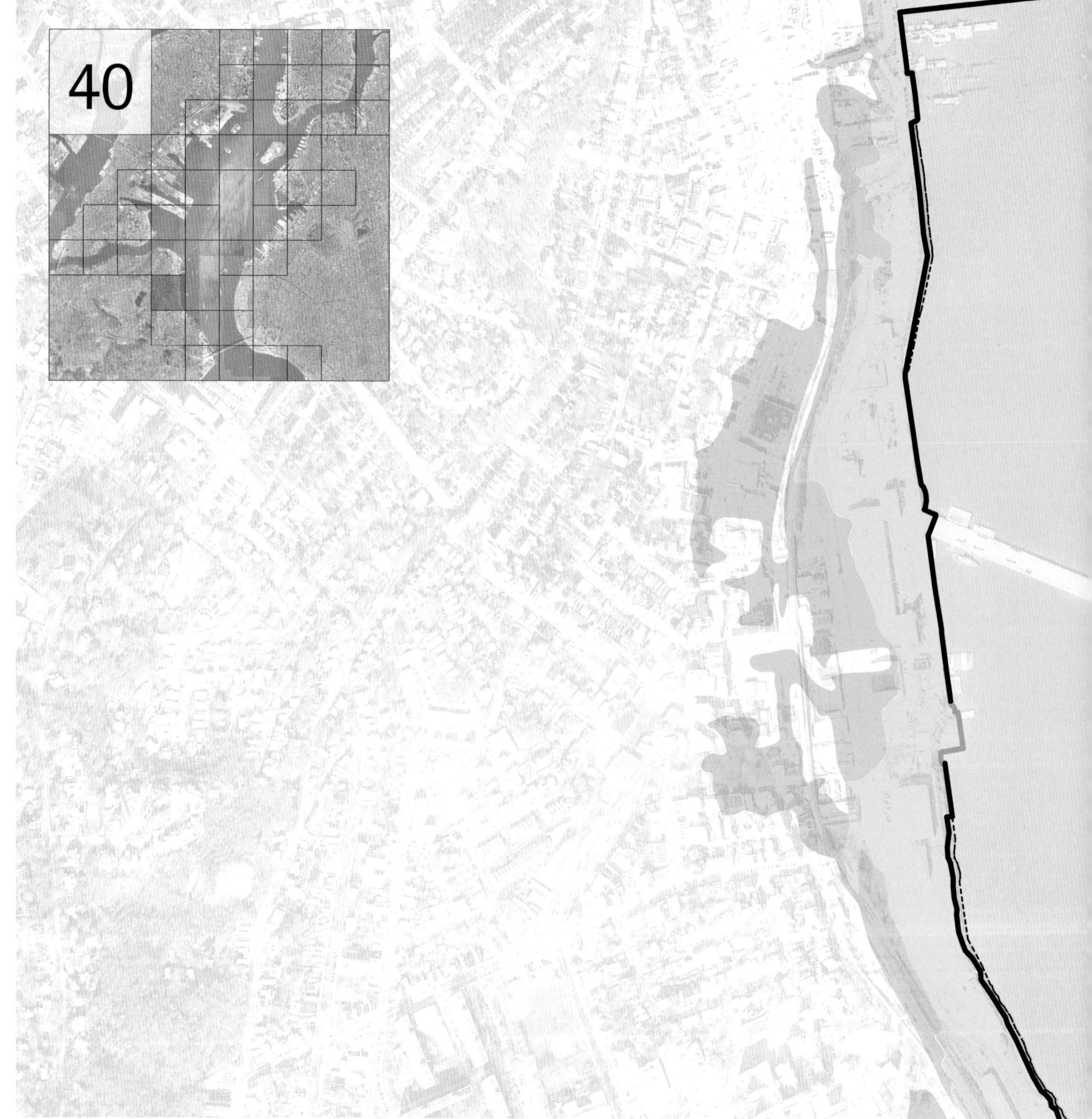
40

0
500
1,000 ft

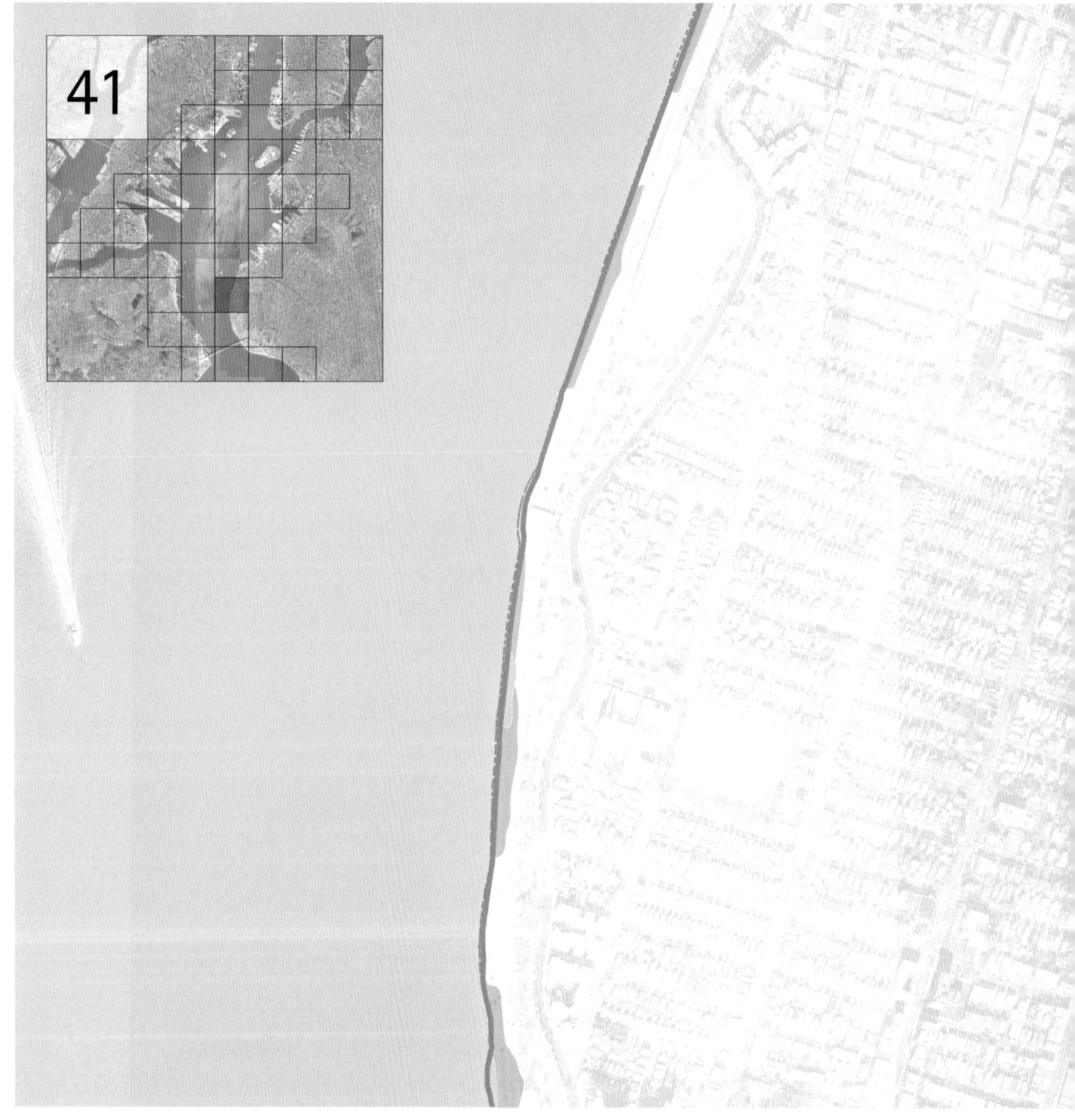
41

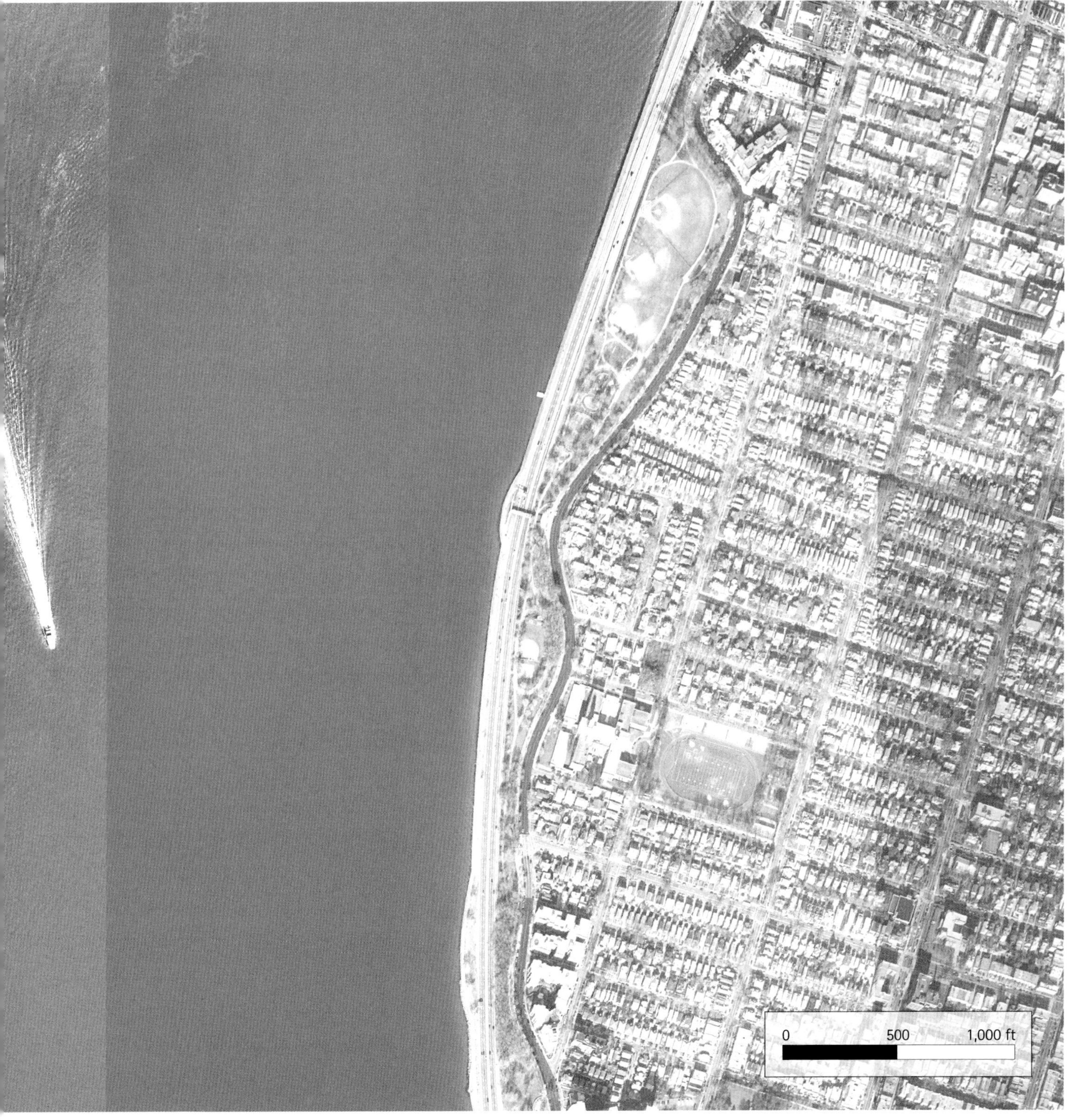
0
500
1,000 ft

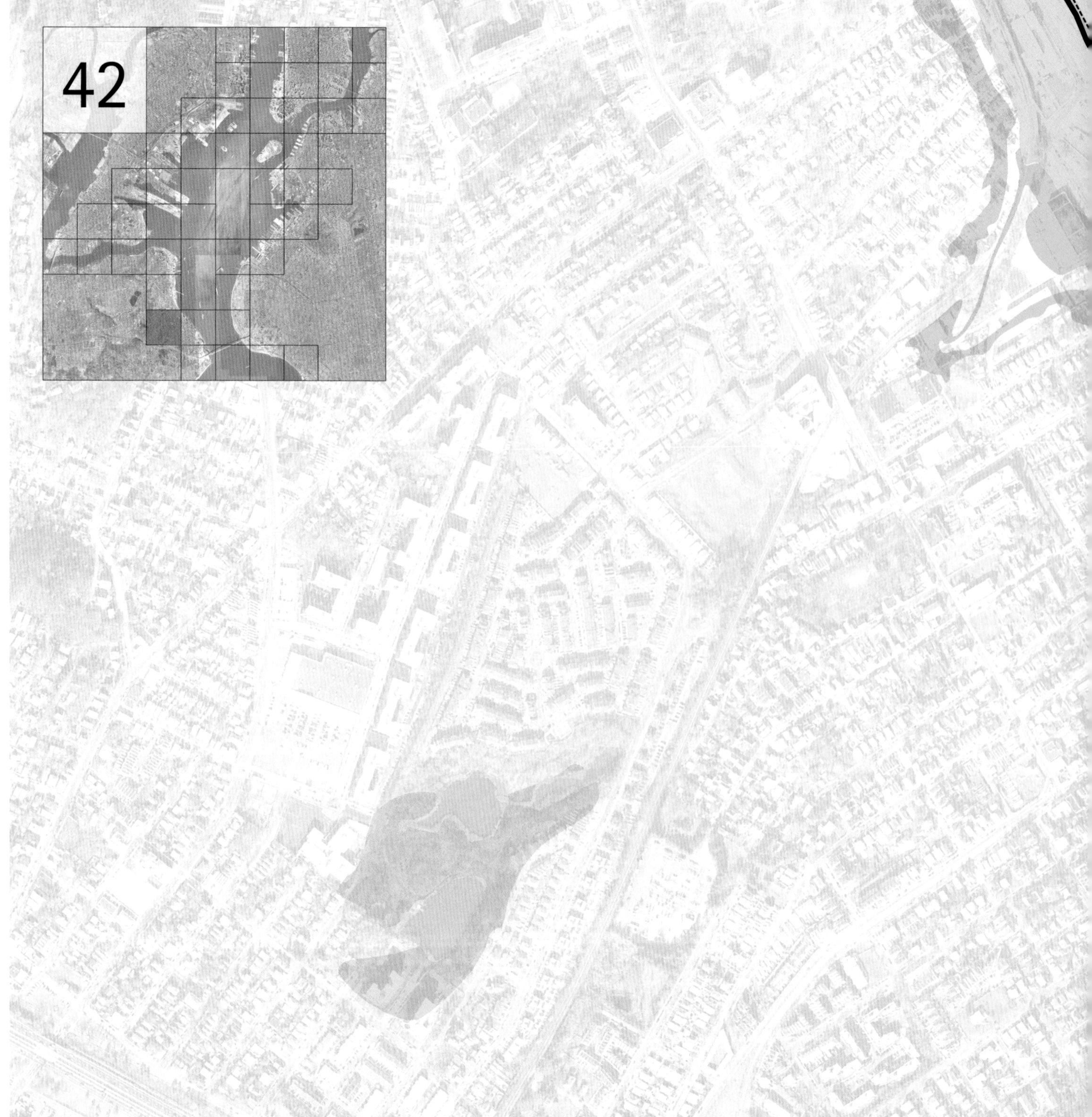
42

0
500
1,000 ft

43

0
500
1,000 ft

44

0
500
1,000 ft

45

0
500
1,000 ft

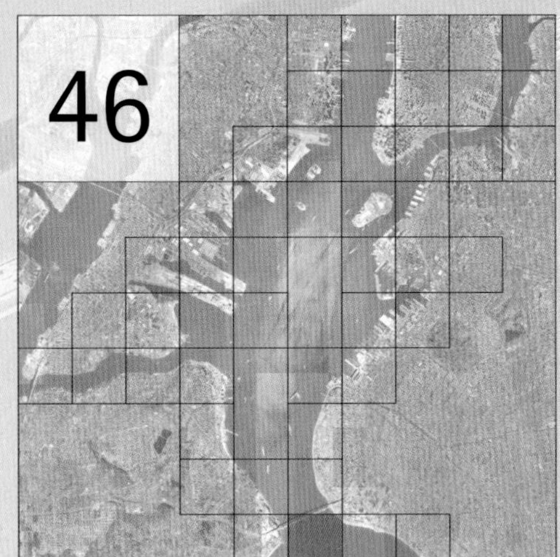
46

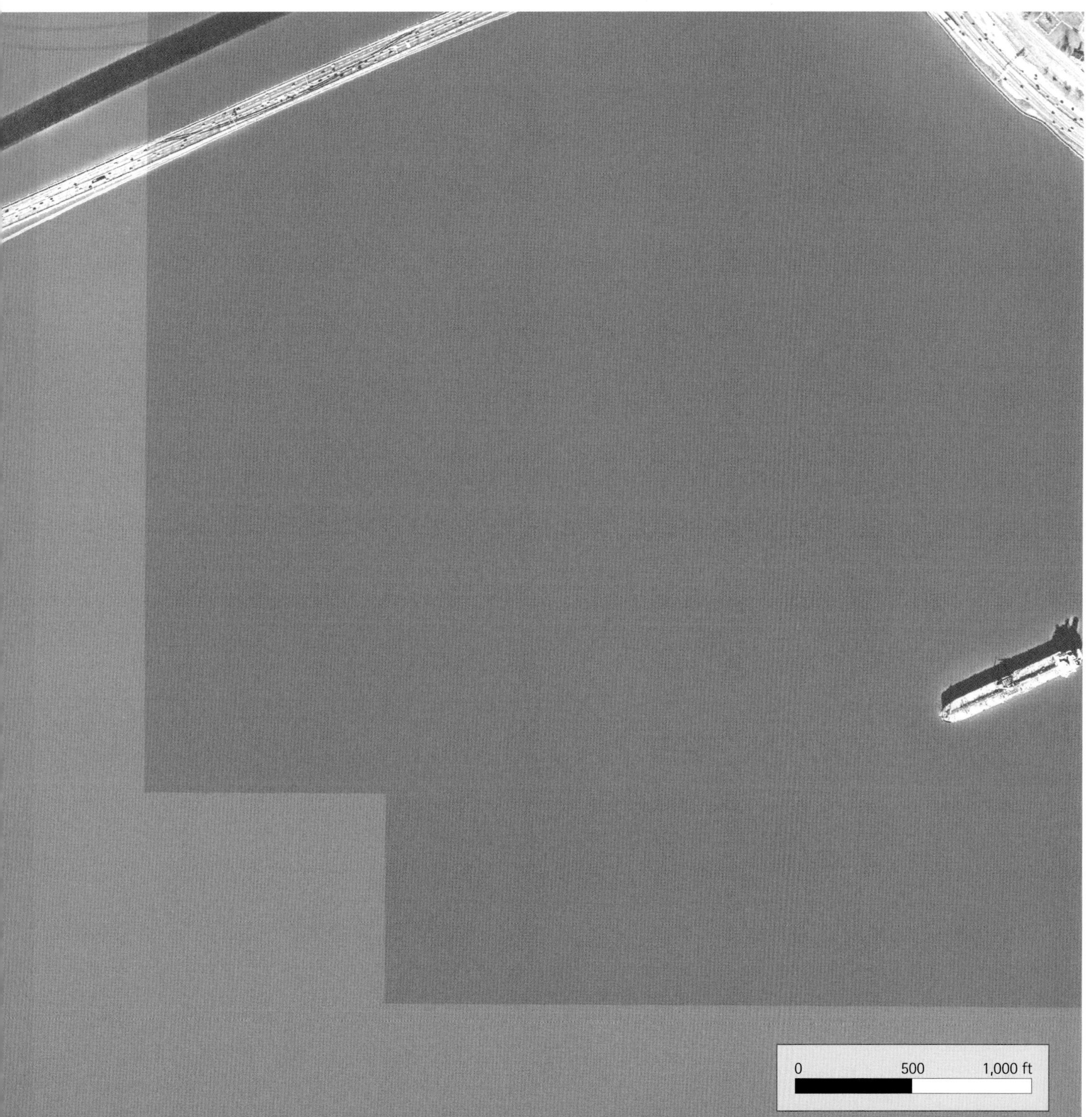
0
500
1,000 ft

47

0
500
1,000 ft

48

0
500
1,000 ft

TOOLS AND RESOURCES

THE REEFBALL FOUNDATION, INC.
www.reefball.org

The Reef Ball Foundation manufactures reef balls for open ocean deployment in sizes which range from one foot in diameter (thirty-five pounds) to eight and one half feet in diameter (8,000 pounds). Made from pH balanced micro silica concrete, reef balls are hollow domes perforated with several holes of various size to closely approximate natural reef conditions. The surface is treated to have a roughened finish to promote the growth of settling marine organisms such as algae, corals, coralline algae, and sponges.

Reef balls promote natural reef rehabilitation and provide habitat and spawning sites for fish. Reef balls are versatile and can be modified to fulfill a variety of developmental needs. For example, they can be used as mangrove planters, breakwaters to prevent beach erosion, oyster reef seed sites, and fishery enhancements. As magnets for marine life, they provide valuable recreational sites for snorkeling, diving, and fishing.

BIO HAVEN FLOATING ISLANDS
www.biofloatingislands.com

Biohaven Floating Islands are a water filtration solution that behaves much like a constructed wetland but which is suitably situated in both shallow and deep waters as well as locations where unobstructed water flow is necessary. The islands are simply anchored to the bottom of a river or attached to a bank. Within a non-woven matrix made of recycled plastic, and injected with foam for initial buoyancy, the islands support aerobic microbes which consume phosphates and ammonia, and anaerobic microbes which convert nitrates to harmless atmospheric gas. This design is extremely efficient; for every 250 square feet of Biohaven, one acre of actual wetland surface area is created.

GEOTUBE

www.tencate.com

Geotube® geocontainment technology is a system for using an engineered textile tube to contain sand and soil. The textile allows water to flow through it but contains the sand and soils from strong currents. As a breakwater, jetty or a sand dune, it is valuable in resisting erosion along vulnerable shorelines. It can also be used to contain land for the creation of artificial islands and still waters to promote wetland habitats. The fill for Geotube® can include sands and soils as well as displaced dredge materials and other spoil materials.

SUBWAY REEF

Decommissioned and cleaned subway car bodies can provide effective artificial reef habitats. Past studies report that charter artificial subway reefs along the Mid Atlantic coast have colonized up to 200 species of fish and invertebrates. These reefs have 800 to 1,000 times more biomass than the open ocean. Because they are perforated by door and window openings, they allow water flow but also deflect strong sea turbulence to provide protection for growing fish. Subway reefs also create a significant textured mass on the ocean floor which creates a drag that lowers storm surge velocities.

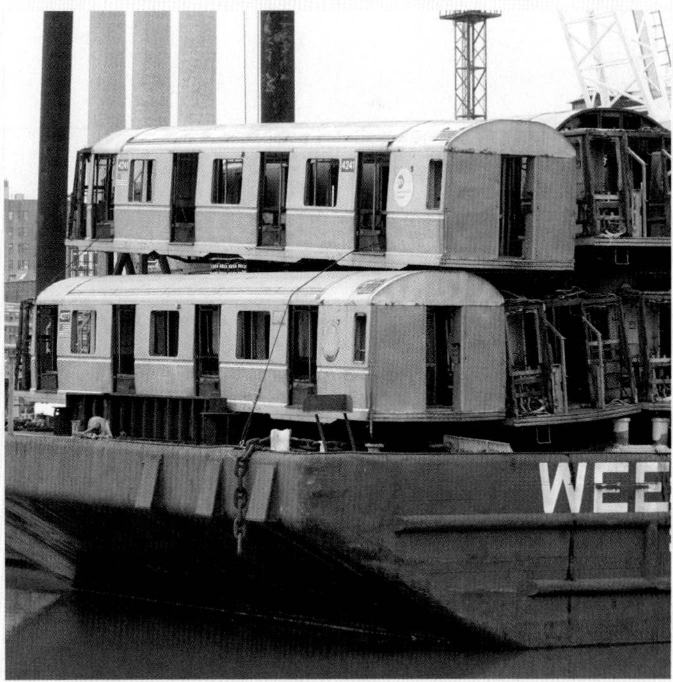

POROUS PAVEMENT AND GRASS PAVERS

Porous pavement and pavers can take on many forms but all are level surfaces suitable for pedestrian and/or vehicular traffic that are still pervious to water. Increasing the pervious surfaces in urban environments would help to absorb storm water and relieve city sewers from overflow and reduce the need for retention ponds, swales, and other large storm water retention devices. Pervious pavement mimics conventional asphalt but uses a controlled mix of water and cementitious materials which are used to create a paste around large aggregate particles. This mix contains little or no sand so that it holds significant voids in the matrix. Grass pavers are a low cost solution and a very simple application suitable for domestic use. They are modular paving blocks made with concrete or plastic which is perforated to combine surface bearing capacity with water absorption. Generally pavers allow for enough filtration of surface water so that additional drainage is not required.

PLANTED SURFACES

www.verticalgardenpatrickblanc.com

Planted vertical and horizontal surfaces unquestionably improve the health, efficiency, and general appearance of urban environments. These surfaces improve air quality, cool city temperatures to reduce energy consumption and catch run-off water to relieve overburdened drains and sewers. They also provide habitat for a variety of birds, butterflies, and other pollinators. A green roof is a lightweight, vegetated system that covers a roof surface. It includes drainage, a protective layer and lightweight soil for low maintenance vegetation. A vertical planted surface is a system for covering a wall surface. It is often developed without a continuous layer of soil and requires selection of plant types that thrive in this conditions as well as watering and fertilization. Often covering several building stories in height, a vertical planted surface acts as an effective sound and thermal barrier in dense urban surroundings.

MODULAR CONSTRUCTED WETLANDS

www.modularwetlands.com

Constructed wetlands on a large scale provide habitat, water filtration, and water retention, all of which are positive contributions to ecological and urban systems. This system is designed to work within existing drain and sewer networks. It simply incorporates a modular plant bed near sewer openings which, through a network of screens, pipes, roots, and soil aggregates embedded in the module, filters the incoming storm water.

The sub surface flow wetland is effective and requires modest operational attention. This ecologically engineered system uses minimal energy and machinery to achieve high quality effluent. The sub surface flow wetland is easily configured to specific aesthetic criteria through layout, construction materials, and plant selection.

GAIASOIL FOR GREEN ROOFS

www.gaiasoil.com

GaiaSoil™ is a lightweight planting soil designed for green roofs. Its main ingredient is a non-toxic, recycled, expanding polystyrene foam coated with an organic pectin which is mixed with finished compost. The GaiaSoil is a proprietary mix which makes green roofs planted with it fifty per cent lighter than roofs that are not. This helps to reduce the capital costs of planting a green roof but also enhances the performance of the roof because it supports more diverse plants and increases storm water capture made possible by greater soil depth allowances.

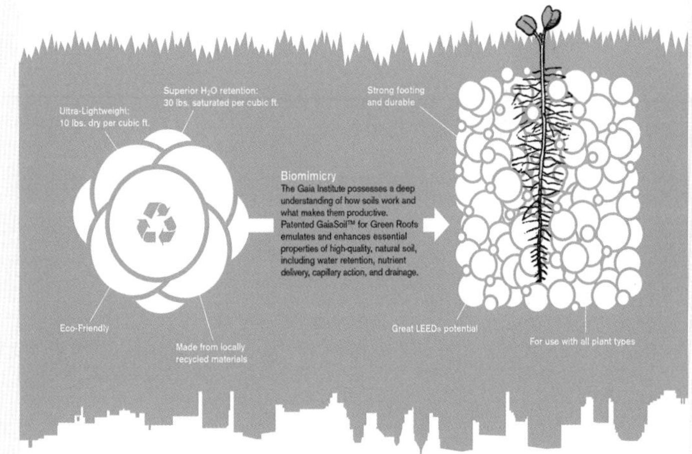

EROSION NETS

www.saicor.com

SUDS Stormwater Drainage systems can be developed in line with the ideals of sustainable development, by balancing the different issues that should be influencing the design. Surface water drainage methods that take account of quantity, quality and amenity issues are collectively referred to as Sustainable Drainage Systems (SUDS). SUDS systems are more sustainable than conventional drainage methods because they reduce the impact of urbanization on flooding by managing runoff flow rate, enhancing water quality, encouraging natural groundwater recharge (where appropriate), are sympathetic to environmental and local community needs, and provide a habitat for wildlife in urban watercourses.

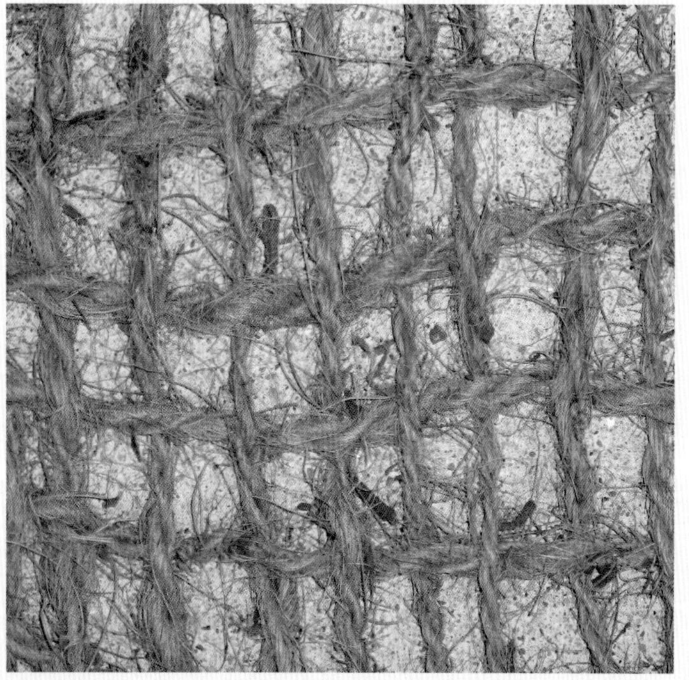

VERMICULTURE

www.wormswrangler.com

Vermicompost is the end product of the breakdown of organic matter by some species of earthworm including Eisenia foetida (Red Wigglers), and Eisenia hortensis (European Nightcrawlers). Containing water-soluble microbes and bacteria, vermicompost is an excellent, nutrient-rich organic fertilizer and soil conditioner. The earthworms species are commonly found in organic-rich soils throughout Europe and North America and live in rotting vegetation, compost and manure piles. As they are shallow dwelling and feed on decomposing plant matter in the soil, they adapt well to living on food or plant waste in the confines of a worm bin. Vermiculture is suitable on domestic and industrial scales for producing rich soil appropriate for agricultural uses.

GABION RETAINING STRUCTURES

Gabions provide a versatile solution to erosion control and land stabilization. They consist of rectangular wire baskets filled with rocks of varying porosity, depending on the specific needs and applications of a project. They can be installed virtually anywhere and are often found along roadsides and beaches.

GROW

www.smit.com

GROW is a hybrid energy delivery device that provides power via the sun and wind, and draws inspiration from ivy growing on a building. It is designed to utilize emerging technology in both the photovoltaic and piezoelectric industries. Based around a modular 'brick' system, GROW is composed of a small number of different parts. Each 'brick' has five solar leaves which have a very flexible piezoelectric generator at their stem. The manufacturing of these bricks could happen in a roll to roll printing process where PV, conductive ink, and piezo generators can be layered quickly and efficiently. The rolls can then be stamped and formed to create leaves and connection points. Each brick is designed so that at the end of its life-cycle the valuable components, (i.e. photovoltaic and piezoelectric), can be stamped out and up-cycled while the reusable material, (i.e. plastic), can be up recycled back into the production stream.

ENERGY ISLANDS

www.inhabit.com

Energy Islands use a concept called Ocean Thermal Energy Conversion (OTEC) which relies on the temperature differential between surface and deep waters to drive a turbine. Their goal is to produce a network of artificial energy islands that would generate electricity from the wind, waves and the sun as well as up to 2,36 million liters per MW per day of desalinated water.

TIDAL ENERGY

www.biopowersystems.com

The tidal power conversion system, bioSTREAM™, is based on the highly efficient propulsion of Thunniform mode swimming species, such as shark, tuna, and mackerel. The bioSTREAM™ mimics the shape and motion characteristics of these species but is a fixed device in a moving stream. In this configuration the propulsion mechanism is reversed and the energy in the passing flow is used to drive the device motion against the resisting torque of an electrical generator.

Due to the single point of rotation, this device can align with the flow in any direction, and can assume a streamlined configuration to avoid excess loading in extreme conditions. Systems are being developed for 250kW, 500kW, and 1000kW capacities to match conditions in various locations.

RESOURCES

RESEARCH INSTITUTIONS

Columbia University, Center for Climate Systems Research, New York, NY

Gaia Institute, Bronx, NY

NASA Goddard Institute for Space Studies (NASA GISS), New York, NY

New York Public Library, New York, NY

Stevens Institute of Technology, Center for Maritime Systems, Hoboken, NJ

Stony Brook University, School of Marine and Atmospheric Sciences, Stony Brook, NY

Woods Hole Oceanographic Institution, Woods Hole, MA

INTERNATIONAL AGENCIES AND ORGANIZATIONS

Intergovernmental Panel on Climate Change (IPCC), Geneva, Switzerland

Project for Public Spaces (PPS), New York, NY

Urban Age, London, United Kingdom

NATIONAL AGENCIES AND ORGANIZATIONS

Federal Emergency Management Agency (FEMA)

National Aeronautics and Space Administration (NASA)

National Audubon Society

National Geographic Society

National Oceanic and Atmospheric Administration (NOAA)

National Weather Service (NWS)

Office of Coast Survey (OCS)

Office of Ocean and Coastal Resource Management

National Park Service

United States Army Corps of Engineers (USACE)

United States Environmental Protection Agency (EPA)

United States Geological Survey (USGS)

REGIONAL AGENCIES AND ORGANIZATIONS

Coalition for a Better Waterfront (CBW)

Metropolitan Waterfront Alliance, New York, NY

New York–New Jersey Baykeeper, Keyport, NJ

New York–New Jersey Harbor Estuary Program (HEP), New York, NY

Port Authority of New York and New Jersey, New York, NY

Regional Plan Association, New York, NY

Riverkeeper, Tarrytown, NY

NEW YORK AND NEW JERSEY AGENCIES

New Jersey Department of Environmental Protection (NJDEP), Trenton, NJ

New Jersey Department of Transportation Office of Maritime Resources (NJDOT/OMR), Trenton, NJ

New York State Department of Environmental Conservation, Albany, NY

New York State Department of State Division of Coastal Resources, Albany, NY

New York State Emergency Management Office (NYSEMO), Albany, NY

New York State Office of Parks, Recreation, and Historic Preservation, Albany, NY

NEW YORK CITY AGENCIES

New York City Department of City Planning (DCP), New York, NY

New York City Department of Environmental Protection (DEP), New York, NY

New York City Department of Information Technology and Telecommunications (DoITT), New York, NY

New York City Department of Parks and Recreation, New York, NY

New York City Office of Emergency Management (OEM), New York, NY

New York City Panel on Climate Change (NPCC), New York, NY

New York City Long Term Planning and Sustainability Office, New York, NY

AFTERWORD

Rising Currents: Projects for New York's Waterfront

Almost two years ago, when Guy Nordenson first presented me with a draft of *On The Water: Palisade Bay*, he and I began discussing ways in which The Museum of Modern Art might build on those findings, and reach a larger public for specific proposals concerning the much-discussed issues of climate change and accompanying sea level rise that already pose serious challenges to major cities world-wide. Evidence has continued to accumulate of the global magnitude of the problem. Indeed, fifteen of the world's largest cities lie in flood zones, and recent reports on the melting underway in Antarctica suggest that the conservative evidences of sea level rise in the next half century used in many studies, including this one, might soon need to be adjusted upward. In addition to the challenges faced by America's largest urban area in the face of climate change, the last year and a half has witnessed an economic recession particularly severe for New York's rich pool of design talent in architecture and landscape design. The opportunity seemed ripe in opening a workshop/exhibition based on the study to address at once two of the most pressing problems facing America's largest metropolis.

While many areas of the world, in particular the Netherlands, have had a tradition of turning to designers to work hand in hand with hydraulic engineers and climate scientists in both hard and soft infrastructure responses, the United States has been remarkably slow in this regard. The debate on climate change has remained largely focused on issues of carbon emissions, although all acknowledge that the process already underway can only be mitigated, not reversed, and the tragic example of the effects of Hurricane Katrina in New Orleans in 2005 still remain vivid, and vividly under-addressed. The necessary work of redesigning the daily landscape of coastal areas, with all its attendant challenges to modes of transportation, has remained largely the work of academic studios. The economic crisis that came fully into focus in the autumn of 2008 has not only rendered many designers idle; it has also resulted in an impressive investment in infrastructure under the Obama administration's federal stimulus package. The pressing needs to get citizens back to work and to stimulate the economy have focused attention and resources on "shovel-ready" projects, assuring that the lion's share of what will be done corresponds to existing paradigms—indeed in many cases involves repairing older infrastructure—and is made up of a patchwork of individual projects. There is little promise for solutions that are paradigmatic in relationship to the environmental challenges that appear to be building to crisis levels, especially when we read of current cases as extreme as the Maldives in the Indian Ocean, an island nation with real chances of disappearing into the sea in coming years. The Palisade Bay team of Nordenson, Seavitt, and Yarinsky propose no such drastic solution, nor do they propose a battery of tools made simply out of defense, although storm barriers and levees might well accompany the manifesto on the possibilities of soft infrastructure they argue for in both realistic analysis and poetic projection. Rather, they propose to work on the coastline of New York and New Jersey to render it more resilient for climatic changes to come and to reorient the perception and the experience of the city around the water, allowing New York to join a host of cities from Copenhagen and Amsterdam to Singapore and Hong Kong, which increasingly focus on an active waterfront of mixed use.

To encourage the type of engaged design work required to move the national climate change and infrastructural debates forward, and to recognize that stimulus money might equally be appropriate to fund research as much as construction work, The Museum of Modern Art's Department of Architecture and Design, aided by a grant from the Rockefeller Foundation, organized an eight-week design workshop in the Fall-Winter of 2009/10 to investigate five large sites in the aqueous study area of the Palisade Bay team's analysis. Each of the sites was assigned to an interdisciplinary team of architects, landscape architects, and designers, for concrete proposals of combinations of new programmatic uses and soft infrastructure design. It was not a matter of picking five designs from research currently underway, but rather an invitation to undertake new

research in an interdisciplinary way on urgent problems global in implication but yet local in application and response. The museum here serves in an almost unprecedented way as the incubator of new ideas. Their work is underway as this book goes to press, but the process and the results are featured on an archived web site/blog at www.moma.org/risingcurrents. All of the results will be exhibited from March 24 to August 9, 2010.

The selection process is worth recording. In September of 2009 invitations went out to some sixty educators and leading practitioners in architecture, landscape architecture, and engineering to nominate emerging design talents with up to ten years experience as head of their own firm who could assemble teams from their own offices and from the pool of talent available in the current recession. A jury was assembled to review the firm portfolios, composed of MoMA and P.S.1 curators, including myself, and invited professionals including Amanda Burden (Chair of the New York City Planning Commission and Director of the Department of City Planning), David Adjaye (Founder, Adjaye Associates, Ltd.), Michael Oppenheimer (Albert G. Milbank Professor of Geosciences and International Affairs at Princeton University), and Guy Nordenson. In October 2009 ten teams were interviewed. The four selected teams, listed below, took up residence in studio space at P.S.1, MoMA's contemporary-arts affiliate in Queens, New York. They were joined by a team headed by Adam Yarinsky of Architecture Research Office, who worked to develop further the project for the tip of Manhattan originally studied in the context of the Palisade Bay study and included in this book. During an intense eight weeks, punctuated by weekly reviews by myself, Guy Nordenson, Catherine Seavitt, and outside guests invited by the teams, they worked in a marvelous spirit of cooperation and exchange of ideas, both within each team and among the teams. On two occasions the general public was invited to open-house days, to imbibe the atmosphere of architectural research and design, and to hear about the team's work in progress and discuss its goals and solutions. The end results will be displayed for six months in 2010 in the Menschel Gallery at The Museum of Modern Art, a gallery usually devoted to works from the permanent collection. Workshop, blog, and exhibition are part of an ongoing experimentation at MoMA with new means of engaging the public in the most pressing current issues, but also the processes of architectural design. At the same time Rising Currents corresponds to a philosophy of working with "glocal" approaches, that is, looking in depth at issues of global importance in a specific local context.

Rising Currents of course refers to two aspects of the experiment: responses to the rising waters of New York harbor and the invitation to relatively young designers. The team leaders in each case are recently established practitioners, most of them dividing practice between a small-to-medium-sized office and teaching in a school of architecture. Although talented designers from New Orleans and San Francisco made interesting presentations during the interviews, the residency aspect of the workshop led the jury to teams assembled by four emerging architectural and landscape studios in New York: SCAPE Studio (Kate Orff Landscape Design), Matthew Baird Architects (Matthew Baird), LTL Architects (Paul Lewis, Marc Tsurumaki, and David Lewis), and nArchitects (Eric Bunge and Mimi Hoang). They joined Architecture Research Office (Adam Yarinsky, one of the principals directing the team), which further developed their initial study for the zone that includes Lower Manhattan. The complete list of participants, both those in residence at P.S.1 and those who participated as ongoing consultants to the teams, are listed on the website and represent an interdisciplinary cross-section of practitioners.

Both the task of the workshop and the exhibition produced by convening a designing think tank to work on a problem are responses to the very real challenges that *On The Water* takes up with both sangfroid and optimism. They present a promise of a New York that can transform itself in productive ways in response to environmental changes larger than any faced before by modern designers.

Barry Bergdoll, Philip Johnson Chief Curator of Architecture and Design,
The Museum of Modern Art, New York

NOTES AND REFERENCES

NOTES

1 New York City Panel on Climate Change, *Climate Risk Information* (February 17, 2009), p. 17. Online version: www.nyc.gov/html/om/pdf/2009/NPCC_CRI.pdf.

2 Ibid., p. 20.

3 Ibid., p. 9.

4 Ibid., p. 3.

5 IPCC, "Summary for Policymakers," in S. Solomon, D. Qin, M. Manning, Z. Chen, M. Marquis, K.B. Averyt, M.Tignor, and H.L. Miller, eds. *Climate Change 2007: The Physical Science Basis. Contribution of Working Group I to the Fourth Assessment Report of the Intergovernmental Panel on Climate Change* (New York, 2007), p. 13.

6 Climate Change Information Resources, New York Metropolitan Region (CCIR-NYC), *What changes in climate are projected for the region?* (New York, 2005), p. 1.

7 New York City Panel on Climate Change 2009 (see note 1), p. 3.

8 Ibid., p. 20.

9 Vivien Gornitz, Stephen Couch, and Ellen K. Hartig, "Impacts of Sea Level Rise in the New York City Metropolitan Area," *Global and Planetary Changes* 32 (2002), p. 65.

10 Ibid., p. 64.

11 Cynthia Rosenzweig and Vivien Gornitz, *Hurricanes, Sea Level Rise, and New York City*, Columbia University, Center for Climate Systems Research.
Online version: http://www.ccsr.columbia.edu/information/hurricanes/

12 Gornitz 2002 (see note 9), p. 65.

13 Ibid., p. 66.

14 Robert Smithson, "A Provisional Theory of Non-Sites," in Jack Flam, ed. *Robert Smithson: The Collected Writings*, (Berkeley, 1996), p. 364.

15 Malcolm Bowman et al., *Hydrologic Feasibility of Storm Surge Barriers to Protect the Metropolitan New York-New Jersey Region: Final Report* (2005), p. 6.

16 John Waldman, *Heartbeats in the Muck: The History of Sea Life and the Environment of New York Harbor* (New York, 1999), p. 26.

17 The Environment Agency, *The Thames Barrier.* Online version: http://www.environment-agency.gov.uk/homeandleisure/floods/105002.aspx.

18 Bowman et. al. 2005 (see note 15), p. 12.

19 Calvert Vaux, *Villages and Cottages: A Series of Designs Prepared for Execution in the United States* (New York, 1872), pp. 49-50.

REFERENCES

Allen, Laura. "Endangered Orbits." *Popular Science* (August 2007).

AP. "Dredging May Not Eliminate Contaminants." *New York Times*. June 5, 2007.

Arcement, G. J., Jr. and V.R. Schneider. *U.S. Geological Survey. Guide for Selecting Manning's Roughness Coefficients for Natural Channels and Flood Plains (Metric).* US Geological Survey Water-Supply Paper 2339. 1989.

Archibold, Randal C. and Kirk Johnson. "No Longer Waiting for Rain, an Arid West is Taking Action." *New York Times*. April 4, 2007.

Arnow, Pat and Mark Berky-Gerard. "New York's Port, Beyond Dubai." *Gotham Gazette*. March 13, 2006.

Arnow, Pat. "Unknown (Unused) Beaches of NYC." *Gotham Gazette*. June 15, 2006.

Arnow, Pat. "Waterfront in Fits and Starts (and Stops)." *Gotham Gazette*. September 27, 2006.

Ascher, Kate. *Works: Anatomy of a City*. New York, 2005.

Bahrampour, Tara. "Frommer's It's Not: Guidebook Burnishes a Rugged Image." *New York Times*. November 19, 2000.

Bahrampour, Tara. "The State Parches Up a Road that Resident Want to Ditch." *New York Times*. September 14, 2003.

Barnett, Jonathan and Kristina Hill. "Design for Rising Sea Level." *Harvard Design Magazine* (Fall 2007/Winter 2008).

Barry, Patrick. "Sooner or Later, the Water Will Arrive." *New Scientist* 190, 2554 (June 3-9, 2006).

Baxter, Roberta. "Shoreline Protection Strategies." *Erosion Control* (July/August 2007).

Baxter, Roberta. "Wetlands–Lose or Restore." *Erosion Control* (May/June 2006).

Berger, Joseph. "Many Gowanus Residents Want Its Collar to Remain Blue." *New York Times*. November 28, 2005.

Bindoff, N.L. et al. "Observations: Oceanic Climate Change and Sea Level." in *Climate Change 2007: The Physical Science Basis. Contribution of Working Group I to the Fourth Assessment Report of the Intergovernmental Panel on Climate Change*. Edited by S. Solomon et al., New York, 2007.

Bohannon, John. "Running Out of Water—and Time." *Science*, 313 (August 25, 2006).

Bone, Kevin, Eugenia Bone, and Mary Beth Betts. *The New York Waterfront: Evolution and Building Culture of the Port and Harbor*. New York, 2004.

Bourne, Joel K., Jr. "New Orleans." *National Geographic*. Vol. 212, No. 2 (August 2007).

Bowman, Malcolm et al. *Hydrologic Feasibility of Storm Surge Barriers to Protect the Metropolitan New York-New Jersey Region: Final Report*. March 2005.

Boyle, Robert H. *The Hudson River: A Natural and Unnatural History.* New York, 1979.

Brustein, Joshua. "In City Waters, Beds (and a Job) for Oysters." *New York Times.* February 24, 2008.

Buttenwieser, Ann L. *Manhattan Waterbound: Planning and Development from the Seventeenth Century to the Present.* New York, 1987.

Cardwell, Diane. "What Rots Beneath: Investigating Exactly What Fouls the Gowanus Canal." *New York Times.* May 19, 2003.

Carter, Nicole T. *Flood Risk Management: Federal Role in Infrastructure. CRS Report for Congress.* October 26, 2005.

Christian, Nichole M. "Ikea Is Said to Consider Gowanus Site for New Store." *New York Times.* March 10, 2001.

City of London Corporation. *Rising to the Challenge: The City of London Corporation's Climate Adaptation Strategy.* January 2007.

The City of New York. *PlaNYC.* April 22, 2007. Online version: http://www.nyc.gov/html/planyc2030/html/home/home.shtml.

The City of New York, Department of City Planning. *Manhattan Waterfront Greenway Master Plan.* November, 2004. Online version: http://www.nyc.gov/html/dcp/html/mwg/mwghome.shtml.

Cohen, Joyce. "Goodbye TriBeCa, Hello Gowanus." *New York Times.* March 20, 2005.

Cohen, Paul E. and Robert T. Augustyn. *Manhattan in Maps: 1527–1995.* New York, 1997.

Cooper, Matthew J.P., Michael D. Beevers, and Michael Oppenheimer. *Future Sea Level Rise and the New Jersey Coast: Assessing Potential Impacts and Opportunities.* Science, Technology and Environmental Policy Program, Woodrow Wilson School of Public and International Affairs, Princeton University. November 2005.

Crooks, Stephen. "The Effect of Sea-Level Rise on Coastal Geomorphology." *Ibis* 146, 1 (September 2004).

Day, Leslie. *Field Guide to the Natural World of New York City.* Baltimore, 2007.

Dean, Cornelia. "Expert Federal Panel Urges New Look at Land Use Along Coasts in Effort to Reduce Erosion." *New York Times.* October 13, 2006.

Dean, Cornelia. "How Little We Know: Will Warming Lead to a Rise in Hurricanes?" *New York Times.* May 29, 2007.

DePalma, Anthony. "City's Catskill Water Gets 10-Year Approval." *New York Times.* April 13, 2007.

DePalma, Anthony. "East River Fights Bid to Harness Its Currents for Electricity." *New York Times.* August 13, 2007.

DePalma, Anthony. "New York's Water Supply May Need Filtering." *New York Times.* July 20, 2006.

DePalma, Anthony. "A Storybook Development With an Uncertain Ending." *New York Times.* January 16, 1990.

De Vriend, Huib. "The Eastern Scheldt Barrier: Environmentally Friendly Engineering?" *Territory and the Environment.* Proc. of the II International Conference on Civil Engineering, September 2004, Colegio de Ingenieros de Camines, Canales y Puertos, Santiago de Compostela, Spain. Pp. 1269-1281.

DeWitt, Godfrey. "Maureen Brennan—Working the System: Red Tape, Bureaucracies, Permits, Insurance, Protocols, Parking, and Port-a-Potties." *Art Journal* 65, 1 (Spring 2006).

Doyle, Rodger. "Darkness on the Water." *Scientific American* 296, 2 (April 2007).

Dybas, Cheryl Lyn. "Nature's Off-Off Broadway: Resuscitating Wild New York Harbor." *Wildlife Conservation* (May/June 2008).

The Environment Agency, *The Thames Barrier.* Online version: http://www.environment-agency.gov.uk/homeandleisure/floods/105002.aspx.

Flam, Jack. *Robert Smithson: The Collected Writings.* Berkeley, 1996.

Garbardine, Rachelle. "Sales Begin at New Phase of Hudson River Complex." *New York Times.* December 3, 1999.

Gastil, Raymond W. *Beyond the Edge: New York's New Waterfront.* New York, 2002.

Gateway National Recreation Area, National Park Service, U.S. Department of the Interior and Jamica Bay Watershed Protection Plan Advisory Committee. *An Update on the Disappearing Salt Marshes of Jamaica Bay, New York.* August 2, 2007.

Geophysical Fluid Dynamics Laboratory, National Oceanic and Atmospheric Administration, United States Department of Commerce. *Computer Model Projections of 21st Century Sea Level Change.* July 2001. Online version: http://www.gfdl.noaa.gov.

Gornitz, Vivien, C. Rosenzweig, and D. Hillel. "Effects of Anthropogenic Intervention in the Land Hydrologic Cycle on Global Sea Level Rise." *Global and Planetary Changes* 14 (1997).

Gornitz, Vivien, Stephen Couch, and Ellen K. Hartig. "Impacts of Sea Level Rise in the New York City Metropolitan Area." *Global and Planetary Changes* 32 (2002).

Greene, Charleton. *Wharves and Piers: Their Design, Construction and Equipment.* New York, 1917.

Handwerk, Brian. "Hundreds of Glaciers Melting Faster in Antarctica." *National Geographic News.* June 6, 2007.

Hartig, Ellen K. and Vivien Gornitz. "The Vanishing Marshes of Jamaica Bay: Sea Level Rise or Environmental Degradation?" *Science Briefs*, December 2001. Online version: http://www.giss.nasa.gov/research/briefs/.

Healy, Patrick. "A Brooklyn Seal's Trick: Surviving the Gowanus." *New York Times.* July 2, 2003.

Heckscher, Morrison. *Creating Central Park.* New Haven, 2008.

Hell, James E. "Currents of Change." *E Magazine: The Environmental Magazine* 10, 3 (May/June 1999).

Hiss, Tony and Christopher Meier. *H2O Highlands to Ocean: A First Close Look at the Outstanding Landscapes and Waterscapes of the New York/New Jersey Metropolitan Region.* Morristown, NJ, 2004.

Hoffman, John S. "Estimates of Future Sea Level Rise." in *Greenhouse Effect and Sea Level Rise: A Challenge for this Generation.* Edited by Michael C. Barth and James G. Titus. New York, 1984.

Intergovernmental Panel on Climate Change. "Summary for Policymakers." In *Climate Change 2007: The Physical Science Basis. Contribution of Working Group I to the Fourth Assessment Report of the Intergovernmental Panel on Climate Change.* Edited by S. Solomon, D. Qin, M. Manning, Z. Chen, M. Marquis, K.B. Averyt, M.Tignor, and H.L. Miller, New York, 2007.

Jet Propulsion Laboratory. *NASA Satellites Measure and Monitor Sea Level.* July 7, 2005.

Kieran, John. *A Natural History of New York City.* Boston, 1959.

Kinetz, Erika. "Residents' Group Sees Big Box as No Boon." *New York Times.* March 25, 2001.

Kunkel, Catherine, Robert Hallberg, and Michael Oppenheimer. *Coral Reefs Reduce Tsunami Impact in Model Simulations.* Geophys. Res. Lett., 33, L23612, doi:10.1029/2006GL027892. 2006.

Kurlansky, Mark. *The Big Oyster: History on a Half Shell.* New York, 2006.

Lavelle, Marianne. "Water Woes." *U.S. News & World Report.* May 27, 2007.

Lewine, Edward. "The Gowanus Canal: An Appreciation." *New York Times.* August 30, 1998.

London Climate Change Partnership. *London's Warming: The Impacts of Climate Change on London: Summary Report.* October 2002.

Lueck, Thomas J. "Neighbors Will Have Voice In Gowanus Road Project." *New York Times.* January 20, 2001.

Lyall, Sarah. "At Risk from Floods, but Looking Ahead with Floating Houses." *New York Times.* April 3, 2007.

Mahler, Jonathan. "Once a Mess, Canal Aspires to Beauty Now." *New York Times.* June 8, 2001.

Margolis, Liat and Alexander Robinson. *Living Systems: Innovative Materials and Technologies for Landscape Architecture.* Basel, 2007.

Martin, Douglas. "Finally, Flushing an Infamous Canal." *New York Times.* May 4, 1999.

"Mayor Bloomberg and Lieutenant Governor Paterson Flip Switch for World's First Free-Flow Tidal Power Turbines." June 11, 2007. Online version: http://www.nyc.gov.

"Mayor Bloomberg and Office of Emergency Management Commissioner Bruno Unveil Revised Coastal Storm Plan." June 28, 2006. Online version: http://www.nyc.gov.

McCully, Betsy. *City at the Waters Edge: A Natural History of New York.* New Brunswick, NJ, 2007.

McManus, Maureen, Keith W. Jones, Nicholas L. Clesceri, and Ivor L. Preiss. "Renewal of Brooklyn's Gowanus Canal Area." *Journal of Urban Technology* 2, 2.

Menard, H.W. *Islands.* New York., 1986.

Merrill, Lynn. "Clearing the Channel: Dredging Operations and Erosion Control." *Erosion Control*, March/April 2003. Online version: http://www.forester.net/ecm.

Milstein, Mati. "Warming to Level Off, then Speed Back Up, New Model Predicts." *National Geographic News.* August 9, 2007. Online version: http://news.nationalgeographic.com/news/index.html.

Minard, Anne. "Global Warming Models Underpredict Increase in Rainfall, Study Says." *National Geographic News.* May 31, 2007. Online version: http://news.nationalgeographic.com/news/index.html.

Mittelbach, Margaret. *Wild New York: A Guide to Wildlife, Wild Places and Natural Phenomena of New York City.* New York, 1998.

Mooney, Jake. "Ah, the Gowanus! Where You Can Walk on Water." *New York Times.* March 20, 2005.

Mooney, Jake. "The Banks of the Gowanus Put the Gleam in a Builder's Eye." *New York Times.* November 14, 2004.

Morocco, Sarah. "Sediment Dredging Has Fallen Short of Achieving Cleanup Goals at Many Contaminate Sites; Better Monitoring Needed to Assess Suitability Results." *NAS News.* June 5, 2007. Online version: http://www.nationalacademies.org/.

Munari, Bruno. *The Sea as Craftsman.* Mantua, 2002.

The National Academy of Sciences. *Sediment Dredging at Superfund Megasites: Assessing the Effectiveness.* June 2007.

National Oceanic and Atmospheric Administration, U.S. Department of Commerce. "NOAA Recognizes New York City as Storm Ready." *News from NOAA.* November 16, 2006.

Newman, Andy. "Stench Is Out, Fish Are In: Gowanus Canal Comes Back to Life After Rescue." *New York Times.* July 29, 1999.

New York City Office of Emergency Management. *Ready New York: Hurricanes and New York City.* 2006.

New York City Office of Emergency Management. *New York City Hurricane Evacuation Zones.* 2006.

New York-New Jersey Harbor Estuary Program. *A Steward's Guide to the Estuary.* April 2003. Online version: http://www.seagrant.sunysb.edu/hep/.

Oki, Taikan and Shinjiro Kanae. "Global Hydrological Cycles and World Water Resources." *Science,* 313 (Aug. 25, 2006).

Owen, James. "Warming May Spur Extinctions, Shortages, Conflicts, World Experts Warn."

National Geographic News. April 6, 2007. Online version: http://news.nationalgeographic.com/news/index.html.

Pacella, Rena Marie. "Five Modest Proposals to Save the Planet." *Popular Science* (August 2007).

Pendleton, Elizabeth A., E. Robert Thieler, and S. Jeffress Williams, U.S. Geological Survey, U.S. Department of the Interior. *Coastal Vulnerability Assessment of Gateway National Recreation Area (GATE) to Sea-Level Rise*. Open-File Report 2004-1257, 2005. Online version: http://pubs.usgs.gov/of/2004/1257.

Pethick, John. "Shoreline Adjustments and Coastal Management: Physical and Biological Processes Under Accelerate Sea-Level Rise." *The Geographic Journal* 159, 2 (July 1993).

Picon, Antoine and Michael Yvon. *L'ingenieur artiste*. Paris, 1989.

Pierre-Pierre, Garry. "Study Backs Tunnel to Replace the Gowanus." *New York Times*. July 1, 1997.

The Port Authority of New York & New Jersey. *Protecting Our Waterways: Creating Jobs, Safeguarding Our Environment*. www.panynj.gov/doingbusinesswith/seaport/pdfs/PANP-1024DredgingBro_m8.pdf

Postel, Sandra L. "For Our Thirsty World, Efficiency or Else." *Science* 313 (Aug. 25, 2006).

Prud'homme, Alex. "There Will Be Floods." *New York Times*. February 27, 2008.

Rahmstorf, Stefan et al. "A Semi-Empirical Approach to Projecting Future Sea-Level Rise." *Science* 315 (January 19, 2007).

Ramirez, Anthony. "Dredging Up a Revived Waterway." *New York Times*. July 12, 1998.

Randolph, Eleanor. "Surviving the Gowanus Canal." *New York Times*. May 23, 1999.

Regional Plan Association. *Northeast Mega Region 2050: A Common Future*. November 2007. Online version: http://www.rpa.org/publications.

Regional Plan Association. *On the Verge: Caring for New York City's Emerging Waterfront Parks & Public Spaces*. Spring 2007. Online version: http://www.rpa.org/publications.

Regional Plan Association and Brooklyn Greenway Initiative. *Brooklyn Waterfront Greenway: A Plan for Community Boards 2 & 6 (Draft)*. February 1, 2005. Online version: http://www.rpa.org/publications.

Roach, John. "Hurricanes Have Doubled Due to Global Warming, Study Says." *National Geographic News*. July 30, 2007. Online version: http://news.nationalgeographic.com/news/index.html.

Rogers, Teri Karush. "How Safe is My Home?" *New York Times*. March 11, 2007.

Royte, Elizabeth. "On the Water Front." *New York Times*. February 18, 2007.

Rosenthal, Elisabeth. "In Italy A Redesign of Nature to Clean It." *New York Times*. September 22, 2008.

Rosenzweig, Cynthia and W.D. Solecki. "Climate Change and a Global City: Learning from New York." *Environment* 43, 3 (April 2001).

Rosenzweig, Cynthia and Vivien Gornitz. *Hurricanes, Sea Level Rise, and New York City.* Columbia University, Center for Climate Systems Research. Online version: http://www.ccsr.columbia.edu/information/hurricanes.

Rudolf, John Collins. "The Warming of Greenland." *New York Times.* January 16, 2007.

Sautner, Stephen C. "Unusual Setting, But Fish Still Bite." *New York Times.* August 3, 2000.

Sawyer, Tom. "Vulnerable Coastal Zones are Focus of Dutch Forum." *Engineering News-Record* 258, 7 (February 19, 2007).

Schiermeier, Quirin. "What We Don't Know About Climate Change." *Nature* 445 (February 8, 2007).

Schwartz, John. "New Orleans Still At Risk, Army Data Shows." *New York Times.* June 21, 2007.

Schwarzenbach, René P. et al. "The Challenge of Micropollutants in Aquatic Systems." *Science* 313 (August 25, 2006).

Service, Robert F. "Delta Blues, California Style." *Science* 317 (July 27, 2007).

Skladony, Robert M. "Lubricant Additive Regains Lost Turbine Capacity." *Power Engineering* 104, 6 (June 2000).

Solecki, W.D. and C. Rosenzweig. "Biodiversity, Biosphere Reserves, and the Big Apple: A Study of the New York Metropolitan Region." *Ann. New York Academy of Science* 1023 (2004).

Stamler, Bernard. "Gowanus Expressway: Trouble Overhead." *New York Times.* December 13, 1998.

Stolberg, Sheryl Gay. "Bush Defends Climate and Missile Plans." *New York Times.* June 7, 2007.

Syvitski, James P.M. "Supply and Flux of Sediment Along Hydrological Pathways: Research for the 21st century." *Global and Planetary Change* 39 (2003).

Tagliabue, John. "Low Country Seeks Higher Ground." *New York Times.* November 7, 2008.

Tal, Alon. "Seeking Sustainability: Israel's Evolving Water Management Strategy." *Science* 313 (August 25, 2006).

Talbot, David. "Saving Holland." *Technology Review* (July/August 2007).

Teal, John and Mildred. *Life and Death of a Salt Marsh.* New York, 1969.

Thompson, Clive. "The Five-Year Forecast." *New York Magazine.* November 27, 2006.

Thumerer, T., A.P. Jones, D. Brown. "A GIS Based Coastal Management System for Climate Change Associated Flood Risk Assessment on the East Coast of England." *International Journal of Geographical Information Science* 14, 3 (2000).

Titus, James G. "Planning for Sea Level Rise before and after a Coastal Disaster." In *Greenhouse Effect and Sea Level Rise: A Challenge for this Generation.* Edited by Michael C. Barth and James G. Titus, New York, 1984.

Titus, James G. "Sea Level Rise." *The Potential Effects of Global Climate Change on the United States: Report to Congress.* U.S. EPA Office of Policy, Planning, and Evaluation, December 1989. Online version: http://www.epa.gov/climatechange/effects/downloads/potential_effects.pdf

Trotta, Daniel. "New York Marshes Vanishing Fast: Study." *Reuters.* August 2, 2007.

U.S. Army Corps of Engineers. *Waterborne Commerce of the United States* (WCUS). 2005. Online version: http://www.iwr.uscare.army.mil/ndc/wcsc/wcsc.htm.

U.S. Army Corps of Engineers, New York District. *Dredged Material Management Plan for the Port of New York and the State of New Jersey: Implementation Report (Draft).* September 1999. Online version: http://www.nau.usace.army.mil/business/prjlinks/dmmp/index.htm.

U.S. Army Corps of Engineers, New York District. *Environmental Assessment of the NY/NJ Harbor Deepening Project on the Remedial Investigation/Feasibility Study of the Newark Bay Study Area (Draft).* April 2007.

U.S. Army Corps of Engineers, New York District. *Wetland Creation: General Investigation Report.* July 2004. Online version: http://www.nau.usace.army.mil/harbor/gowanus/reports.htm.

U.S. Environmental Protection Agency. *Wetlands: Protecting Life and Property from Flooding.*

Vandam, Jeff. "In an Industrial Neighborhood, Grim Signs That Families Live There." *New York Times.* February 6, 2005.

Vandam, Jeff. "Some See Venice, Some See a Canal." *New York Times.* October 30, 2005.

Van Lenten, Christine. "Bracing for Super Floyd: How Storm Surge Barriers Could Protect the New York Region." *New York Academy of Sciences eBriefings.* May 31, 2005. Online version: http://www.nyas.org/superfloyd.

Vaux, Calvert. *Villages and Cottages: A Series of Designs Prepared for Execution in the United States.* New York, 1872.

"Vegetation Significantly Affects Water Flow and Transportation" *CEE at MIT Newsletter* 21, 2 (November 2007).

Waldman, Amy. "Evening Cruise on the Gowanus Canal, Clothespins Optional." *New York Times.* August 3, 1997.

Waldman, John. *Heartbeats in the Muck: The History of Sea Life and the Environment of New York Harbor.* New York, 1999.

Walsh, K.J.E. et al. "Using Sea Level Rise Projections for Urban Planning in Australia." *Journal of Coastal Research* 20, 2 (Spring 2004).

Walter, Robert C. and Merritts, Dorothy J. "Natural Streams and Legacy of Water Powered Mills." *Science* 319 (January 18, 2008).

Weggel, J. Richard et al. "The Cost of Defending Developed Shorelines Along Sheltered Waters of the United State from a Two Meter Rise in Mean Sea Level." *The Potential Effects of Global Climate Change on the United States: Report to Congress.* U.S. EPA Office of Policy, Planning, and Evaluation, December 1989. Online version: http://www.epa.gov/climatechange/effects/downloads/potential_effects.pdf.

Wilber, Pace and Linda E. Iocco. "Using a GIS to Examine Changes in the Bathymetry of Borrow Pits and in Lower Bay, New York Harbor, USA." *Marine Geodesy* 26 (2003).

Yozzo, David J., Pace Wilber, and Robert J. Will. "Beneficial Use of Dredged Material for Habitat Creation, Enhancement, and Restoration in New York-New Jersey Harbor." *Journal of Environmental Management* 73 (2004).

Zedler, Joy B. "Compensating for Wetland Losses in the United States." *Ibis* 146, 1 (September 2004).

CREDITS

GIS DATA CREDITS

Data used in GIS-generated maps is within the public domain and was sourced from the following government agencies:

Federal Emergency Management Agency (FEMA)

National Oceanic and Atmospheric Administration (NOAA)

New Jersey Department of Environmental Protection (NJDEP)

New York City Department of Information Technology and Telecommunications (DoITT)

New York State Emergency Management Office (NYSEMO)

United States Fish and Wildlife Service (USFWS)

United States Geological Survey (USGS)

IMAGE CREDITS

Palisade Bay Team: 25, 26–33, 50 (bottom), 62–63, 64, 66–83, 86–91, 92–93, 94–103 (top), 104–06, 111, 112, 120–23, 125, 127, 130 (bottom), 132–39, 141, 145, 146 (bottom), 147–49, 152–53, 155, 170 (top), 182–83, 185, 189, 190–289, 319

Architecture Research Office: 158–59, 160 (top), 162 (bottom), 163 (top), 164, 165, 166, 167, 168 (bottom), 169, 171, 172–73, 174, 175–179, 180–81

NASA: 50 (top), 51 (top), 52 (top), 53 (top), 54 (top), 55 (top), 56 (top), 57 (top), 58 (top), 59 (top), 60–61, 113, 160 (bottom)

National Oceanic and Atmospheric Administration/Department of Commerce: 14, 53 (bottom), 58 (bottom), 126 (bottom), 128, 148, 150, 170 (bottom)

National Oceanic and Atmospheric Administration/Office of Coast Survey: 107, 186–87

15, 17: Columbia Center for Climate Systems Research

16: Phyllis Cooper/US Fish and Wildlife Service

18: Seth Wenig/The New York Times/Redux

19: New York City Office of Emergency Management

20 (top): William Van Dorp

20 (middle): Art © Estate of Robert Smithson/Licensed by VAGA, New York NY

20 (bottom): Photo by Atto © 1994, Courtesy isisuf, istituto internazionale di studi sul futurismo

22 (top): Steve Rider

22 (bottom): UNLV School of Life Sciences

23: Emmet Collection, Miriam and Ira D. Wallach Division of Arts, Prints and Photographs, The New York Public Library, Astor, Lenox and Tilden Foundations

24: Kenzo Tange Associates

34–35: The Lionel Pincus and Princess Firyal Map Division, The New York Public Library, Astor, Lenox and Tilden Foundations

36: Rutgers University Special Collections

37: Lawrence H. Slaughter Collection, The Lionel Pincus and Princess Firyal Map Division, The New York Public Library, Astor, Lenox and Tilden Foundations

38–39: Collection of the New York Historical Society, negative no. 74563

40: The Lionel Pincus and Princess Firyal Map Division, The New York Public Library, Astor, Lenox and Tilden Foundations

41: Collection of the New York Historical Society, negative no. 82152d

42–43: The Lionel Pincus and Princess Firyal Map Division, The New York Public Library, Astor, Lenox and Tilden Foundations

44–45: Regional Plan Association

46: Michael Van Valkenburgh Associates, Inc

47: West 8/Rogers Marvel Architects/Diller Scofidio + Renfro/Quennell Rothschild/SMWM

48 (top): Susannah C. Drake, dlandstudio LLC

48 (middle): Marpillero Pollak Architects/WRT

49 (top): Nathan Kensinger

49 (bottom): ©James Corner Field Operations

51 (bottom): Peter Visontay/Earth Photography

52 (bottom): AFP/Stringer/Getty Images

54 (bottom): Dennis Sennikovski

55 (bottom): Nancy Nehring/iStockphoto

56 (bottom): Zhang Zhang

57 (bottom): Nils van der Burg

59 (bottom): District of Columbia, Office of Planning

84 (top): Queens Museum of Art

84 (bottom): Center for Land Use Interpretation photo archive

85: Center for Land Use Interpretation photo archive

103 (bottom): John Dunstan

108: New York City Municipal Archives

109: Picture Collection, The New York Public Library, Astor, Lenox and Tilden Foundations

110: (top) Board of Engineers for Rivers and Harbors, Map no. 13

110: (bottom) North German Lloyd Co., Hoboken, NJ, from Carleton Greene, Wharves and Piers: Their Design, Construction, and Equipment, New York, 1917

114: Nik Wheeler

115: Ecole Nationale des Ponts et Chaussées (ENPC)

116: Tony Shi

117: Hulton Archive/Getty Images

118: Plan of Chicago, Prepared under the direction of The Commercial Club, by Daniel H. Burnham and Edward H. Bennett, 1909

119: Paul Scharff

124: Bill Gill/US Fish and Wildlife Service

126 (top): US Department of Agriculture

129: Jeffrey Kirsh

130: Wikimedia Commons/Chris 73, GNU Free Documentation License, http://www.gnu.org/copyleft/fdl.html

131: Ben Gertzfield

140: UTEX The Culture Collection of Algae at The University of Texas, Austin

142: Picture Collection, The New York Public Library, Astor, Lenox and Tilden Foundations

143: Collection of the New York Historical Society, negative no. 4383

144: Picture Collection, The New York Public Library, Astor, Lenox and Tilden Foundations

146: (top) Wikimedia Commons/Ibagli/Public Domain

150: Ian Hamilton/iStockphoto

151: Canaletto; Bacino di San Marco, Venice, about 1738; oil on canvas; 124.5 x 204.5cm; Museum of Fine Arts, Boston; Abbott Lawrence Fund, Seth K. Sweetser Fund, and Charles Edward French Fund; 39.290

156 (top): Kristin Brenneman Eno

156 (bottom): Mario Burger

157: © 2007 Michael Light

162 (top): TenCate Geosynthetics North America

163 (bottom): TenCate Geosynthetics North America

184 (top): New York City Municipal Archives, Department of Ports and Trade, neg. 32

184 (bottom): Wharves and Piers: their design, construction, and equipment by Carleton Greene, 1917

290–91: Vin Crosbie

292 (left): Reef Ball Foundation

292 (right): Howard Bright, Ion Exchange, Inc

293 (left): TenCate Geosynthetics North America

293 (right): Brian Blakely

294 (left): Karin Lau/iStockphoto

294 (right): © Patrick Blanc

295 (left): Modular Wetland Systems

295 (right): Gaia Soil/The Gaia Institute

296 (left): Eco Fabriks, Maryland

296 (right): Suzanne Carter-Jackson/iStockphoto

297 (left): Dominic Michaelis and Alex Michaelis, Architects

297 (right): © 2009 BioPower Systems

298 (left): Maccaferri, Inc.

298 (right): © SMIT–Sustainably Minded Interactive Technology

The publication of this book coincides with the exhibition
Rising Currents: Projects for New York's Waterfront

The Museum of Modern Art, New York
March 24, 2010 – August 9, 2010

By Guy Nordenson, Catherine Seavitt, and Adam Yarinsky with Stephen Cassell, Lizzie Hodges, Marianne Koch, James Smith, Michael Tantala, and Rebecca Veit

Editing: Rebecca Veit

Coordination: Cristina Steingräber, Julika Zimmermann, Hatje Cantz

Copyediting: Kirsten Weiss with Else Schlegel

Graphic design: Lizzie Hodges with René Selpin

Typeface: Rotis Sans Serif

Production: Stefanie Langner, Hatje Cantz

Reproductions: LVD Gesellschaft für Datenverarbeitung mbH

Paper: Eurobulk, 115 g/m^2

Binding: Conzella Verlagsbuchbinderei, Urban Meister GmbH, Aschheim-Dornach

Printed by Dr. Cantz'sche Druckerei, Ostfildern

Published by
Hatje Cantz Verlag
Zeppelinstrasse 32
73760 Ostfildern
Germany
Tel. +49 711 4405-200
Fax +49 711 4405-220
www.hatjecantz.com
and
The Museum of Modern Art
11 West 53 Street
New York, New York 10019
United States
Tel. +1 212 708 9400
Fax +1 212 333 6575
www.moma.org

Hatje Cantz books are available internationally at selected bookstores. For more information about our distribution partners, please visit our homepage at www.hatjecantz.com.

ISBN 978-3-7757-2578-1
Distributed outside the United States and Canada by Hatje Cantz

Library of Congress Control Number: 2009944219
MoMA Edition: ISBN 978-0-87070-785-8
Distributed in the United States and Canada by D.A.P./
Distributed Art Publishers, Inc.
155 Sixth Avenue, 2nd floor
New York, New York 10013
United States
www.artbook.com

Printed in Germany

Cover illustrations:
Front: NOAA, "Historical North Atlantic Tropical Cyclone Tracks 1851–2004" and "Historical North Atlantic Hurricane Tracks—Major Storms with Landfall in the United States 1851–2004" in *National Atlas of the United States*, September 2005
Back: Lower Manhattan and Palisade Bay as envisioned by the Palisade Bay Team